MORPHOLOGY
The Descriptive Analysis of Words

MORPHOLOGY

The Descriptive Analysis of Words

(Second Edition)

EUGENE A. NIDA

Ann Arbor: The University of Michigan Press

PREFACE

The present volume is a complete revision of a work of the same title published in 1946 in the University of Michigan Publications in Linguistics. But instead of setting up morphological and phonological processes as basic to the descriptive methodology, it treats the morpheme together with its allomorphs as the fundamental feature. In the first edition most of the language problems consisted of hypothetical data. In this book practically all of the illustrative data used in Chapters 1-9 are from actual languages. Occasionally it has been advisable to introduce hypothetical data into the discussion in order to illustrate a particularly complicated type of structure, but for the most part the hypothetical problems have been placed in the Appendix. These problems should, however, prove to be a valuable supplement to the text, and teachers will discover that their use in classroom discussions and for assignments will greatly improve the student's ability to handle linguistic data. It is felt that the use of actual-language problems in the text is a distinct improvement over the earlier presentation, since the student learns about the structure of real languages at the same time as he studies methodology. There is an inevitable increase in interest when actual languages are being examined, and complications which may be considered "impossible" by the student when presented in the form of hypothetical data are more readily received when they appear as genuine linguistic phenomena.

The data contained in such actual-language problems are derived from a number of sources. Frequently the material comes from other publications; when this is so, the bibliographical information is given in the footnotes. Some of the problems are from my own field notes, and a considerable number are based on data supplied by my colleagues of the Summer Institute of Linguistics and other missionary friends. Without such aid it would have been impossible to prepare this text, and I wish to express my thanks to the following people for their contributions of language data: Aztec (Tetelcingo dialect), Richard and Kay Pittman; Aztec (Veracruz dialect), Howard and Joan Law; Aztec (Zacapoaxtla dialect), Arch McKinlay, Harold and Mary Key; Chatino, Howard and Barbara McKaughan; Cuicatec, Marjorie Davis and Doris Needham; Futa-Fula, Harry Watkins; Huave, Milton and Clara Warkentin; Huichol, John and Genevieve McIntosh; Ilamba, George Anderson; Kekchi, William Sedat; Loma, Wesley Sadler; Mam, Edward Sywulka; Mazahua, Elinor Briggs and Hazel Spotts; Mazatec, Eunice Pike and Florence Cowan; Mongbandi, Quentin and Ruth Nelson; Otomi (Mesquital dialect), Donald and Isabel Sinclair; Pame-Chichimeca, Anne Blackman and Lorna Gibson; Popoluca, Ben and Adelle Elson; Tarascan, Max and Elizabeth Lathrop; Tlapanec, Hubel and Mildred Lemley; Tojolabal, Julia Supple and Celia Douglass Mendenhall; Totonac, Herman and Bessie Aschmann; Tsotsil, Kenneth and Nadine Weathers; Yipounou, Leroy Pierson; Zapotec (Isthmus dialect), Velma Pickett and Marjory MacMillan Nyman; Zapotec (Sierra dialect), Neil and Jane Nellis; and Zoque, William and Dorothy Wonderly.

Because the data have been taken from so many different sources, it has been necessary to change some details of the phonemic transcriptions. Otherwise, the student would be confronted with a wide variety of phonetic values for the various symbols. Even as it is, a number of alternatives have been employed (see Table of Phonetic Symbols, Part II of the Appendix), and this has been done so as to preserve in so far as possible the symbolization used by the linguists who have described the particular language structures.

Since some of the language data are derived from field notes which have not been completely phonemicized, a number of phonemic errors exist in the data. For example, in certain of the Mayan languages there are occasional inaccuracies in the length of vowels, the tone-stresses, and the distinctions in velar fricatives. This is undoubtedly true of certain minor details in other languages. Such phonemic inadequacies do not materially affect the descriptions of the morphological structures, however, and in no way do they change the methodology illustrated by the treatment of the data.

The phonemic writing of English follows essentially the system employed by Bloomfield[1] and Bloch and Trager[2] in that it recognizes the two-segment value of diphthongal syllabics.[3] But my own speech, upon which the transcriptions in this volume are based, is much simpler than many varieties of American English because it lacks certain syllabic contrasts (see Appendix, Part III).

The present book is primarily a text for teaching descriptive linguistics. Consequently the arrangement of materials and the rate of progression reflect pedagogical requirements. An attempt has been made to indicate alternative ways of describing data, but it has been impossible to consider all the possibilities. Furthermore, such a study would be too advanced for the average student employing this text. The treatment of theory has, for the most part, followed a single line of approach and has not included a critical examination of alternatives advanced by various scholars. A discussion of that type would be beyond the scope of a textbook designed for introducing descriptive linguistic methods to beginning students. However, I wish to acknowledge my great indebtedness to the outstanding recent contributions of such structuralists as Bernard Bloch, Charles F. Hockett, Zellig S. Harris, C. F. Voegelin, and Rulon S. Wells.

I have been greatly assisted in working out many of the pedagogical features and methodological procedures by my associates in the Department of Morphology and Syntax in the Summer Institute of Linguistics. William L. Wonderly and Velma Pickett have been particularly helpful in the development of this text.

E. A. N.

New York
April, 1949

---

[1]Leonard Bloomfield, Language (New York: Henry Holt and Co., 1933).

[2]Bernard Bloch and George L. Trager, "The Syllabic Phonemes of English," Language, 17 (1941), 3: 223-46.

[3]This interpretation of English syllabics is maintained by most phonemicists.

TABLE OF CONTENTS

Chapter   Page

PREFACE   v

TABLE OF PROBLEMS   xiii

1. INTRODUCTION TO MORPHOLOGY   1
1.1 Morphology   1
1.2 Principles of Descriptive Analysis   1
    A. Descriptive Analysis Must Be Based upon What People Say   1
    B. The Forms Are Primary, and the Usages Secondary   2
    C. No Part of a Language Can Be Adequately Described without Reference to All
        Other Parts   2
    D. Languages Are Constantly in the Process of Change   3
1.3 Relationship of Descriptive Linguistics to Historical and Comparative
        Linguistics   3
1.4 Terminology of Descriptive Linguistics   4
1.5 Arrangement of Contents of This Book   4
1.6 Language Problems in the Present Volume   5

2. THE IDENTIFICATION OF MORPHEMES   6
2.1 Morphemes as Minimal Units   6
2.11 Isolation of Morphemes by Comparing Forms   6
2.12 The Definition of the Morpheme   6
2.2 Principles Employed in the Identification of Morphemes   7
2.21 Principle 1   7
2.21.1 The Meaning of Principle 1   7
2.21.2 The Application of Principle 1   8
    A. Steps in Procedure   8
    B. Problems of Residues   9
    C. The Tentative Nature of an Analyst's Correlations   10
    D. Supplementary Problems Illustrative of Principle 1   11
2.22 Principle 2   14
2.22.1 The Meaning of Principle 2   14
2.22.2 The Application of Principle 2   15
    A. Where the Sounds Involved Exhibit Some Phonetic Similarities   15
    B. Where the Sounds Involved May Not Exhibit Phonetic Similarities   15
    C. Where Sequences of Phonemes Are Involved   16
    D. Problems Illustrative of Principle 2   17
    E. Steps in Procedure for Problems Involving Principle 2   18
    F. Writing up the Answers to Problems   19
    G. Types of Phonological Environment Described in Terms of Processes . . .   21
        1. Assimilation   21
        2. Dissimilation   23
        3. Assimilation of Tonemes   24
        4. Loss of Consonant Phonemes   26
        5. Loss of Vowel Phonemes   30
        6. Palatalization   35
    H. Supplementary Problems Illustrative of Principle 2   37
2.23 Principle 3   41

Chapter   Page

2.23.1 The Meaning of Principle 3   42
2.23.2 The Application of Principle 3   44
        A. Determination of Allomorphs by Complementary Distribution   44
        B. Basis of Complementation   44
        C. Degree of Phonological Difference between Allomorphs   44
        D. Basic and Nonbasic Allomorphs   45
        E. Types of Zero   46
        F. Supplementary Problems Illustrative of Principle 3   46
2.24   Principle 4   54
2.24.1 The Meaning of Principle 4   54
2.24.2 The Application of Principle 4   55
2.25   Principle 5   55
        A. Definition of Homophonous Forms   56
        B. Definition of Related Forms   56
        C. Types of Related Areas of Meaning   56
        D. Types of Distributional Differences   57
        E. Problems Illustrative of Principle 5   57
2.26   Principle 6   58
        A. Condition 1   59
        B. Condition 2   59
        C. Condition 3   60

3. TYPES OF MORPHEMES   62
3.1 Internal Composition of Morphemes   62
3.11 Types of Phonemes Which Compose Morphemes   62
3.11.1 Morphemes Consisting of Segmental Phonemes   62
3.11.2 Morphemes Consisting of Suprasegmental Phonemes   62
3.11.3 Morphemes Consisting of Segmental and Suprasegmental Phonemes   65
3.12 Different Shapes and Sizes of Morphemes   65
3.13 Formal Relationships of the Parts of Morphemes   67
3.2 Formal Relationships of Morphemes to Each Other   68
3.21 Structural Relationships of Morphemes to Each Other   69
3.21.1 Additive Morphemes   69
3.21.2 Replacive Morphemes   71
3.21.3 Subtractive Morphemes   75
3.22 Positional Relationships of Morphemes to Each Other   76

4. THE DISTRIBUTION OF MORPHEMES   78
4.1 Significance of the Distribution of Morphemes   78
4.2 Types of Morphemes as Determined by Their Distribution   81
        A. Bound vs. Free Forms   81
        B. Roots vs. Nonroots   82
        C. Roots vs. Stems   83
        D. Nuclei vs. Nonnuclei   83
        E. Nuclear vs. Peripheral Structures   84
        F. Morphemes of the Same Order vs. Morphemes of Different Orders   84
        G. Mutually Exclusive Morphemes   84
        H. Mutually Obligatory Morphemes   84
        I. Obligatory vs. Nonobligatory Morphemes   85
        J. Closing vs. Nonclosing Morphemes   85
4.3 Formal Combining of Morphemes   85
4.4 Immediate Constituents   86
4.41 Significance of Immediate Constituents   86
4.42 Positional Relationships between Immediate Constituents   88
        A. Combinations of Two Immediate Constituents   88
           1. Continuous Nuclear and Peripheral Immediate Constituents   88
              a. With All Successive Peripheral Constituents on One Side of the
                 Nucleus   88

        b. With Successive Peripheral Constituents on More than One Side of or
            within the Nucleus   89
        2. Discontinuous Immediate Constituents--Nuclear, Peripheral, or Both . .   90
    B. Combinations of More than Two Immediate Constituents   90
4.43 Principles of Procedure in Determining Immediate Constituents   90
4.43.1 Principle 1   91
4.43.2 Principle 2   91
4.43.3 Principle 3   92
4.43.4 Principle 4   92
4.43.5 Principle 5   92
4.44 Functional Relationships between Immediate Constituents   94
4.44.1 Endocentric vs. Exocentric Constructions   94
4.44.2 Coördinate vs. Subordinate vs. Noncoördinate and Nonsubordinate
            Constructions   95
4.5 Types of Morphological Structure   97
4.6 Primary Structural Layers   98
4.7 The Limits of Morphological Structures   102
4.71 Structural Contrasts   102
4.72 Phonological Criteria for Establishing the Limits of Morphological
            Structures   102
4.73 Distributional Criteria for Establishing the Limits of Morphological
            Structures   103
4.74 Overlapping between Phonological and Morphological Criteria   104
4.75 Overlapping between Morphological and Syntactic Distributional Data   104
4.76 The Practical Limits of the Word   106

5. STRUCTURAL CLASSES   107
5.1 Types of Structural Classes   107
5.11 Form Classes   107
5.12 Sequence Classes   108
5.13 Distribution Classes   110
5.13.1 Definitions of Significant Features   110
5.13.2 Types of Distributional Arrangements   111
5.13.21 Distributional Arrangements in Single Sequence Classes   111
5.13.21.1 Forms Occurring in Determiner-Determined Series   112
5.13.21.11 Structural Series with No Subclasses of Determiner and No Subclasses
            of Determined   112
5.13.21.12 Structural Series with Subclasses of Determiner and No Subclasses of
            Determined   112
5.13.21.13 Structural Series with No Subclasses of Determiner but Subclasses of
            Determined   117
5.13.21.14 Structural Series with Subclasses of Determiner and Subclasses of
            Determined   125
5.13.21.2 Forms Not Occurring in Determiner-Determined Series   127
5.13.22 Distributional Arrangements in Multiple Sequence Classes   130
5.2 Systems of Structural Classes   147

6. THE MEANING OF MORPHEMES AND SEQUENCES OF MORPHEMES   151
6.1 Semantic Principles   151
6.11 Principle 1   151
6.12 Principle 2   152
    A. Nonlinguistic Environments   152
        1. Objective Environments   152
        2. Subjective Environments   152
    B. Linguistic Environments   153
        1. Structural Environments   153
        2. Contextual Environments   154
6.13 Principle 3   157

Chapter   Page

6.2   The Use of Symbols 161
6.3   Definability of Meaning 161
6.4   Procedures in Determining the Meanings of Morphemes 162
6.5   The Labeling of Morphemes 165
6.6   Grammatical Categories Expressed by Bound Forms 166
6.7   The Meaning of Grammatical Sequences 174

7.   FIELD PROCEDURES 175
7.1   Monolingual Approach 175
7.2   Bilingual Approach 178
7.21 The Data 178
7.21.1 Simple Object Words 178
7.21.2 Object Words in Possible Morphological Categories 180
7.21.3 Simple Process Words 181
7.21.4 Process Words in Possible Morphological Categories 182
7.21.5 Combinations of Object and Process Words 183
7.21.6 Texts 186
7.22 Recording the Data 188
7.23 The Informant 189
7.23.1 Dialect Differences among Informants 189
7.23.2 Qualifications of Informants 190
7.23.3 Handling of Informants 190

8.   ANALYTICAL PROCEDURES 192
8.1   Relationship of Analytical to Field Procedures 192
8.2   Steps in Analytical Procedure 192
8.21 Initial Observations 192
8.21.1 Phonetic Observations 193
8.21.2 Identificational Observations 193
8.21.3 Distributional Observations 194
8.22 Filing of Data 195
8.22.1 Purpose of Filing Data 195
8.22.2 Form of the Filing Slip 195
8.22.3 Relationship of Filing to Analysis 196
8.22.4 Nature and Quantity of the Data to be Filed 198
8.22.5 Number of Files 199
8.22.6 Form of the Structural File 199
8.22.61 Morphophonemic Section 200
8.22.62 Morphology Section 200
8.3   Determining the Relative Order of Morphemes 205
8.4   Use of Arbitrary Symbols in Identifying Forms 207

9.   THE DESCRIPTIVE STATEMENT OF THE MORPHOLOGY 222
9.1   Structural Difficulties 222
9.11 Illustrative Outlines 222
9.11.1 Chichewa, by Mark Hanna Watkins 223
9.11.2 Chiricahua Apache, by Harry Hoijer 225
9.11.3 Delaware, by C. F. Voegelin 226
9.11.4 French, by Robert A. Hall, Jr. 227
9.11.5 Hebrew, by Zellig S. Harris 229
9.11.6 Potawatomi, by Charles F. Hockett 230
9.11.7 Southern Paiute, by Edward Sapir 231
9.11.8 Tzeltal, by Marianna C. Slocum 234
9.11.9 Yuma, by A. M. Halpern 235
9.12 Discussion of Illustrative Outlines 237
9.2   Technical Difficulties 239
9.21 Systems of Outlining 239

Chapter   Page

9.22 Terminology 240
9.23 Types of Descriptive Statements 240
9.3   Illustrative Language Problems 243

   APPENDIX 283
   Part I: Supplementary Problems 283
      A.   Problems Supplementary to Section 2.22.2 283
      A.1 Assimilation and Dissimilation 283
      A.2 Medial Voicing 290
      A.3 Final Unvoicing 290
      A.4 Assimilation and Dissimilation of Tonemes 291
      A.5 Reduction of Word-Medial Consonant Clusters 293
      A.6 Reduction of Word-Final Consonant Clusters 296
      A.7 Reduction of Vowel Sequences 297
      A.8 "Weakening" of Consonants 301
      A.9 "Weakening" of Vowels in Unstressed Syllables 302
      A.10 Loss of Vowels in Unstressed Syllables 303
      A.11 Differences of Vowel Length Due to Open and Closed Syllables . 306
      A.12 Compensatory Lengthening 306
      A.13 Developed Phonemes 307
      A.14 Palatalization 308
      A.15 Nasalization 310
      A.16 Verner's Phenomenon 311
      A.17 Metathesis 312
      B.   Problems Supplementary to Section 2.23.2 313
      C.   Problems Supplementary to Chapter 3 315
      D.   Problems Supplementary to Chapter 5 320
      E.   Problems Supplementary to Chapter 6 324
   Part II: Table of Phonetic Symbols 329
   Part III: Phonemic Writing of English 332

   BIBLIOGRAPHY 335

   INDEX 339

TABLE OF PROBLEMS

(Exclusive of those based on hypothetical data.)

Language	Page
Arabic (Egyptian)	
Problem 53	68
Arabic (Sudan Colloquial)	
Problem 34	41
Aztec (Guerrero Dialect)	
Problem 82	117
Aztec (Tetelcingo Dialect)	
Problem 127	216
Aztec (Veracruz Dialect)	
Problem 1	8
Problem 3	11
Problem 30	38
Problem 42	58
Problem 110	157
Aztec (Zacapoaxtla Dialect)	
Problem 2	11
Problem 109	156
Problem 115	169
Chatino (Restricted)	
Problem 48	64
Chichewa	
Problem 92	126
Problem 102	141
Chiluba (Luba-Lulua Dialect)	
Problem 32	39
Cuicatec	
Problem 17	24
English	
Problem 9	17
Problem 22	30
Problem 40	55
Problem 41	57
Problem 45	59
Problem 57	72
Problem 59	74
Problem 66	83
Problem 67	90
Problem 68	93
Problem 69	95
Problem 73	100
Problem 79	115
Problem 80	115
Problem 84	117
Problem 85	119
Problem 86	120
Problem 87	122

Language   . Page

English (continued)
    Problem 88   123
    Problem 95   127
    Problem 96   128
    Problem 106   153
    Problem 107   154
    Problem 108   155
Eskimo (Barrow Dialect)
    Problem 63   78
French
    Problem 60   75
Futa-Fula
    Problem 39   53
    Problem 78   114
Greek (Classical)
    Problem 18   27
Hausa
    Problem 13   22
    Problem 26   36
    Problem 56   70
Huave
    Problem 8   17
    Problem 50   66
    Problem 77   112
Huichol
    Problem 112   164
Ilamba (Restricted)
    Problem 38   51
Kekchi
    Problem 31   39
    Problem 37   49
Loma
    Problem 103   144
    Problem 104   145
    Problem 105   146
Mam
    Problem 136   258
Mazahua
    Problem 27   36
Mazatec
    Problem 113   164
    Problem 114   165
Mongbandi
    Problem 47   63
Navaho
    Problem 19   28
    Problem 20   29
Ngbaka
    Problem 46   63
Otomi (Mesquital Dialect)
    Problem 130   219
Pame-Chichimeca
    Problem 128   216
    Problem 129   217
Popoluca (Restricted)
    Problem 28   37

Language   Page

Quechua
    Problem 64   79
Samoan
    Problem 61   76
Shilluk
    Problem 58   72
Spanish
    Problem 83   117
    Problem 90   124
    Problem 91   125
    Problem 99   130
    Problem 100   136
Swahili, Congo (Elisabethville Dialect)
    Problem 5   12
Tarahumara
    Problem 14   22
Tarascan
    Problem 131   220
Tlapanec
    Problem 24   32
Tojolabal
    Problem 10   18
    Problem 51   67
    Problem 55   70
    Problem 126   214
Tonkawa
    Problem 25   34
    Problem 71   96
Totonac
    Problem 11   18
Tsotsil
    Problem 15   23
Turkish
    Problem 65   79
Turu
    Problem 33   40
Tzeltal
    Problem 7   16
    Problem 16   23
    Problem 35   46
    Problem 70   95
    Problem 74   100
    Problem 81   116
Yipounou
    Problem 6   13
Zapotec (Isthmus Dialect)
    Problem 29 (Restricted)   38
    Problem 123 (Restricted)   210
    Problem 137   262
Zapotec (Sierra Dialect)
    Problem 89   123
    Problem 111   163
Zoque
    Problem 4   12
    Problem 12   21
    Problem 21   29

Language   Page

    Zoque (continued)
        Problem 23   30
        Problem 52   67
        Problem 72   99
        Problem 116   171

MORPHOLOGY
The Descriptive Analysis of Words

C H A P T E R   1

INTRODUCTION TO MORPHOLOGY

1.1 Morphology

Morphology is the study of morphemes and their arrangements in forming words.[1] Morphemes are the minimal meaningful units which may constitute words or parts of words, e.g. re-, de-, un-, -ish, -ly, -ceive, -mand, tie, boy, and like in the combinations receive, demand, untie, boyish, likely. The morpheme arrangements which are treated under the morphology of a language include all combinations that form words or parts of words. Combinations of words into phrases and sentences are treated under the syntax.

It would be quite wrong to assume, however, that morphology and syntax constitute airtight compartments in the structure of any language. This is by no means true. In some languages there is constant overlapping of structure, and in a few instances it seems almost impossible to draw a line between word structure and phrase structure.[2]

1.2 Principles of Descriptive Analysis

The descriptive analyst must be guided by certain very fixed principles if he is to be objective in describing accurately any language or part of any language. It would be excellent if he could adopt a completely man-from-Mars attitude toward any language he analyzes and describes. None of us, however, can completely dissociate himself from the knowledge of languages he has already acquired or from the apparatus which has been used to describe the grammar of such languages. Despite this fact, the descriptive linguist must divest himself of the tourist's viewpoint, which consists in judging everything strange and different on the basis of things found at home. To help reorient oneself to the new approach, it is important to bear in mind constantly the following fundamental principles:

A. Descriptive analysis must be based upon what people say.

The implications of this principle are greater than a beginner may realize. In the first place, it means that the written form of the language is entirely secondary (in fact, quite irrelevant) so far as the descriptive linguist is concerned. His description of English, French, Arabic, or Chinese will treat first and foremost the spoken forms of the language. He may consider it pertinent to note the extent to which the conventional orthography conforms to a scientific symbolization of the structural units, but the descriptive linguist as such is only indirectly concerned with conventional or practical alphabets.[3]

---

[1] We are using "word" in this chapter in the usual traditional sense. See Chapters 4 and 8 for further discussion and a more precise definition of "morphology."

[2] Such problems are treated in Chapters 4 and 8.

[3] Of course the descriptive linguist also deals with practical problems involving alphabets and methods of writing, but the practical results should be based upon scientific analysis, rather than the scientific analysis upon the existent orthography.

In the second place, this principle of basing description on the spoken form of the language means that the linguist records the actual forms employed, rather than regularizing the data or evaluating utterances on the basis of some literary dialect. In other words, it is what people say rather than what some people think they should say that is important to the descriptive linguist.[4] Furthermore, the descriptive linguist is interested in all types of speakers, representing different educational, social, economic, and racial groups. For the linguist any dialect of a language is intrinsically as good as any other, and all varieties of language are equally "correct" in that they represent the dialect of the speaker. The descriptive linguist simply describes languages, all kinds of languages, and all types of dialects of any language. If any judgments are to be passed upon the acceptability or so-called correctness of some usage, these are left either to the anthropologist and sociologist for an objective statement of the factors in the society which make certain persons more socially prominent and hence make their speech more acceptable, or to the man on the street, who is thoroughly accustomed to forming judgments upon the basis of his own egocentric attitudes and limited knowledge.[5] Of course, the descriptive linguist notes such forms as It's me and It's I. He finds that English-speaking members of all social, economic, and educational classes say It's me, and that an occasional person says It's I. He may also care to note that the form It's I is regarded by many persons of all classes as distastefully pedantic. The descriptive linguist, however, does not go beyond this point in describing such alternative forms.

B. The forms are primary, and the usages secondary.

The descriptive linguist starts from forms and then proceeds to describe the grammatical positions in which the forms occur. In describing English, for example, he would not say that there are gerunds and gerundives, but rather that there are certain verbals ending in -ing and that these have a distribution which is parallel to that of nouns (these are the so-called gerunds) and to that of adjectives (these are the so-called gerundives). In describing the Greek cases, the descriptive linguist lists five sets of forms,[6] and then describes how these forms are used. He does not base a description of Greek on the eight cases which are revealed by historical and comparative study,[7] since in the functioning of Greek the formally contrastive sets are the distinctive features.

C. No part of a language can be adequately described without reference to all other parts.

This principle means that the phonemics, morphology, and syntax of a language cannot be described without reference to each other. A language is not a departmentalized grouping of relatively isolated structures; it is a functioning whole, and the parts are only

---

[4]It is perfectly possible to describe an artificial literary dialect, but such a description must be recognized for precisely what it is, namely, a description of a dialect of a language, not the language.

[5]For a fuller discussion of such problems see Eugene A. Nida, Linguistic Interludes (Glendale, Calif.: Summer Institute of Linguistics, 1947), pp. 1-32.

[6]The vocative is quite defective, but it is nevertheless formally distinguishable in some declensions.

[7]Certain scholars, beginning with A. T. Robertson in A Grammar of the Greek New Testament (New York: Hodder and Stoughton, 1914), have attempted to describe Koine Greek on the basis of eight cases. This may be pedagogically defensible, but it is structurally misleading and theoretically unjustifiable, since, once the formal criteria have been set aside, there are no functional criteria which will enable one to restrict the number of cases to eight. For example, why should not a further subdivision of cases be made between subjective, objective, appositive, attributive, and predicative genitives?

fully describable in terms of their relationship to the whole. Nor are languages like simple geometric figures which can be described by beginning at one fixed point and methodically plotting the structure from there. Languages are exceedingly complex structures and they constitute their own frame of reference. Though one language should not be described in terms of any other language, no part of a single language can be described adequately without reference to the other parts. This fact becomes most fully evident when we attempt to determine the relationships between words and phrases. We usually say that a suffix unites into a single word everything with which it occurs, but in the expression the king of England's (hat), we have a "feeling" that the king of England is not a single word, despite the fact that -s occurs with the entire phrase. The answer to such a relatively basic question as "What constitutes a word?" can be answered only by examining the morphological, syntactic, and phonemic structure of the language.

D. Languages are constantly in the process of change.

Our descriptions of languages tend to give the impression that they are static, fixed structures. This is, of course, the attitude of the average speaker of a language, and yet we do realize that there are (1) fluctuations of forms, e.g. roofs vs. rooves, hoofs vs. hooves, proven vs. proved, and dove vs. dived, and (2) new items of vocabulary, e.g. video, skreeno, cyclotron, and commies.[8] The existence of fluctuations in forms means that certain structures are winning out over others, for alternative forms never stay in equilibrium for long. The increased use of proved and dived in preference to proven and dove means that the regular formations are gaining at the expense of the irregular. The descriptive linguist does not attempt to take into account the tendencies and trends of a language, but when he records in his data that there are alternative forms and that these exhibit a certain relative frequency of occurrence, he is touching upon the dynamics of language change.

One must not think that only written languages change or, on the contrary, that written languages change less than unwritten ones. All languages change, and the rate varies at different times in the history of any one language. We must be aware of such tendencies and, in describing a language, recognize the significance of fluctuating forms. In a language like Maya of Yucatan we find a relatively large number of alternative formations, and in a language such as Navaho they are conspicuously fewer. The proportion of alternative forms tells us something about the rate of change, but without some knowledge of the history of the language, we do not know whether such changes are increasing or diminishing in number.[9]

1.3 Relationship of Descriptive Linguistics to Historical and Comparative Linguistics

Descriptive linguistics may be said to underlie historical and comparative linguistics; it is not dependent upon them. Historical linguistics consists in the study of data from two or more historical periods in a language. Comparative linguistics consists in the study of the data from two or more dialects of a single language or from two or more languages. In every case the data which historical and comparative linguistics employ should be descriptive, in the sense, that is, that the data are described entirely in terms of their relationship to contemporary material or in terms of their relationship to the one dialect or language involved. For valid results, the historical and comparative linguist is dependent upon descriptive data, but the descriptive linguist is not dependent upon historical and comparative findings.

---

[8]The elements out of which such words are constructed are not new, but the words themselves are recent formations.

[9]The practical linguist is frequently called upon to decide which types of alternatives will be employed in a written literature. These problems have been discussed by me in Bible Translating (New York: American Bible Society, 1947).

This does not mean that training in historical and comparative linguistics is not valuable to the descriptive linguist, but it means that the systematic organization of the data of any one language is not dependent upon facts which come from a historical or comparative knowledge of that language or of related languages. In a descriptive analysis of English, for example, we do not speak of a subjunctive form of the verb, for there are no verb forms in English which are distinctively subjunctive and nothing else. All the so-called subjunctive forms, e.g. be in I move he be elected and were in if he were here are formally identical with infinitives or past-tense forms. Historically there was at one time a formally distinct subjunctive in English, but it exists no longer. Hence, we no longer talk of subjunctive forms, though we do, of course, describe the particular situations in which forms such as be and were occur.[10] Similarly, we do not talk about dative-case forms in English simply because German, a cognate language, has such a formally distinct case. In the expression I gave him a ball, the word him is not a dative-case form in contrast with a so-called accusative him in I hit him. In both sentences the word him is just an objective form; in the first sentence it is the first of two grammatical objects and in the second sentence it is structurally equivalent to the second type of grammatical object. For convenience we may call these indirect and direct objects, but there is just one form. The fact that German (or any other language for that matter) has two case forms, ihm 'dative' and ihn 'accusative,' to distinguish such structural contrasts is not pertinent to the description of English.

1.4 Terminology of Descriptive Linguistics

Every science must have an adequate specialized terminology to permit identification and discussion of the various features pertinent to its scope. There is always a tendency (particularly in any comparatively new scientific endeavor) to increase the technical vocabulary very rapidly. Such words as "macromorph," "schismeme," and "homolog" all have a value, but it is true that perhaps one could employ terms (whether single words or phrases) which would be more easily recognizable. On the one hand, the student may be confused, even overwhelmed, by many new terms or may think that a knowledge of the technical vocabulary is a substitute for recognizing the underlying principles. On the other hand, the use of already existing words in meanings which are not traditional may be even more disconcerting or may give the student a false assurance that he has understood their meanings. At any rate, it is quite impossible to avoid all specialized, technical vocabulary, and no text should attempt to do so even if it were possible, for the student must be introduced to the terminology which is current in present-day linguistic discussions.

A number of new words and phrases are used in this text, e.g. "replacive," "subtractive," "suprafix," and "polyallomorphic." They are not introduced in order to be novel, but to call attention to structure. Simply because the reader does not find such traditional terms as "dative," "accusative," "gerund," "infinitive," "supine," "subjunctive," and "participle" frequently in this book, he is not justified in concluding that all conventional terms are taboo. It simply means that the science of descriptive linguistics is not predominantly concerned with features of Greek and Latin grammar but with structural relationships in any and all languages. Wherever the traditional terms are applicable they should be and are most certainly used.

1.5 Arrangement of Contents of This Book

The following chapters of this book exhibit a structurally important sequence. Chapter 2 treats the identification of morphemes. This chapter is basic to any subsequent analysis, for we cannot discuss the ways in which morphemes combine until we understand the means by which we may identify the fundamental structural units of the language. Chapter 3,

---

[10]This is precisely analogous to the problem involving the Greek case system discussed in section 1.2, principle B.

dealing with the types of morphemes, is an extension of Chapter 2, and together they constitute the presentation of analytical theory. Chapter 4 introduces the synthetic part of the structural procedures by discussing the distribution of morphemes. Chapter 5 is a continuation of Chapter 4 and treats the same type of data from the standpoint of the structural classes. These classes are the forms which result from the various types of distributions. Chapter 6, on the meanings of morphemes, considers in detail various semantic factors which have only been touched upon in other parts of the book, or merely assumed, in order that the more systematic treatment might be taken up after sufficient background had been acquired. Theoretically, Chapter 9, on the organization of the descriptive statement of the morphology, should follow Chapter 6, but the actual procedures of analysis of a language are quite different from the schematic approach suggested by Chapters 2-6. Accordingly, it was necessary to introduce first a chapter on field procedures and one on analytical procedures.

In brief, we learn to "break down" the language structure in Chapters 2 and 3, and to "reassemble" it in Chapters 4 and 5. Chapter 6 enables us to label the parts and the combinations. Chapters 7 and 8 likewise show us how to break down the structure and to reassemble the pieces, but this time from the standpoint of the actual field task and not from the standpoint of nicely classified data found in a textbook. Chapter 9 introduces us to the methods of organizing the description of field data so that it will reveal the essential structure of the language.

1.6 Language Problems in the Present Volume

There are two types of language problems employed in this text: (1) those using data from actual languages and (2) those using hypothetical data. The materials from actual languages are found for the most part in the text proper, and the hypothetical data in the Appendix.

In some instances the data of actual languages are so complex that it is necessary to eliminate some of the complexities for the sake of the illustration or because they introduce difficulties considered much later in the text. Problems that have been somewhat simplified in this fashion are marked "restricted."

Even at best the problems are rather artificial, for no one ever begins by collecting forms with all the phonemic problems already solved. Furthermore, the problems give an unnatural impression that morphology and syntax can be easily distinguished, and this is by no means true. But in any textbook approach to the study of language structure, we must begin with simple data and gradually take on the more complicated.

Indirectly the problems do much more than illustrate the particular structure in question, for they reveal many other features at the same time. A simple problem such as number 5 is introduced to give the student practice in isolating morphemes, but it also reveals the three primary sets of prefixes characteristic of Bantu verb structure.[11]

The structure of some languages is amazingly simple and regular and that of other languages is incredibly complicated and irregular. Despite the degrees of complexity and the vast differences of structure, however, there are always definite patterns of formation, each demanding strict adherence if the speaker is to be understood. No languages are unorganized jumbles of sounds, as some people have thought. It is the purpose of morphology to enable the analyst to discover and describe that part of the language structure which forms words or parts of words.

---

[11]See the Preface for further information concerning the language problems in this text.

C H A P T E R 2

THE IDENTIFICATION OF MORPHEMES

2.1 Morphemes as Minimal Units

One of the first tasks which confront the linguist in examining a new language with a view to discovering and describing its structure is the identification of the minimal meaningful units of which the language is composed. These minimal units are called "morphemes," and in many instances they are readily recognized. For example, in the English words boy-ish, maddening, condense, receive, and up, we have little difficulty in identifying the various component units: boy, -ish, mad, -en, -ing, con-, -dense, re-, -ceive, and up. With practically no complications we have thus "broken down" these longer expressions (i.e. words) into their constituent parts. The process by which this is accomplished appears at first to be almost instinctive, but if we consider closely what we have done, we recognize that we compared words, or at least drew upon our knowledge of such comparisons. In order to identify the morphemes we must have certain partially similar forms in which we can recognize recurring partials. What we need for comparison would be provided by the following series: boy, girlish, mad, fatten, fattening, constrain, density, return, deceive, start up. These forms contain each of the morphemes in a different situation. By this means we compare and isolate, and it is only by such comparison with other forms that we can discover morphemes.

2.11 Isolation of Morphemes by Comparing Forms

The necessity of comparison becomes perfectly obvious when we examine a foreign language. In Kekchi, a Mayan language of Guatemala, the form tinbeq means 'I will walk.' By just looking at such a form it is impossible to know which part of the word corresponds to which part of the meaning suggested by the English translation. We have no way of knowing how many morphemes exist in this form, or what parts of the form constitute such morphemes. By comparison, however, we can soon discover the units which make up this word. The forms tatbeq 'you (sg.) will walk' and ninbeq 'I am walking' enable us to isolate three morphemes in the first form, tinbeq. These are t- 'future tense' (this is in contrast with n- 'present progressive tense'), -in- 'first person singular subject' (in contrast with -at- 'second person singular subject'), and -beq, meaning 'to walk.' It is possible that the stem -beq might prove to be made up of more than one part. It happens that it is a single morpheme, but we can know this only by comparison with many other forms.

To judge from the illustrations just given, the procedure for identifying morphemes would appear to be relatively easy, but this is not true of languages. Just looking about for similar forms with approximate meanings is helpful and very much a part of the linguist's procedure, but such a rather naïve approach will not be satisfactory in difficult situations.

2.12 The Definition of the Morpheme

The definition of the morpheme which is most widely accepted and most practical in application is the one stated by Bloomfield: "A linguistic form which bears no partial

6

phonetic-semantic resemblance to any other form is ... a morpheme."[1] This definition
seems rather strangely worded. Instead of being a positive statement about forms being
similar and having similar meanings, e.g. like the -ish in boyish, mannish, piggish, girlish, and the -en in fatten, broaden, widen, deepen, the definition describes the relationships in a negative fashion. It means that forms belonging to the same morpheme may not
consist of identically the same phonemes and they may not have precisely equivalent meanings, but if these varying forms with correspondingly different meanings still do not overlap on other sets of forms with their respective meanings, then they may be regarded as
constituting a single morpheme. This is because, as the definition states, they bear no
partial phonetic-semantic resemblance to other forms. The significance of this negative
type of definition will become more obvious as we consider the various principles which
determine the identification of morphemes.

2.2 Principles Employed in the Identification of Morphemes

There are six principles which we may apply in isolating and identifying morphemes.
None of the principles is complete in itself; each is supplementary to the basic definition
and must be considered so. If each were interpreted as being exclusive of all situations
not specifically noted in the principle, the statements would be contradictory.

2.21 Principle 1

Forms which have a common semantic distinctiveness and an identical phonemic form in
all their occurrences constitute a single morpheme.

2.21.1 The Meaning of Principle 1

Principle 1 means that such a form as -er added to verbs in such constructions as
worker, dancer, runner, walker, and flier is a morpheme. It always has the same phonetic
form, and always has essentially the same meaning, namely, that of 'the doer of the action'
(also called 'agentive'). The principle used the phrase "common semantic distinctiveness"
as a way of indicating that the meaning which is in common to all the occurrences of the
suffix -er contrasts with (or is distinctively set off from) the meaning of all other similar forms. In the definition of the morpheme and in the statement of this first principle
we were very careful to indicate that the meaning of -er in all these positions is not necessarily identical. In fact, no science has made available to us the tools by which we can
test degrees of difference in meaning. It is necessary, however, for us to make certain
distinctions between types of meaning. For example, in English there is another suffixal
morpheme with the form -er, that is, the -er in comparative adjectives such as wider, broader, smaller, deeper, cleaner. But there is no common semantic distinctiveness in the series
of suffixal forms occurring in worker, dancer, runner, wider, broader, smaller. Despite,
therefore, an identity of form, we may distinguish two morphemes on the basis of meaning.[2]

At times the difficulty of accurately and comprehensively defining the common semantic
features of distinctiveness in any set of forms may be very acute. For example, in the
series boyish, girlish, old-maidish, mannish, heathenish, dampish, bearish, slavish, book-
ish, the morpheme -ish may be said to denote 'a quality of.' Or if we identify the stems
as A and the suffix as B, then we may say that B "qualitativizes" A. But that is not all

---

[1]Leonard Bloomfield, Language (New York: Henry Holt and Co., 1933), p. 161.

[2]There are, of course, other distinguishing distributional features which are pertinent
to the distinction between the two suffixal morphemes, but these are covered by other principles.

the meaning, for this suffix generally adds an unfavorable connotation to the word.   The suffix -ly also identifies a quality, e.g. <u>manly</u>, <u>friendly</u>, <u>worldly</u>, <u>cowardly</u>, <u>princely</u>, but there are no unpleasant situations necessarily associated with words having this -ly suffix.   Such problems of defining the meanings of forms are very complicated and the whole of Chapter 6 is given to a consideration of various difficulties.   Principle 5 will treat some of the complications involved when identical forms have widely differing meanings.

2.21.2   <u>The</u> <u>Application</u> <u>of</u> <u>Principle</u> <u>1</u>

In order to understand the procedures we should employ in isolating morphemes in accordance with Principle 1, we may examine the following set of forms in an Aztec dialect of Veracruz:

<u>Problem 1</u>

  1. ničoka   'I cry'

  2. ničoka°   'I cried'

  3. nimayana   'I am hungry'

  4. nimayana°   'I was hungry'

  5. nimayanaya   'I was hungry (and may still be)'

  6. timayana   'you (sg.) are hungry'

  7. nimayanas   'I will be hungry'

  8. tičoka   'you (sg.) cry'

  9. ničokaya   'I was crying (and may still be)'

  10. ničokas   'I will cry'

There are several possible steps in procedure in isolating the morphemes in this series of Aztec words.   After practice one may go about such a task almost instinctively, but the beginner frequently needs to have some helpful hints.   The exact order in which the steps are carried out is not fixed, but the following suggestions may prove valuable:

A. <u>Steps</u> <u>in</u> <u>Procedure</u>

  1. Compare forms and meanings, beginning with the first of the series.

  2. Having isolated a possible form-meaning distinction, check it throughout the
     series.

  3. Isolate and check all possible form-meaning distinctions.

  4. Look for residues, and assign these to morphemes or reserve them for further
     check.

In carrying out these four points of procedure the analyst would note forms 1 and 2 in the data.   The form-meaning distinction is the final glottal stop -°, with the apparent meaning of past tense, in contrast with the present-tense form.   Having isolated this prob- able morpheme, he should then check down the series for a similar form with a correspond- ing meaning.   It may be found in form 4 (compare form 3), but there are no other occur- rences of this final glottal stop.

The third step in procedure is essentially a repetition of the first two steps until all the forms have been discovered. The next contrast will be found in comparing forms 2 and 3. The chances are that as a result of this comparison the initial ni- will be isolated as meaning 'I.' It is also possible, however, that the final or prefinal -a denotes the first person, but a quick check of all the forms will confirm the deduction that ni- is probably the first person singular element.

B. Problems of Residues

If this procedure is followed through the entire series, a number of forms may be isolated:

1. ni- (or possibly only n-) as first person indicator.

2. ti- (or possibly only t-) as second person indicator.

3. -čok- the stem meaning 'to cry.'

4. -mayan- the stem meaning 'to be hungry.'

5. The suffix -y-, or -ay- or -ya indicating past incomplete action.

6. The suffix -s or -as indicating future time.

These forms of the suffixes and prefixes show that we have some residues which have not been adequately assigned. It may be that the forms ni- and ti- both contain a common element -i- meaning, for example, that the subject is singular. It may be that the final -a, or in some words the prefinal -a-, indicates that the verbs are intransitive. Before we can adequately determine the forms of the prefixes and suffixes we must treat these two possible residues i and a.

Assigning these residues is only possible if we find other forms which show contrasts. Accordingly, let us add the following forms to the series above:

Problem 1 (cont.)

11. aŋkwake   'you (pl.) ate'

12. nitehkawi   'I climb'

13. titehkawi?   'you (sg.) climbed'

14. nitehkawiya   'I was climbing (and may still be)'

15. nitehkawis   'I will climb'

16. nikwake   'we ate'

These forms make it clear that the i before the verb stems is not an indicator of a singular subject, for it appears in form 16 with a plural subject. Furthermore, the i is not an indicator of some aspect,[3] since it does not occur throughout the series (cf. form 11), as we would expect if that were true. The a after the stem can no longer be regarded as some indicator of the kind of action, since it does not appear in all the words in the series, as may be seen from forms 12-15.

---

[3]Aspect means the kind of action, e.g. habitual, frequent, repeated, beginning (see Chapter 6).

C. The Tentative Nature of an Analyst's Correlations

It would be possible to argue that we are not absolutely sure of these morphemes in Problem 1. Perhaps it could be said that we have jumped to conclusions. That is true, and it is precisely what we do constantly in linguistic analysis, but we introduce into our overall approach features which protect us from mistakes. We may describe this more inclusive procedure as follows:

1. We look for every possible correspondence of forms to discover morphemes.

2. We isolate these units in their simplest and most obvious forms.

3. We realize that we may be mistaken, so we are constantly on the lookout for supplementary data which will confirm or disprove our tentative analyses.

In Problem 1 we still have reason to be suspicious of some of the forms, especially the long verb stems mayana 'to be hungry' and tehkawi 'to climb.' We frequently cannot break down such forms into constituent parts, but we should be constantly watchful for possibilities to do so. That is to say, we must look to see if some part of these stems does not occur in other words. In fact, our entire analytical procedure consists in discovering the recurring parts of utterances and classifying them. The recurring minimal meaningful parts of utterances are morphemes. A recurring partial may be any part of a language, i.e. a phoneme, a morpheme, a grouping of morphemes. The recognition of certain of these recurring partials is the means by which we isolate morphemes.

Following the procedures which have been outlined, isolate and identify the form and meaning of the morphemes in all of Problem 1, including the series below.

Problem 1 (cont.)

17. nimayanati   'I go to be hungry'[4]

18. nimayanato   'I went to be hungry'

19. nimayanaki   'I come to be hungry'[4]

20. nimayanako   'I came to be hungry'

21. nikmayanati   'I cause him to be hungry'[5]

22. nikmayanati?   'I caused him to be hungry'

23. nimicmayanatis   'I shall cause you (sg.) to be hungry'

The morphemes of Problem 1 may be listed as follows:

1. ni-   'I'

2. ti-   'you (sg.)'

3. -čoka   'to cry'

   etc.

---

[4]The forms translated with the help of the verbs 'to come' and 'to go' indicate direction away from and toward the speaker.

[5]The causative -ti may be considered distinct from the directional -ti.

Employ hyphens to indicate the way in which morphemes are connected with each other. A form which always occurs initially is followed by a hyphen. A form which always occurs finally is preceded by a hyphen. Forms which never occur initially or finally are preceded and followed by hyphens. A morpheme such as -čoka, which never occurs initially in this series but which does occur finally, is preceded by a hyphen. The opposite would be true of a form which may occur initially but never occurs finally. This use of hyphens is, however, restricted to these introductory analyses. Other systems may be employed in treating various series of affixes. These will be considered specifically in Chapter 4.

D. Supplementary Problems Illustrative of Principle 1

Problem 2 (data [restricted][6] from the Zacapoaxtla dialect of Aztec, a language of Mexico)

1. -ita   stem of the verb 'to see'   9. nikinitak   'I saw them'

2. nikita   'I see it'   10. kitakeh   'they saw it'

3. kita   'he sees it'   11. kinitakeh   'they saw them'

4. kinita   'he sees them'   12. tikitas   'you (sg.) will see it'

5. kitas   'he will see it'   13. kitaya   'he was seeing it'

6. kitak   'he saw it'   14. tikitaya   'you (sg.) were seeing it'

7. tikinita   'you (sg.) see them'   15. kitaskia   'he would see it'

8. nikitak   'I saw it'   16. nikitaskia   'I would see it'

Supplementary information: The third person singular subject is not expressed. This may be called a zero morpheme (see Principle 3).

Problem 3 (data from a Veracruz dialect of Aztec, a language of Mexico)

Instructions:

   a. List all morphemes.

   b. Give the meaning of each.

1. ikalwewe   'his big house'   9. petatci·n   'little mat'

2. ikalsosol   'his old house'   10. ikalmeh   'his houses'

3. ikalci·n   'his little house'   11. komitmeh   'cooking-pots'

4. komitwewe   'big cooking-pot'   12. petatmeh   'mats'

5. komitsosol   'old cooking-pot'   13. ko·yameci·n   'little pig'

6. komitci·n   'little cooking-pot'   14. ko·yamewewe   'big male pig'

7. petatwewe   'big mat'   15. ko·yameilama   'big female pig'

8. petatsosol   'old mat'   16. ko·yamemeh   'pigs'

---

[6] "Restricted" indicates that some of the complexities due to phonologically and morphologically defined distributions (see Principles 2 and 3) are omitted.

Problem 4 (data from Zoque, a language of Mexico)

Instructions:

    a. List all morphemes.

    b. Give the meaning of each.

1. pən	'man	19. yomotaʔm	'women'
2. pəntaʔm	'men'	20. yomohiʔŋ	'with a woman'
3. pənkəsi	'on a man'	21. yomotih	'just a woman'
4. pənkotoya	'for a man'	22. yomoʔune	'girl'
5. pənhiʔŋ	'with a man'	23. kahšiʔune	'chick'
6. pənkəsitaʔm	'on men'	24. kahši	'hen'
7. pənkəsišeh	'as on a man'	25. libru	'book'
8. pənšeh	'manlike'	26. libruʔune	'booklet'
9. pənšehtaʔm	'like men'	27. wetu	'fox'
10. nanah	'mother'	28. wetuʔune	'fox whelp'
11. nanahtaʔm	'mothers'	29. teʔ pən	'the man'
12. nanahkotoya	'for a mother'	30. maŋu teʔ pən	'the man went'
13. ʔunehiʔŋ	'with a child'	31. maŋpa teʔ pən	'the man goes'
14. ʔunehiʔŋtaʔm	'with children'	32. maŋkeʔtpa teʔ yomo	'the woman also goes'
15. naka	'skin, leather'	33. minpa teʔ ʔune	'the child comes'
16. nakapit	'by means of leather'	34. minu teʔ ʔune	'the child came'
17. nakapitšeh	'as if by leather'	35. maŋkeʔtu	'he also went'
18. yomo	'woman'	36. maŋutih	'he went (and did nothing more)'

Problem 5 (data from the Elisabethville dialect of Congo Swahili, a language of the Belgian Congo)

Instructions:

    a. List all morphemes.

    b. Give the meaning of each.

1. ninasema	'I speak'	4. ninaona	'I see'
2. wunasema	'you (sg.) speak'	5. ninamupika	'I hit him'
3. anasema	'he speaks'	6. tunasema	'we speak'

(Continued on next page.)

7. munasema   'you (pl.) speak'   19. wutakapikiwa   'you (sg.) will be hit'

8. wanasema   'they speak'   20. ninapikiwa   'I am hit'

9. ninapika   'I hit'   21. nilipikiwa   'I have been hit'

10. ninanupika   'I hit you (pl.)'   22. nilipikaka   'I hit (remote time)'

11. ninakupika   'I hit you (sg.)'   23. wunapikizwa   'you (sg.) cause being hit'

12. ninawapika   'I hit them'   24. wunanipikizwa   'you (sg.) cause me to be
                                                                             hit'

13. ananipika   'he hits me'   25. wutakanipikizwa   'you (sg.) will cause
                                                                       me to be hit'
14. ananupika   'he hits you (pl.)'   26. sitanupika   'I do not hit you (pl.)'

15. nilipika   'I have hit'   27. hatanupika   'he does not hit you (pl.)'

16. nilimupika   'I have hit him'   28. hatutanupika   'we do not hit you (pl.)'

17. nitakanupika   'I will hit you (pl.)'   29. hawatatupika   'they do not hit us'

18. nitakapikiwa   'I will be hit'

Supplementary information:

1. The future -taka- and the negative -ta- are not related.

2. The final -a may be treated as a morpheme. Its meaning is not indicated in this series.

3. The passive morpheme may be described as having two forms -iw- and -w-. Its form depends on what precedes it (see Principles 2 and 3).

Problem 6 (data from Yipounou, a language of the Gabon, Africa)

Instructions:

a. List all morphemes.

b. Give the meaning of each.[7]

1. gobul-   'to save'   6. nyigobulu   'I am saved'

2. gobulu   'state of being saved' 7. nyimagobulu   'I was saved'

3. ugobulu   'to be saved'   8. nyimagobula   'I saved'

4. nyugobulu   'I will be saved'   9. nyimamugobula   'I saved him'

5. nyugobula   'I will save'   10. nyimakegobula   'I saved myself'

(Continued on next page.)

---

[7]It will be perfectly evident that it is impossible on the basis of these few data to indicate adequately the meaning of certain morphemes. The student is expected to base his judgments only on the data given here. In Yipounou the -a suffix actually has a usage which is more extensive than is suggested by the contrast with -u, but this contrast is enough to isolate the morpheme -a and to assign it at least some meaning.

11. nyukegobula   'I will save myself'   13. amamugobula   'he saved him'

12. amagobula   'he saved'   14. amakegobula   'he saved himself'

Supplementary information:

1. The first person singular prefix has two forms, ny- and nyi-. The difference is accounted for by Principle 2.

2. There is no overt form to indicate the present tense.

3. The stem gobul- is derived from a combination of two morphemes, but may be treated here as a single morpheme.

2.22 Principle 2

Forms which have a common semantic distinctiveness but which differ in phonemic form (i.e. the phonemes or order of the phonemes) may constitute a morpheme provided the distribution of formal differences is phonologically definable.

2.22.1 The Meaning of Principle 2

Principle 2 may at first seem difficult to understand, but really it is quite simple. It means that when we discover forms with some common semantic distinctiveness but with different phonemes or arrangements of phonemes, we can still put these various forms together as a single morpheme provided we can discover phonological conditions which "govern" the occurrence of such phonologically different forms. In English, for example, one negative prefix has more than a single form. Compare intolerable and impossible. The forms in- and im- bear a partial phonetic-semantic resemblance and the positions in which they occur are determined by the type of consonant following. Before alveolar sounds such as t and d, the alveolar nasal n occurs, e.g. intangible, indecent. Before a bilabial sound such as p, the bilabial nasal occurs, e.g. impracticable, impersonal. We may say that the form of the word to which the prefix is added "determines" the form of the prefix. This is just another way of saying that the distribution (i.e. positions of occurrence) of in- and im- can be defined by the phonological characteristics of the forms with which they occur.

A slightly more extensive type of assimilation[8] occurs in the series comparable, context, congregate /kaŋgrǝgeyt/.[9] Here the bilabial nasal precedes a bilabial consonant; an alveolar nasal precedes an alveolar consonant; and a velar nasal precedes a velar consonant. Though this prefix has three forms /kam-, kan-, kaŋ/, their distribution can be phonologically defined, i.e. it is definable by the phonemes which occur in the construction. We may symbolize this type of relationship between these forms as /kam- ~ kan- ~ kaŋ/. The wavy symbol ~ means that the difference of distribution between the alternant forms of a single morpheme is phonologically definable. We may call the forms morphemic alternants or allomorphs. The second term is convenient because it is shorter than the full phrase and because it follows an analogy: allophone is to phoneme as allomorph is to morpheme. The relationships are not completely parallel, but they are sufficiently so to constitute a valuable association.

------

[8]This term identifies situations in which phonemes are phonologically similar, whether in terms of point of articulation or manner of articulation. See the Appendix, Part I, for a discussion of assimilation.

[9]Unless otherwise noted, all transcriptions of English are based on my own dialect.

2.22.2 The Application of Principle 2

A. Where the Sounds Involved Exhibit Some Phonetic Similarities

That morphemes should differ in form depending upon the phonological surroundings is only to be expected. In Totonac, for example, a somewhat similar situation exists as in the English example cited just above. The first person singular objective prefix occurs in three different forms: kin-~ kim-~ ki-: kinta·wáɬ 'he treated me,' kimpa·ški·ɬ 'he loved me,' and kiwaniɬ 'he said to me.' The first allomorph kin- occurs before stems beginning with t, c, č, k, and g; the second allomorph occurs before stems beginning with p; and the third allomorph occurs before continuants.

In some instances the phonologically conditioned forms seem quite different from each other. For example, in the formation of the Greek perfect forms /leluka, bebouleuka, gegrap^{h}a, dedo·ka, teth^{h}ɛ·ka, keklɛ·ka, meme·na/ from stems meaning 'loose,' 'consider,' 'write,' 'give,' 'place,' 'call,' 'rage,' respectively, the phonological differences in the reduplicated portion are very great: /le, be, ge, de, te, ke, me/. Nevertheless, we can define the distribution of these forms by the phonological characteristics of the stems to which they are added. In each case, except when stems begin with aspirated consonants, the initial consonant of the stem is repeated with the vowel /e/. When stem-initial consonants are aspirated, the reduplicated consonant has the same point of articulation, except that it is unaspirated. In fact, a survey of Greek soon reveals that there are no sequences of aspirated consonants in successive syllables.[10] If, then, we can define the distribution of these variants, all having the semantic value of forming the perfective stem of the verb, we may combine such forms into a single morpheme, and each individual form becomes a phonologically conditioned allomorph. We may symbolize the entire morpheme as /C$_1$e-/, by which we mean that the first consonant of the stem (including the change from aspirated to unaspirated) is repeated and followed by /e/.[11] The relationship of the various allomorphs may be symbolized as /le- ~ be- ~ ge- ~ de- ~ te- ~ ke- ~ me-/.

B. Where the Sounds Involved May Not Exhibit Phonetic Similarities

Sometimes there is a degree of phonetic likeness present in the phonological conditioning of occurrence, but phonetic likeness may not explain all the phonologically defined distributions. For example, in English the regular plural morpheme has three forms: /-əz/, /-z/, and /-s/. The last form always follows voiceless phonemes which have no s-like quality:[12] /piks, siyts, lips, blufs/ picks, seats, lips, bluffs. The form /-z/ follows voiced phonemes which have no s-like quality: /legz, bedz, tuwbz, siynz/ legs, beds, tubes, scenes. We can readily understand how a voiceless phoneme /-s/ would follow voiceless phonemes and how /-z/ would follow voiced phonemes, but we have no such easy explanation of why /-əz/ follows phonemes with an s-like quality: /rowzəz, liyčəz, brijəz, beysəz, læšəz, gəražəz/ roses, leeches, bridges, bases, lashes, garages. As descriptive linguists we need not be

---

[10]This is the so-called Grassmann's law.

[11]It may be argued that these reduplicated elements bear partial resemblances to their stems, and that hence they cannot be considered separate morphemes. It must be remembered, however, that this resemblance is one of phonetic form alone, not of meaning, too. The meaning of the reduplicated elements in this Greek series has nothing to do with the meanings of the stems. The reduplication signifies quite another matter, namely, the tense, and is as semantically different as if it were a distinct prefix having no phonetic resemblance. It is for this reason that the definition of a morpheme requires an absence of phonetic-semantic resemblance to other forms. The features of both form and meaning must be involved.

[12]Phonemes with s-like quality are called sibilants.

concerned about explaining the "why's" of certain forms. There are a number of observed relationships between sounds which we call by such names as assimilation, dissimilation, reduction of clusters, palatalization, and nasalization (these are discussed at length in the Appendix), but even these types of relationships are not "reasons" for modification. They are just observed situations, and it makes no difference whether we can discover some phonological "conditioning" or not for the forms we find. If we can define the distribution of alternants in terms of the phonological situations in which they occur, then we may combine such forms as allomorphs of the same morpheme, provided, of course, that they fulfill the requirement of "common semantic distinctiveness." In English the indefinite article a and an has two forms in unstressed positions: /ə/ a and /æn/ an. The first occurs before words beginning with a consonant, and the second before words beginning with vowels. We cannot "explain" the reasons for this difference, but we can define the distribution of these forms in terms of the phonological surroundings, in this case, the following phonemes. Compare the sets of forms in Tzeltal:[13]

Problem 7

1. hk'ab	'my hand'		1a. k'ab	'hand'
2. kakan	'my leg'		2a. akan	'leg'
3. alumal	'your land'		3a. lumal	'land'
4. awinam	'your wife'		4a. inam	'wife'
5. sk'op	'his language'		5a. k'op	'language'
6. yat'el	'his work'		6a. at'el	'work'

In this Tzeltal material the possessive pronouns occur in two different forms, depending upon whether the following noun begins with a vowel or a consonant. Note that h- occurs before the consonant-initial stem k'ab and k- before the vowel-initial stem akan. These two prefixal forms may be combined into a single morpheme on the basis of this phonologically defined distribution. The first person possessive morpheme may be symbolized as h- ~ k-. Similarly, the second and third person pronouns have alternant forms: a- ~ aw- and s- ~ y-. There does not seem to be much rhyme or reason to this type of alternation, and we need not look for it. Our concern is with the distribution; if we can discover the basis of the distribution we have fulfilled the requirements of our descriptive analysis. Perhaps students of comparative and historical Mayan could provide clues to past changes which have resulted in these differences where we might expect greater similarities. But such problems are beyond the scope of our descriptive procedures.

C. Where Sequences of Phonemes Are Involved

In some instances there is no actual change in the phonemes which occur, but the phonemes are arranged in different orders. For example, in Sudan Colloquial Arabic[14] the second person singular feminine possessive pronoun has two forms: -ik after consonant-final stems, e.g. kita·bik 'your book,' and -ki after vowel-final stems, e.g. axu·ki 'your brother.' In this instance the phonemes of the alternant forms are identical; it is just the order which is different. The distribution of these alternants is phonologically definable, and accordingly we may symbolize this morpheme as -ik ~ -ki.

---

[13]These data are taken from Marianna C. Slocum, "Tzeltal (Mayan) Noun and Verb Morphology," International Journal of American Linguistics, 14 (1948), 2: 77-86. Word-initial prevowel glottal stops have been omitted so as to simplify the problem.

[14]See J. Trimingham, Sudan Colloquial Arabic (London: Oxford University Press, 1946).

It may be that the phonemes of some morphemes do not remain in uninterrupted sequence. For example, in Zoque if the suffix -pa 'present tense indicator' is added to the stem kenhay-, the resultant form is kenhapya 'he looks for his benefit.' The expected order yp becomes py. This type of exchange of position is called metathesis. It is very common in Zoque. The fact that morphemes occur in such forms as -hay- ~ -ha...y- and -pa ~ -p...a is not difficult for us to describe, for we may readily state the phonological circumstances under which these changes take place. There is no change in the phonemes themselves, just in the order of their occurrence.

D. Problems Illustrative of Principle 2

Examine the following problems for various types of phonologically definable distributions of allomorphs.

Problem 8 (data from Huave, a language of Mexico)

Instructions:

    a. Identify the morpheme having allomorphs.

    b. Describe the phonologically defined distribution.

1. nahimb	'broom'	5. -hta	'female'
2. nahndot	'dust'	6. -šei	'male'
3. našei	'man'	7. nahta	'woman'
4. ahimb	'to sweep'	8. ahndot	'to dust'

Problem 9

Instructions:

    a. Rewrite the English phonemically.

    b. Discover three morphemes with three allomorphs each.

    c. Describe the phonologically definable distribution of each allomorph.

    d. Point out the distributional similarities between the three sets of allomorphs.

1. Fred goes to the playground every day.

2. The ragged tramp walked under the bridges.

3. Some students enjoy finding morphemes.

4. A reddish-haired flapper dashes down the highway in a speedster.

5. Fifteen boys jumped noisily into the newly finished swimming pool.

6. The wrinkled little old man wobbled uneasily along the slippery sidewalk.

7. The employer angrily dispatched a message to the workman's home.

8. The hungry creature creeps stealthily through the dark.

(Continued on next page.)

9. The faithful dog showed the greatest of love to his unkind master.

10. The fool crowded ten persons into the car.

Problem 10 (data from Tojolabal, a language of Mexico)

Instructions:

    a. Identify the morphemes.

    b. List all morphemes having allomorphs.

    c. Describe the distribution of all allomorphs having phonologically definable positions of occurrence.

1. hman	'I buy'	7. awal	'you (sg.) say'
2. ak'an	'you (sg.) want'	8. -il	'to see'
3. -man	'to buy'	9. -lap	'to dress'
4. slap	'he dresses'	10. yuʔ	'he drinks'
5. -k'an	'to want'	11. -al	'to say'
6. kil	'I see'	12. -uʔ	'to drink'

Problem 11 (data from Totonac, a language of Mexico)

Instructions:

    a. Identify the morphemes.

    b. List all morphemes having allomorphs.

    c. Describe the distribution of all allomorphs having phonologically definable positions of occurrence.

1. pašwi	'we (incl.) bathed'	7. pášti	'you (sg.) bathed'
2. kpašwi	'we (excl.) bathed'	8. wánti	'you (sg.) said it'
3. paš-	'to bathe'	9. wan-	'to say'
4. cukuw	'we (incl.) began'	10. wát	'you (sg.) ate it'
5. cukuya·w	'we (incl.) begin'	11. wa-	'to eat'
6. cuku-	'to begin'		

Supplementary information: The glottalization of the vowel (cf. forms 7, 8, and 10) constitutes a type of morpheme in Totonac (see Chapter 3), but should be omitted in this analysis.

E. Steps in Procedure for Problems Involving Principle 2

    In analysing any of the problems above there are certain procedural steps which may prove very valuable. These involve finding answers to the following questions.

1. What tentative morphemes have only one form?

2. What tentative morphemes appear to have more than one form, i.e. have allomorphs?

3. Are the phonological surroundings of the allomorphs of any one tentative morpheme different?

4. Are there other morphemes with similar types of allomorphs?

5. Are the phonological surroundings of these other allomorphs correspondingly different?

By following these steps in Problem 11, we may gather and analyze the following data:

Step 1: The tentative morphemes cuku- 'to begin' and (if we omit from the analysis the glottalization of the stem vowels, as suggested in the supplementary information) wan- 'to say' and wa- 'to eat' have only one form.

Step 2: The tentative morphemes -wi ~ -w and -ti ~ -t appear to have allomorphs.

Step 3: After consonant-final stems the form -wi occurs and after vowel-final stems the form -w occurs.

Step 4: As indicated by the data gathered under step 2, the tentative morphemes -wi ~ -w and -ti ~ -t have similar types of allomorphs.

Step 5: The phonological surroundings of the allomorphs -ti ~ -t are correspondingly different (cf. -wi ~ -w, step 3). In regard to both these morphemes we may state that the form -CV (C stands for any consonant and V for any vowel) follows consonant-final forms and -C follows vowel-final forms.

This approach may seem over simplified and unnecessarily tedious, but in complicated problems these steps, in the suggested order, are very helpful. The systematic procedure involves discovering (1) the forms which remain unchanged and which thus offer no problems, (2) those forms which are different and yet which may presumably constitute morphemes, (3) the possible correspondence of differences of phonological surroundings to differences of form, (4) any parallelism of different sets of allomorphs, and (5) the relationship of different phonological surroundings to different (and possibly parallel) sets of allomorphs. Steps 4 and 5 are designed to insure as comprehensive an analysis of the divergences as possible.

F. Writing up the Answers to Problems

Anyone who reads the descriptions of languages in such journals as Language, the International Journal of American Linguistics, Word, or the Journal of the American Oriental Society, will immediately discover that there are a number of systems for describing languages or particular details of languages. There are, however, certain facts essential to the problems we treat here, and there are certain ways in which these facts may be conveniently indicated and discussed. Of course, the instructions differ considerably for the various problems, but when they stipulate that one is to list and describe the distributions of the allomorphs (as in Problem 10), it is convenient and practical to employ the following type of statement:

The morphemes having allomorphs include: h- ~ k- 'I,' a- ~ aw- 'you (sg.),' and s- ~ y- 'he.'

The distributions are as follows:

h- ~ k- 'I'

    h- occurs before consonant stems: hman 'I buy.'

    k- occurs before vowel stems: kil 'I see.'

a- ~ aw- 'you (sg.)'

    a- occurs before consonant stems: ak'an 'you (sg.) want.'

    aw- occurs before vowel stems: awal 'you (sg.) say.'

s- ~ y- 'he'

    s- occurs before consonant stems: slap 'he dresses.'

    y- occurs before vowel stems: yuʔ 'he drinks.'

Several significant points should be noted in this presentation of the solution to Problem 10:

1. The first statement fulfills instruction b and the second fulfills instruction c.

2. With each listing of the morpheme we indicate its meaning. This is a method of identification and is frequently necessary, since different morphemes may have identical forms.

3. The allomorphs are listed in a structurally corresponding fashion. First is given the preconsonant form and secondly the prevowel form, but the reverse order would have been just as accurate. Regardless of the order employed, all three sets should indicate the parallelisms by the way in which they are listed.

4. The form in which the solution is given follows the general pattern of an outline. Such outlining is not very economical in publications, but for analysis it is helpful in indicating parallelisms or contradictions in structure.

5. Illustrations are provided with each statement of structure. Since the data of Problem 10 include just one illustration of each combination, only one illustration can be given. Such illustrative data may be introduced by the conventional symbol "e.g.," but a colon is usually preferred.

6. In this problem one could list illustrative data simply by referring to the stems, but in describing combinations of forms such as these, it is preferable to give the entire form. If necessary, one could expand the illustrative data to read:

    h- occurs before consonant stems: hman 'I buy' (< h- 'I' + -man 'to buy').[15]

It is impossible to indicate all the details involved in writing up all types of problems, but certain general principles should be noted. These principles may be summed up in the parody, "Describe the facts, all the facts, and nothing but the facts." This means, first, that we must record precisely what the findings are in view of the data actually used (that no plural formations occur in Problem 10 is, for example, unimportant); secondly, that we must record all the essential findings (that is, all the allomorphs must be listed, but not necessarily all the illustrations); and, thirdly, that we must exclude all irrelevant considerations (speculations as to why there are allomorphs, why they have the particular forms they have, and so on).

---

[15]The symbol < means "comes from," and, conversely, the symbol > means "becomes."

Another way of stating the principles of descriptive presentation is to say that we aim at comprehensiveness, clarity, and conciseness. This means (1) that all the facts should be described, (2) that they should be clearly described and all the relationships to other forms adequately indicated (both by what is said and the manner in which the description is organized), and (3) that the facts about a language should be concisely expressed. These principles will occupy our attention at other points in the text, especially in Chapter 9.

G. Types of Phonological Environment Described in Terms of Processes

In attempting to describe the phonological environment of various types of allomorphs we soon discover that the kinds of phonological environment differ greatly, but that some kinds tend to recur more frequently than others. We have already mentioned the processes of assimilation and dissimilation, in which the allomorphic distribution may be defined in terms of similarities or dissimilarities of point of articulation or manner of articulation. We also find that allomorphic differences of tone may be described in terms of different tonal surroundings, since contiguous tones tend to be alike. We find, too, that when consonants are lost in certain clusters, there is often a regular pattern for such a loss. Certain phonemes, furthermore, tend to "fuse" together, so that a combination such as dy may become ǰ. Compare /did yuw/ and /diǰuw/ Did you?

In order to explain in a measure the relationships of such phonological differences, the changes which take place have been spoken of in terms of processes. This is perhaps the easiest and most practical manner in which we can discuss them. In this section we shall note only the processes of assimilation, dissimilation, loss of phonemes, and palatalization. The Appendix contains a fuller account of these processes and discusses a number of others. The treatment in this chapter is designed only to make one aware of such phonological relationships and of how they may be described.

1. Assimilation

Assimilation denotes a process by which phonemes are made similar. Examine the following set of forms in Zoque:

Problem 12

1. ʔəs mpama	'my clothes'		1a. pama	'clothes'
2. ʔəs ŋkayu	'my horse'		2a. kayu	'horse'
3. ʔəs ntuwi	'my dog'		3a. tuwi	'dog'
4. ʔəs mpoco	'my younger sibling'		4a. poco	'younger sibling'
5. ʔəs ŋkose	'my older sister'		5a. kose	'older sister'
6. ʔəs ncin	'my pine'		6a. cin	'pine'

The prefixal forms which occur in this series are m-, n-, and ŋ-. We say that they are assimilated to the following consonant, by which we mean that the alternant m- precedes the bilabial stop p, the alternant n- precedes the dental phonemes t and c, and the alternant ŋ- precedes the velar k. In the history of Zoque this prefixal morpheme may have had at one time a single form.[16] Perhaps it was n-, but from this data we have no way of knowing, or even a valid way of guessing. Regardless of the original form, the two other allomorphs could have developed by a process of assimilation. That is to say, the n before p might

---

[16]These changes could also have occurred by analogy with some other prior set of forms.

have become increasingly like the p in the closure of the lips. At one time in the history of the language some of the Zoque people might have used the combination np and others the form mp, but the form mp apparently prevailed. This reconstruction of the history is, however, guesswork, and is quite beyond the scope of our descriptive analysis. Nevertheless, from the numerous instances in which we do know the history of forms we can suggest some of the possible stages in the process of change. For the descriptive linguist, however, the important thing is the end product, and though we may talk about assimilation as a kind of historical process, our primary interest is simply in being able to recognize types of phonological environment which may be determinative in defining the relationship of allomorphs.

Problem 13 (data from Hausa, a language of the Sudan)[17]

Instructions:

    a. Describe the phonological environment of all allomorphs.

    b. Describe the kind of assimilation involved.[18]

1. ʔùbankà	'your father'		8. ʔùwakkà	'your mother'
2. ʔùbankì	'your (f.) father'		9. ʔùwakkì	'your (f.) mother'
3. ʔùbanšì	'his father'		10. ʔùwaššì	'his mother'
4. ʔùbantà	'her father'		11. ʔùwattà	'her mother'
5. ʔùbammù	'our father'		12. ʔùwammù	'our mother'
6. ʔùbankù	'your (pl.) father'		13. ʔùwakkù	'your (pl.) mother'
7. ʔùbansù	'their father'		14. ʔùwassù	'their mother'

Supplementary information:

    1. Regard ʔùba- 'father' and ʔùwa- 'mother' as stems.

    2. The possessive suffixes consist of a -CV pattern.

    3. The morphemes which undergo assimilation (they consist of the form C) are elements which define certain syntactic and morphological relationships. Their meaning is unimportant to this problem.

Problem 14 (data from Tarahumara, a language of Mexico)

Instructions:

    a. Describe the phonological environment of all allomorphs.

    b. Describe the kind of assimilation involved.

---

[17]These data are taken from Carleton T. Hodge, An Outline of Hausa Grammar, Language Dissertation No. 41 (Baltimore: Linguistic Society of America, 1947).

[18]If necessary, consult the Appendix for a more detailed classification and explanation of types of assimilation.

1. mičiru	'to make shavings'	7. reme	'to make tortillas'[19]
2. sikwiči	'anthill'	8. remeke	'tortillas'
3. sikwiki	'ant'	9. pači	'to grow ears of corn'
4. mičiruku	'shavings'	10. pačiki	'an ear of corn'
5. ritu	'to be icy'	11. opača	'to be dressed'
6. rituku	'ice'	12. opačaka	'garment'

2. Dissimilation

Phonologically defined distributions may reflect differences of types of phonemes, as well as similarities. The following problems illustrate such dissimilative patterns.

Problem 15 (data from Tsotsil, a language of Mexico)

Instructions:

a. Identify all morphemes.

b. List the morphemes having allomorphs.

c. Describe the phonological distribution of these allomorphs.

1. -k'uši	'to put a wedge in'	1a. -k'uš	'wedge'
2. -šik'u	'to put a prop under'	2a. -šik'	'prop used beneath an object'
3. -šoni	'to put a prop against'	3a. -šon	'prop used against an object'
4. -vovi	'to go crazy'	4a. vov	'crazy'
5. -t'uši	'to become wet'	5a. t'uš	'wet'
6. -sakub	'to become white'	6a. sak	'white'
7. -lekub	'to become good'	7a. lek	'good'
8. -ʔik'ub	'to become black'	8a. ʔik'	'black'
9. -tuib	'to become smelly'	9a. tu	'smelly'

Supplementary information: For this analysis it is preferable to consider that there are two different verbalizing suffixes, one consisting of the structure -V and the other of -VC.

Problem 16 (data from Tzeltal, a language of Mexico)[20]

Instructions:

a. Identify all morphemes.

---

[19]Tortillas are a type of pancake made of ground corn.

[20]Slocum, op. cit., p. 81.

b. List the morphemes having allomorphs.

c. Describe the phonological distribution of these allomorphs.

1. sčay   'his fish'

2. čay   'fish'

3. pak'   'cloth'

4. swicul   'its hill'

5. swic   'his hill'

6. wic   'hill'

7. slewul   'its fat'

8. spak'ul   'its cloth'

9. slumil   'its ground'

10. lew   'fat'

11. si?   'his firewood'

12. spošil   'its medicine'

13. lum   'ground'

14. si?ul   'its firewood'

15. poš   'medicine'

Supplementary information: The translation 'its' refers to an inanimate possessor. 'Its firewood' could thus refer to the firewood possessed by the fire.

3. Assimilation of Tonemes

Assimilative as well as dissimilative patterns may also be found in the relationships of tonemes to one another. For example, in Mazatec,[21] a language of Mexico, the verb v?esko[1] 'to gather' ends normally in the highest of the four phonemic tones.[22] This may be called tone 1. The first person plural inclusive suffix -a normally occurs with tone 2, the second from the highest tone. When, however, this suffixal morpheme occurs with v?esko[1], the form is not v?esko[1]a[2], but rather v?esko[1]a[1], with the entire last syllable pronounced on a high tone. The suffixal morpheme thus has two allomorphs -a[2] and -a[1]. The distribution of these may be stated in terms of the phonological environment and is illustrative of assimilative patterns.[23]

Problem 17 (data from Cuicatec, a language of Mexico)

Instructions:

a. List the allomorphic tonemic patterns of the stems.

b. List the allomorphic tonemic patterns of the pronominal suffixes.

c. Determine whether there is any way of stating the types of collocations without identifying particular morphemes. This may be done by formulating (1) rules of change or (2) types of allomorphic sequences (this second type of solution will be considered in Chapter 5).

---

[21] These data are taken from a paper read by Eunice V. Pike at a meeting of the Linguistic Society of America, 1948, Ann Arbor, Michigan.

[22] For the purposes of this illustration only the word-final tones are indicated and discussed.

[23] See Kenneth L. Pike, Tone Language (Ann Arbor: University of Michigan Press, 1948), for many illustrations of assimilative as well as dissimilative patterns in the tonal structure of languages.

The following list consists of present-tense forms meaning 'to write' (A), 'to make' (B), 'to divide' (C), 'to sew' (D), 'to spy out' (E). In the first column the numbers 1, 2, 3 indicate first, second, and third person. The abbreviations are: s. 'singular,' p. 'plural,' fa. 'familiar,' fo. 'formal,' f. 'feminine,' m. 'masculine,' incl. 'inclusive,' and excl. 'exclusive.'

	A	B	C	D	E
1s.	1a. idahúú	1b. idíí	1c. inˀtaá	1d. inˀteiyǫ́	1e. héénú
2sfa.	2a. idahúudi	2b. idįidi	2c. inˀtaadi	2d. inˀteiyǫdi	2e. héénúdí
2sfo.	3a. idahúunì	3b. idíínì	3c. inˀtaànì	3d. inˀteiyǫ́nì	3e. héénúnì
3sm.	4a. idahúusa	4b. idįisa	4c. inˀtaasa	4d. inˀteiyǫsa	4e. héénúsá
3sf.	5a. idahúutá	5b. idįitá	5c. inˀtaatá	5d. inˀteiyǫtá	5e. héénútá
3sfa.	6a. idahúuyà	6b. idííyà	6c. inˀtaàyà	6d. inˀteiyǫ́yà	6e. héénúyà
1p. incl.	7a. idahúuˀ	7b. idiǫˀ	7c. inˀtaaoˀ	7d. inˀteiyǫˀ	7e. héénúˀ
1p. excl.	8a. idahúunu	8b. idįinu	8c. inˀtaanu	8d. inˀteiyǫnu	8e. héénúnú

Supplementary information:

1. Verbs A, B, C, and D belong to a class which takes the prefix i- in the present-tense formation. Verb E belongs to another class.

2. The morpheme of the first person singular is a high tone replacing (or identical with) the tone of the stem. This type of morpheme will be considered in Chapter 3. It is possible to symbolize it here as -V́.

3. Regard the stems as single morphemes (they are actually complex formations).

4. Omit from consideration the vocalic alternations and reductions in the first person inclusive suffix. Symbolize this morpheme as -oˀ.

5. Mid tones are left unmarked.

Procedure in analysis:

1. Determine the morphemes which do not change.

2. List the morphemes which change.

3. Reconstruct a set of forms which would reflect a hypothetical situation prior to any assimilative changes. Observe the following directions:

   a. Leave in their unchanged form the forms which do not change.

   b. When there are alternant forms, base the reconstruction on that form which is apparently least affected by its surroundings. For example, the suffix -nì in forms 3a, 3b, 3c, 3d, and 3e follows mid, low, and high tones. Stems A and E show no change (except 1a, in which the first person singular suffix accounts for the change), but stems B, C, and D do exhibit changes. We set up the stems of cross section 3 as representing the basic forms, and add the suffixes as they occur in series A, B, C, and D. These series are selected rather than E, since the greater diversity of tonal forms occurs in A-D. In E only high and low occur on the suffixes.

The reconstructed forms would be of the following type:

A	B	C	D	E
1a. *idahú… + V́	1b. *idįí + V́	1c. *inˀtaà + V́	1d. *inˀtęįyó̜ + V́	1e. *héénú + V́
2a. *idahúudí	2b. *idįídi	2c. *inˀtaàdi	2d. *inˀtęįyó̜di	2e. *héénúdi

4. If in comparison with actual forms the reconstructed forms exhibit substantial correlations which will permit a description of perfectly automatic changes, one may conclude that the reconstruction is correct. This does not mean that the reconstructed forms represent actual historical forms, but that for the sake of our descriptive analysis these reconstructed forms may serve as basic ones. If the reconstruction does not provide adequate correlations, one should set up other stem forms as basic. The procedure, however, must always be systematic; choices may not be made at random. After two or three types of reconstructions have been worked out and the correlations compared, the selection of the "right" reconstruction will depend upon the number and value of the correlations. For this problem apply the suggestions under procedure 3b, but the student should attempt a reconstruction from forms of cross section 4 and the suffixal forms from E. This will show immediately the differences in results.

The solution to Problem 17:

In the solution below, the rules requested in the first part of instruction c are not completely formulated. The descriptive statement is, however, set up; the student should fill in the rest.

1. Final vowels of stems before a zero-vowel high-tone morpheme become ... or remain ...

2. Stems consisting of one or more mid tones followed by a high tone or a low tone preserve the stem-final tones before low tones, and undergo a change of the stem-final tone to a ... tone in all other occurrences.

3. Stems consisting of high tones or a high tone plus a mid tone ...

4. Suffixes of mid tone become high after stems consisting of all ... tones.

4. Loss of Consonant Phonemes

When morphemes occur next to each other, one or the other, and sometimes both, may lose one or more of their contiguous consonant phonemes. For example, in Tojolabal the combination of the stem oč 'to enter' and the stem caan 'behind' becomes ocaan 'to put behind,' rather than *oččaan, which we might expect. Compare the following constructions:

sutut 'he whirls around' < š- 'tense-aspect prefix' + sutut 'to whirl around'

suunil 'its paper' < s- '3d sg. possessive prefix' + huun 'paper'

In two combinations the first of two phonemes is lost and in one the second is lost: čc > c, šs > s, sh > s. In some constructions the clusters in Tojolabal reduce, but undergo assimilation at the same time. For example, oč 'to enter' + siˀ 'wood' becomes ociˀ 'to put in wood.' The alveopalatal affricative č has been shifted front to the dental position of the s. The resulting affricative is dental c. This type of assimilation-loss combination is sometimes called "fusion." The total number of phonemes is reduced, but the evidence of the original combination is still preserved.

<u>Problem 18</u> (data from Classical Greek)[24]

Instructions:

   a. Compare the nominative (subject) forms (1-9) with the corresponding genitive forms (1a-9a).

   b. Determine the assimilations which are exhibited in the nominative series.

   c. Describe the reductions in consonant clusters occurring in the same series.

1. ait^{h}íops   'Ethiopian'   1a. ait^{h}iopos   'of an Ethiopian'

2. p^{h}léps   'vein'   2a. p^{h}lebós   'of a vein'

3. p^{h}úlaks   'watchman'   3a. p^{h}úlakos   'of a watchman'

4. aíks   'goat'   4a. aigós   'of a goat'

5. t^{h}ɛ́·s   'serf'   5a. t^{h}ɛ·tós   'of a serf'

6. elpís   'hope'   6a. elpídos   'of hope'

7. órni·s   'bird'   7a. órni·t^{h}os   'of a bird'

8. gíga·s   'giant'   8a. gígantos   'of a giant'

9. hrí·s   'nose'   9a. hri·nós   'of a nose'

Supplementary information:

   1. The stresses (perhaps combinations of tone and stress) are not pertinent to the problem.

   2. The genitive series exhibit the basic forms of the stems (see section 2.23.2, D).

One of the best ways to analyze such a problem as this is to reconstruct the forms as they might have existed before the presumed changes took place. The principles of procedure are simple:

   1. Take the fullest forms of each possible morpheme (or combinations of morphemes).

   2. Arrange these in their respective positions.

   3. Compare these reconstructed forms with the forms actually in use. This comparison may consist of replies to the following series of questions:

   a. What forms are unchanged?

   b. What forms are changed (that is, lost, fused, changed in quality, quantity, and so on)?

   c. Are there similarities of change?

   d. How may such changes be described?

---

[24]The phonemic transcription follows Edgar H. Sturtevant, <u>The Pronunciation of Greek and Latin</u> (Baltimore: Linguistic Society of America, 1940).

We may assume that the genitive forms exhibit the basic stems, for they appear to be the least modified by their phonological surroundings. There are no phonological processes which would account for (1) the differences between p and b and between k and g in such an intervocalic position, and (2) the intrusion of consonants between the stem vowel and the suffix vowel o. On the other hand, we can readily discover the phonological "conditioning" for the assimilation of b to p and g to k before s and the loss of a consonant in final clusters of the type Cs or CCs. On the basis of these general observations we may proceed to reconstruct the hypothetical forms (marked by a star) as follows:

1. *ait^híops 'Ethiopian'   6. *elpíds   'hope'

2. *p^hlébs   'vein'   7. *órni·t^hs 'bird'

3. *p^húlaks 'watchman'   8. *gígants 'giant'

4. *aígs   'goat'   9. *hrí·ns   'nose'

5. *t^hέ·ts 'serf'

The test of such a reconstruction is in the number and significance of the correlations which may be discovered. By comparing the reconstructed forms with those in actual use we may say that bilabial and velar consonants before final -s are assimilated as to manner of articulation (i.e. voiced + voiceless becomes voiced + voiced) and that dental consonants before final -s are lost, with compensatory lengthening of a short to a long vowel if one of the consonants is n. Long vowels, of course, remain long. Such regular developments of phonological change are sufficient to warrant the selection of the stems in the genitive series as basic. This is not, however, obligatory, and one could, if he so desired, select the stems in the nominative series. But, if this is done, the resultant description is very complicated, for one must list those stems which change p to b and k to g, and those stems which add the phonemes -t, -d, -t^h, -nt, and -n before the genitive -os. This listing of morphemes is much more complicated than the simple statements about the regular changes which occur under phonologically definable circumstances.

In the following two problems from Navaho[25] the actual forms occur in the first columns and the reconstructed forms in the second. Instructions are given below Problem 20.

Problem 19

1. dìsé·h   'I belch'   1a. *dišzé·h

2. yìšàš   'I'm wearing out'   2a. *yišžàš

3. náhìšlá·h   'I pick them up'   3a. *náhišlá·h

4. hònìsą́   'I am discerning'   4a. *honišyą́

5. ʔàšą́   'I eat'   5a. *ʔašyą́

6. yìšxą́   'I kill them'   6a. *yišgą́

7. dìšá·h   'I start to go'   7a. *dišhá·h

Supplementary information:

1. The tones are not pertinent to the problem. The unmarked vowels of series 1a-7a

---

[25]These data are taken from Harry Hoijer, Navaho Phonology (Albuquerque: University of New Mexico Press, 1945), p. 46.

constitute a special morphophonemic (see section 8.22.61) class.

2. The differences in items 4 and 5 are illustrative of Principle 3.

Problem 20

1. yìsé·h   'he tans it'   1a. *yiɬzé·h

2. yìyì·šàh   'he hooks it'   2a. *yiyì·ɬžàh

3. yìǰò·ɬá   'he hates him'   3a. *yiǰò·ɬlá

4. nìnísᶇ   'I have raised you'   4a. *niníɬyᶇ

5. yìɬxà·ɬ   'he beats it with a stick'   5a. *yiɬgà·ɬ

6. yéɬá·h   'he overtakes him'   6a. *yéɬhá·h

Supplementary information: The tones are not pertinent to the problem.

In describing the changes (reduction and assimilation) in Problems 19 and 20, chart the changes in the type of square indicated below rather than attempt to state the different allomorphs:

Second members of the consonant clusters

	z	ž	l	y	g	h
š						
ɬ						

First members of the consonant clusters

Having charted the types of resultant forms in Problems 19 and 20, point out any parallels between the two series of reductions and assimilations. The following questions may be helpful in finding significant correlations:

1. What is the result of a voiceless phoneme plus a voiced phoneme?

2. What is the result of a more front phoneme plus a more back phoneme?

3. Which types of combinations reduce to one phoneme and which remain two?

Problem 21 (data from Zoque, a language of Mexico)

Instructions:

a. Identify the morphemes.

b. List the morphemes having allomorphs.

c. Describe the types of reductions without referring to any specific phoneme. This can be done in two statements.

d. Describe the phonological distribution of the allomorphs.

1. kenu   'he looked'   1a. kenpa   'he looks'

2. sihku   'he laughed'   2a. sikpa   'he laughs'

(Continued on next page.)

3. wihtu   'he walked'   3a. witpa   'he walks'

4. ka?u˙   'he died'   4a. ka?pa   'he dies'

5. nahpu   'he kicked'   5a. nahpa   'he kicks'

6. cihcu   'it tore'   6a. cicpa   'it tears'

7. sohsu   'it cooked'   7a. sospa   'it cooks'

Supplementary information: The difference in translation between 'he' and 'it' reflects only the differences in the types of subjects which normally occur with such verbs. It has no bearing upon the phonological problem.

Problem 22

Instructions:

    a. Rewrite the forms phonemically.

    b. Identify the stems minus the suffixes.

    c. State what has happened to the stems in the free forms listed in column 1 (omit, however, any change of vowels or stress).

1. hymn   1a. hymnal

2. solemn   2a. solemnize

3. condemn   3a. condemnation

4. damn   4a. damnation

5. autumn   5a. autumnal

Problem 23

Instructions:

    a. Add the following forms to the data of Problem 12.

    b. State the types of reductions which occur for all the data.

7. ?əs ?aci   'my older brother'   7a. ?aci   'older brother'

8. ?əs mok   'my corn'   8a. mok   'corn'

9. ?əs ?inu   'my zapote'   9a. ?inu   'zapote' (a kind of fruit)

5. Loss of Vowel Phonemes

In the same way that consonants may be lost, whether singly or in clusters, so vowels may be lost. Generally this loss results from (1) reduction of a cluster of vowels, (2) some type of stress, or (3) the position of the vowel at the end of the word or phrase.

In some languages and with certain morphemes the reductions may be very extensive. For example, in Mazatec[26] the stem-final vowels of verbs combine with dependent subject pronouns in the following manner (numerals refer to discussion below):

---

[26]These data are from E. V. Pike, as cited in footnote 21.

Chart of Reductions

Vowels of dependent subject pronouns

		-a	-i	-o
Stem vowels	i	ia[1]	i[5]	io[9]
	e	e[2]	ai[6]	ao[10]
	a	a[3]	ai[7]	ao[11]
	o	oa[4]	oi[8]	o[12]

For convenience in describing the relationships of the four phonemic vowels to each other, we may chart their relative positions as follows:

Chart of Vowel Positions

	Front	Back
High	i	o
Low	e	a

This chart does not correspond precisely to the type of chart usually employed in describing the articulatory relationships of vowels, but for our purposes it is very useful, and the morphological validity of such a plotting of relationships will be evident from the correlations which it reveals.

By listing the actual reduction (the first chart) and by correlating these reductions with the structural placements (the second chart), several significant facts may be observed:

1. Sequences of identical vowels reduce to a single vowel of the same quality, i.e. i plus i becomes i; cf. 3, 5, 12.

2. In sequences of nonidentical vowels, high vowels are never lost; cf. 1, 4, 6, 7, 8, 9, 10, and 11.

3. The low-front vowel e in combination with high vowels becomes a low-back vowel; cf. 6 and 10.

4. A sequence of low-front vowel plus low-back vowel becomes a low-front vowel, cf. 2.

A hasty glance at the Mazatec data from which the first chart is compiled and even some attention given to the chart itself may tend to leave the impression that the reductions and changes have no rhyme or reason. It is true that the changes are arbitrary, just as all linguistic changes are fundamentally arbitrary, but there are some definite parallelisms. That is to say, the changes are not random changes without relationship to each other.

In the following data from Tlapanec, a language of Mexico, there are similar types of reductions and assimilations.

Problem 24

Instructions:

    a. Reconstruct the fuller forms in view of the supplementary information.

    b. Chart the reductions in accordance with the first chart of the Mazatec data.

    c. Chart the vowel relationships in accordance with the second chart of the Mazatec data.

    d. List all the parallelisms of change.

    e. Attempt to classify these parallelisms in terms of types of change. The text which follows the supplementary information indicates how each of these instructions is to be carried out.

1. guˀdo·	'I have'		1a. štaˀda·	'you (sg.) have'
2. ndayo·	'I see'		2a. nataya·	'you (sg.) see'
3. narugo·	'I close'		3a. natarugwa·	'you (sg.) close'
4. naruˀho·	'I tie'		4a. nataruˀhwa·	'you (sg.) tie'
5. nariˀku·	'I translate'		5a. natariˀkwi·	'you (sg.) translate'
6. na·tanabu·	'I justify'		6a. naratanabi·	'you (sg.) justify'
7. na·štu·	'I lick with the tongue'		7a. narašti·	'you (sg.) lick with the tongue'

Supplementary information:

    1. The tones are not written, as they are not pertinent to this problem.

    2. The unsuffixed stems of 1 and 2 end in <u>a</u>.

    3. The unsuffixed stems of 3 and 4 end in <u>o</u>.

    4. The unsuffixed stem of 5 ends in <u>u</u>.

    5. The unsuffixed stems of 6 and 7 end in <u>i</u>.

    6. The suffix of the first person has a form -<u>o</u> in situations not involving such reductions.

    7. The suffix of the second person has a form -<u>a</u> in situations not involving such reductions.

    8. The supplementary information under numbers 2-7 above is supplied only through other occurrences, ones which do not involve the changes listed in Problem 24.

    9. None of the phonemes up to and including the last consonant of the stem have any relationship to the phonological changes of the stem vowel and the personal suffix.

    On the basis of the original data and the supplementary information, one may readily proceed to follow the instructions, as shown below.

a. The reconstruction of the fuller forms:

By combining the stem forms and the suffixal forms, the following type of series may be constructed:

1. *guˀdao   1a. *štaˀdaa

2. *ndayao   2a. *natayaa

etc.

b. The charting of reductions:

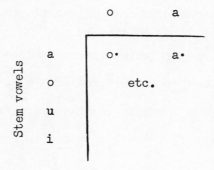

Suffixal vowels

c. The charting of vowel relationships:

Since there are only four vowels in Tlapanec, the charting of articulatory and structural relationships is parallel with that in Mazatec.

d. Parallelisms of change:

There are numerous parallelisms of change. The following statements point out some of these:

1. The reduction of identical vowels to a long vowel of the same quality occurs in 3, 4, 1a, and 2a.

2. Combinations of back vowels plus -a result in consonant-vowel sequences; cf. 3a, 4a, and 5a.

3. When the stem vowel is low (1, 2, 3, 4) the final vowel is low, but when the stem vowel is high (5, 6, 7), the final vowel is high.

e. Classification of the parallelisms of change:

These parallelisms should be classified according to sequences of identical vowels and of nonidentical vowels, then according to low vowels plus high vowels, high vowels plus low vowels, front vowels plus back vowels, low-front plus low-back, and so on, including any combination which is significant in this series.

One may readily ask what the value of this type of analysis is for the practical description of a language, since, as we shall find in accordance with Principle 3, we could simply list the various forms of the first person suffix (-o· and -u·) and then list all the verbs with which they occur. Similarly, we could list the forms of the second person suffix (-a·, -wa·, -wi·, and -i·) and then list the verbs with which these occur. This is a perfectly possible and legitimate procedure, but it is quite clumsy and involves the making of long lists of forms in order to indicate the combinations which occur. By means of the techniques we have indicated in Problem 24 we may eliminate this listing of forms and in a few simple statements indicate that all the changes take place "automatically," given the phonologically basic[27] forms of the stems and of the suffixes. There is a very practical consideration for the person learning such a language: he need not memorize long lists of forms, but if he knows the form of the stem (which he will find in other combinations), he can immediately determine the proper form of the personal pronominal ending. Furthermore, these same types of changes in vowel clusters occur in many parts of the language. For this reason, such changes are generally described in the first part of the morphological section of a grammar in order that the details need not be repeated over and over again for the numerous instances in which the same phonological facts are pertinent.[28]

In Tonkawa[29] the vowels in certain morphemes and combinations of morphemes[30] are reduced or lost according to regular patterns:

1. Short vowels occurring in even-numbered syllables (counting from the beginning of the word) are lost.

2. Long vowels in even-numbered syllables are reduced to short vowels.

3. All stem-final vowels before vowel suffixes are lost.

4. All stem-final vowels before consonant suffixes are retained.

5. When final to the word, the last vowel of the stem is lost and the next to the last vowel is retained.

Situations described in 3, 4, and 5 constitute exceptions to "rule" 1.

Examine closely the following set of forms.

Problem 25 (data from Tonkawa, an Indian language of the United States)

Instructions:

a. Reconstruct the fuller forms, as was done in Problem 18, e.g.:

2a. *yamaxao°

8a. *keyamaxano°

etc.

b. Place over the vowels of the reconstructed series the number of the "rule" (1-5) by which we may account for its loss or retention (by exception), e.g.:

---

[27]By "phonologically basic" we mean those forms which may be most conveniently employed to describe other related forms.

[28]See Chapter 9.

[29]See Harry Hoijer, "Tonkawa" in Linguistic Structures of Native America (Viking Fund Publications in Anthropology, Vol. 6) (New York, 1946), p. 294. Used by permission.

[30]There is a morphophonemically different class of vowels which do not undergo these changes (see Chapter 5).

$$\overset{1\ \ 3}{2a.\ *yamaxao^{\gamma}}$$

$$\overset{1\ \ 4}{8a.\ *keyamaxano^{\gamma}}$$

etc.

This is the reverse of the procedure employed in most problems, but it assists us in understanding the techniques of analysis and the significance of the final description.

1. yamaxa-	'to paint someone's face'	8. keymaxano?	'he is painting my face'
2. yamxo?	'he paints his face'	9. notsono?	'he is hoeing it'
3. keymaxo?	'he paints my face'	10. notos	'hoe'
4. ka·na-	'to throw away'	11. notoso-	'to hoe'
5. ka·no?	'he throws it away'	12. wentoso?	'he hoes them'
6. xakano?	'he throws it far away'	13. notso?	'he hoes it'
7. yamxano?	'he is painting his face'		

Supplementary information: Stem forms 1, 4, and 11 exhibit no losses.

It should be obvious that the method employed in describing the phonological differences in the morphemes of Problem 25 is very much simpler than if we should first list the various allomorphs, e.g. ymaxa-, yamxa-, ymax-, and yamx-, and then list all the different combinations in which these variant forms occur. By discovering the phonological distribution of these allomorphs (i.e. by position within the word) we may succeed not only in identifying the morphemes in question but in greatly simplifying our subsequent description of their distribution (see Chapters 4 and 5).

6. Palatalization

Palatalization consists in replacing a consonant by one of a more palatal (or sometimes, alveopalatal) position, because of the presence of a front vowel or y. Historically such changes have taken place very frequently, and can be seen in many English words. For example, the suffixation of -ion /-yən/ (cf. communion) to the word act /ækt/ results in /ækšən/, rather than the form /*æktyən/, which we might have expected. Similarly, divide /divayd/ plus /-yən/ becomes /divižən/ and convulse /kənvəls/ plus /-yən/ becomes convulsion /kənvəlšən/. Also, did you /did yuw/ may be optionally /dijuw/.

There are many different types of palatalization, but the most common are:

1. Replacement of a stop consonant by an affricate with sibilant type of off-glide, e.g. ti > či, ki > či, di > ji, gi > ji.[31]

2. Replacement of stops or affricate consonants by sibilant continuants, e.g. ti > si, ki > ši, di > zi, gi > ži, č > š, ʒ > ž.

---

[31]In some combinations the high front vowel (or consonant) is fused with the preceding consonant and is thus lost, but in others the so-called palatalizing element is retained. There is a tendency for phonemes to be replaced by ones of the same voiced or voiceless quality, but this by no means always happens.

3. Replacement of dental or velar continuants by alveopalatal or palatal sibilant continuants, e.g. si > ši, θi > ši, xi > ši, zi > ži, gi > ži.

Problem 26 (data from Hausa, a language of West Africa)[32]

Instructions:

a. Identify as many morphemes as possible.

b. List all morphemes of which one or more allomorphs involve palatalization.

c. List all the types of palatalization.

1. šaat-   'to comb'

2. mašaačii   'a comb'

3. b'aat-   'to spoil'

4. yaab'aačì   'he's spoiled'

5. b'add-   'to lose'

6. yaab'aččèè   'he's lost'

7. gid-   'house'

8. gijìì   'house'

9. buus-   'to blow'

10. mabùùšii   'player of a wind instrument'

11. mabùùsaa   'players of wind instruments'

12. rans'-   'to swear an oath'

13. yaaranč'èè   'he swore an oath'

14. z-   'to go'

15. yaajee   'he went'

16. čiiz-   'to bite'

17. mačììjii   'snake'

Supplementary information:

1. The tones are not pertinent to the problem.

2. Though the replacement of s' (12) by č' (13) is the reverse of what has been described as the second principal type of palatalization, yet the shift in articulatory position is toward the more palatal position.

Problem 27 (data from Mazahua, a language of Mexico)

Instructions: List the types of palatalization.

1. njišu   'women'

2. njɔhɔ   'singers'

3. njoˀyi   'bones'

4. njæčhɔ   'corn (pl.)'

5. njʉNʋ   'flowers'

6. njɔˀɔ   'eyes'

1a. ndišu   'woman'

2a. ndɔhɔ   'singer'

3a. ndoˀyi   'bone'

4a. ndæčhɔ   'corn'

5a. ndʉNʋ   'flower'

6a. ndɔˀɔ   'eye'

(Continued on next page.)

---

[32]See Hodge, op. cit., pp. 25-26.

7. čʰɔmæč'i 'bread (pl.)'   7a. tʰɔmæč'i 'bread'

8. č'i?i 'boys'   8a. t'i?i 'boy'

9. č'æzi 'metals'   9a. t'æzi 'metal'

10. č'æ?bi 'grasses'   10a. t'æ?bi 'grass'

11. čʰæ?mæ 'charcoal (pl.)'   11a. tʰæ?mæ 'charcoal'

12. njæčʰi 'sheep (pl.)'   12a. ndæčʰɨ 'sheep'

Supplementary information:

1. Tones are not given in the data.

2. The plural morpheme has an allomorph y-, which combines with the forms of column 2 to produce the replacements occurring in column 1.

3. It is possible to regard the initial clusters beginning with a nasal as constituting unit phonemes.

H. Supplementary Problems Illustrative of Principle 2

Problem 28 (data [restricted] from Popoluca, a language of Mexico)

Instructions:

a. Identify all the morphemes.

b. List all morphemes having allomorphs.

c. Describe the distribution of all allomorphs having phonologically definable positions of occurrence.

1. ?iŋku?tpa 'you (sg.) eat it'   9. ?iñhokspa 'you (sg.) are hoeing it'

2. ?anhokspa 'I hoe it'   10. no·mi 'boss'

3. ?iku?t 'he ate it'   11. ?ano·mi 'my boss'

4. ?imo·ya 'his flower'   12. ?ika·ma 'his cornfield'

5. mo·ya 'flower'   13. ?iŋka·ma 'your (sg.) cornfield'

6. ?ampetpa 'I sweep it'   14. ?amo·ya 'my flower'

7. ?impet 'you swept it'   15. ?ino·mi 'your (sg.) boss'

8. ?antek 'my house'

Supplementary information:

1. The same morphemes are used as subjects of transitive verb forms and as possessives of nouns.

2. The phonological processes include assimilation and reduction of consonant clusters.

Problem 29 (data [restricted] from Zapotec of the Isthmus, a language of Mexico)

Instructions:

    a. Identify all morphemes.

    b. List all morphemes having allomorphs.

    c. Describe the distribution of all allomorphs having phonologically definable positions of occurrence.

1. geta	'corncake'	1a. sketabe	'his corncake'	1b. sketaluʔ	'your corncake'
2. bere	'chicken'	2a. sperebe	'his chicken'	2b. spereluʔ	'your chicken'
3. doʔo	'rope'	3a. stoʔobe	'his rope'	3b. stoʔoluʔ	'your rope'
4. ya·ga	'wood'	4a. sya·gabe	'his wood'	4b. sya·galuʔ	'your wood'
5. diʔiǰa	'word'	5a. stiʔiǰabe	'his word'	5b. stiʔiǰaluʔ	'your word'
6. palu	'stick'	6a. spalube	'his stick'	6b. spaluluʔ	'your stick'
7. ku·ba	'dough'	7a. sku·babe	'his dough'	7b. sku·baluʔ	'your dough'
8. tapa	'four'	8a. stapabe	'his four'	8b. stapaluʔ	'your four'

Problem 30 (data [restricted] from a Veracruz dialect of Aztec, a language of Mexico)

Instructions:

    a. Identify all morphemes.

    b. List all morphemes having allomorphs.

    c. Describe the distribution of all allomorphs having phonologically definable positions of occurrence.

1. tiwi	'you (sg.) come'	7. nikmanatih	'we (excl.) are going to cook it'
2. niwi	'I come'	8. tikmanatih	'we (incl.) are going to cook it'
3. nikmana	'I cook it'	9. kimana	'he cooks it'
4. nikmanaʔ	'I cooked it'	10. kimanah	'they cook it'
5. tikmanas	'you (sg.) will cook it'	11. momana	'it cooks itself'
6. kimanati	'he is going to cook it'		

Supplementary information:

    1. The third person subject pronoun is not overtly expressed.

    2. The combination ti-...-h (8) means 'we including you.' The second person plural subject morpheme is aŋ- (see Problem 1).

Problem 31 (data from Kekchi, a language of Guatemala)

Instructions:

    a. Identify all morphemes.

    b. List all morphemes having allomorphs.

    c. Describe the distribution of all allomorphs having phonologically definable positions of occurrence.

1. šinsak'	'I hit him'		9. šril	'he saw it'
2. šasak'	'you (sg.) hit him'		10. šqil	'we saw it'
3. šsak'	'he hit him'		11. šeril	'you (pl.) saw it'
4. šqasak'	'we hit him'		12. šeʔril	'they saw it'
5. šesak'	'you (pl.) hit him'		13. teʔril	'they are going to see it'
6. šeʔsak'	'they hit him'		14. -sak'	'to hit'
7. šgwil	'I saw it'		15. tiškut	'he will throw it'
8. šagwil	'you (sg.) saw it'			

Supplementary information:

    1. The third person object is not overtly indicated.

    2. One allomorph of the third person subject morpheme is -š- (15), but in form 3, a reduction of cluster takes place.

    3. The verb 'hit' (1-6) is a past-tense form.

Problem 32 (data from the Luba-Lulua dialect of Chiluba, a language of the Congo)

Instructions:

    a. Identify all morphemes.

    b. List all morphemes having allomorphs.

    c. Describe the distribution of all allomorphs having phonologically definable positions of occurrence.

1. ǹsùmá	'I, biting'		8. ǹtú ŋá·sùmá	'I am always biting'
2. úsùmá	'you (sg.), biting'		9. útú wá·sùmá	'you (sg.) are always biting'
3. ùsùmá	'he, biting'		10. ùtú wà·sùmá	'he is always biting'
4. ǹdí ǹsùmá	'I am biting'		11. m̀bá·sùmú	'I bit (indefinite past)'
5. ídí úsùmá	'you (sg.) are biting'		12. ǹdí músùmé	'I have bitten'
6. ùdí ùsùmá	'he is biting'		13. údí músùmé	'you (sg.) have bitten'
7. ǹčǐdí ǹsùmá	'I am now biting'			

Supplementary information:

1. Forms 1-3 are participial forms.

2. The allomorphic form of the first person pronoun in the second word of item 8 is not characteristic of prevowel position, but should be treated as such in terms of these limited data.

3. Form 11 is primarily a Baluba dialect form. The final -u may be disregarded.

4. The second forms in items 12 and 13 are past participles. The prefix mú- is a person indicator, employed with all singular persons.

5. A tone mark written over a consonant indicates that it is syllabic.

6. Vowels such as u and i may become consonants w and y in certain situations. See forms 9 and 10.

7. The tonal part of a morpheme may be transferred to some contiguous phonemes. The allomorphic structure may be symbolized as C'..-.

Problem 33 (data from Turu, a language of Tanganyika)

Instructions:

a. Identify all the morphemes.

b. List all morphemes having allomorphs.

c. Describe the distribution of all allomorphs having phonologically definable positions of occurrence.

1. nahé·ya	'I take away'	9. ogo·mohé·ya	'he will take him away'
2. nagehé·ya	'I take it away'	10. nahé·yua	'I was taken away'
3. namóhe·ya	'I take him away'	11. wahé·yua	'he was taken away'
4. wamóhe·ya	'he takes him away'	12. gó·mohe·ya	'we will take him away'
5. goagehé·ya	'we take it away'	13. beómohe·ya	'they will take him away'
6. ŋgó·gehé·ya	'I will take it away'	14. behé·yɛ	'let them take away'
7. ŋgó·mohe·ya	'I will take him away'	15. ŋé·yɛ	'let me take away'
8. ogo·ŋé·ya	'he will take me away'	16. ohe·ya	'to take away'

Supplementary information:

1. Turu has high and low tones. Only high tones are marked here. Usually there is only one high tone on each word, but there may be two (6), or none (16). The factors which govern the placement of tone are very complicated, and need not be considered in this problem.

2. The a occurring in the prefixal portion of items 1-5, 10, and 11 should be described as a morpheme.

3. Analyze the alternant forms occurring in 8 and 15 as resulting from assimilation and reduction.

4. Item 12 exhibits a reduction of two similar syllables, gogo· > go·. This type of reduction is not uncommon and is called "haplology."

Problem 34 (data from Sudan Colloquial Arabic)[33]

Instructions:

a. Identify as many morphemes as the data indicate.

b. List all morphemes having allomorphs.

c. Describe the distribution of all allomorphs having phonologically definable positions of occurrence.

1. kita·bi	'my book'		1a. axu·y	'my brother'
2. kita·bak	'your (m. sg.) book'		2a. axu·k	'your (m. sg.) brother'
3. kita·bik	'your (f. sg.) book'		3a. axu·ki	'your (f. sg.) brother'
4. kita·bu	'his book'		4a. axu·hu	'his brother'
5. kita·ba	'her book'		5a. axu·ha	'her brother'
6. kita·bna	'our book'		6a. axu·na	'our brother'
7. kita·bkum	'your (m. pl.) book'		7a. axu·kum	'your (m. pl.) brother'
8. kita·bkan	'your (f. pl.) book'		8a. axu·kan	'your (f. pl.) brother'
9. kita·bum	'their (m.) book'		9a. axu·hum	'their (m.) brother'
10. kita·bin	'their (f.) book'		10a. axu·hin	'their (f.) brother'

Supplementary information:

1. With regard to form 1a, see Problem 32, supplementary information 6.

2. The stem vowels of Arabic may constitute morphemes, but the requisite data are not given in this problem. Hence the stems should be treated here as single morphemic units.

The problems which have been discussed in this section do not begin to cover all the types of phonologically definable situations. The Appendix, however, does offer a fairly comprehensive treatment of the various, commonly observed patterns affecting phonological distribution.

2.23 Principle 3

Forms which have a common semantic distinctiveness but which differ in phonemic form in such a way that their distribution cannot be phonologically defined constitute a single morpheme if the forms are in complementary distribution in accordance with the following restrictions:

---

[33]See Trimingham, op. cit., p. 34.

1. Occurrence in the same structural series has precedence over occurrence in different structural series in the determination of morphemic status.

2. Complementary distribution in different structural series constitutes a basis for combining possible allomorphs into one morpheme only if there also occurs in these different structural series a morpheme which belongs to the same distribution class as the allomorphic series in question and which itself has only one allomorph or phonologically defined allomorphs.

3. Immediate tactical environments have precedence over nonimmediate tactical environments in determining morphemic status.

4. Contrast in identical distributional environments may be treated as submorphemic if the difference in meaning of the allomorphs reflects the distribution of these forms.

2.23.1 <u>The Meaning of Principle 3</u>

A. "Common semantic distinctiveness" is here identical in meaning and application with this phrase as it is used in the development of Principles 1 and 2.

B. The clause "but which differ in phonemic form in such a way that their distribution cannot be phonologically defined" means that the differences of form cannot be treated under Principle 2, whereby we reconcile such formal contrasts by determining the phonological distribution.

C. "Complementary distribution" means that differences of form are paralleled by differences of distribution. For example, let us assume that a morpheme has three allomorphs 1, 2, 3, and that these allomorphs occur with stems A through J in such a way that not more than one allomorph ever occurs with a single stem, e.g. A1, B1, C3, D2, E1, F3, G2, H1, I3, J2. In accordance with this type of distribution, we may say that the allomorphs 1, 2, and 3 are in complementary distribution with stems A through J.

D. Certain "restrictions" are necessary to the general principle of complementary distribution. Otherwise we would be involved in many contradictory types of analyses.[34]

E. The phrase "same structural series" in restriction 1 identifies a series of forms which are structurally related, both by contrast with other series and by virtue of their having certain common features. These problems will be treated fully in Chapter 5, but may be illustrated here. We may say that in English the forms <u>roses</u>, <u>boys</u>, <u>lips</u>, <u>oxen</u>, and <u>sheep</u> belong to the same structural series. The formational elements of the plural are not identical, but this series contrasts with all other series in English and exhibits the common feature of having singular nouns as stems and plural formatives consisting of a single allomorphic series. The genitive morpheme /-ǝz ~ -z ~ -s/ is in a different structural series in that it occurs with both singular and plural nouns, e.g. <u>man's</u> and <u>men's</u>.

   In Kekchi the morpheme in 'first person pronominal substitute' occurs as a prefix before the stem in <u>tinbeq</u> 'I will walk' and as a suffix following the stem in <u>yašin</u> 'I am sick.' These forms represent different structural series in that the verb stems are of different classes and the order of the constituent parts is different. There are also other formal and structural contrasts (see Problem 37).

---

[34]See Eugene A. Nida, "A System for the Identification of Morphemes," <u>Language</u>, 24 (1948), 4: 414-41.

F. In order to understand the meaning of restriction 2, we may consider a purely hypothetical problem involving the following sets of pronouns:

	Subject Pronouns (always following the verb)	Object Pronouns (always preceding the verb)
1st per.	-na	fi-
2d per.	-so	ka-
3d per. animate	-ri	po-

These pronominal affixes are in complementary distribution and are in different structural series. They do not, however, meet the requirements of restriction 2 for permitting the combination of the six forms into three sets of bi-allomorphic morphemes (i.e. morphemes with two allomorphs), since there is no one morpheme in both structural series which has the same form or allomorphs whose distribution may be phonologically defined. If, however, we could add to this set the affixal form zo as a third person inanimate pronoun, both subjective and objective, then we would have the data which would permit the combining of the subjective and objective forms.[35] (See Problem 37 for such a situation in Kekchi.)

G. The phrase "immediate tactical environments" in restriction 3 identifies the immediate construction in which any morpheme occurs. (See Chapter 4 for the analysis of immediate constituents.) For example, in the boys died the immediate tactical environment of -s is boy-. Any combination of boys, such as the boys or the boys died is the nonimmediate tactical environment of -s.

"Tactical" refers to the meaningful relationship of forms to each other. This relationship is definable in terms of form (the order and junctures) and function (the relationship of the parts to the whole).

To understand the meaning of restriction 3, we may take another hypothetical situation. Let us assume that all nouns have a suffix -ma when occurring as subjects and have a suffix -li when occurring as objects. We may also assume that nouns as subject expressions precede the verb and as object expressions follow the verb. This would mean that -ma and -li would be in complementary distribution in their nonimmediate environments, but would not be in complementary distribution in their immediate environments, since a single noun stem would occur with either -ma or -li. If this situation existed, we would regard -ma and -li as separate morphemes, despite the fact that they are in complementary distribution in their nonimmediate environments. Restriction 3 is specifically adopted so as to set up immediate tactical environments as of higher priority than nonimmediate environments in determining morphemic status.

H. "Contrast in identical distributional environments" in restriction 4 means that more than one form may occur in a particular situation; e.g. the verb show occurs with two "past participial" formations: shown and showed. The distributions of -n and -ed are not complementary at this point, i.e. they contrast. According to

---

[35] Restriction 2 is structurally very important and reflects the problem of signification. If we should have a situation such as is indicated by the six hypothetical forms first given, it would be impossible to know whether the distinction between subject vs. object relationships is "signaled" by the position of the forms or by their formal differences. Without other evidence, we would have to conclude that both form and position are meaningful. But once we are given the supplementary data that a single form may occur in both positions and that the positions alone are sufficient to "signal" the subject-object distinction, we have structural evidence for the uniting of formally different items into single morphemes.

restriction 4 this contrast is not sufficient to force us to regard -n and -ed as separate morphemes (note that for the most part they are in complementary distribution), since whatever difference of meaning there is between -n and -ed is a reflection of their differences of distribution. (See Chapter 6 for a fuller discussion of these problems of meaning.)

2.23.2 The Application of Principle 3

A. Determination of Allomorphs by Complementary Distribution

The plural forms of English nouns illustrate a number of points in the application of Principle 3. The predominant pattern of formation consists in the suffixation of /-əz ~ -z ~ -s/, but there are other ways of forming the plural. For example, the noun ox suffixes -en. There is absolutely nothing in the phonological form of the stem ox to indicate that it does not take the regular plural suffixal set. A word such as box, which is phonologically similar, does take the suffix /-əz/. The only way in which we may know which words occur with which suffixes is to make a list, and the specific class for oxen contains just this one word. Since, however, the allomorphic set /-əz ~ -z ~ -s/ and the form /-ən/ are in complementary distribution and have a common semantic distinctiveness (i.e. they are indicators of pluralization), we may combine all these forms as allomorphs. Some plural nouns do not differ in any overt way from the singular nouns, e.g. sheep, trout, elk, salmon and grouse. For the sake of descriptive convenience we may say that these words occur with a zero suffix.[36]

B. Basis of Complementation

The three types of plural formatives (1) /-əz ~ -z ~ -s/, (2) /-ən/, and (3) -0 (0 = zero) are all in complementary distribution.[37] If they are combined as a single morpheme, then each of these forms constitutes an allomorph. Nevertheless, the relationships between these allomorphs are quite different because the basis of complementation is very different. The allomorphs /-əz ~ -z ~ -s/ are in complementation on the basis of phonological environment. This type of complementation we symbolize by ~. The complementation which exists between the three types of plural formatives[38] is based upon the morphological environment. That is to say, we can describe the environment only by specifically identifying particular morphemes. This type of complementation we may symbolize by ∞. Accordingly, the series noted above may be written as /(-əz ~ -z ~ -s) ∞ -ən ∞ -0/.

C. Degree of Phonological Difference between Allomorphs

There are absolutely no limits to the degree of phonological difference between allomorphs.[39] Allomorphs may consist of very different phonemes as in the plural formatives /(-əz ~ -z ~ -s) ∞ -ən ∞ -0/ or they may be quite similar. For example, some nouns have an allomorphic bound stem which occurs before plural formatives. In treating such a series

---

[36]A zero is a significant absence of something. See section E, below, for further explanation.

[37]There are certain apparent exceptions to this statement, e.g. The Elks held a meeting in the city hall, but such problems are handled under restriction 4, above, or under Principle 5, which deals with homonyms.

[38]There are other types of morphemes, but these will not be considered until Chapter 3.

[39]In this respect morphological and phonemic analyses differ. For example, in English the sounds [ŋ] and [h] are in complementary distribution, but they are not subsumed under the same phoneme as allophones because of their phonological differences. No such restriction exists in morphological analysis.

as wife : wives, thief : thieves, wreath : wreaths, bath : baths, house : houses, we set
up a series of allomorphs which are phonologically very similar: /wayf ∞ wayv-, θiyf ∞
θiyv-, riyθ ∞ riyð-, bæθ ∞ bæð-, haws ∞ hawz-/.

There is no correlation between the degree of phonological difference and the basis
of complementation. Allomorphs whose distribution may be phonologically defined, e.g. /ə/
a ~ /æn/ an, may be utterly different in phonological form (see data under Principle 2).
On the other hand, phonologically defined allomorphs[40] may be phonologically very similar,
e.g. /-əz ~ -z ~ -s/: roses, boys, and lips. In the same way, allomorphs whose distribution may be morphologically defined may be very different in phonological form, e.g. /(-əz
~ -z ~ -s) ∞ -ən/ (in addition, see problems below), or quite similar, e.g. /wayf ∞ wayv-/
wife ∞ wiv-.

D. Basic and Nonbasic Allomorphs

In treating phonologically defined allomorphs it is sometimes helpful to select a
single form as phonologically basic, i.e. one from which the other allomorphs may be phonologically "derived."[41] For example, of the three allomorphs /-əz ~ -z ~ -s/ we may set
up /-əz/ as phonologically basic. This is done in view of two types of data: (1) comparison with other similar series in English, e.g. /iz ~ z ~ s/, atonic forms of is: Rose's
dead, Bill's dead, Dick's dead, /əz ~ z ~ s/, atonic forms of has: Rose's done it, Bill's
done it, and Dick's done it, and (2) congruence with general patterns of phonological
change, by which we note that it is "phonologically simpler"[42] to explain or describe the
loss of a phoneme than the addition of one. For the most part, however, we do not concern
ourselves greatly about the rank of allomorphs as determined by their possible phonological
relationships.

There is much greater value in determining the basic or nonbasic character of morphologically defined allomorphs.[40] The basic allomorph is defined in terms of three characteristics: statistical predominance, productivity of new formations, and regularity of
formation. An allomorph which occurs in more combinations than any other may generally be
selected as being the basic form.[43] A form which is statistically predominant is also
likely to be productive of new combinations. For example, in English the so-called s-
plural is productive of new plural formations, e.g. radios and videos. Whether a form is
regular (i.e. consists of phonologically defined allomorphs) may also be a factor in determining its allomorphic rank.

The determining of the basic form of a morpheme makes it possible to refer to the entire morpheme by a single allomorphic form. For example, in discussing the English plural
formatives we may refer to the allomorphic series as a whole by using the symbols { } to
enclose the basic allomorph, e.g. { -əz }. In many instances, there is no foundation for, or

---

[40]"Phonologically defined allomorphs" means that the distribution of the allomorphs
in question may be phonologically defined. Similarly, "morphologically defined allomorphs"
means that the distribution of the allomorphs may be morphologically defined.

[41]This does not mean that there is any essential relationship between the descriptive
(synchronic) treatment and the historical (diachronic) development, though the correlation
is usually close.

[42]By "phonologically simpler" we mean that the description of loss may usually be
made without identifying any phoneme, but the description of additions demands the indication of the specific phoneme added. The description of loss is also phonologically simpler
in that the loss of a phoneme is a more commonly observed phonological process than the
addition of one. For a fuller treatment of these problems, see the Appendix.

[43]This is analogous to the usual procedure in the selection of allophones.

particular value in, attempting to set up a basic allomorph, but one may arbitrarily select a particular characteristic form of an allomorphic series and use it to refer to the entire series.

E. Types of Zero

When the structure of a series of related forms is such that there is a significant absence of a formal feature at some point or points in the series, we may describe such a significant absence as "zero." For example, with the words sheep, trout, elk, salmon, and grouse, there is a significant (meaningful) absence of a plural suffix. We determine that there is an absence because the total structure is such as to make us "expect" to find a suffix. This absence is meaningful, since the form with the absence (i.e. with zero) has a meaning which is different from the singular form, which has no such absence. A significant absence in an allomorphic series may be called an allomorphic zero.

Sometimes the general structure suggests a zero element. For example, in Totonac the subject pronouns are as follows:

k- first person singular	-tit second person plural
-wi first person plural	-- third person singular
-ti second person singular	-qu· third person plural

The third person singular is never indicated overtly, i.e. it has no obvious form. The absence of some other form is what actually indicates the third singular. Structurally, this is a type of significant absence; it is not, however, an allomorphic zero, but, rather, a morphemic zero. That is to say, this significant absence does not occur in a series of allomorphs, but in a series of morphemes. Both types of zeros are structurally and descriptively pertinent, but should be carefully distinguished.[44]

F. Supplementary Problems Illustrative of Principle 3

Problem 35 (data from Tzeltal, a language of Mexico)[45]

Instructions:

   a. Identify the stems[46] to which the verb-forming suffix is added.

   b. List the allomorphic alternants of the stems (see supplementary information 1).

   c. List the allomorphs of the verb-forming suffix and under each allomorph the stem or stems with which it occurs.

---

[44]It is possible to say that in English the nouns have a zero morpheme for singular and {-əz} for plural. This would mean that sheep in the singular would have a morphemic zero and in the plural an allomorphic zero. One should, however, avoid the indiscriminate use of morphemic zeros. Otherwise, the description of a language becomes unduly sprinkled with zeros merely for the sake of structural congruence and balance.

[45]See Slocum, op. cit., p. 82.

[46]A distinction is made between (1) stems, which may consist of any number of morphemes but which include a root and underlie further formations, and (2) roots (see Chapter 3).

1. -betan	'to loan'	1a. bet	'debt'
2. -ʔipan	'to nourish'	2a. ʔip	'strength'
3. -ʔelkʼan	'to steal'	3a. ʔelekʼ	'stealing'
4. -kʼopan	'to speak with'	4a. kʼop	'speech'
5. -ʔabatin	'to serve'	5a. ʔabat	'servant'
6. -ʔinamin	'to take a wife'	6a. ʔinam	'wife'
7. -helolin	'to be one's namesake'	7a. helol	'namesake'
8. -mulin	'to commit sin'	8a. mul	'sin'
9. -wayčin	'to dream of'	9a. wayič	'dream'
10. -wayibin	'to use for bed'	10a. wayib	'bed'
11. -makʼlin	'to provide food for'	11a. -makʼ	'to divide in pieces'
12. -cʼaklin	'to accompany'	12a. -cʼak	'to join'
13. -hawcʼun	'to fall backwards'	13a. -hawcʼ-	'fall backwards'

Supplementary information:

1. Some of the stems consist of more than one morpheme, but for the sake of this description treat the stems as single units.

2. The allomorphs of the suffix have morphologically definable distributions. Because of the limited data of this problem it would be possible to construct some phonologically definable conditions of occurrence, but these are invalid for the structure as a whole.

3. The second column does not necessarily give the forms of the stems. The stem-formative -l- constitutes a morpheme.

Solution to Problem 35:

Having followed the instructions for Problem 35, it is possible to describe the solution in one of the following ways:

Alternative A

-in ∞ -an ∞ -un,[47] verb-forming suffix, has the following distribution:

-in occurs with

---

[47]The order of listing allomorphs is not particularly significant in this problem, but for the sake of some systematic treatment it is convenient to base the order on numerical superiority of occurrence.

?abat 'servant'[48]

?inam 'wife'

etc.

-an occurs with

bet 'debt'

?ip 'strength'

?elk'- (∞ ?elek')[49] 'stealing'

etc.

-un occurs with

-hawc'- 'fall backwards'

Alternative B

-in ∞ -an ∞ -un, verb-forming suffix, occurs in the following distribution:

-in: -?abatin 'to serve,' -?inamin 'to take a wife,' etc.

-an: -betan 'to loan,' -?ipan 'to nourish,' etc.

-un: -hawc'un 'to fall backwards'

Alternative C

-in ∞ -an ∞ -un, verb-forming suffix, occurs in the following distribution:

-in:

-?abatin 'to serve' (< ?abat 'servant')

-?inamin 'to take a wife' (< ?inam 'wife')

etc.

-an:

-betan 'to loan' (< bet 'debt')

-?ipan 'to nourish' (< ?ip 'strength')

etc.

---

[48] All the resultant forms (those in the first column) are bound (i.e. do not occur as full words in isolation, but must have prefixes added), but the stems to which the verb-forming suffix is added are not necessarily bound. Those that are free words should be written without hyphens. Those that are bound should have hyphens.

[49] Where a stem is an allomorph of a free form, it is frequently valuable to indicate this relationship.

-un:

-hawc'un 'to fall backwards' (< -hawc'- 'fall backwards')

There is no fixed format which must be employed in stating the solutions to linguistic problems. The details which are to be included or excluded depend greatly upon (1) the type of data, (2) the extent of the data, and (3) the type of publication for which one is writing. We are here considering only the first two factors. For our purposes in studying the techniques discussed in this text, it is preferable to use some sort of outline presentation. Whether, however, one should give lists of forms in sequence on the same line (alternative B) or should list by columns (alternatives A and C) depends entirely upon one's personal taste. Usually, however, it is better to list by columns, for forms may be located more readily and parallelisms or discrepancies may be more easily detected.

The alternative descriptions above differ principally in the data given under each allomorph. In alternative A the stems are listed, but no indication is made of the considerable differences of meaning between the stem forms and the suffixed forms. Alternative B is similar, but here only the resultant forms are listed and the stems are not given. Alternative C lists both, but gives the suffixed forms first, and then the stems from which these are derived. Where there are extensive differences of meaning, it is important to note both the stems and the resultant forms. In a series such as that for the affixation of the -er agentive suffix to verbs, e.g. walker, worker, dancer, player, finisher, there is no particular necessity to identify both the stem and the affixed combination, for the meaningful relationships are perfectly regular.

Unless otherwise stated, the student should list all forms which illustrate the distribution of any allomorph or morpheme. This means that "etc." should not be used. It is also to be avoided in indicating illustrative examples (i.e. where the entire membership of a class is not included). Its use in these alternative solutions is simply to call attention to the fact that the lists are not complete; the student is supposed to supply the additional data.

Problem 36 (the data consist of items 1-24 of Problem 5).

Instructions:

a. Reëxamine the sets of subject and object pronouns.

b. Describe the differences in distribution for each set.

c. List the sets of morphologically defined allomorphs.

d. State the particular restrictions involved and the way in which they operate.

Supplementary information:

1. The negative forms 26-29 introduce problems which are beyond the scope of this problem. They should be omitted from this analysis.

2. As the data now stand it would be possible to formulate a phonological basis for the distributions of subject and object pronouns, but this phonological distribution is not valid for the language as a whole.

Problem 37 (data from Kekchi, a language of Guatemala)

Instructions:

a. Add the following data to Problem 31.

b. List the three series of potential allomorphs.

c. Determine the restrictions which are applicable to possible complementation of these series.

d. Symbolize the relationships of the allomorphs.

16. šinkam   'I died'

17. šatkam   'you (sg.) died'

18. škam   'he died'

19. šokam   'we died'

20. šeškam   'you (pl.) died'

21. še'kam   'they died'

22. yašin   'I am sick'

23. yašat   'you (sg.) are sick'

24. yaš   'he is sick'

25. yašo   'we are sick'

26. yašeš   'you (pl.) are sick'

27. yaše'p   'they are sick'

28. gwinkin   'I am a man'

29. ciat   'you are a dog'

30. išk   'she is a woman'

31. gwinko   'we are men'

32. šuleš   'you (pl.) are animals'

33. peke'p   'they are stones'

34. inci   'my dog'

35. agwink   'your (sg.) man'

36. ššul   'his animal'

37. qapek   'our stone'

38. ešul   'your (pl.) animal'

39. ššule'p   'their animal'

40. gwočoč   'my house'

41. agwočoč   'your (sg.) house'

42. ročoč   'his house'

43. qočoč   'our house'

44. eročoč   'your (pl.) house'

45. ročoče'p   'their house'

Supplementary information:

1. There is no third person singular morpheme in forms 18, 24, and 30.

2. Form 30 is also the word meaning 'woman.'

Discussion of Problem 37:

The sets of allomorphs of pronominal morphemes are as follows:

Subjects of Transitive Verbs, and Possessives with Nouns		Subjects of Intransitive Verbs, and Objects of Transitive Verbs
Before Vowels	Before Consonants	
A	B	C
1s. gw-	in-	in- (-in)
2s. agw-	a-	at- (-at)

(Continued on next page.)

3s.	r-	š-	---
1p.	q-	qa-	o- (-o)
2p.	er-	e-	eš- (-eš)
3p.	eʔr- (verbal)	eʔ- (verbal)	eʔ- (-eʔp)
	r-...-eʔp (nominal)	š-...-eʔp (nominal)	

There are some very important facts to be considered before giving a final answer to this problem:

1. These sets of pronouns may occur in quite different structural series. Note that sets A and B occur as subjects of transitive verbs and as possessive pronouns with nouns. These are different types of constructions. Our restrictions (cf. 1, 2, and 3) do not, however, eliminate the possibility of combining elements which occur in such widely differing structural series.

2. Pronominal set C differs in distribution from A and B. It may occur as a subject of intransitive verbs, both of process (e.g. forms 16 ff.) and state (e.g. forms 22 ff.). Nouns may also be considered a subtype of verbs of state (e.g. forms 28 ff.).

3. Set C differs from sets A and B in being preposed or postposed to the stem. The positions of occurrence are dependent upon the morphological class of the stem.

4. There is only one triplet of pronominal forms which meets the requirements of restriction 2 of Principle 3.

Problem 38 (data [restricted] from Ilamba, a language of Tanganyika)

Instructions:

a. Identify all the prefixal morphemes in the subject expressions and the verbs.

b. Determine the sets of allomorphs.

c. Describe the distribution of the allomorphs in terms of phonological and morphological environment. Treat the subject and object elements as two different sets of forms.

The following sentences are arranged in two sets, the first are singular and the second plural. The noun subjects and objects are different in each sentence, but the attributives and the verb are the same throughout. Sentence 1 means, 'His one big man is greater than (literally 'surpasses') the child.' Similarly, sentence 2 means, 'His one big arm is greater than the thing.' The second set represents the plural forms, and the form -bele means 'two.' After the first sentence in each series, only the meanings of the nouns are given.

1. mo·nto wa·koe moko·lu omoe wakake·la eka·na

   'man   his   big   one surpasses child'

2. mokɔnɔ wa·koe moko·lu omoe wakeke·la eke·nto   'arm ... thing'

3. ke·nto kiakoe keko·lu kemoe kiameke·la eno·mba   'thing ... house'

4. nsi·mba ya·koe ŋko·lu emoe yameke·la eŋo·mbɛ   'lion ... cow'

(Continued on next page.)

5. li·no	liakoe	kio·lu	lemoe	liaoke·la	oo·ta	'tooth ... bow'
6. ulɔ·gwa	wa·koe	uko·lu	umoe	waoke·la	ootɛ·ndi	'love ... deed'
7. lokani	loakoe	loko·lu	lomoe	loaoke·la	omole·mɔ	'word ... wood'
8. kazo·mba	kakoe	kako·lu	kamoe	kameke·la	eno·mba	'little house ... house'

1a. a·nto	a·koe	ako·lu	abele	a·ke·la	ia·na	
'men	his	big	two	surpass	children'	
2a. mekɔnɔ	ya·koe	meko·lu	ebele	yaike·la	i·nto	'arms ... things'
3a. i·nto	ya·koe	iko·lu	ibele	yazike·la	ino·mba	'things ... houses'
4a. i·nsi·mba	za·koe	ŋko·lu	zibele	zazike·la	iŋo·mbɛ	'lions ... cows'
5a. mi·no	ma·koe	mako·lu	mabele	mamake·la	emata	'teeth ... bows'
6a. malɔ·gwa	ma·koe	mako·lu	mabele	mamake·la	ematɛ·ndi	'love(s) ... deeds'
7a. iŋkani	za·koe	ŋko·lu	zibele	zameke·la	emele·mɔ	'words ... woods'
8a. pizo·mba	piakoe	piko·lu	pibele	piazike·la	ino·mba	'little houses ... houses'

Supplementary information:

1. Tones are not indicated since they are not pertinent to this problem.

2. All vowels are long before a nasal-stop cluster within the same word.

3. The nouns employed as subjects represent eight different noun classes, each requiring a different type of concord in succeeding words. In order to use representatives of the eight different classes in the same type of structural framework, the meanings of the resultant sentences are, of course, somewhat forced.

4. Regard the noun stems, except -ino 'tooth,' as beginning with a consonant, and all that precedes (except when dealing with object nouns, see supplementary information 10) as being the class prefix indicating singular or plural number.

5. Regard -akoe 'his' as the stem. The resultant long vowels are derived from the reduction of vowel clusters or from compensatory lengthening when vowels become consonantalized. The prefix occurring with -akoe in sentence 1 may be symbolized as wV·-, meaning that the initial vowel of the stem is lengthened.

6. In the third word of sentence 5 there is an instance of metathesis.

7. The verbs have three prefixes: (1) the subject prefix, (2) the tense prefix -a-, and (3) the object prefix, which shows grammatical agreement with the noun object. In the verb of sentence 1a, regard the object prefix as zero.

8. There are two principal groups of allomorphs indicated in the subject elements: (1) those occurring with nouns and adjectives such as -ko·lu 'big' and (2) those occurring with other types of adjectives and verbs.

9. The following phonological changes take place: i or e before other vowels and not preceded by a consonant becomes y; o before other vowels and not preceded by a consonant becomes w; changes of oa to wa· or ea to ya· result in the compensatory lengthening of the a·.

10. Certain of the object nouns occur with prefixes e- or o- preceding the classifying prefixes. These prefixes e- and o- do not occur on any of the subject nouns in this problem.

Problem 39 (data from Futa-Fula, a language of French Guinea)

Instructions:

a. Identify the stems and the suffixal morphemes.

b. List all morphemes having allomorphs.

c. Describe the morphological distribution of the allomorphs.

1. a·deŋ 'person'		1a. o· a·deŋ 'this person'	
2. paikuŋ 'child'		2a. ku'uŋ paikuŋ 'this child'	
3. gertogal 'chicken'		3a. ŋga'al gertogal 'this chicken'	
4. puttyu 'horse'		4a. ŋgu'u puttyu 'this horse'	
5. ŋgurndaŋ 'life'		5a. da'aŋ ŋgurndaŋ 'this life'	
6. fena·ndɛ' 'lie'		6a. dɛ'ɛ fena·ndɛ' 'this lie'	
7. d'yi·d'yaŋ 'food'		7a. da'aŋ d'yi·d'yaŋ 'this food'	
8. gomd'iŋd'o' 'believing'		8a. o· gomd'iŋd'o' 'this believing'	
9. nyala·ndɛ' 'day'		9a. dɛ'ɛ nyala·ndɛ' 'this day'	
10. d'oudi 'shadow'		10a. di'i d'oudi 'this shadow'	
11. bi·niri 'bottle'		11a. di'i bi·niri 'this bottle'	
12. nya·wo·rɛ' 'judgment'		12a. dɛ'ɛ nya·wo·rɛ' 'this judgment'	
13. yurmɛ·ndɛ' 'mercy'		13a. dɛ'ɛ yurmɛ·ndɛ' 'this mercy'	

1b. a·deŋ go·to 'one person'	1c. a·deŋ mo'd'yə' 'good person'
2b. paikuŋ go·tuŋ 'one child'	2c. paikuŋ mo'd'yuŋ 'good child'
3b. gertogal go·tal 'one chicken'	3c. gertogal mo'd'yal 'good chicken'
4b. puttyu wo·tu 'one horse'	4c. puttyu mo'd'yu 'good horse'
5b. ŋgurndaŋ go·taŋ 'one life'	5c. ŋgurndaŋ mo'd'yaŋ 'good life'

(Continued on next page.)

6b. fena·ndɛˀ wo·tɛrɛ   'one lie'   6c. fɛna·ndɛˀ moˀd'ya   'good lie'

7b. d'yi·d'yaŋ go·taŋ   'one food'   7c. d'yi·d'yaŋ moˀd'yaŋ   'good food'

8b. gomd'iŋd'oˀ go·to   'one believing' 8c. gomd'iŋd'oˀ mo'd'yoˀ 'good believing'

9b. nyala·ndɛˀ wo·tɛrɛ   'one day'   9c. nyala·ndɛˀ moˀd'yɛrɛ   'good day'

10b. d'oudi wo·tiri   'one shadow'   10c. d'oudi moˀd'iri   'good shadow'

11b. bi·niri wo·tiri   'one bottle'   11c. bi·niri moˀd'iri   'good bottle'

12b. nya·wo·rɛˀ wo·tɛrɛ 'one judgment'   12c. nya·wo·rɛˀ moˀd'yɛrɛ   'good judgment'

13b. yurmɛ·ndɛˀ wo·tɛrɛ 'one mercy'   13c. yurmɛ·ndɛˀ moˀd'ya   'good mercy'

Supplementary information:

1. Phonemic pitch-stress is not indicated since it is not pertinent to this problem.

2. The words in the first column consist of stems plus certain class suffixes. These suffixes indicate only the grammatical class of the words.

2.24 Principle 4

An overt formal difference in a structural series constitutes a morpheme if in any member of such a series, the overt formal difference and a zero structural difference are the only significant features for distinguishing a minimal unit of phonetic-semantic distinctiveness.

2.24.1 The Meaning of Principle 4.

A. "An overt formal difference" means a contrast which is indicated by differences in phonemes or in the order of phonemes. The distinction between foot /fut/ and feet /fiyt/ is an overt difference, since it consists in a difference of phonemes. The contrast between the singular sheep /šiyp/ and the plural sheep /šiyp/ consists of a zero and is covert.

B. A member of a structural series may occur with a zero structural difference and an overt formal difference. For example, feet /fiyt/ as the plural of foot /fut/ has a structural zero similar to the zero occurring with sheep /šiyp/ as the plural of sheep /šiyp/. This zero consists in a significant absence of the suffix {-əz}, which occurs in the vast majority of plural formations. The overt difference between foot and feet is the replacement of /u/ by /iy/. According to Principle 4, this replacement acquires the status of a morpheme because it is the only overt difference between foot and feet. Principle 4 does not mean that there is no zero occurring in the word feet /fiyt/, but only that the replacement constitutes a morpheme. We may say that feet actually consists of three morphemes: (1) the stem, (2) the replacement of /u/ by /iy/, and (3) the zero suffix.

If it were not for the occurrence of such forms as sheep, deer, grouse, and salmon with structural zeros and no other overt differences, we should describe feet as consisting of only two morphemes: the stem and the replacement. The replacement would then constitute an allomorph in the {-əz} series.

2.24.2 The Application of Principle 4

Problem 40

Instructions:

a. Identify the morphemes by comparing the stems as found in the corresponding infinitives.

b. List those forms which have a structural zero.

c. List those forms which have a structural zero and some other overt difference.

d. List the overt differences. In listing the replacements, it is convenient to employ the symbolization /V ← V/. The arrow reads "replaces." Hence, in the example feet as a plural of foot we may describe the replacement as /iy ← u/. Such morphemes are called "replacives" (see Chapter 3).

1. walked	12. spit
2. played	13. sang
3. ran	14. bled
4. hit	15. kept
5. met	16. meant
6. worked	17. rang
7. fought	18. swam
8. jumped	19. rode
9. pounded	20. slept
10. cut	21. bought
11. split	

Supplementary information:

1. There are four important types of structures:

   a. Unchanged stems plus suffixes

   b. Unchanged stems plus zero

   c. Changed stems plus suffixes

   d. Changed stems plus zero

2. The replacements in the stems consist of vowels or vowels plus consonants /y/ or /w/.

2.25 Principle 5

Homophonous forms are identifiable as the same or different morphemes on the basis of the following conditions:

1. Homophonous forms with distinctly different meanings constitute different morphemes.

2. Homophonous forms with related meanings constitute a single morpheme if the meaning classes are paralleled by distributional differences, but they constitute multiple morphemes if the meaning classes are not paralleled by distributional differences.

A. Definition of Homophonous Forms

Homophonous forms are phonemically identical. For example, in English pear, pare, and pair are homophonous, and, as such, they may be called homophones.

B. Definition of Related Forms

It is difficult to define degrees of difference in meaning, and there are no simple means of deciding whether forms are "distinctly different" or "related" in meaning. There are, however, some forms which appear to be obviously related, for example, the word run in the expressions they run and their run. Even in the phrase the run in her stocking the form run appears to be related in meaning to the preceding occurrences of this homophonous form. Similarly, the fish and to fish appear to contain a meaningfully similar item, fish. On the other hand, in the phrases to pare and the pear there appears to be no meaningful relationship between pare and pear. We may explain such similarities and differences by saying that fish in the phrases to fish and the fish identifies a characteristically associated aspect of a single process, whereas the word pare is not characteristically associated with pear.

Despite the difficulty in finding an entirely satisfactory definition of "related meanings" (and of the converse, "distinctly different meanings"), it is possible for us to employ the following, generally usable definition: Homophonous forms have related meanings when they identify regularly associated aspects of the same object, process, or state.

C. Types of Related Areas of Meaning

There are a great number of possible semantic relationships between homophonous forms, but the following brief series will give some idea of the range of more common occurrences:

1. Form and function: horn of an animal and horn as an instrument for providing sounds.[50]

2. Process and result: to run and a run in her stocking.

3. Process and characteristically associated object: to fish and the fish.

4. State of being and causative of a state: foul (adjective) and to foul up the job.

5. Agent and process: the man and to man the ship.

6. Instrument and process: a spear and to spear.

7. Object and associated characteristic: it is a pill and he is a pill.

8. Form and process: a cross and to cross.

There are many phrases in which one is in doubt as to the meaningful relationships of forms. For example, there are several uses of board: board and room, to board a ship, I bought a pine board, and the board of directors. Should all these occurrences of board be

---

[50]Form and function may be related in a single object, namely, a ram's horn used as an instrument for making a noise.

regarded as related in meaning, or not? The decision rests with the native speaker of the language, and to this extent the description of any language will be subjective.[51] However, if there is doubt, it is preferable to regard the forms as not related.

D. Types of Distributional Differences

There is no limitation on the types of distributional differences, but the most common situations involve occurrence in different major word classes. For example, we have no difficulty in English in assigning fish, meaning an object, and fish, meaning a process, to the same morpheme, for these differences in meaning are paralleled by distributional differences; the first is a noun and the second a verb. They occur in different grammatical constructions and with different suffixes. Similarly, we may combine into the same morpheme the verb run and the noun run. On the same basis, we also combine the adjective foul with the verb foul.[52]

In analyzing the distribution of the semantically related forms of horn designating (A) an animal's horn (and by extension such things as the horns of the moon), and (B) an instrument for producing sound, it soon becomes evident that they are not in complementary distribution. The form with meaning A occurs as both a noun, e.g. the animal's horn, and as a verb, he horned in, and the form with meaning B occurs as a noun, e.g. the car's horn. In the sentence I bought a horn there is no way of knowing whether meaning A or meaning B is intended. Hence, these forms are not in complementary distribution. The differences of meaning under A, as reflected in the noun and verb usage, are in complementary distribution and consequently these differences may be combined in the same morpheme.

E. Problems Illustrative of Principle 5

Problem 41

Instructions:

    a. Determine whether or not the following sets of underlined forms are related in meaning.

    b. If the forms are related in meaning, describe the relationship.

----

[51]This subjectivism in the analysis of a language is completely legitimate, since it reflects the actual usage of the language by the native speaker and reveals the live associations, which are constantly operative in producing new formations and in giving rise to new analogical series. In a paper read before the Linguistic Society of America, at Ann Arbor, Michigan (1948), Allen Walker Read pointed out a number of words which exhibit forms considered semantically related by some speakers of American English: groom and bridegroom, sand and sandblind, pun and pundit, fake and fakir, bust and robust, noise and noisome, gyp and gypsy, grease and ambergris, mist and mysticism, sex and sextette, nigger and niggardly. Such data are in conflict with the history of the language, but are pertinent to a descriptive analysis.

[52]There are two other solutions to this type of problem: (1) setting up certain forms, e.g. man, horse, fish, as nouns and other forms, e.g. swim, run, jump, as verbs, and then deriving the related forms from these by zero, and (2) listing all homophonous forms with different distributions as different morphemes. The first procedure introduces innumerable errors, since it is impossible to arrive at any valid basis for determining the basic class memberships of homophonous forms, and the second procedure necessitates repetitions of forms in listing. The method advocated in this text has the advantage of recognizing all phonetic-semantic resemblances, but it simplifies the procedure by listing such forms as man, horse, fish, swim, run and jump as having two class memberships, namely, those of nouns and of verbs.

    c. If the forms are related in meaning, determine whether the forms are in complementary distribution. (Supplementary data must be supplied by the student.)

    d. List all sets of forms which occur in complementary distribution, and describe the type of distribution.

1. He is <u>faint</u>.

1a. They <u>faint</u> frequently.

2. He shot a <u>crow</u>.

2a. Some always <u>crow</u> about it.

3. He bought a <u>board</u>.

3a. <u>Board</u> and room is expensive.

4. Dick'<u>s</u> done it.

4a. Dick'<u>s</u> here.

5. first-night<u>er</u>

5a. danc<u>er</u>

6. <u>by</u>-law

6a. <u>by</u>-path

7. He went a<u>long</u>.

7a. It is a <u>long</u> way.

8. He went <u>aboard</u>.

8a. He wants a <u>board</u>.

9. We <u>run</u> the place.

9a. They had a <u>run</u> on the market.

10. I hate cray<u>fish</u>.

10a. I love to <u>fish</u>.

Problem 42 (data from a Veracruz dialect of Aztec, a language of Mexico)

Instructions:

    a. Identify the morphemes.

    b. Determine the homophonous forms which constitute more than one morpheme, and state the reasons for this conclusion.

1. nikwa·   'I eat'

8. nikwah   'I ate'

2. tikwa·   'you (sg.) eat'

9. tikwah   'you (sg.) ate'

3. kwa·   'he eats'

10. kwah   'he ate'

4. nikwah   'we (excl.) eat'

11. nikwake   'we (excl.) ate'

5. tikwah   'we (incl.) eat'

12. tikwake   'we (incl.) ate'

6. aŋkwah   'you (pl.) eat'

13. aŋkwake   'you (pl.) ate'

7. kwah   'they eat'

14. kwake   'they ate'

2.26 Principle 6

A morpheme is isolatable if it occurs under the following conditions:

    1. In isolation.

    2. In multiple combinations in at least one of which the unit with which it is combined occurs in isolation or in other combinations.

3. In a single combination provided the element with which it is combined occurs in isolation or in other combinations with nonunique constituents.

A. Condition 1

On the basis of the first condition of isolatability we may identify as morphemes such forms as boy, cow, run, jump, up, he, this, and ouch, since it is possible to utter all these forms in isolation.

Problem 43 (data consist of data for Problem 9)

Instructions:

   a. List all the morphemes which may be identified because they occur in isolation.

   b. Indicate by number the forms in which all such morphemes occur.

B. Condition 2

Certain morphemes never occur in isolation, e.g. the -er in such words as dancer, worker, jumper, and provider. Nevertheless, we can identify -er as a morpheme, since the elements with which it occurs may be found in isolation, e.g. dance, work, jump, and provide. The second condition of isolatability does not require that all combining elements have an independent occurrence, but only that at least one form in any such structural series have the capacity of occurrence in isolation or in other combinations. The prefix con- occurs only in combinations, e.g. conceive, consume, contain, condense, but the form dense occurs in isolation. This provides justification for considering con- a morpheme. Added evidence is available in the fact that the stem forms occur in other combinations, e.g. perceive, resume, detain.

Problem 44 (data consist of data for Problem 4)

   Instructions: List those morphemes which are isolatable on the basis of condition 1 and condition 2.

Problem 45

Instructions:

   a. Determine the conditions of isolatability of the prefixal and suffixal morphemes.

   b. Test the stems for occurrence in isolation or in other combinations, but do not add other words with the same prefixes or suffixes in order to determine the basis of isolatability.

1. inky	1a. milky	1b. cheeky	1c. sticky
2. friendly	2a. manly	2b. cowardly	2c. womanly
3. president	3a. correspondent	3b. student	3c. regent
4. adulterous	3a. vociferous	4b. venous	4c. anonymous
5. directness	5a. rightness	5b. stillness	5c. illness
6. detachment	6a. merriment	6b. torment	6c. shipment

(Continued on next page.)

7. archaism	7a. methodism	7b. theism	7c. fetishism
8. regal	8a. legal	8b. frugal	8c. conjugal
9. realize	9a. moralize	9b. actualize	9c. atomize
10. denude	10a. deodorize	10b. delouse	10c. debunk
11. beguile	11a. behold	11b. belabor	11c. belittle
12. impart	12a. intend	12b. import	12c. infect
13. intolerable	13a. impossible	13b. improbable	13c. intangible
14. evolve	14a. evoke	14b. evade	14c. erode
15. retain	15a. revolve	15b. resist	15c. retail

C. Condition 3

There are some morphemes which occur in only one combination, e.g. cran- in cranberry, rasp- in raspberry, and cray- in crayfish. According to condition 3 for isolatability, the morphemes cran-, rasp-, and cray- are isolatable because the elements berry and fish occur in isolation or in other combinations.

There are certain types of structures which Principle 6 specifically excludes from morphemic status: (1) constituent parts of such words as hammer, ladder, otter, badger, under, linger, bitter[53] and (2) phonetic symbolism, e.g. such a series as slide, slush, slurp, slip, slop, slime, slobber, and slick.

The descriptive analysis of a language may be extended to include such forms as hammer, ladder, and otter, but the method of isolating the possible stems and suffixes is dependent upon two factors: (1) canonicity of forms (see section 3.12) and (2) frequency of occurrence.[54] By comparing many words in English it is possible to state that a high percentage of stem morphemes consist of a single syllable, and hence that in such words as hammer, ladder, and otter, the initial syllables may be taken as the stems and the element -er, which occurs in over one hundred such combinations, may be considered the suffixal morpheme. Furthermore, there is a certain structural parallelism between the set hammer, ladder, otter and the forms dancer, walker, worker.

Despite this measure of structural validity for distinguishing morphemes on the basis of canonicity of forms[55] and frequency of occurrence, however, there are some important

---

[53]This series is specifically excluded by condition 3, since the -er with which such forms as hamm-, ladd-, ott-, and so on occur, combines only with unique constituents, i.e. forms occurring only in this combination. This -er is not semantically relatable to the agentive -er in dancer, player, runner, and worker.

[54]This is the procedure employed by Bloomfield, op. cit., pp. 240-41. In the first edition of the present text (1946), these methods are also employed.

[55]This is not intended to deny the existence or the relevance of canonical forms in the analysis and description of languages. In many of the Sudanic languages the most common stem structure is CV; in the Nilotic languages the CVC structure appears predominant; in Bantu CVCV is more usual; and in Semitic languages the roots are usually CCC, with various vowels inserted in the derivational and inflectional forms. But in all these languages there are numerous and important exceptions. Despite this fact, however, the analyst does employ such structural features in identifying morphemes and in describing them (see section 3.12).

practical and theoretical liabilities in such a procedure. In the first place, there is no language which has absolutely fixed forms of morphemes and, in the second place, there is no way of determining the number of instances which must occur before one is justified in assigning morphemic status. Accordingly, in adopting Principle 6, we are restricting the analysis to units which may be isolated in terms of the distribution. This is a far more practical basis for procedure and seems to reflect more accurately the functional relationships of forms.

Phonetic symbolism is common, especially in certain Bantu languages. In the English series slide, slush, slurp, slip, slop, slime, slobber, and slick we can recognize a common phonemic element sl and a common meaningful relationship which may be defined as 'smoothly wet.' A series such as flash, flare, flame, flicker, and flimmer have an analogous relationship involving the meaning 'moving light.'[56] Despite these partial phonetic-semantic resemblances, however, we do not isolate either sl- or fl- as morphemes, since they do not occur with free forms or with forms which occur in other combinations.

---

[56]See Bloomfield, op. cit., p. 245, for these and other similar series in English.

C H A P T E R   3

TYPES OF MORPHEMES

Morphemes differ in the types of phonemes which comprise them, the relationship of the parts of morphemes to each other, and the manner in which morphemes are formally connected with each other. Our discussion is divided between (1) the internal composition of morphemes and (2) the formal relationships of morphemes to each other.

3.1 Internal Composition of Morphemes

The internal composition of morphemes may be treated in terms of (1) the types of phonemes which compose morphemes, (2) the different phonemic shapes and sizes of morphemes, and (3) the formal relationships of the parts of morphemes to each other.

3.11 Types of Phonemes Which Compose Morphemes

Morphemes may be composed of (1) segmental phonemes, (2) suprasegmental phonemes, and (3) combinations of segmental and suprasegmental phonemes.

3.11.1 Morphemes Consisting of Segmental Phonemes

Morphemes consisting of segmental phonemes are the most numerous in occurrence and have been abundantly illustrated in the preceding problems. Review especially Problems 1, 4, 5, 7, 25, and 34, comprising data from Aztec, Zoque, Congo Swahili, Tonkawa, and Arabic.

3.11.2 Morphemes Consisting of Suprasegmental Phonemes

One type of morpheme consisting solely of suprasegmental phonemes is very common. This type is composed of the morphemic units of intonational patterns. For example, in English the sentence-final glides which follow the last intonationally stressed syllable constitute morphemes. Whether the glide goes up or down from any one of four intonational levels to another or is sustained on any one of these levels is meaningful.[1] One important fact to note about such glides is that they are not the structural property of the particular morpheme or group of morphemes with which they occur; rather, they have an independent structural value, quite separate from the segmental phonemes to which they are added. These intonational glides are not significant on a morphological level or analysis, however, but on a syntactic one. Accordingly, they will not be treated further in this volume.

Morphemes which are structurally significant to the morphology of a language and which consist wholly of suprasegmental phonemes are relatively rare. We have, however, already encountered two instances in the previous data. In the Cuicatec of Problem 17 we noted that the indicator of the first person was a suffix consisting solely of a high tone. This morpheme is symbolized as -V̄, indicating that regardless of the vowel of the stem the tone

---

[1]See Kenneth L. Pike, The Intonation of American English (Ann Arbor: University of Michigan Press, 1945).

is high. In the Totonac data of Problem 11 we indicated that the glottalization of the vowel could constitute a type of morpheme. Sometimes this glottalization occurs together with a second person suffix, but in other instances it is the only overt distinguishing characteristic. Hence, according to Principle 4 governing the identification of morphemes, it acquires the status of a morpheme. Compare the two Totonac forms pasa 'he bathes' and pasá 'you (sg.) bathe.' Both forms occur with the suffix -a 'neutral or durative aspect.' The third person singular subject morpheme is always a zero morpheme (see section 2.23.2, E), and the second person subject morpheme consists in the glottalization of the final vowel, which in turn glottalizes the preceding vowel in a regular, automatic development. This structure in Totonac, in which the glottalization alone serves as a second person indicator, is, however, very restricted. Nevertheless, it is identifiable as a morpheme having suprasegmental characteristics, since it is not the property of any particular vowel or morpheme, but a superimposed structural feature.

In a number of Sudanic languages there are many morphemes which consist wholly of suprasegmental features. For example, in Ngbaka, spoken in the northeastern part of the Belgian Congo, there are four principal forms of every verb,[2] consisting (1) of a low tone or tones on the root, (2) of a mid tone or tones on the root, (3) of a low-high glide on monosyllabic roots and a low tone followed by a high tone on dissyllabic roots, and (4) of a high tone or tones on the roots.

Problem 46 (data from Ngbaka, a language of the Belgian Congo)

1. à	1a. ā	1b. ǎ·	1c. á	'to put (more than one thing)'
2. wà	2a. wā	2b. wǎ·	2c. wá	'to clean'
3. gbòtò	3a. gbōtō	3b. gbòtó	3c. gbótó	'to pull'
4. kpòlò	4a. kpōlō	4b. kpòló	4c. kpóló	'to return'
5. b'ìlì	5a. b'īlī	5b. b'ìlí	5c. b'ílí	'to cut'
6. kà̰	6a. kā̰	6b. kǎ̰·	6c. ká̰	'to look'

In this series of Ngbaka words the segmental phonemes constitute the morphemes which "carry" the meanings 'to put,' 'to clean,' 'to pull,' and so on. The differences of tones indicate four principal tense-aspect contrasts.

Problem 47 (data from Mongbandi, a language of the Congo)

Instructions: Determine the allomorphs of the morpheme consisting solely of suprasegmental phonemes.

Forms with Singular Subjects	Forms with Plural Subjects	
1. ŋgbò	1a. ŋgbó	'swam'
2. gwè	2a. gwé	'went'
3. mā	3a. má	'heard'
4. kpē	4a. kpé	'fled'

(Continued on next page.)

---

[2] The investigations into the tonal structure of Ngbaka are not complete, and further research may reveal a few exceptions to this statement.

5. yó	5a. yó	'carried'
6. yé	6a. yé	'agreed'
7. bàtà	7a. bātá	'guarded'
8. hùlù	8a. hūlú	'jumped'
9. hākà	9a. hāká	'taught'
10. dīrì	10a. dīrí	'answered'
11. kōló	11a. kōló	'pierced'
12. sīgí	12a. sīgí	'went out'
13. díkò	13a. dīkó	'read'
14. gbíŋgà	14a. gbīŋgá	'translated'

Supplementary information:

    1. All forms are in the completive aspect.

    2. The series in column 1 represent the basic forms of the roots. The tones written
on this series are a fundamental part of the root morphemes.

Special attention must be called to the differences between the Mongbandi words in
column 1 and those in column 2. Words which occur in the completive aspect with singular
subjects exhibit seven different tonal forms,[3] and by regarding these forms as basic, we
can predict in almost all instances what the forms of the verb will be for other aspects
and numbers. Because of this fact and because there is no phonetic-semantic resemblance
between the forms of this first series, we consider the tones to be integral parts of the
morphemes. The second series exhibits a different situation. There is a phonetic-semantic
resemblance consisting of tonal similarities and agreement with plural subjects. This
structural phonetic-semantic feature constitutes a morpheme.

Problem 48 (data [restricted] from Chatino, a language of Mexico)

    Instructions:

        a. Identify the morphemes.

        b. List all suprasegmental morphemes.

1. ku	'he eats'	6. nda·wą	'you (pl.) are giving'
2. ku·wą	'you (pl.) eat'	7. ndá	'you (sg.) are giving'
3. kǘ	'I eat'	8. nda	'he is giving'
4. kú	'you (sg.) eat'	9. ta	'he gives'
5. tá	'you (sg.) give'	10. ku·tu	'he will eat'

(Continued on next page.)

---

[3]These constitute the major tonal classes of Mongbandi verbs.

11. ku·tú	'I will eat'	14. ta·tu	'he will give'
12. ku·tú	'you (sg.) will eat'	15. ta·tú	'you (sg.) will give'
13. ta·tú	'I will give'	16. ndá	'I am giving'

Supplementary information:

1. Only those tones are indicated which are pertinent to this particular problem.

2. On the basis of these limited data we may describe the prefinal long vowel as a part of one of alternant roots: CV ~ CV·-. The alternation depends upon whether or not the forms are word-final. On the other hand, the length may be described as part of the property of the following morphemes, e.g. -·tu and -·wa.

3. Third person singular subjects are indicated by a zero morpheme.

There are two types of answers possible to Problem 48. One may regard the suprasegmental phoneme of tone as one morpheme and the suprasegmental[4] phoneme of nasalization as another morpheme, in which case, there is a degree of overlapping in meaning. If, on the other hand, one considers one morpheme to consist of tone and nasalization and the other morpheme to consist solely of tone, then there is a degree of overlapping in form. In some constructions the nasalization is a part of the basic forms of the morpheme, e.g. -wa 'you (pl.),' but in others its structural independence is evidenced by the fact that it may be added to stems or suffixes.

3.11.3 Morphemes Consisting of Segmental and Suprasegmental Phonemes

Morphemes consisting of segmental and suprasegmental phonemes have already been illustrated in previous material, e.g. Problems 13, 17, 19, 20, 26, 32, and 47, which include data from Hausa, Cuicatec, Navaho, Luba-Lulua, and Mongbandi. They also exist in English; e.g. the words boy, girl, goulash consist not only of certain segmental phonemes, but also have a phoneme of stress. In Chinese each morpheme consists of segmental phonemes plus any one of a number (depending on the dialect) of suprasegmental phonemes.

In some languages which exhibit distinctive stress this suprasegmental feature serves primarily to distinguish morphological units. For example, in Kekchi the stress always occurs at the end of the word. In Congo Swahili the stress is always on the next to the last syllable. For the most part, this is true in Quechua, also. We usually say that such stress is not phonemic, for by writing the juncture (space) between words we automatically indicate the placement of the stress. In reality, the stress is a phonetic part of this juncture phoneme.

3.12 Different Shapes and Sizes of Morphemes

Theoretically, there is no restriction on the shape and size of morphemes. For example, in English there are morphemes such as goulash and talmud[5] and ones such as -s in lips and -d in told. Between these extremes there are morphemes consisting of the following patterns of segmental phonemes: V, a-long; VC, im-possible; CV, de-ceive; CVC, fish; CVCV, lava; and CVCVC, hammer /hæmər/. Of course, there are a number of morphemes

---

[4]"Suprasegmental" does not mean that the symbol for a suprasegmental phoneme must necessarily be written above the line. It merely denotes that the phonemic feature is phonologically a part of one or more segmental units.

[5]These are, of course, borrowed words, but they are no less a part of English.

involving various types of consonant clusters, so that this inventory could be extended greatly. But if we begin to list and number the types of morphemes in English, we find that there are three major types: C, VC, and CVC (in the formula CVC, C stands for either a consonant or a consonant cluster). The morphemes C and VC tend to be affixes, e.g. -s in lips, -s in John's, -d in sold, in- in intention, un- in untie, en- in enable, -ish in mannish, /-iy/ in baby, /-ər/ in dancer, /-əl/ in formal. The CVC morphemes include both affixes and roots, but the greater number of such structures are roots. One of the reasons for the great diversity in the shapes and sizes of morphemes in English is the fact that English has borrowed so many words from other languages, and these words frequently represent different types of basic structure; but no language is completely free from borrowing, and no language has completely regular types of morphemes.

In the Mayan languages roots are predominantly of the CVC type, while affixes are usually shorter and consist of all sorts of consonant and vowel combinations.

Bantu languages exhibit a root structure which is predominantly CVCV; the affixes are almost always shorter and, for the most part, of a CV type. But it is very difficult to generalize in regard to Bantu, for there are many exceptions.

In Hebrew (and all Semitic languages) the basic root consists of a CCC structure, e.g. /*sbr/ 'to break.' But one must also recognize other types of morphemes:[6] (1) those consisting of vowels, vowels plus ·, or vowels plus a consonantal affix: CCuC 'active action,' CaCi·C 'object having a particular quality,' CaC·aC 'transitive intensive action,' nCaCiC 'middle action,' and (2) those consisting of sequences of consonants and vowels: mi· 'who?,' -tim 'you (m. pl.),' balti· 'without.'

The various types of morphemes may be referred to as "canonical" forms. In all languages there are different classes of such forms, and the principal distinction is usually between roots and affixes. In some languages word classes differ from each other. For example, in Ngbaka the verb roots consist of canonical forms composed entirely of segmental phonemes, but the noun roots have both segmental and suprasegmental phonemes, e.g. lí 'face,' lî 'name,' lì 'water.'

Problem 49

Instructions:

a. List the canonical forms of the morphemes of the following languages:

1. Veracruz dialect of Aztec (Problems 1 and 3)

2. Ilamba (Problem 38)

3. Zoque (Problems 4 and 12)

4. Kekchi (Problems 31 and 37)

b. List all parallelisms between types of canonical forms and distributional types of morphemes, e.g. roots vs. affixes, prefixes vs. suffixes, and nouns vs. verbs.

Problem 50 (data from Huave, a language of Mexico)

Instructions: List the different canonical forms of root morphemes. This should be done by employing the symbols C and V.

---

[6]See Zellig S. Harris, "Linguistic Structure of Hebrew," Journal of the American Oriental Society, 61 (1941): 143-67.

1. keh 'blood'	6. kət 'fish'	11. dwat 'spider'
2. lu 'jaguar'	7. mim 'fly'	12. so 'pig'
3. kənč 'crab'	8. yo 'water'	13. med 'blouse'
4. m̌bat 'lice'	9. pimb 'pumpkin'	14. tiət 'road'
5. nẕa 'gum'	10. heng 'arrow'	15. miok 'butterfly'

Problem 51 (data from Tojolabal, a language of Mexico)

Instructions: List the different canonical forms of the root morphemes. This should be done by employing the symbols C and V.

1. -čon 'to sell'	8. -ʔal 'to say'
2. -heʔ 'to show'	9. -ʔiʔ 'to take'
3. -k'an 'to want'	10. -hutp' 'to push'
4. -ʔelk' 'to steal'	11. -ce·n 'to laugh'
5. -p'i·š 'to stretch'	12. -ʔašw 'to be bored'
6. -ʔalp' 'to loiter'	13. -k'eʔ 'to get up'
7. -k'a·tn 'to warm'	14. -hutp' 'to push'

3.13 Formal Relationships of the Parts of Morphemes

The parts of morphemes usually occur in continuous sequence if all of them are segmental; they are superimposed if they include segmental and suprasegmental phonemes. These features have been abundantly illustrated in the preceding data. Sometimes, however, parts of morphemes consisting of segmental phonemes do not occur in continuous sequence. For example, compare the following forms in Zoque.

Problem 52

1. kenu 'looked'

2. kenpa 'he looks, he will look'

3. kyenhayu 'he saw it for him (on his behalf)'

4. kyenhapya 'he sees it for him (on his behalf)'

5. kento̱ʔyu 'he wanted to look'

6. kento̱ʔpya 'he wants to look'

The basic forms of the morphemes in this series are:

     ken-   'to look'

     y-   'third person subject in transitive verbs'

     -hay-   'benefactive'

-to͗y-   'desiderative'

-u   'past tense'

-pa   'present (or future) tense'

It will be noted that these basic forms do not always occur in continuous sequence. The stem ken- may be broken by -y-, the subject prefix. Similarly, -hay- may be -ha...y-, and -pa may be -p...a. Compare also -to͗y- and -to͗...y. All these allomorphic differences are the result of metathesis of y in certain combinations, but the result is a discontinuous morpheme.

In Tzeltal[7] there is an intransitivizing verbal infix -h-: kuhč' 'to endure' < -kuč' 'to carry,' puhk' 'to spread the word' < -puk' to divide among,' k'ehp 'to be clear (as of the weather)' < -k'ep 'to clear away.' Any infix results in the splitting of a morpheme. In the Semitic languages the root morphemes CCC are constantly split by infixes. Note the following series:

Problem 53 (data from Egyptian Arabic)[8]

1. *ktb 'write'		7. yektub 'he is writing'
2. katab 'he wrote'		8. *gls 'sit'
3. ka·tib 'writing (person)'		9. galas 'he sat'
4. kita·b 'book'		10. ga·lis 'sitting (person)'
5. maka·tib 'places for writing'		11. maga·lis 'councils'
6. maktab 'place for writing'		12. maglas 'council'

When replacive morphemes (see section 3.21.2) occur, they may likewise cause a morpheme to be split and hence to occur in a discontinuous form. For example, the replacement of /u/ by /iy/ in feet /fiyt/ results in the discontinuous allomorph /f...t/.

There are, moreover, some rare forms, whose parts never occur in continuous sequence in a single word, but at the same time never occur without each other. For example, in Kissi there are two interrogative particles yὲ and nɛ̄. If one of these forms occurs, the other also occurs, e.g. yὲ yá gbɛ́ngbɛ́lá yὲ ndū sísὲ̀ nɛ̄ 'how I see (interrogative particle) him now (interrogative particle)?' In this case we may describe the interrogative morpheme as yὲ ... nɛ̄.[9]

3.2 Formal Relationships of Morphemes to Each Other

The formal relationships of morphemes to each other are structural and positional.

---

[7] See Marianna C. Slocum, "Tzeltal (Mayan) Noun and Verb Morphology," International Journal of American Linguistics, 14 (1948) 2: 83.

[8] These data are taken from Leonard Bloomfield, Language (New York: Henry Holt and Co., 1933), pp. 243-44.

[9] These are not structurally equivalent to French ne ... pas, for ne may occur without pas, e.g. ne ... rien, ne ... point, ne ... que; and pas may occur without ne, e.g. pas du tout and pourquoi pas.

3.21 Structural Relationships of Morphemes to Each Other

The structural relationships of morphemes are of three different morphemic types: (1) additive, (2) replacive, and (3) subtractive. These represent three basic morphological processes: addition, replacement, and subtraction.

3.21.1 Additive Morphemes

Additive morphemes include roots, prefixes, suffixes, infixes, suprafixes, and reduplicatives. Roots constitute the basic core of most words (see Chapter 4). Prefixes are bound elements (i.e. they never occur in isolation) which precede the root. Suffixes are bound elements which follow the root. Infixes occur within the root. Suprafixes are morphemes which consist wholly of suprasegmental phonemes and which are added to the root or stem. For example, the tones on the Ngbaka verbs (Problem 46) are suprafixes. Similarly, the tones and the nasalization in Problem 48 are suprafixes, in terms of the data given.[10] The suprasegmental morphemes of Mongbandi plural verbs (Problem 47) are not suprafixes, but suprasegmental replacive morphemes.[11]

Problem 54

Instructions: From any of the preceding data in this text give examples of the following types of morphemes, listing for each example the language and the problem from which it is taken; only one example of each type is to be taken from any one language:

1. Prefixes, 5 examples

2. Suffixes, 5 examples

3. Infixes, 2 examples

4. Suprafixes, 2 examples

Reduplication consists in the repetition of all or of part of a root or stem. If the entire stem is repeated (e.g. Tojolabal -oč 'to enter' becomes -očoč 'to enter little by little'), we generally treat such a structure as a repetitive compound. In some constructions roots may be repeated three times; e.g. in San Blas, a language of Panama, the stem mu·a 'to rise and fall' occurs also as mu·amu·a 'to rise and fall successively (as of large waves)' and mu·amu·amu·a 'to rise and fall successively (as of little ripples).'

Where only a part of the root or stem is repeated, the repeated portion may be called a "reduplicative." Such reduplicatives may occur preposed, interposed, and postposed to the root or stem, and they may consist of just the morphemes of the stem or there may be some added elements, e.g. the /Ce-/ reduplicative in the Greek perfect tense (see section 2.22.2, A).

---

[10]In actuality the tones indicated in Problem 48 replace other basic tones of the roots or stems. Accordingly, they are replacives (see section 3.21.2).

[11]Alternative terminology may be used in describing such structures. For example, we may speak of "additive suprafixes" (the Ngbaka data) and "replacive suprafixes" (the Mongbandi data). Similarly, we may speak of "additive prefixes, infixes, and suffixes," and "replacive prefixes, infixes, and suffixes."

Problem 55 (data from Tojolabal, a language of Mexico)

Instructions:

    a. List those forms which consist of repetitive compounds and those which contain reduplicatives.

    b. Symbolize the types of reduplicatives in accordance with the following precedure:

        1. Assign C and V values to the roots.

        2. Number these C and V constituents. For example, a stem -not would have the symbolization $-C_1V_2C_3$.

        3. Assign numbered C and V symbols to the reduplicative portions, e.g. if -not occurs in a reduplicated form -notot this reduplicated form would be symbolized as $-C_1V_2C_3V_2C_3$. The reduplicative would have the form $-V_2C_3$.

    c. Classify the reduplicatives in terms of their symbolic types.

1. -oč	'to enter'	1a. -očoč	'to enter little by little'
2. -set	'to go around'	2a. -setet	'to go around and around'
3. -ših	'to unbend'	3a. -šihših	'to unbend little by little'
4. -hur	(unique constituent stem)	4a. -hurur	'to move (as of an animal or bird)'
5. -muh	(unique constituent stem)	5a. -muhmun	'to moo'
6. -tim	'to spread out'	6a. -timim	'to lightning'
7. -lok	'to boil'	7a. -loklon	'to boil (continuously)'

Supplementary information:

    1. The final n should be treated in the same way as the e in the Greek perfect tense reduplicative series (see section 2.22.2, A).

    2. It should be noted that there is a different semantic value in the partial as compared to the complete reduplication.

Problem 56 (data from Hausa, a language of the Sudan)[12]

Instructions:

    a. Distinguish between complete and partial reduplication.

    b. Classify reduplicatives according to whether they are preposed or postposed.

    c. Classify reduplicatives according to the structural order of phonemes which are reduplicated. Employ numbers to identify the phonemes.

---

    [12]See Carleton T. Hodge, An Outline of Hausa Grammar, Language Dissertation No. 41 (Baltimore: Linguistic Society of America, 1947), pp. 39-40.

1. ʔayàà   'tiger nut'   1a. ʔayààʔayàà   'a similar but inedible nut'

2. *šikee   2a. šiššikèè   'supporting timber'

3. *fikee   3a. fiffikèè   'feather'

4. sʔawrii   'retarded growth'   4a. sʔàsʔawraa   'one of retarded growth'

5. mòòriyaa   'usefulness'   5a. mammooraa   'usefulness'

6. gawčʔii   'brittleness'   6a. gàggaẃsʔaa   'a brittle one'

7. tawrii   'toughness'   7a. tàttawraa   'a tough person'

8. muunìì   'ugliness'   8a. mùmmuunaa   'an ugly person'

9. kʔumčii   'dense brush'   9a. kʔunkʔumčii   'a narrow one or place'

10. *zaroo   10a. zànzaroo   'wasp'

11. *giǰee   11a. gilgiǰèè   'cloud'

12. *piloo   12a. pilpilòò   'butterfly'

13. gaašii   'hair'   13a. gàlgaasàà   'hairy person'

14. mààtaa   'woman'   14a. màlmaatàà   'eunuch'

15. ʔàlǰanaa   'jinni'   15a. ʔàlǰanǰanii   'one possessed of jinni'

16. kʔibàà   'fat'   16a. kʔibààkʔibàà   'a fat person'

Supplementary information:

1. Stems with preposed * are reconstructed.

2. The differences of tone may be omitted from the description of the reduplicatives, though there are certain tonal patterns which are pertinent to these formations.

3. Palatalization occurs in forms 6 and 13 (see Problem 26).

4. Reduplication in 8a belongs to the same structural type as that in 7a.

5. Reduplication in 9a belongs to the same structural type as that in 10a.

6. Reduplication in 12a belongs to the same structural type as that in 11a.

7. Omit the suffixes -aa and -ii in determining the type of reduplication in set 15-15a.

3.21.2 Replacive Morphemes

Certain morphemes replace parts of stems. These are structurally different from the additive morphemes, which are added to the stems.

Replacive morphemes have already been discussed under Principle 4 (see section 2.24) of the preceding chapter, and in connection with Problem 47, illustrating a Mongbandi structure.

Replacive morphemes may consist of any phonemic form. That is to say, they may be vowels, consonants, tones, nasalization, or combinations of such segmental and suprasegmental features. In English replacive morphemes are abundantly illustrated in the verbs which undergo a change of syllabic in the past-tense and participial formations (see Problem 40), but they also occur in other structures.

Problem 57

Instructions:

    a. Rewrite the data phonemically.

    b. Determine the types of consonant replacements.

    c. Investigate the possibilities of phonologically defined distribution.

    d. Determine the form of the verbalizing morpheme.

1. bath	1a. bathe	8. grief	8a. grieve
2. sheath	2a. sheathe	9. half	9a. halve
3. wreath	3a. wreathe	10. shelf	10a. shelve
4. teeth	4a. teethe	11. serf	11a. serve
5. safe	5a. save	12. advice	12a. advise
6. strife	6a. strive	13. house	13a. house (v.)
7. thief	7a. thieve		

Supplementary information:

    1. Treat the change of syllabic in set 1-1a as a part of the allomorphic alternant of the stem: /bæθ ∞ bey...-/. In symbolizing the allomorphs of the stems, the position of the replacive morpheme may be indicated by three dots. The hyphen follows the form, since it is bound.

    2. Regard the noun forms as basic and the verb forms as derived from these.

Discussion of Problem 57:

    There are three types of replacives: /d ← θ/ in bathe, sheathe, wreathe, teethe, /v ← f/ in save, strive, thieve, grieve, halve, shelve, serve, and /z ← s/ in advise and house (verb).

    These replacives occur in phonologically defined environments. That is to say, the form of the verbalizing series may be determined by the form of the noun stem. Accordingly, by the use of Principle 2 in the determination of morphemes, we may combine these different forms into a single replacive morpheme: /(d ← θ) ~ (v ← f) ~ (z ← s)/.

Problem 58 (data from Shilluk, a Nilotic language of the Anglo-Egyptian Sudan)

    Instructions: Determine the replacive morphemes which form the plural and the combinative forms. Series 1-11 are singular absolute forms; 1a-11a are plural absolute forms; and 1b-11b are singular combinative forms.

1. wāt 'house'	1a. wàt 'houses'	1b. wán 'house'
2. kwàm 'chair'	2a. kwàmì 'chairs'	2b. kwām 'chair'
3. pūk 'jar'	3a. pūkī 'jars'	3b. pūŋ 'jar'
4. pyēn 'bed'	4a. pēnĻ 'beds'	4b. pyén 'bed'
5. yίʈ 'ear'	5a. yīʈ 'ears'	5b. yίŋ 'ear'
6. tā·k 'hat'	6a. tākì 'hats'	6b. tāŋī 'hat'
7. tίk 'chin'	7a. tīk 'chins'	7b. tίŋ 'chin'
8. tóŋ 'spear'	8a. tōŋ 'spears'	8b. tóŋ 'spear'
9. čúŋ 'knee'	9a. čāŋ 'knees'	9b. čúŋ 'knee'
10. bàt 'arm'	10a. bà·t 'arms'	10b. bān 'arm'
11. ógāʈ 'cloth'	11a. ógàʈ 'cloths'	11b. ógān 'cloth'

Supplementary information:

1. The plural formations in Shilluk are very irregular, that is to say, there are many classes of plural forms and a number of these classes have very few members.

2. Regard the singular forms of the first column as basic.

3. The stem form pēn- (4a) is an allomorph of the stem.

4. The shorter vowels in forms 6a and 6b represent allomorphic differences in the stems.

5. The dots beneath vowels indicate a breathy character. This may acquire suprasegmental morphemic status in some forms (but not in this series).

6. The circumflex beneath consonants indicates an interdental series.

7. The change of vowel in 9a may be treated here as submorphemic (i.e. a part of the stem allomorph), though in the plural formations as a whole such changes of vowel acquire the status of morphemes.

8. The length in form 10a may be considered a suprafix.

9. The initial ó- in set 11-11a-11b is a prefix.

10. The lower tones which distinguish the plural forms from the singular may be regarded as suprasegmental replacives.

11. The higher tones which distinguish the singular combinative forms from the singular noncombinative forms are suprasegmental replacives.

12. The forms in the third column are only one type of combinative formation.

13. A form such as 10b bān 'arm' exhibits two replacive morphemes: the final nasal and the change of tone. Two morphemes which are structurally significant in a single structural series may be called "supplementary morphemes."[13]

---

[13] These morphemes are complementary in the forms 2b and 5b, but this complementation

The shift of stress which occurs in English nouns derived from verbs is a replacive morpheme.

Problem 59

Instructions:

    a. Write out phonemically the verb and corresponding noun forms.

    b. Determine the pattern of stress change.

1. inlay	6. insult	11. convict
2. impact	7. insert	12. project
3. import	8. protest	13. rebel
4. increase	9. convert	14. conflict
5. contrast	10. transfer	

Supplementary information:

    1. Most of the verb forms in this series occur with stress on the second syllable. The forms import, increase, contrast, transfer occur as verbs with stress on either the first or second syllable. Historically this is due to (1) the derivation of the noun from the verb by shift of stress and (2) the reversed derivation of the verb from a noun by zero modification (cf. fish, man, angle). Descriptively, we may say that in some instances the shift of stress results in a noun and in other instances results in a form belonging to both noun and verb distributional classes.

    2. In some pairs there are differences of segmental phonemes, e.g. /rəbél ~ rebəl/. The second form is a bound allomorph occurring with the replacive stress morpheme /CVCVC/.

Discussion of Problem 59:

    The relationship of the verb series to the noun series is parallel to the relationship of forms with singular and plural subjects in the Mongbandi data of Problem 47. The Mongbandi forms with singular subjects consist of segmental and suprasegmental phonemes. The allomorphs which occur in the forms with plural subjects consist entirely of segmental phonemes, and the suprasegmental phonemes are structurally a different morpheme. Similarly in English the verb rebel /rəbél/ consists of segmental and suprasegmental phonemes, but the allomorph /rebəl/, which occurs with the noun-forming morpheme /CVCVC/, consists wholly of segmental phonemes.[14]

------

does not exist throughout. Hence both formations acquire morphemic status, but since they are semantically and structurally supplementary, they may be called supplementary morphemes.

    [14]Some morphemes may be described as both additive and replacive. For example, the suffix -ity may be said to have segmental and suprasegmental features. The segmental form would be /-itiy/ and the suprasegmental feature consists in the occurrence of a presuffixal stress: ability, legálity, frigídity, electrícity. The morpheme may be symbolized as /VCitiy/. The allomorphic forms of the stems (i.e. consisting of one or more morphemes) would be /éybəl ∞ əbil-, líygəl ∞ liygæl-, fríjid ∞ frijid-, eléktrik ∞ elektris-/. However, it would also be possible to treat the shift of stress as a property of the stem allomorph, e.g. /éybəl ∞ əbil-/. This second treatment is preferable.

3.21.3 Subtractive Morphemes

Phonemes may be subtracted from stems as well as added to them to signify some difference in meaning. Such subtractions are, however, much rarer than additions. They usually result from a historical process of sound change which becomes morphologically meaningful.

Problem 60 (data from French)

Feminine Forms	Masculine Forms (phrase-final or before consonants)	
1. /movɛz/ mauvaise	1a. /movɛ/ mauvais	'bad'
2. /œrøz/ heureuse	2a. /œrø/ heureux	'happy'
3. /grãd/ grande	3a. /grã/ grand	'big'
4. /frwad/ froide	4a. /frwa/ froid	'cold'
5. /šod/ chaude	5a. /šo/ chaud	'hot'
6. /ptit/ petite	6a. /pti/ petit	'little'
7. /bɔn/ bonne	7a. /bɔ̃/ bon	'good'
8. /fos/ fausse	8a. /fo/ faux	'false'
9. /gras/ grasse	9a. /gra/ gras	'fat'
10. /lɔ̃g/ longue	10a. /lɔ̃/ long	'long'
11. /žãtiy/ gentille	11a. /žãti/ gentil	'nice'
12. /distɛkt/ distincte	12a. /distɛ/ distinct	'distinct'
13. /sul/ soûle	13a. /su/ soûl	'drunk'
14. /frɛš/ fraîche	14a. /frɛ/ frais	'fresh'

Supplementary information: Historically, the feminine forms ended in -e, but this final vowel was lost. Previous to this loss of final vowel, the final consonants of the masculine forms were lost. The loss of final -n resulted in the nasalization of the preceding vowel.

Discussion of Problem 60:

There are two ways[15] in which to describe the relationships of these French forms. It would be possible to assume that the masculine forms represent the basic forms of the stems and that the feminine forms are derived by the suffixation of /-z ∞ -d ∞ -t ∞ -n ∞ -s ∞ -g ∞ -y ∞ -kt ∞ -l ∞ -s/. It would be necessary, however, to list the

---

[15] A third alternative has been suggested to me by my colleague William L. Wonderly. This would involve setting up stems on the pattern of the feminine forms, and then, by means of a morphophonemic final /-ə/ added to the feminine forms, describing all the differences in terms of phonologically definable distributions. These would, however, be very complex. Such a procedure introduces techniques described in Chapter 5. This alternative does, however, have the advantages of representing more easily the dialectal variants and of taking into account the masculine forms occurring before vowels.

stems which occur with each of these morphologically defined allomorphs. The second procedure consists in setting up the feminine forms as basic and deriving the masculine forms by a subtractive morpheme consisting of the last consonant or consonant cluster. This is a much simpler way of treating such a structure, and it reveals an important set of relationships.

Not all instances of loss of phonemes may be regarded as subtractive morphemes. For example, in Samoan[16] there are the following sets of forms:

Problem 61

1. tani	'weep'		1a. tanisia	'wept'	
2. inu	'drink'		2a. inumia	'drunk'	
3. ulu	'enter'		3a. ulufia	'entered'	

It is obvious that the simpler procedure here is to take the stems from the series having the suffix -ia. The forms of the first column can then be described as having lost the final consonant of the stem. This difference is not, however, morphemic, for there are no final consonants in Samoan, and thus such a loss is phonologically "conditioned" by the environment. Accordingly, we may list the stem alternants as tanis- ~ tani, inum- ~ inu, and uluf- ~ ulu. The feature which distinguishes this Samoan problem from the French problem cited above is that in French there is no such phonologically definable distribution for alternative forms, since some adjectives ending in a consonant do not lose any final consonant in the formation of the masculine, e.g. national /nasyɔnal/, naturel /natürɛl/, jeune /žœn/, raisonnable /rezɔnabl/, riche /riš/.

3.22 Positional Relationships of Morphemes to Each Other

Morphemes have the following positional types of occurrence: (1) successive, (2) included, and (3) simultaneous.

Most morphemes occur in succession. These have been abundantly illustrated in the preceding data.

Some morphemes occur in included positions, either partial or complete. The Zoque morphemes -hay- 'benefactive' and -pa 'present tense' (see Problem 52) may occur in the sequence -hapya. Here each morpheme occupies a partially included position within the other. Infixes, on the other hand, are completely included within other morphemes, e.g. the intransitivizing -h- in Tzeltal (see section 3.13).

Suprasegmental morphemes always have simultaneous occurrence with some segmental units. In some instances morphemes consisting of segmental phonemes may have a partial or a complete simultaneous occurrence. For example, in the English form /miyčuw/, as an optional variant of /miyt yuw/ meet you, the phoneme /č/ is actually a part of two morphemes, in that the /t/ and the /y/ of the basic forms of the morphemes have coalesced and another phoneme has taken their place. In describing such a series as /kišuw, hičuw, bežuw, liyǰuw/ kiss you, hit you, buzz you, lead you we usually list such alternants as /kis ∞ kiš, hit ∞ hič-, bəz ∞ bəž-, liyd ∞ liyǰ-/, and /yuw ∞ -uw/,[17] and then describe the circumstances in which they occur. We could, theoretically, list the allomorphs as /kis ∞

---

[16] These data are taken from Bloomfield, op. cit., p. 219.

[17] The hyphens in this series indicate relationships of the clitic /-uw/ to the verbs. A clitic is a form which phonologically combines with an element with which it does not form a morphological construction (see Chapters 4 and 5).

ki-, hit ∞ hi-, bəz ∞ bə-, liyd ∞ liy-/ and /yuw ∞ -šuw ∞ čuw ∞ -žuw ∞ -ǰuw/, but we usually avoid this type of division since it makes for a more awkward description. If we are to
be perfectly correct in our symbolization of allomorphs, we should list them as /kis ∞
ki͟š-, hit ∞ hi͟č-, bəz ∞ bə͟ž-, liyd ∞ liy͟ǰ-/ and /yuw ∞ (-šuw ~ -čuw ~ -žuw ~ -ǰuw)/. The
underlining indicates phonemes shared by the allomorphs of two different morphemes. Usually, however, we find it simpler to list allomorphs without indicating such matters as partial simultaneous occurrence.

Problem 62

    Instructions: List the morphemes in Problems 24, 26, 27, and 32 which have partial
        simultaneous occurrence with other morphemes.

    There are some instances in which morphemes have a complete simultaneous occurrence.
For example, in French the word au /o/ 'to the' results from a combination of a 'to' and
le 'the.' It would be possible for us to describe the allomorphs of le as /le͞ ∞ -o/,[18]
and of a as /a ∞ o-/. The relationship of the allomorphs is symbolized by ∞, since the
occurrence of such an allomorph is dependent upon the morphemes which occur. Hyphens are
employed to indicate (1) the relative order of the allomorphs and (2) the fact that the
allomorphs occur only in combination. Such instances of complete simultaneous occurrence
are very rare.[19]

------

[18]These are not the only allomorphs of le.

[19]It is not legitimate to consider that a suffix such as /-ɔ·/ in Greek /lu·ɔ·/ 'I
loose' represents the complete simultaneous occurrence of five morphemes because this one
form /-ɔ·/ indicates person, number, tense, mode, and voice. Allomorphs may not be construed as having the capacity of simultaneous occurrence unless they are relatable to overt
allomorphs occurring in structurally parallel situations.

CHAPTER 4

THE DISTRIBUTION OF MORPHEMES

4.1 Significance of the Distribution of Morphemes

In the analysis of any language we are concerned with two primary features: (1) the morphemic inventory (i.e. the morphemes which exist) and (2) their distribution. The so-called grammar of a language consists largely in describing the kinds of morphemes which go together. In general, if these combinations constitute words, they are described in the morphology; if they constitute phrases, they are described in the syntax. The description of the types of morphemes in any given language is relatively simple in comparison with the description of the meaningful constructions in which these morphemes occur.

Each language has a different system for the combining of morphemes, and within each system there are rigid restrictions. In the syntax there may be such alternative orders as John ran away, Away ran John, and Away John ran, but in the morphology of most languages the order is fixed, and in some languages it is very complicated. Even in English we find rather complex structures, e.g. the word formalizers, consisting of five morphemes. The shift in order of one morpheme makes the word quite unintelligible, e.g. *formizalers.

In some languages, for example, Eskimo, Quechua, and Turkish, the roots are initial and all bound forms are suffixed.

Problem 63 (data from the Barrow [Alaska] dialect of Eskimo)

1. nigiiñ   'eat (sg.)'

2. nigipkagiñ   'you (sg.) feed him (cause him to eat)'

3. nigipkaŋagiñ   'you (sg.) fed him'

4. nigipkagaŋa   'he feeds me'

5. nigipkaktuŋa   'I feed myself (I eat)'

6. nigipkaŋazuŋa   'I fed myself'

7. nigisuktuŋa   'I want to feed myself'

8. nigiyumazuŋa   'I intend to feed myself'

9. iglu   'house'

10. iglukpiiñ   'build (you sg.) a house!'

11. iglukpisuktuŋa   'I want to build a house'

12. iglukpiyumazuŋa   'I intend to build a house'

13. iglukpiyumalaaktuŋa   'I am anxious to build a house'

Supplementary information:

    1. The reflexive morpheme is -tu ~ -zu.

    2. The subject-object suffixes are irregularly fused.

Problem 64 (data from Quechua, a language of South America)

    1. t'ika   'flower'

    2. t'ikay   'my flower'

    3. t'ikaykuna   'my flowers'

    4. t'ikaykunaman   'to my flowers'

    5. t'ikaykunamanta   'of my flowers'

    6. t'ikaykunamantapača   'from my flowers'

    7. t'ikaykunamantapačal^{y}a   'from my flowers also'

    8. t'ikaykunamantapačal^{y}apis   'also from my flowers only'

Supplementary information: The postposed elements -al^{y}a and -pis are clitics.

Problem 65 (data from Turkish)[1]

1. git- ~ gid-	'to go'		9. gitseydi	'if he had gone'	
2. gidejektim	'I would have gone'		10. gittíyseler	'if they went'	
3. gidejéksem	'if I am to go'		11. gittilérse	'if they went'	
4. gidejekmiš	'he would probably have gone'		12. gitmeli	'he ought to go'	
5. gítmiyejegim	'I will not go'		13. gítmemeli	'he must not go'	
6. gitmišti	'he probably had gone'		14. gitmeliydim	'I was obliged to go'	
7. gitmedi	'he did not go'		15. gitmeliymiš	'he probably had to go'	
8. gittíyse	'if he had gone'		16. gitmíssem	'if I went'	

Supplementary information:

    1. Morphemes may differ in form depending upon whether they occur before a vowel or a consonant.

    2. Certain morphemes have allomorphs with or without an initial y, e.g. -di ∞ -ydi, -mis ∞ -ymis, -se ∞ -yse, -ejek ∞ -yejek.

    3. The vowels of the suffixes are dependent upon the vowel of the stem. The phoneme e before y becomes i.

---

[1]These data are taken from C. F. Voegelin and M. E. Ellinghausen, "Turkish Structure," _Journal of the American Oriental Society_, 63 (1943), 1: 54-56.

4. In certain instances suffixes may belong to different orders, as in items 8-9 and 10-11.

In other languages the bound forms may be largely prefixal. In Navaho,[2] for example, all the bound forms occurring in finite forms of the verb are prefixes.[3] There are eleven relative orders of prefixes which are closely bound in structure to the verb stem:[4]

1. Adverbial prefix: ?á- 'thus,' ná- 'back,' naa- 'around.'[5]

2. Theme prefix: dah- 'to start off,' ?álah- 'together,' dah- 'up on.'

3. Iterative mode: ná- 'again and again.'

4. Number: da- 'distributive plural.'

5. Direct object: ši- 'me,' bi- 'third person,' yi- 'third person (when subject is also third person),' ha-, ho- 'time, place.'

6. Deictic prefix: ?a- 'someone, something,' ji- 'third person.'

7. Adverbial prefix: ni- 'completive,' di- 'inceptive.'

8. Tense: di- 'future.'

9. Mode: si- 'perfective,' go- 'optative,' yi- 'progressive.'

10. Subject pronoun: š- 'I,' ni- 'you (sg.).'

11. Classifiers: zero, d-, ł-, and l-.

12. The stems, which occur in several different possible forms: -?aah 'momentaneous imperfective,' -?áh 'continuative imperfective,' -?á 'perfective, -?áál 'progressive and optative,' and -?ááh 'iterative,' of the stem meaning 'to handle one round or bulky object.'

The following words illustrate the ways in which these constituents of various orders combine:

1. ?áhodoolííł 'he will make the place thus' (< ?á- 'thus,'[1] ho- 'place,'[5] doo [< di- 'future'[8] + yi- 'progressive'[9]], O- 'zero classifier,'[11] -lííł [progressive stem][12] 'to make').

---

[2] See Harry Hoijer, "The Apachean Verb, Part I: Verb Structure and Pronominal Prefixes," International Journal of American Linguistics, 11 (1945), 4: 193-203, and Robert Young and William Morgan, The Navaho Language (Phoenix, Arizona: United States Indian Service, 1943).

[3] Certain noun-forming elements are suffixal.

[4] There are two preceding orders, consisting of an indirect object pronoun plus a postpositional element, but these need not be considered a part of the essential verb structure, even though they do occur in a fixed position.

[5] The illustrative data listed under each structural order are incomplete except for orders 3, 4, 7, 8, and 11. The allomorphs and homophonous morphemes are not listed for a number of the forms.

2. ńdadidoot'ááł 'he will forgive you' (< ń- [< ná- 'back'], da- 'distributive plural,
di- 'inceptive,' doo- [< di- 'future' + yi- 'progressive'], t' 'classifier' [< d-
'classifier' + ? of the stem -?ááł], -?ááł [progressive stem] 'to handle').

Rather than having predominantly or exclusively a prefixal or suffixal structure, the majority of affixing languages have both prefixes and suffixes. These have been abundantly illustrated in Chapters 2 and 3. Where languages have both prefixes and suffixes, certain categories may be expressed by prefixes and others by suffixes. For example, in most Bantu languages the verb prefixes indicate person (subject and object), tense, and negation, while the suffixes indicate voice (active or passive), mode, and aspect (see Problems 5, 6, 32, and 33).

The description of the distribution of morphemes is not easy, and there are many different factors involved. These will be taken up in the following sections, which deal with (1) the types of morphemes as determined by their distribution, (2) the ways in which morphemes combine formally, (3) the pertinence of the distributional environment in terms of immediate constituents, (4) the types of morphological structures which result from various combinations of immediate constituents, (5) primary structural layers, and (6) the limits of morphological structures.

4.2 Types of Morphemes as Determined by Their Distribution

The distribution of morphemes differentiates a great many classes of morphemes and combinations of morphemes: (A) bound vs. free, (B) roots vs. nonroots, (C) **roots vs. stems,** (D) nuclei vs. nonnuclei, (E) nuclear vs. peripheral, (F) same order vs. different orders, (G) mutually exclusive, (H) mutually obligatory, (I) obligatory vs. nonobligatory, (J) closing vs. nonclosing.

A. Bound vs. Free Forms

Bound morphemes never occur in isolation, that is, are not regularly uttered alone in normal discourse.[6] Such bound forms include prefixes, suffixes, suprafixes, infixes, replacives, subtractives, and some roots. Free morphemes are those which may be uttered in isolation, e.g. boy, girl, man. They always consist of a root. Stems, which consist of a root or a root plus some other morpheme, are by definition always bound, e.g. -ceive (cf. receive) and recep- (cf. reception), manli- (cf. manliness) and formaliz- (cf. formalizer). Such stems as /mænliy-/ in /mæliynes/ and /fowrməlayz-/ in /fowrməlayzər/ differ from the corresponding free forms only because of the postposed juncture (see section 4.3). The forms /mænliy-/ and /fowrməlayz-/ are potentially free, though in the combinations /mænliynes/ and /fowrməlayzər/ they are actually bound. A distinction may thus be made between potentially free, actually free, and bound. For example, the word boy is actually free in such an utterance as Boy! (an exclamation of enthusiasm or a vocative, depending upon the intonation), but it is only potentially free in such a word as boyish. "Actual freedom," however, always involves some combining intonational morphemes. What we usually mean to indicate by distinguishing free morphemes from bound morphemes is the potential freedom of forms, not their actual free occurrences. Some morphemes are always bound, e.g. -ceive, whereas others may have a bound allomorph, e.g. /əbíl-/ (the bound allomorph of /éybəl/ able) in ability /əbílitiy/.

---

[6]In special contexts it is always possible to employ a bound form in isolation. For example, in response to the question, "What is this suffix?" one may reply "-ly."

B. Roots vs. Nonroots

Roots constitute the nuclei (or cores) of all words.[7] There may be more than one root in a single word, e.g. blackbird, catfish, and he-goat, and some roots may have unique occurrences. For example, the unique element cran- in cranberry does not constitute the nucleus of any other words, but it occurs in the position occupied by roots; cf. redberry, blueberry, blackberry, and strawberry. All other distributional types of morphemes constitute nonroots.

It is not always easy to distinguish between roots and nonroots. This is because some roots become nonroots and vice versa. For example, the nonroot -ism in such words as fatalism, pragmatism, fascism, and communism, has become a full root, e.g. (I'm disgusted with all these) isms. We may say that ism fills the position of both a root and a nonroot. As a suffix it is a nonroot, and as a noun it is a root. Conversely, the root like became the bound form -ly. Historically, a form such as man-like became manly, but a new formation man-like was reintroduced. There is no difficulty in this instance, because there is so little phonetic-semantic resemblance between like and -ly, and hence we consider them two morphemes. But in the words disgraceful and bucketful we recognize elements which have phonetic-semantic resemblance to the root full. There are actually three allomorphs: (1) /fól/ full, (2) /fòl/ -ful having secondary morphological stress and combined with the preceding word with an open juncture (see section 4.3) as in /péyl-fòl/ pailful, /békət-fòl/ bucketful, and (3) /fəl/[8] with zero stress and combined with close juncture, as in /disgréysfəl/ disgraceful. Allomorph 1 occurs in syntactic constructions, and allomorph 2 combines in the same way as do compounding roots (see sections 4.44 and 4.5), but allomorph 3 combines in the same formal and structural manner as do suffixes, and hence it is a suffix. Combinations with allomorph 2 result in nouns, e.g. bucketful, handful, cupful, spadeful (typical root-plus-root constructions), but combinations with allomorph 3 result in adjectives, e.g. plentiful, bountiful, careful, tasteful, spiteful (typical root-plus-nonroot constructions).

Criteria for determining roots include the following:

1. Positions of occurrence, e.g. in Eskimo, Quechua, Turkish.

2. Occurrence with certain prosodic features. Roots frequently have different prosodic characteristics of stress or tone from those of other morphemes.

3. Occurrence with different bounding junctures, e.g. full and the suffix -ful in disgraceful.

4. Statistical frequency. There are many more roots than bound forms, i.e. by morphological listing, not necessarily by occurrence in context.

5. Parallelism of structure. Having determined the structure of most morphological constructions, the same patterns may be employed to establish the roots and nonroots where there may be some doubt.[9]

---

[7]There are some very rare instances in which it may be necessary to postulate a zero stem, and sometimes the stems may have empty meanings (see Morris Swadesh, "Nootka Internal Syntax," International Journal of American Linguistics, 9 (1939), 2-4: 90).

[8]It is frequently valuable to be able to distinguish a phonemic juncture from a structural one orthographically. The phonemic external juncture may be indicated by a regular hyphen, and a structural juncture, e.g. the relationship of suffix to root, by a slanted hyphen. Allomorphs 2 and 3 could then be written /-fòl/ and /ᷧfəl/.

[9]There is, of course, always the possibility of unique constructions, but these are rare.

6. <u>Meaning</u>. The root (or roots, in compounds) are usually, but not always, the principal "carriers" of the meaning.[10]

<u>Problem</u> <u>66</u>

Instructions:

    a. Write the forms phonemically.

    b. Underline each morpheme.

    c. Indicate under each morpheme the following distinctions: B "bound," F "free," R "root," and NR "nonroot."

1. football	8. bandageless	15. peaches
2. friends	9. resourcefulness	16. fanatical
3. foolish	10. glueyness	17. greenhouses
4. fisherman	11. bombsights	18. old-maidish
5. guardedly	12. blackberry	19. provide
6. leaderless	13. disappoint	20. involve
7. distasteful	14. angelic	21. fish

C. Roots vs. Stems

All bound roots are stems, but not all stems (they are all bound) are roots. A stem is composed of (1) the nucleus, consisting of one or more roots, or (2) the nucleus plus any other nonroot morphemes, except the last "structurally added" morpheme that results in a word. The form <u>man-</u> in <u>manly</u> is at the same time a root and a stem. The form <u>breakwater</u> is the stem of <u>breakwaters</u>, but it is not a single root. There are two root morphemes, <u>break</u> and <u>water</u>. The stem /əbil-/ in <u>ability</u> is a bound alternant of a root morpheme /éybəl ∞ əbíl-/. A form such as <u>men's</u> may never constitute a stem since the genitive morpheme <u>-s</u> always closes any morphological construction in English.

D. Nuclei vs. Nonnuclei

The nucleus of a morphological construction consists of (1) a root or (2) a combination of roots (including possible nonroots attributive to respective roots). The nonnucleus is made up of nonroots. In the construction <u>boyishness</u> the element <u>boy</u> is the nucleus and <u>-ishness</u> constitutes the nonnucleus. In <u>breakwaters</u> the nucleus <u>breakwater</u> consists of two roots.

Some nuclei are bipartite, with dependent nucleus-nonnucleus included constituents. For example, the nucleus of the Greek word /hippopotamos/ 'hippopotamus (lit. horse-river)' consists of (1) the root /hipp-/ (cf. /hippikos/ 'horsey') plus its stem formative -o and (2) the root /potam-/ (cf. /potamios/ adj. 'of a river') plus its stem formative -o. The final declensional suffix -s is added to the combination. The construction /hippo-/, consisting of a root and a nonroot (also a nucleus and a nonnucleus), is not a nucleus. The construction /potamo-/ is similarly not a nucleus, but the combination /hippopotamo-/

---

[10]In actual practice, the criterion of meaning is most frequently employed, but it is not reliable and must be substantiated by structural criteria.

constitutes a bipartite nucleus. The significance of such a division will become more obvious after we consider immediate constituents, in section 4.4.

A nucleus may be tripartite; e.g. the San Blas word mu·amu·amu·a 'to rise and fall successively and quite rapidly' consists of three identical roots. Here the nucleus is also a word. Tripartite nuclei of nonidentical roots are quite rare, e.g. foot-pound-second, a unit of measurement, franco-anglo-américaine (cf. la déclaration franco-anglo-américaine 'the French, English, and American declaration'), rouge-blanc-bleu (cf. le drapeau rouge-blanc-bleu 'the red, white, and blue flag'), and suouetaur(ilia) (Latin) 'a sacrifice of a pig, a sheep, and a bull.'[11]

E. Nuclear vs. Peripheral Structures

A nuclear structure consists of or contains the nucleus, or constitutes the head of a subordinate endocentric construction (cf. 4.44.1). A peripheral morpheme usually consists of a nonroot and is always "outside" of the nuclear constituent.[12] In the word formal the nuclear element is form- and the peripheral element -al. In the word formalize the nuclear structure is formal- and the peripheral element is -ize. Similarly in formalizer the nuclear constituent is formalize- and the peripheral element is -er. "Nuclear" and "peripheral" are simply names for the immediate constituents (see section 4.4).

The Greek word /hippopotamos/ (cited above, under D) has a structure which may be symbolized as [(N + P) + (N + P) = N] + P in which N stands for nuclear and P for peripheral elements. In the first two instances of N the nuclear element is also both a nucleus and a root, but that is not pertinent to the problem here.

F. Morphemes of the Same Order vs. Morphemes of Different Orders

In the structure of words we find morphemes which belong to the same order or to different orders. In Problem 5, for example, the subject pronouns ni- 'I,' wu- 'you (sg.),' a- 'he,' tu- 'we,' mu- 'you (pl.),' and wa- 'they' all belong to the same order. As such, they belong to a particular order class. They are in contrast with the tense morphemes which all belong to the same order and the object pronouns which all belong to the same order. The morphemes ni- 'I' and wu- 'you (sg.)' belong to the same order, but ni- 'I' and na- 'present tense' belong to different orders. Similarly, the subject pronoun wu- 'you (sg.)' is of a different order from the object pronoun ku- 'you (sg.).'

G. Mutually Exclusive Morphemes

Morphemes of the same order are always mutually exclusive.

Morphemes of different orders may also be mutually exclusive. For example, of the Navaho prefixes listed in section 4.1, those in orders 3 and 9 are mutually exclusive, and so are those in orders 6 and 10. That is to say, if ná-, the prefix of the iterative mode, occurs in the word, then none of the modal prefixes in order 9 occur. Similarly, if a deictic prefix from order 6 is employed, then none of the subject prefixes of order 10 are employed.

H. Mutually Obligatory Morphemes

If the occurrence of one morpheme requires the occurrence of another, then the two morphemes are mutually obligatory. If forms are mutually obligatory in all situations,

---

[11]The French and Latin examples are cited by Henry Frei, "Note sur l'analyse des syntagmes," Word, 4 (1948) 2: 66.

[12]Note, however, that infixes and some replacives are "peripheral" even though they are formally included within the nuclear constituent.

then they constitute a single discontinuous morpheme, but some forms may be mutually obligatory in some constructions and not in others.

I. Obligatory vs. Nonobligatory Morphemes

Certain morphemes may be obligatory to a structural class and others not. For example, in the finite verb forms of Bantu (cf. Problem 33) there are usually only two obligatory affixal morphemic classes, namely, the subject indicator and the suffixal modal indicator. In Kekchi a finite verb must consist of a verb stem and a subject, though in the third person singular the subject may be indicated by a zero morpheme. All the other order classes are optional.

J. Closing vs. Nonclosing Morphemes

Certain morphemes "close" the construction to further formation. For example, in English the use of a genitive suffix closes the noun to further suffixation. No suffix may follow the genitive. In Greek the addition of /-o/ to the root /hipp-/ 'horse' does not prevent further derivation, e.g. /hippotɛ·s/ 'horseman' and /hippodromos/ 'racecourse,' but the addition of a declensional ending such as the nominative singular /-s/ closes the word to any further derivation. Nothing like /-tɛ·s/ can be added to /hippos/. The morpheme /-o/ is a nonclosing morpheme, and /-s/ is a closing morpheme.

There are two distinct degrees of closure in some languages. For example, a morpheme such as -ize in formalize and legalize does not close the form to further word formation, e.g. formalizer and legalization. But the addition of the plural -s closes any form to further derivation by such suffixes as -ment, -ity, -ence, -ion, -ian, -ize, -er. A genitive suffix does the same thing. This break in structure in English coincides with the division between inflectional and derivational formations (see section 4.6).

4.3 Formal Combining of Morphemes

The formal combining of morphemes involves two factors: order and juncture. The various possible orders have already been discussed in Chapter 3.

By "juncture" we mean the type of transition between morphemes. These junctures between morphemes are of two important kinds: (1) phonemic (i.e. contrastively perceptible in utterance) and (2) structural.

There are two (rarely more) degrees of phonemic juncture which are morphologically pertinent: (1) open juncture and (2) close juncture. Open juncture is generally equivalent to the "break" occurring between words, and close juncture is what we normally find within words. In English there are two words (1) recover, meaning 'to recuperate,' and (2) recover, meaning 'to cover again.' These words are phonemically different, and this difference may be symbolized as (1) /riykévər/ and (2) /rìy-kévər/. The acute accent indicates a primary stress, the grave a secondary stress, and the hyphen denotes a type of open transition. There is no actual phonetic break (i.e. cessation of sound) in /rìy-kévər/, but the phonemes /iy/ preceding the hyphen are pronounced with more emphasis (this is to be expected from the secondary stress), and somewhat longer, and the consonant following it exhibits a different "attack." The transition in /rìy-kévər/ is equivalent to the one in the sequence see Cuthbert. This may be phonemically symbolized as /sìy kə́θbərt/.[13]

---

[13]The accents in the two expressions are written in the same way so as to point out the phonological similarities, but the phonological identity is the result of different structural features. In /rìy-kévər/ the accentual pattern is morphologically determined, but in /sìy kə́θbərt/ the secondary stress is the result of an intonational pattern which may be readily shifted. The secondary accent on /sìy/ is an intonationally reduced primary stress, whereas the secondary accent on /rìy-/ is the property of the morpheme as a

One must not assume a one-to-one correspondence between types of phonetic open and close transition and open and close phonemic junctures. Such a correspondence is usual, but in Chitimacha[14] a sequence of identical consonants is pronounced with open phonetic transition within a word and with close phonetic transition between words. For example, each p of the cluster pp in kappa 'light' is aspirated, but in the phrase ni·hkup pešk 'flying downward' the sequence pp is pronounced with a single closure of the lips.

Structural junctures are of two types: (1) overt and (2) covert.

Overt structural junctures are marked by formal contrasts in types of sequences. For example, in the English word kingdom the sequence /ŋd/ is structurally distinctive, because it never occurs within a single morpheme; the sequence /nd/, on the other hand, does occur within morphemes, e.g. sandy, landed. A sequence such as nn is also structurally distinctive. Since no single morpheme occurs with such a cluster, it always marks a morphemic juncture, e.g. unnatural /ənnǽčərəl/ and meanness /míynnes/.

Covert structural junctures involve potential and nonpotential pauses. The potential position of intonational pauses[15] is important for the analysis of word and phrase units. These potential positions of pause are also very significant in syntactic analysis. The fact that such intonational pauses do not occur within words provides the covert evidence of the morphological and phonological unity of a word. A form such as blackbird /blǽk-bə̀rd/ has a phonemic open juncture between the morphemes, and two structural junctures. The overt structural juncture (quite apart from the phonemic /-/) consists of the cluster /kb/, which never occurs within a single morpheme, and the covert structural juncture consists in the fact that an intonational pause never comes between the morphemes when they occur in this structural relationship.[16]

4.4 Immediate Constituents

4.41 Significance of Immediate Constituents

The distribution of any morpheme must be given in terms of its environment, but some of its environment may be important and the rest relatively unimportant. This is true of

---

whole. The junctures are phonetically identical, but one is written with a hyphen to indicate the structurally pertinent fact that an intonational pause never coincides with it. An open juncture of the type /-/ is phonemically a part of both contiguous morphemes. (A sequence of a preposed and a postposed open juncture reduces to a single open juncture.) The difference between night-rate and nitrate is that night- and -rate have open junctural phonemes. Such a juncture phoneme does not belong to the form nit- in nitrate. The fact that the juncture is a part of the morpheme has already been noted in the discussion of full and -ful in section 4.2, B. One morpheme in English has the characteristic of inducing a noncontiguous open juncture. Compare effigy /éfijiy/ and refugee /réfyuw-ǰìy/. The suffixal morpheme in the second word may be symbolized as /-Cìy/. A pertinent part of the description of all allomorphs of morphemes is the type of juncture which may precede and follow.

Intonational pauses, which normally occur only between words, are morphemes and belong to the intonational structure, which is syntactically pertinent.

[14]See Morris Swadesh, "The Phonetics of Chitimacha," Language, 10 (1934), 4: 346-47.

[15]These are not hesitations which mark a speaker's indecision as to what to say next, for such hesitations may occur within words, as well as between words, though they do so much less frequently. See Kenneth L. Pike, The Intonation of American English (Ann Arbor: University of Michigan Press, 1945), for a discussion of intonational pauses.

[16]In a phrase structure it is possible to find such a pause. For example, in a

both morphology and syntax, and perhaps it is more easily illustrated by the syntax. For example, in the sentence <u>Peasants</u> <u>throughout</u> <u>China</u> <u>work</u> <u>very</u> <u>hard</u> we could describe the environment of <u>very</u> as bounded by a preposed <u>work</u> and a postposed <u>hard</u> and of <u>work</u> as bounded by a preposed <u>China</u> and a postposed <u>very</u>, but this kind of description of the environment does not seem to be quite pertinent. We "feel" that <u>very</u> goes first with <u>hard</u> and that <u>very hard</u> then goes with the verb. Similarly, <u>throughout</u> and <u>China</u> appear to "go together," and these in turn "modify" <u>peasants</u>. We unite the subject <u>peasants throughout China</u> with all of the predicate <u>work very hard</u>. What we have done in this simple sentence is to discover the pertinent environment of each word or group of words. These sets of pertinent environments correlate with what we shall call immediate constituents, i.e. the constituent elements immediately entering into any meaningful combination. In terms of the above sentence we would describe the most inclusive set of immediate constituents as consisting of <u>Peasants throughout China</u> | <u>work very hard</u>.[17] The successive sets of immediate constituents may be marked as follows: <u>Peasants</u> ‖ <u>throughout</u> ‖‖ <u>China</u> | <u>work</u> ‖ <u>very</u> ‖‖ <u>hard</u>. This may be diagramed somewhat differently as:

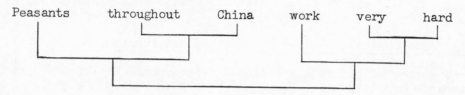

The situation in morphology is analogous to what we find in syntax, though the immediate constituents are usually not so involved and there are fewer successive sets. We have already noted in section 4.2, E that nuclear constituents may be of different sizes. In the following series the nuclear constituent occurring with the peripheral -er varies in morphemic size:

    1. dancer

    2. condenser

    3. formalizer

In describing the distribution of -er we need to know the pertinent environment. We could, of course, say that in 1 -er follows the root <u>dance</u>-, in 2 it follows another root, -<u>dense</u>-, and in 3 it follows a suffix, -<u>ize</u> /-ayz/. But these environments are not particularly pertinent ones. What is important is that all the nuclear constituents with which the peripheral -er occurs are verbs. The -er combines structurally with the entire nuclear constituent and not with just the preceding morpheme. Accordingly, we may say that -er constitutes the peripheral immediate constituent and all the forms which precede constitute the nuclear immediate constituents.

Note that the nuclear immediate constituents may in themselves contain nuclear and peripheral elements. For example, <u>condense</u> consists of a nuclear immediate constituent -<u>dense</u> and a peripheral <u>con</u>-. Similarly, <u>formalize</u> consists of a nuclear[18] <u>formal</u>- and the peripheral -<u>ize</u>. <u>Formal</u> consists of a nuclear <u>form</u>- and a peripheral -<u>al</u>.

---

deliberate, emphatic utterance of the sentence <u>We</u> <u>saw</u> <u>a</u> <u>gigantic</u> <u>black</u> <u>bird</u> <u>hovering</u> <u>over</u> <u>us</u>, intonational pauses may occur following <u>gigantic</u> and <u>black</u>, though their occurrence in these positions is admittedly not frequent.

[17]Upright bars mark the successive breaks.

[18]It is unnecessary to repeat "nuclear immediate constituent" and "peripheral immediate constituent," for in discussing a particular construction "nuclear" and "peripheral" are synonymous with "nuclear immediate constituent" and "peripheral immediate constituent."

In establishing these sets of nuclear and peripheral constituents we have been identifying the pertinent environment of each morpheme. It would be quite hopeless to describe
all words such as formalizer as strings of morphemes, each with an equal rank or attachment
to all the other morphemes. Such a description would be entirely too long and involved,
and furthermore, it would not reveal the essential structure. It is a fact that in formalizer /-ayz/ follows /-əl/ and precedes /-ər/, but it is not the pertinent fact we need to
know. These divisions into immediate constituents will become even more meaningful when we
consider the organization of the grammar in Chapter 9, for there we shall see that the combinations which make up formalizer are discussed in entirely different parts of the grammar.
For example, the root form is discussed as a morpheme with two class memberships, namely,
noun and verb. The combination formal is discussed, elsewhere, as a derived form having
two class memberships, namely, noun and adjective. The word formalize is treated under
verb derivation, and formalizer is treated in still another section, under noun derivation.
At no one place in the grammar is a word such as formalizer "pulled apart" (or "put together") layer by layer, but the various layers (sets of immediate constituents) are discussed
in those parts of the grammar where all similar formations are discussed.

4.42 Positional Relationships between Immediate Constituents

There are a number of possible positional relationships between the nuclear and the
peripheral immediate constituents. These may be classified on the basis of constructions
with two immediate constituents and those with more than two immediate constituents. The
first class may be subdivided between constructions in which the nuclear and the peripheral
immediate constituents are each continuous and those in which either may be discontinuous.

A. Combinations of Two Immediate Constituents

1. Continuous Nuclear and Peripheral Immediate Constituents

a. With All Successive Peripheral Constituents on One Side of the Nucleus

In the Eskimo, Quechua, and Turkish data cited in Problems 63-65 the peripheral constituents all follow the nucleus. In the English word formalizers the successive peripheral constituents are all on one side of the nucleus, and each successive morpheme combines
with the preceding element or elements to form a construction. This is the usual situation,
but there are some exceptions. For example, two peripheral constituents may combine to form
a unit, and then this unit is in turn combined with the rest. Note the following series in
Taos:[19]

    1. ʔą̈npˌuywaʔi   'my friend'

    2. ką̈pˌuywaʔi   'your (sg.) friend'

    3. ką̈npˌuywaʔi   'the friend of us two'

The element kąn- is a combination of the morphemes of the first and second persons singular,
and though it is a combination of two morphemes, it fills the same structural position as a
single morpheme. Hence, in analyzing these peripheral morphemes we would first combine
them into a construction kąn- and then unite this complex peripheral immediate constituent
with the following nuclear immediate constituent. When all nonnuclear constituents are on
one side of the nucleus, the immediate constituents are generally successive series with
each morpheme adding another layer to the morphological "concretion."

---

[19]See George L. Trager, "An Outline of Taos Grammar" in Linguistic Structures of Native America (Viking Fund Publications in Anthropology, 6) (New York, 1946), p. 206. Used
by permission.

b. With Successive Peripheral Constituents on More than One Side of or within the Nucleus

In languages having many bound forms we usually find nonnuclear elements on more than one side of the nucleus. We could say both sides, except for the fact that there are prefixes, suffixes, infixes, and suprafixes. Accordingly, there are four relative positions. The word condenser consists of a nucleus dense and two nonnuclei con- and -er. The manner of dividing condenser into immediate constituents may be complicated by the fact that the apparent partials condense and denser both make sense, but we immediately recognize that the form denser contains quite a different morpheme, namely, the homophonous comparative -er (cf. fuller, meaner, darker, blacker). If we "combine" con- with -dense and then "add" to condense the suffix -er, we do not violate any such meaningful relationship, and hence we "feel" assured that this latter division is correct. The meaning is, of course, a very important guide, but it is not the only one and in some instances it is not too reliable. What does count is the substitutability. A verb such as condense may be substituted for by a verb of a single morpheme, e.g. dance, and since the form dancer consists of only two morphemes, there is no difficulty in deciding upon sets of immediate constituents. There is also a structural fact to help us, namely, that con- does not combine with other comparative adjective forms, e.g. *conbetter, *confuller, and *conmeaner.

The decision is not always so easy. For example, in deciding upon the immediate constituents of disgraceful (and hence the pertinent environment of the morphemes), we can select the alternatives (1) disgrace plus -ful and (2) dis- plus graceful. It would seem at first that either division could be made, since the potential nuclears disgrace and graceful are meaningful combinations, and since dis- may occur with single morphemes, e.g. discount, and -ful may occur with single morphemes, e.g. faithful. There are two ways of resolving this apparent contradiction: (1) by analyzing the meaningful relationships[20] and (2) by studying the structural parallels.

By analyzing the meaningful relationships, we may decide that -ful as a modifier of disgrace, meaning 'full of disgrace,' is more in keeping with the total meaning of disgraceful than the division dis- plus graceful, which would mean 'not graceful.'

The structural analysis by substitutes will give us the same results. By comparing all the various types of combinations in which dis- occurs and all the combinations in which -ful occurs, we find that dis- and -ful both combine primarily with nouns and verbs, e.g. discolor, discord, discount, disfigure, bountiful, plentiful, careful, tasteful. However, the resultant combinations with dis- are usually nouns or verbs and the resultant combinations with -ful[21] are adjectives. The only way in which these structural parallels may be preserved is to combine dis- with grace and then -ful with disgrace.

---

[20]To employ the meaningful relationships of forms as criteria in determining sets of immediate constituents is entirely justifiable. There are meaningful relationships between forms, and it is essential to adhere to these in analyzing the structure. Furthermore, there are some expressions which are identical in form, but which are different in meaning depending upon differences of immediate constituents. For example, in the sentence I hit the man with the cane the phrase with the cane may be an immediate constituent with the phrase the man, in which case the meaning is 'I hit the particular man who had a cane.' On the other hand, with the cane may be an attributive of the entire preceding verb expression, in which case it means 'I hit the man by means of a cane.' In some instances, only an appeal to the meaning of a construction will enable us to determine the sets of immediate constituents. In the analysis of foreign languages one constantly employs meaning as the first and most important criterion, but divisions made on the basis of meaning must be confirmed by supporting structural evidence.

[21]This form must be distinguished from the allomorph -ful which occurs in handful, hatful, and the like, and which has a different type of juncture and a secondary stress rather than a zero stress (see section 4.2, B).

Problem 67

Instructions:

    a. Determine sets of immediate constituents.

    b. List the semantic and structural criteria employed.

1. manliness	6. unmanly
2. old-maidishness	7. distasteful
3. harshly	8. resourceful
4. surpassing	9. engaging
5. untruly	10. confining

2. Discontinuous Immediate Constituents--Nuclear, Peripheral, or Both

Nonnuclear constituents may combine to form a discontinuous peripheral immediate constituent. For example, in the Kekchi data of Problem 37, we noted that the third person plural possessor consists of a prefix and a suffix, e.g. ročoče^ʔp 'their house' r-...-e^ʔp 'their' and očoč 'house.' The two peripheral morphemes are structurally equivalent to a single morpheme in the form qočoč 'our house.' For this reason we consider r-...e^ʔp a discontinuous immediate constituent.[22]

The nuclear immediate constituent may also occur in a discontinuous form. For example, in the word sons-in-law the nuclear immediate constituent is son...-in-law and the peripheral immediate constituent is -s. Such inclusion of a peripheral immediate constituent within a nuclear one is not common, and the "pressure" of the structural pattern in English, in which nuclear and peripheral immediate constituents are in sequence rather than included, results in the alternative son-in-laws.

B. Combinations of More than Two Immediate Constituents

Combinations of more than two immediate constituents are rare, and so far as is known involve only nuclear elements. Certain illustrations of these have already been cited in section 4.2, D. To these may be added some repetitive compounds from Lingombe, a Bantu language of the Belgian Congo:

    1. kŏ·kŏ·kŏ·, an ideophone denoting the noise of rapping

    2. gbágbágbá, an ideophone denoting continuity

    3. kpíkpíkpí, an ideophone denoting pulsation

    4. gbákùgbákùgbákù 'gobble, gobble, gobble'

4.43 Principles of Procedure in Determining Immediate Constituents

Principles of procedure employed in determining immediate constituents have already been touched upon in the preceding sections. The principles are not many and they appear comparatively simple, but their application is not easy. This is because we cannot say

---

[22]The form ročoče^ʔp may also mean 'his houses'; when it has this meaning the immediate constituents are r- and -očoče^ʔp.

that one division of morphemes is inherently right and another wrong, but only that one division produces a relatively simple, coherent description of a language and that another division produces a more complicated and contradictory type of description. This difficulty is reflected in the very way in which the principles are stated:

1. Divisions should conform to meaningful relationships.

2. Divisions are made on the basis of the substitutability of larger units by smaller units belonging to the same or a different external distribution class.

3. Divisions should be as few as possible.

4. Divisions should be supported by the total structure of the language.

5. Other things being equal, a division into continuous immediate constituents has precedence over a division into discontinuous immediate constituents.

4.43.1 Principle 1

Divisions should conform to meaningful relationships.

This principle has already been illustrated in the preceding discussions of condenser and disgraceful (section 4.42, B). In practical analysis it is more frequently employed than any other. This is because we are more accustomed to thinking in terms of meaningful units than in terms of structural units. We must not allow ourselves, however, to follow blindly what seems to be a valid meaningful relationship when this contradicts the structural relationships. Furthermore, there are some words, e.g. untruly, in which we cannot obtain any very satisfactory leads from the meaningful relationships.

4.43.2 Principle 2

Divisions are made on the basis of the substitutability of larger units by smaller units belonging to the same or a different external distribution class.

The principle of division on the basis of substitutability is of primary importance. We found, for example, that in the word formalizer it was possible to substitute dance, a verb of a single morpheme, for the three-morpheme verb formalize. By reducing the overall number of morphemes to two, we remove the difficulty in deciding where to divide the immediate constituents. Note that in substituting the verb dance for the verb formalize we are employing a word of the same general external distribution class.[23] In some instances we may employ a substitute of a different external distribution class, though different external distribution classes occurring in the same environment are much rarer in the morphology of a language than in the syntax.[24] We may, however, decide to divide naturalism between natural and -ism, rather than between natur- and -alism, because of the form

---

[23]A class whose members have some internal morpheme in common, e.g. dancer, player, walker, worker, constitutes an internal distribution class. A class whose members occur in the same external environment, e.g. all verbs which may occur before the suffix -ing, constitutes an external distribution class. However, once the suffix -ing has been added, we describe such a series as an internal distribution class, since they all have the same morpheme in common. Such a group, however, constitutes another external distribution class in that its members may all follow the verb form is: is working, is walking, is playing, is dancing.

[24]This part of the principle is, consequently, much more applicable to syntactic analysis.

snobbism. Snob, a noun, belongs to a different external distribution class from the adjective natural. The word purism contains a substitute of the same external distribution class as natural, and this confirms the pattern of substitution and the validity of the division. Substitution by members of the same external distribution class is far more important than substitution by members of different classes, for in substitutions from the same class there is much greater likelihood of preserving the same meaningful relationships.

4.43.3   Principle 3

Divisions should be as few as possible.

Because we find from experience that linguistic structure tends to be binary (i.e. to consist of two-divisional constructions), we assume in analysis that a particular construction consists of two immediate constituents unless we cannot find substitutional patterns which will make such a division possible. There is, for example, no adequate manner in which we can describe the French adjective rouge-blanc-bleu 'red-white-blue' as anything but three immediate constituents. The same is true of the English foot-pound-second and of the Lingombe kpíkpíkpí, the ideophone of 'pulsation.' No two of these sets of constituents may be regarded as structurally prior to a third.[25]

4.43.4   Principle 4

Divisions should be supported by the total structure of the language.

This principle requiring any division to be supported by the total structure of the language is of course the most difficult to apply, for it necessitates a comprehensive knowledge of the various structures. It is the principle we employed in the discussion of condenser and disgraceful (section 4.42, B). No division of data may be made without consideration of the other similar and different structures. If, for example, we should describe the object pronouns in Congo Swahili (see Problem 5) in terms of their relationships to the tense prefixes or to the subject prefixes, our description would be more or less meaningless. Even if we described the relationship of the object pronouns to the roots, it would still not be enough. We must describe the distribution of the object pronouns in combination with the entire verb stem, for the occurrence or nonoccurrence of an object pronoun can be determined by whether or not the verb stem contains a simple passive suffix. Hence, it is not only a matter of the kind of root, but whether the root may occur with the suffix -iw that is important. The overall structural relationships make it valuable to describe all the suffixal formations in Congo Swahili (these form immediate constituents beginning with the root), before taking up the prefixal formations.

4.43.5   Principle 5

Other things being equal, a division into continuous immediate constituents has precedence over a division into discontinuous immediate constituents.

It is doubtful if there is ever a situation in which a perfect balance exists between continuous vs. discontinuous immediate constituents. The purpose of this principle, however, is to call attention to the fact that in analyzing the structures of strange languages, we must assume that forms which are juxtaposed are more likely to go together than ones which are not juxtaposed. A translation into English frequently violates such an

---

[25]Coördinate series in syntax may consist of more than two immediate constituents, e.g. Father, mother, Jack and sister (went away). The subject expression is made up of four immediate constituents, of which the first three are single words and the last consists of two words. Such series are uncommon in morphology.

arrangement of constituents, but no analysis of a language can be based upon its translation in another language.

Problem 68

Instructions:

    a. Rewrite the forms phonemically.

    b. Determine all the sets of immediate constituents.

    c. List the principles which are applicable in any division and illustrate the use of each principle employed.

1. football	7. greenhouses
2. unfriendly	8. resourceful
3. foolish	9. surpassing
4. fisherman	10. ungentlemanliness
5. glueyness	11. unpretentiousness
6. angelic	12. attractive

Supplementary information:

    1. Where there are only two morphemes, none of the five principles listed above need be employed.

    2. Regard the noun pretense as being one of the constituent elements in item 11.

    3. The types of answers required may be illustrated with unfriendly:

The sets of immediate constituents are /ənfréndliy/.

This division into immediate constituents involves the following principles:

    a. Conformance to meaningful relationships. The present division means 'not friendly.' The alternative division /ənfréndliy/ would mean 'the quality

of not being a friend.' Either meaningful relationship is possible, but the division chosen does not violate the meaning of the word as a whole.

    b. The nuclear constituent friendly is readily substitutable by many monomorphemic adjectives, e.g. unkind, untrue, unchaste, uneven, unjust, unfair. The potential nuclear constituent *unfriend is not readily identifiable as to class, but, assuming that it is analogous to the noun unbelief, one may substitute nouns, e.g. manly, godly, cowardly, timely.

    c. On the basis of either division there would be only two immediate constituents on any level of analysis.

d. The first division is more fully supported by the total structure of the language, since un- combines with many adjectives, and -ly combines with many nouns. The alternative division has only unbelief as a structural parallel, and this does not occur with -ly.

4.44 Functional Relationships between Immediate Constituents

Functional relationships between immediate constituents are defined here as denoting (1) the relationships of the parts to the whole, and (2) the relationships between parts. The first type of relationship may be defined as endocentric or exocentric and the second as subordinate, or coördinate, or nonsubordinate and noncoördinate.

4.44.1 Endocentric vs. Exocentric Constructions

Endocentric constructions are those in which the unit as a whole belongs to substantially the same external distribution class as the nuclear immediate constituent or both immediate constituents (there are rarely more than two). The word blackbird consists of two morphemes black and bird, and in terms of the syntactic structure of English, bird constitutes the nucleus of such a construction. The unit blackbird belongs to substantially the same distribution class as bird, i.e. it takes the same suffix -s and occurs in the same positions as the noun bird occurs. We must, however, say that the classes are "substantially the same," rather than "identical," since blackbird obviously does not combine with red in *redblackbird as bird does in redbird.

In some instances the resultant combination belongs to substantially the same class as both constituents. For example, the word queen-mother is a noun and both immediate constituents are nouns. A compound such as foot-pound-second is also endocentric.

Certain combinations appear to be endocentric, but are not. For example, Redcoat is a noun, and the nuclear immediate constituent, coat, is also a noun. But this nuclear constituent belongs to a class for which the pronominal substitute is it, whereas the construction Redcoat has the pronominal substitute he. Coat and Redcoat are to this extent not members of the same external distributional classes, and we treat such forms as Redcoat as exocentric. Similarly, butterfingers, though it is a noun, does not belong to the same external distribution class as the nuclear immediate constituent fingers, for the nuclear form occurs with plural agreement, e.g. those fingers, but butterfingers occurs with singular agreement, e.g. (Here comes) that butterfingers.

Exocentric constructions are those in which the unit as a whole belongs to a different external distribution class from the nuclear constituent or from both of the immediate constituents. For example, pickpocket consists of a verb and a noun, of which the verb is the nuclear immediate constituent.[26] The noun pickpocket belongs to a different external distribution class from the verb nuclear constituent pick, and hence the construction pickpocket is exocentric. In the word income the immediate constituents are an adverb in and a verb come; the resulting combination, being a noun, is exocentric, in that it does not belong to the class of either immediate constituent.

Both endocentric and exocentric constructions may consist wholly of roots or may include nonroots as immediate constituents. For example, eyelet is an endocentric root-plus-nonroot construction. It belongs to substantially the same external distribution class as the nuclear constituent eye. The adjective fishy is an exocentric root-plus-nonroot construction, because the resultant combination does not belong to the same class as the noun nuclear constituent fish.

---

[26] In the analysis of predicate constructions in the syntax of English the verb constitutes a nuclear and the direct object a peripheral.

4.44.2 Coördinate vs. Subordinate vs. Noncoördinate and Nonsubordinate Constructions

Coördinate constructions are those in which the immediate constituents are of equal structural rank and belong to substantially the same external distribution classes. For example, the adjective bittersweet consists of two coördinate nuclear constituents. The same is true of queen-mother and God-man.

In the constructions eyelet and fishy the peripheral elements -let and -y are subordinate to the nuclear constituents. In blackbird the peripheral black is subordinate to the nuclear bird.

In the word overall, as in the phrase the overall appearance, the immediate constituents over (a preposition) and all (a pronoun), exhibit a noncoördinate and nonsubordinate relationship. In the syntax of English the parallel prepositional phrases constitute exocentric constructions, since the units as a whole do not belong to the same external distribution class as either immediate constituent.

Coördinate immediate constituents must consist entirely of nuclei or of nonnuclei. Subordinate immediate constituents consist of nuclei, combinations of nuclei and nonnuclei, or combinations of nonnuclei. The Kekchi immediate constituent r-...-e?p 'their' in ročoče?p 'their house' is a combination of nonnuclei.

Problem 69

Instructions:

    a. Write out the forms phonemically.

    b. Underline the primary set of immediate constituents.

    c. Identify the functional relationships of the immediate constituents as endocentric or exocentric and as coordinate or subordinate, or noncoordinate and nonsubordinate.

1. ability	7. haystack	13. baseball
2. funny	8. unable	14. cheerful
3. playground	9. greenhouses	15. figurehead
4. jumpy	10. goldfish	16. thoroughbred
5. postman	11. setup	17. lazybones
6. jackknife	12. upset	18. know-all (noun)

Problem 70 (data from Tzeltal, a language of Mexico)[27]

Instructions:

    a. Identify the external distribution classes of the immediate constituents: adjective, noun, or verb. This may be done from the English translation.[28]

---

[27]These data are from Marianna C. Slocum, "Tzeltal (Mayan) Noun and Verb Morphology," International Journal of American Linguistics, 14 (1948), 2: 79-80.

[28]In the actual analysis of a language the translation cannot be used with any degree of accuracy. Only a knowledge of the structural types of the language in question will allow the assigning of external distributional class membership.

b. Identify the constructions as exocentric or endocentric and as coördinate or subordinate, or noncoördinate and nonsubordinate.

1. tomut   'egg' < ton   'stone' + mut   'hen'

2. pante?   'bridge' < pam   'flat' + te?   'wood'

3. k'atimbak   'hell' < k'atim   'to heat' + bak   'bone'

4. čik'pom   'incense-burner' < čik'   'to burn' + pom   'incense'

5. holwic   'summit' < hol   'head' + wic   'mountain'

6. ničk'ahk'   'spark' < nič   'flower' + k'ahk'   'fire'

7. č'ultat   'god' < č'ul   'holy' + tat   'father'

8. mel?ot'an   'sadness' < mel   'to explain' + ?ot'an   'heart'

9. k'anpatan   'tax-collector' < k'an   'to ask for' + patan   'tax'

10. ?ancil?al   'daughter' < ?ancil   'female' + ?al   'child'

11. muk'ha?   'river' < muk'   'big' + ha?   'water'

12. ha?č'uht'   'diarrhea' < ha?   'water' + č'uht'   'stomach'

Supplementary information: In combinations of noun plus noun, the second noun is attributive to the first.

Problem 71 (data from Tonkawa, an Indian language in the United States)[29]

Instructions: By analyzing the meanings of the resultant combinations in comparison with the constituent parts, determine which element is nuclear and which peripheral.[30]

1. hawawne-taxka-   'to carry (several) to this place' < hawawne-   'to carry a burden' + taxka-   'several arrive'

2. yakaw-ka·na-   'to kick away' < yakaw-   'to kick' + ka·na-   'to throw away'

3. so·l-to·xa-   'to drip onto' < so·l-   'to drip' + -to·xa-   '(to fall) on'

4. ho·s-taxsew-   'to be morning' < ho·s   'early' + taxsew-   'day breaks'

5. yako·n-yapal?-   'to knock down' < yako·n-   'to strike' + -yapal?-   'down'

6. na·x-sokna-   'to guide, reconnoitre' < na·x   'road' + sokna-   'to put away, to have'

7. ?a·x-pix   'cider' < ?a·x   'water' + pix   'sweet'

(Continued on next page.)

---

[29] See Harry Hoijer, "Tonkawa" in Linguistic Structures of Native America (Viking Fund Publications in Anthropolgoy, Vol. 6) (New York, 1946), pp. 296-97. Used by permission.

[30] Such a procedure is not conclusive and must always be tested by structural patterns. Nevertheless, it is helpful in selecting nuclears.

8. tan-maslak   'rabbit' < tan   'tail' + maslak   'white'

9. tan-ʔok-apay   'opossum' < tan   'tail' + ʔok   'hair' + kapay   'none'

10. cʔaxʷ-yapec   'thread' < cʔaxʷ   'cloth' + yapce-   'to sew'

Supplementary information: In combinations of verb plus verb, the second modifies the
    first.

4.5 Types of Morphological Structure

Morphological structure may be simple or complex. Simple structures consist of a
single morpheme, free or bound. Complex structures consist of more than one morpheme.
Simple structures may be called "monomorphemic" and complex structures "polymorphemic."

A simple structure always consists of a root. This may be potentially free, e.g. boy,
John, run, and up, or it may be bound. A bound root may be either a stem, e.g. -ceive,
-tain, -veal (cf. receive, retain, reveal) or a clitic, e.g. /ə-, -ə, -l/, atonic forms of
a, you, and will. These bound allomorphs of free forms never occur in isolation, but they
do not necessarily form morphological constructions with the constituents with which they
are phonologically bound. For example, the clitic a in a bored person /əbówrd pérsən/
phonologically "leans"[31] on the form bored, but it constitutes an immediate constituent
with bored person. Similarly, you and will occur in atonic allomorphic forms in I'll hit
yuh (you) /áyl híčə/, in which /-l/ 'll is an immediate constituent with the verb form hit,
and /-ə/ is the object of the verb phrase will hit.

In many instances clitics are not relatable to free alternants. For example, in the
Chanca dialect of Quechua there is a postposed element -ña 'already' which is phonologically a part of many different types of words. There is no doubt about its phonological dependence, because it always occurs within a phonological unit accented on the next to the
last syllable. The following are a few of the combinations in which it occurs:

1. With a free particle, manaña 'no already'

2. With a nominalized verb, tukuruspanña 'already his finishing'

3. With an adjective-like word, miskiña 'already sweet'

4. With a verb, toqyaroqočkanña 'already it is blown up'

5. With a pronoun, kayña 'already this'

6. With a noun, wataña 'year already'

An investigation of the structures in which this -ña occurs reveals that it is an immediate constituent with entire phrases and not necessarily with the word immediately preceding. The very fact that it is postposed to all types of words leads us to suspect that
it has the same sort of positional freedom as syntactic items have. In the inventory of
morpheme classes we must list these simple types of clitic structures, but their distribution is described in the syntax, since they form immediate constituents with phrases.

Complex morphological structures include the following types:

1. Bound stem plus bound periphery

---

[31]This is the literal meaning of the Greek derivative clitic.

2. Free stem plus bound periphery

3. Bound or free stem plus bound or free stem[32]

The results of these three structural types may be either bound or free.

A bound stem plus a bound periphery[33] may be illustrated by English receive, detain, ability,[34] function, all Ngbaka verbs (see Problem 46), Mongbandi plural verbs (see Problem 47), and Eskimo verbs (see Problem 63). In Barrow Eskimo one may add a causative -pka- to the stem nigi- 'to eat,' but the resultant form is still bound. Even the further addition of the third person subject -ga- results in a bound stem. Only the suffixation of an objective form such as -ŋa 'me' results in a free form. Nigipka- 'to cause to eat' and nigipkaga- 'to cause him to eat' and nigipkagaŋa 'he causes me to eat' are all illustrative of this first type of complex structure. The bound stem in such constructions may consist of more than one root, e.g. Greek /hippopotamo-/ literally 'horse-river' to which is added /-s/ (see section 4.2, D).

Free stems plus bound peripheries may be illustrated by English formal, retake, disgraceful, Kekchi gwočoč 'my house' (< gw- 'my' + očoč 'house') (Problem 37), and Popoluca ʔimo·ya 'his flower' (< ʔi- 'his' + mo·ya 'flower') (Problem 28). The free stems may consist of more than one root, e.g. blackbirds, in which the immediate constituents are the free stem blackbird and the suffix -s.

Constructions consisting of free stems plus bound peripheries may themselves be either free or bound, e.g. formal /fówrməl/ or formal- /fowrméel-/ in formality /fowrmélitiy/. The suffix -al is polyallomorphic /-əl/ and /-æl/. The first allomorph constitutes an immediate constituent of free forms (words) and the second of bound stems.

Morphological structures consisting of bound or free stems plus bound or free stems may be illustrated by blackbird, whatnot, upset, and gocart. Each stem may in turn consist of a root plus a nonroot, e.g. Greek /hippopotamo-/ in which the derivative suffix /-o/ is added to each root /hipp-/ and /potam-/. The resultant combination of free stems may be bound, e.g. first-night- /fórst-nàyt-/, which combines with -er /fórst-nàytər/.

4.6 Primary Structural Layers

Languages with an extensive morphological structure frequently exhibit well-defined structural layers. The principal division is between derivational and inflectional formations. The derivational formations may in turn be divided between formations of the nuclei (these are compounds) and constructions consisting of nuclei and nonnuclei.

Complex structures which belong to the same general external distribution class[35] as the simplest member of the class in question are derivational formations. For example, farmer, refusal, formalizer, instrumentalist are all English nouns consisting of two, three,

---

[32]There may be more than two immediate constituents consisting of such stems (see section 4.2, D), but these are rare.

[33]The particular order is not pertinent.

[34]Bound alternants of free forms are considered bound. Polyallomorphic morphemes having a bound and a free form are common. In some descriptions it is convenient to distinguish between the two types of bound stems: (1) those with free alternants and (2) those without free alternants.

[35]These are the so-called parts of speech, e.g. nouns, verbs, adjectives, adverbs, and particles.

four, and five[36] morphemes, but all belong to the same external distribution class, in that they occur with plural formations: <u>farmers</u>, <u>refusals</u>, <u>formalizers</u>, and <u>instrumental-ists</u>. These plural formations also occur with the simplest members of the class, e.g. <u>boys</u>, <u>girls</u>, <u>houses</u>. A word such as <u>boys</u> does not belong to the same distribution class as the simplest member of the noun class. There is no single morpheme which is structurally a plural noun. Even the plural form of the word <u>sheep</u> occurs with a zero morpheme.

The derivational formations are usually, but not always, "inner-layer" formations, and the inflectional formations are usually "outer-layer" formations. Note the following series in Zoque.

<u>Problem 72</u> (data from Zoque, a language of Mexico)

1. kaʔ-   'to die'

2. kaʔu   'he died'

3. kaʔyahu   'they died'

4. kaʔuwə   'a dead person'

5. kaʔyahuwə   'dead persons'

6. kaʔuwəʔs   'of the dead person'

7. kaʔyahuwəʔs   'of the dead persons'

8. yomo   'woman'

9. yomoʔs   'of the woman'

The inflectional suffixes are -yah- 'pluralizer' and -u 'past tense.' To the inflected forms may be added the nominalizing[37] suffix -wə. The resultant nominalized verb belongs to the same external distribution class as the simple monomorphemic noun <u>yomo</u> 'woman,' and both of these occur with the genitive inflectional suffix -ʔs.

Certain features are characteristic of derivational and inflectional formations.

<u>Derivational Formations</u>:

1. Belong to substantially the same general external distribution classes as the simplest member of the class in question.

2. Tend to be "inner" formations.

3. Tend to be statistically more numerous.[38]

4. Have derivational morphemes with more restricted distribution.[39]

5. May exhibit changes in major distribution class membership.[40]

<u>Inflectional Formations</u>:

1. Do not belong to substantially the same general external distribution classes as the simplest member of the class in question.

2. Tend to be "outer" formations.

3. Tend to be statistically less numerous.

4. Have inflectional morphemes with more extensive distribution.

5. Exhibit no changes in major distribution class membership.

---

[36]There are, of course, many longer words.

[37]"Nominalizing" means "to make a noun of."

[38]That is, statistically more numerous in terms of morphological listing, not necessarily in terms of any particular context.

[39]A derivational morpheme, e.g. -<u>let</u> in <u>eyelet</u>, <u>armlet</u>, <u>eaglet</u>, <u>hamlet</u>, tends to have a more restricted distribution than an inflectional one, e.g. -<u>s</u> plural suffix. Derivational morphemes tend to be more numerous, but to occur in a smaller number of combinations.

[40]For example, derivational morphemes may verbalize adjectives, e.g. <u>enable</u>, <u>endear</u>;

6. "Form" words.   6. May show a grammatical relationship be-
                                        tween words.

Problem 73

Instructions:

a. Determine the primary sets of immediate constituents.

b. Indicate whether the formation is inflectional or derivational.

1. boys	6. sang	11. sees
2. men's	7. walked	12. ran
3. freshman	8. runner	13. smarter
4. first-nighter	9. jigsaw	14. fullest
5. baby	10. manly	15. John's

Problem 74 (data from Tzeltal, a language of Mexico)[41]

Instructions:

a. Indicate whether the formation is derivational or inflectional.[42]

b. List the characteristics which provide the basis for your decision.

1. h-čamel	'sick person'	1a. čamel	'illness'
2. šiwel	'fright'	2a. šiw	'to be afraid'
3. lumal	'land'	3a. lum	'earth'
4. mahk'il	'lid'	4a. mahk'	'to close'
5. awinam	'your (sg.) wife'	5a. ʔinam	'wife'
6. čenk'ultik	'bean patches'	6a. čenk'ul	'bean patch'
7. h-ʔuʔel	'influential person'	7a. ʔuʔel	'power'
8. č'uunel	'offering'	8a. č'uun	'to believe, obey'
9. k'abal	'custody'	9a. k'ab	'hand'

(Continued on next page.)

---

nominalize verbs, e.g. dancer, inheritance; adjectivize nouns, truthful, gracious; nominalize adjectives, e.g. truth, fatalism; and adverbialize adjectives, e.g. truthfully, really.

[41]See Slocum, op. cit., pp. 77-83.

[42]It is obvious that not enough data are given to provide an adequate basis for judgment, but the characteristics listed above furnish practically all that is needed for most
examples. The Tzeltal data are purposely chosen for their simplicity.

22892

10. haʔal	'rain'	10a. haʔ	'water'
11. bihil	'intelligence'	11a. bih	'intelligent'
12. tatab	'fathers'	12a. tat	'father'
13. nič'nab	'sons'	13a. nič'an	'son'
14. miltomba	'war'	14a. -mil	'to kill'
15. pak'hom	'potter'	15a. -pak'	'to mold clay'
16. ti'bal	'meat'	16a. -tiʔ	'to eat meat'
17. milaw	'murder'	17a. -mil	'to kill'
18. nawil	'housebuilder'	18a. na	'house'
19. ʔewil	'carrier'	19a. -ʔe-	'to transport corn'
20. pamleh	'level place'	20a. -pam	'to flatten'
21. kušleh	'life'	21a. kuš	'to live'
22. awil	'you (sg.) see'	22a. ʔil	'to see'
23. awiloh	'you (sg.) have seen'	23a. ʔil	'to see'
24. manohel	'creator'	24a. -man	'to create'
25. k'ešlal	'shame'	25a. k'eš	'to be shy'
26. tontikil	'stony-place'	26a. ton	'stone'

Supplementary information: Nouns in the sets 1-1a, 3-3a, 7-7a, 9-9a, 10-10a, 18-18a, and 26-26a belong to substantially the same external distribution class.

The distinction between primary structural levels is most important in the organization of the grammar, for it makes it possible for one to distinguish the pertinent from the nonpertinent environments of many forms. Any other type of description becomes hopelessly involved and exceedingly long. For example, in a language such as Totonac, spoken in Mexico, there are many complex structures and only a careful division into derivational and inflectional layers will enable one to make a concise and accurate description. In the word kilila·pa·ški·qú·t 'my necessity of loving them reciprocally' there are the following morphemes: ki-, first person possessive prefix added to nouns, li-...-t, a noun formative meaning 'it is necessary,' la·-, reciprocal prefix added to verbs, pa·ški·, the stem 'to love,' -qú·, third person object suffix added to verbs. The sets of immediate constituents are as follows:

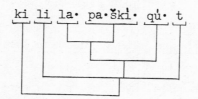

In a descriptive grammar of Totonac the first construction la·pa·ški· would be discussed under the derivation of verbs; the second construction la·pa·ški·qú· would be described under the inflection of verbs; the third construction lila·pa·ški·qú·t belongs under the derivation of nouns, and the last construction <u>kilila·pa·ški·qú·t</u> would be described under the inflection of nouns. Only be describing such complex structures according to their types and according to some systematic arrangement can we possibly reveal the essential structure.

4.7 <u>The</u> <u>Limits</u> <u>of</u> <u>Morphological</u> <u>Structures</u>

There are two limits of morphological structures: lower, which is the level of the morpheme, and upper, the point at which the structure becomes syntactic. The lower limits have been treated in Chapters 2 and 3, and, on the whole, there is not too much difficulty in establishing the morphemes. It is by no means so easy to determine the point at which the morphology of a language divides from the syntax, for there is constant overlapping, especially in such languages as Bantu.

4.71 <u>Structural</u> <u>Contrasts</u>

There are certain important distinctions between the morphological and the syntactic structural levels:

1. Relative order in morphological structures is more rigid.

2. Morphological structures are more fused phonologically.

3. The internal distribution classes in morphological structures are smaller, especially in derivational formations.

4. Morphological distribution classes are less open to new members (i.e. they are less productive of new combinations).

5. Morphological structures are smaller.

6. Morphological structures do not readily admit internal pauses.

7. Morphological structures have a more limited substitutability of expanded expressions.

4.72 <u>Phonological</u> <u>Criteria</u> <u>for</u> <u>Establishing</u> <u>the</u> <u>Limits</u> <u>of</u> <u>Morphological</u> <u>Structures</u>

In the analysis of any language phonological and distributional data are relevant in establishing the limits of morphological units. Phonological data include:

1. Occurrence of <u>open</u> vs. <u>closed</u> <u>junctures</u>. Open junctures mark certain phonologically and morphologically pertinent points.

2. The <u>distribution</u> <u>of</u> <u>phonemes</u> <u>within</u> <u>juncture</u> <u>limits</u>. For example, certain clusters may occur medially between such junctures but may not occur contiguous to such junctures.

3. The <u>distribution</u> <u>of</u> <u>allophones</u> <u>within</u> <u>juncture</u> <u>limits</u>. (See example from Chitimacha in section 4.3.)

4. <u>Stress</u> <u>patterns</u>. Forms bounded by open junctures may exhibit certain stress characteristics. For example, each such unit in English has at least one primary or secondary stress.

5. <u>Potential pause</u> vs. <u>nonpotential pause</u>. An intonational pause may occur at the point of some external junctures and not of others. For example, in English the juncture which we write with a hyphen never coincides with an intonational pause, but the juncture which we may write with a space may coincide with such a pause.

6. <u>Patterns</u> of <u>phonological change</u>. These include loss of vowels, as in Tonkawa (see Problem 25), alternating unvoicing and reduction as in Southern Paiute,[43] vocalic harmony as in Turkish (see Problem 65), and more frequent assimilative changes within external junctures than across such juncture points. All these types of changes may be related to external junctures, though often there is not a complete correlation.

These phonological criteria supplement each other and give us the basis for determining what may be called "the phonological word." In some instances phonological words are equivalent to phrases or entire sentences. For example, the French expression <u>il faut prendre deux cabines</u> 'it is necessary to take two cabins' is written by Hall as /ilfoprədrədøkabin/ [44] In this expression the phonological junctures are not helpful in distinguishing the morphological structure from the syntactic. Furthermore, French has no word stress as English does, but rather a phrase stress. Hence, there are no phonological features (except possibly positions of potential pause) which materially assist us in determining the borders of morphological structures. We are thus dependent entirely upon distributional data.

4.73 <u>Distributional</u> <u>Criteria</u> <u>for</u> <u>Establishing</u> <u>the</u> <u>Limits</u> <u>of</u> <u>Morphological</u> <u>Structures</u>

Distributional data include:

1. <u>Occurrence</u> <u>of</u> <u>bound forms</u>. Such bound forms are either (1) nonclitics--additives, replacives, subtractives--or (2) clitics. Nonclitics have a more restricted distribution and occur (for the most part) as immediate constituents with items with which they are phonologically bound. Clitics have a greater freedom of distribution and only accidentally form immediate constituents with the items with which they are phonologically bound.

2. <u>Occurrence</u> <u>of</u> <u>free forms</u>. All minimal free forms constitute the limits of some <u>morphological</u> <u>structure</u>.

3. <u>Occurrence</u> <u>of</u> <u>nonsyntactic sequence classes</u>.[45] Certain sequence classes consisting of potentially free forms may be abundantly illustrated in phrases. There are other sequence classes of similar types of constituents which show marked contrast in (a) order, (b) juncture, (c) morphemic content, and (d) relative imperviousness to internal expansion.

    a. The constructions <u>outcast</u> and <u>sight-see</u> differ in order from the corresponding syntactic sequence classes <u>cast</u> <u>out</u> and <u>see</u> <u>sight(s)</u>.

---

[43]See Edward Sapir, "The Southern Paiute Language," <u>Proceedings</u> <u>of</u> <u>the</u> <u>American</u> <u>academy</u> <u>of</u> <u>Arts</u> <u>and</u> <u>Sciences</u>, 65 (1930), 1: 27.

[44]Robert A. Hall, Jr., <u>French</u>, Language Monograph No. 24, Structural Sketches 1 (1948), p. 14.

[45]Sequence classes are discussed in Chapter 5. In brief, they are any sequence of forms constituting a construction. For example, the combination <u>good</u> <u>man</u> belongs to an adjective-noun sequence class, to which such phrases as <u>red house</u>, <u>bad chimney</u>, and <u>fishy story</u> also belong. This sequence class differs from such sequence classes as adverb-adjective <u>very</u> <u>good</u>, noun-verb (or subject-predicate) <u>John</u> <u>ran</u>, and preposition-object <u>for</u> <u>me</u>.

   b. The constructions greenhouse /gríyn-hàws/ and blackbird /blǽk-bə̀rd/ have
      the same order as the corresponding syntactic sequence classes green house
      and black bird, but the juncture /-/ never coincides with an intonational
      pause.

   c. The Greek word /nea·póleɔ·s/ 'of Naples (lit. new city)' differs in mor-
      phemic content from the syntactic phrase /néa·s póleɔ·s/ 'of the new city'
      in that the adjectival attributive /nea·/ has no genitive suffix /-s/.[46]
      Similarly, in the English compound thoroughbred there is lacking the mor-
      pheme -ly which occurs in the corresponding syntactic sequence class
      thoroughly bred. The word cutthroat differs in morphemic content from the
      corresponding syntactic sequence class cut the throat.

   d. Morphological structures such as greenhouse and blackbird do not permit
      internal expansion to give such forms as *greenerhouse and *blackestbird.
      However, there are some exceptions, e.g. fathers-in-law.

4. Occurrence of sequence classes with different external distribution class membership from what they have in syntactic constructions. For example, the verbal-
   adverb sequence castaway does not belong to the external distribution class of
   the nuclear verbal, but rather to the noun class. The word sobersides belongs
   to a singular external distribution class, e.g. an old sobersides, whereas the
   syntactic parallel sober sides belongs to the same class as the nuclear sides.

5. Occurrence of unique constituents. Morphemes which occur only in one construction are usually part of a morphological structure, e.g. cran- in cranberry,
   and cray- in crayfish.

4.74 Overlapping between Phonological and Morphological Criteria

   In general, the phonological and morphological data supplement each other in determining divisions between morphological and syntactic structures. In French this is not
true, and in English we have a number of nonconformities. For example, I'll is homophonous with aisle, though there is an important structural break in the first and not in the
second. Similarly, a board is homophonous with aboard, but the first /ə/ is a clitic and
the second a prefix. The occurrence of clitics always involves an overlap between phonological and morphological criteria.

4.75 Overlapping between Morphological and Syntactic Distributional Data

   In English there is one frequent overlap between morphological and syntactic distributional data. The genitive -s may occur with single morphological units, as in John's,
his, and everybody's, or it may occur with phrases, e.g. the old man's (aches and pains)
and the king of England's (hat).[47] This morpheme is considered a suffix rather than a
clitic because its distribution is limited to occurrence with nouns and pronouns[48] and because the resultant construction belongs to one of two external distribution classes: (1)
attributive to nouns, e.g. the king of England's (hat) or (2) a substitute for nouns, e.g.

---

[46]There is also, of course, difference in stress, and undoubtedly one of juncture.

[47]Statistically according to context, the genitive -s occurs more frequently with
phrases.

[48]Certain other combinations are theoretically possible, e.g. the man we saw there's
(hat).

the king of England's was there. The second expression is possible in a context in which the thing possessed by the king of England has already been named. The distributional behavior of the genitive -s is quite different from that of the usual clitic, which may be combined with any number of classes of forms and with numerous resultant external distribution class memberships.

In Bantu languages there is a great deal of overlapping in the concordant system. For example, in the Yipounou phrase dibaandu dibilimba biandi 'beginning of his signs,' dibaandu 'beginning' consists of the concordant prefix di- and the stem -baandu; dibilimba 'signs' consists of a double concordant prefixal set di- which shows agreement with the preceding dibaandu and bi- the basic concord of the noun; and the adjective biandi 'his' shows agreement with bilimba by means of the prefix bi-. The immediate constituents of the series are as follows:

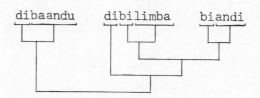

The prefix di- in its second occurrence is an immediate constituent with the entire following phrase. These bound forms which combine with phrases are not, however, clitics, for they are rigidly restricted in positions of occurrence and may occur with single morphemes or words in the same way that all other concordant prefixes occur, e.g. dibaandu diandi 'his beginning.'

The limits of morphological structures may be defined as: All single morphemes, or combinations of morphemes of which at least one immediate constituent is a bound form (including bound alternants of free forms) and of which the peripheral immediate constituent is not a clitic, or combinations of free forms in nonsyntactic arrangements (see section 4.73).[49]
Three features of this definition are important: (1) the distributional contrast between clitics and nonclitics (the nonclitics include additives, replacives, and subtractives), (2) the characteristics of the bound form, including (a) phonemes, segmental and suprasegmental, and (b) junctures, and (3) the form of the immediate constituent which may not be bound. Forms may be bound in the sense that (1) they never occur alone, e.g. the plural suffix in English, (2) they are bound alternants of free forms, e.g. /wayv-/ (cf. wives) in contrast with wife /wayf/, (3) they occur with certain junctures, e.g. fresh- in freshman /fréšmən/, which is bounded by an internal (unmarked) juncture, and (4) they occur with certain suprasegmental features, e.g. -bird in blackbird /blǽk-bə̀rd/, which occurs with a secondary stress. The particular type of external juncture is also pertinent.

The immediate constituents which combine with such bound forms may be wholly bound or include free forms. In the king of England's there is (1) a phonologically free form /ðəkíŋ/, consisting of a clitic plus a potentially free noun, and (2) a potentially free form /əvíŋglənd/.

In the morphological section of the grammar we discuss all the morphological structures, and this includes some phrases as immediate constituents with nonclitic bound forms. There are two other alternatives: (1) setting up a special section of the grammar to deal with all instances of overlap or (2) discussing all constructions which include phrases in

---

[49]The term "word" cannot be conveniently used as an equivalent of "morphological structure," for it has too many other traditional associations. In this text "word" is used to define morphological structures which do not include phrases phonologically identical with parallel syntactic formations, but which may include clitics having no corresponding free forms. Thus, the king of England's would not be considered a "word," but the Quechua expressions in section 4.5 would be words.

the syntax. Either alternative would necessitate describing the same bound morphemes more than once, and this is neither economical nor consistent with the structure.

4.76 The Practical Limits of the Word

Because we discuss all the morphological structures under the morphology or because we write clitics together with the forms with which they are phonologically combined does not mean that in the practical orthography of a language for native speakers we should write all such structures as single undivided elements. It must be remembered that reading is in many respects strikingly different from listening, and the process of isolating and assimilating visual impressions contrasts with auditory recognition. A great deal of essential research is lacking in this field, but those who have dealt with the practical problems of language show a remarkable degree of agreement in their manner of writing words.[50]   In summary, the basic principles may be stated as follows:

1. Clitics which are bound alternants of free forms are written separately. These would include English a, the, of, will, would.[51]

2. Clitics which are not relatable to free alternants are written in combination with other words, e.g. Quechua enclitics.

3. Nonclitics are combined, but any included phrases are left separated, e.g. the king of England's.

4. When there is doubt as to whether or not potential free forms constitute a single morphological structure, the forms are written separately.[52]

---

[50]There are some notable exceptions to this in the arguments for and against conjunctive writing of Bantu.

[51]The apostrophe is a device for indicating a special type of separation in writing, but its use is not recommended.

[52]Theoretically there should be no doubt, but the analyst frequently works for many years in a language before discovering all the pertinent data. This fourth principle is a safeguard against the tendency to unite forms into long words simply because they may translate a single word in English.

C H A P T E R 5

STRUCTURAL CLASSES

5.1 Types of Structural Classes

Structural classes consist of form classes, sequence classes, and distribution classes.[1] Form classes are determined purely by their phonological forms; sequence classes and distributional classes are determined by the identification of morphemes.

5.11 Form Classes

Any set of forms[2] which exhibits some phonological similarity may constitute a form class. Such phonological groupings may be based on:

1. Form and number of syllables. Forms ending in open syllables contrast with those ending in closed syllables, and those consisting of one syllable differ from those having more than one syllable.

2. Sequence of segmental phonemes. Differences of clusters and arrangements of segmental phonemes differentiate forms.

3. Occurrence of specific segmental phonemes. Forms beginning with a consonant such as a glottal stop contrast with those beginning with some other consonant.

4. Occurrence of suprasegmental phonemes. Differences of form may be based upon positions and types of stresses and tones.

5. Junctures. Forms with only internal junctures contrast with those including external junctures.

These five types of phonological features are the principal ones, and in every language they distinguish hundreds of form classes, but only a relatively small number of these classes are morphologically significant. In English, for example, there are monosyllabic and polysyllabic verbs. These constitute two different form classes, but this distinction is not structurally significant, for it is not the basis of any distributional facts. In Kissi, a language of French Guinea, West Africa, the distinction between monosyllabic and polysyllabic verbs is pertinent, since there are parallel differences of tone classes. In Maya there are verbs ending in bilabial, dental, and velar consonants, but no distinction is made, as there is in English, between (1) those which palatalize before a following /y/, e.g. /hičə/ hit yuh, /liyǰə/ lead yuh, /kišə/ kiss yuh, /bežə/ buzz yuh, and (2) those which do not palatalize. In Maya these form classes based upon final

---

[1]This is a departure from the traditional usage, in which "form class" has been employed to include formally and distributionally determined classes. Sequence classes are a special type of distribution class.

[2]It is, of course, possible to have a class with a single member, if there is a contrast with other forms.

consonants are simply not significant. One of the primary tasks of the linguist is to discover which form classes are pertinent to the structure and which are not.

The morphological significance of a form class is frequently manifest by its relevance in the following circumstances:

1. Change of phonemes. Certain form classes may undergo such phonological processes as palatalization, loss of a final vowel, reduction of clusters, or assimilation, whereas others may not.

2. Definition of a sequence class by a form class. If, for example, stems should always consist of CVC patterns and affixes of VC patterns, then formal classes could define sequence classes. A form CVCVC would constitute a stem-suffix sequence class.

3. Definition of a distribution class by a form class. If, as in Ngbaka, verb stems consist of segmental phonemes only and noun stems consist of segmental and suprasegmental phonemes, then formal distinctions define distributional classes. If, as in Kekchi, certain allomorphs of the pronominal affixes occur before consonant-initial stems and others before vowel-initial stems, a form-class distinction determines a distribution class. That is to say, a form-class contrast in the stems determines the distribution of the allomorphs.

4. Junctures. Certain formally distinctive items may always occur with open junctures and others with closed junctures.

5. Order. The order and arrangement of morphemes may be identified by formal distinctions. For example, in Zoque the metathesis of y occurs with certain consonants and not with others.

Problem 75

Instructions:

a. Determine the morphologically pertinent form classes in the following problems: 7, 8, 10, 11, 12, 14, 18, 20, 24, 26, 32, 33, 34, and 37.

b. State the basis of this pertinence in terms of the preceding five types of circumstances.

5.12 Sequence Classes

Sequence classes consist of sequences of morphemes in which the corresponding immediate constituents belong to structurally parallel external distribution classes. Structural parallelism is defined as occurrence with the same class of constituents and in the same order. Morphological sequence classes are of two principal types: (1) those which have at least one nonroot immediate constituent and (2) those which have only root-containing immediate constituents. The second type of sequence class has syntactic parallels.

Morphological sequence classes of the first type may include the following:

1. Stem plus affix; e.g. contain, deceive, and remit belong to the same sequence class, since they consist of the verb derivational prefixes con-, de-, and re- and the bound stems -tain, -ceive, and -mit.

2. Stem plus replacive, e.g. mice, feet, and geese.

3. Stem plus subtractive, e.g. French /movɛ/ mauvais < /movɛz/ mauvaise 'bad' and /šo/ chaud < /šod/ chaude 'hot.'

4. Stem plus reduplicative, e.g. choo-choo and tut-tut.

5. Stem plus derivative formative,[3] e.g. truth and kindness.

6. Stem plus inflectional formative,[3] e.g. boys, oxen, and sheep (pl.).

Sequence classes of the second type are parallel to or contrast with the syntactic structure. In English they may be illustrated by the following:

Syntactic sequence classes in morphological constructions:

1. Adjective plus noun, e.g. blackbird, greenhouse, and Redcoat.

2. Noun plus noun, e.g. goldfish, beefsteak, and seacoast.

3. First (i.e. -ing) verbal plus noun, e.g. drawing-room, walking-stick, spinning-wheel.

4. Verb plus adverb, e.g. go-between, holdup, and setup.

5. Noun plus phrase, e.g. father-in-law and cat-o'-nine-tails.

6. Limiting attributive plus noun, e.g. everybody, nobody, and something.

Nonsyntactic sequence classes in morphological constructions:

1. Adverb plus verb, e.g. backfire, upset, and outcry.

2. Verb plus noun, e.g. playground, gocart, and driveway.

3. Pronoun plus noun, e.g. he-goat, she-goat.

4. Noun plus noun, e.g. God-man, queen-mother.

Problem 76

Instructions: Determine the sequence classes in the following problems: 3, 5, 7, 14, 16, 20, 28, 34, 37, 40, 47, and 55.

Supplementary information:

1. Sequence classes should be determined by sets of immediate constituents, but where it is impossible to decide upon the immediate constituents on the basis of the data given, one may identify each type of morpheme in the sequence.

2. The sequence classes of Problem 3 may be described as follows:

a. Noun plus attributive, e.g. komitwewe 'big cooking-pot' and petatsosol 'old mat.'

b. Noun plus pluralizer, e.g. komitmeh 'cooking-pots' and petatmeh 'mats.'

c. Possessive prefix plus noun, e.g. ikalwewe 'his big house' and ikalsosol 'his old house.'

In terms of immediate constituents there are three sets of sequence classes, but

---

[3]Types 5 and 6 are structural subdivisions of 1-3.

if one were unable to determine the immediate constituents the sequence series[4] would be as follows:

a. Possessive prefix plus noun plus attributive, e.g. ikalwewe 'his big house.'

b. Noun plus attributive, e.g. komitwewe 'big cooking-pot.'

c. Possessive prefix plus noun plus pluralizer, e.g. ikalmeh 'his houses.'

d. Noun plus pluralizer, e.g. petatmeh 'mats.'

5.13 Distribution Classes

5.13.1 Definitions of Significant Features

An internal distribution class consists of a set of forms all of which have the same morpheme for one of the immediate constituents. Members of an internal distribution class must consist of at least two morphemes.

An external distribution class consists of a set of forms which occur in the same environment. Every internal distribution class (except, of course, the discourse) has an external distribution.[5]

Supplementary morphemes have identical meanings and overlap in distribution with the same external distribution class. For example, in the past-tense formation there are the supplementary morphemes /e ← iy/: bled, read, met, and /-d ~ -t/: flowed, walked, with supplementation in /fled/ fled and /kept/ kept. Supplementary morphemes occurring in the same form comprise a single immediate constituent. That is to say, the immediate constituents of kept are the nuclear /k...p/ plus the complex peripheral /e ← iy + -t/.

Complementary morphemes have differences of meaning, but within the same semantic category, and are in complementary occurrence in at least one series. For example, the class suffixes in Futa-Fula (Problem 39) and in Ilamba (Problem 38) are complementary morphemes in that they indicate the noun classes and with nouns (but not with attributives and verbs) are in complementary distribution.

A structural series consists of a single internal distribution class or of multiple distribution classes united by means of supplementary or complementary morphemes. For example, the past-tense and the plural formations in English constitute two structural series, each containing supplementary morphemes. The Futa-Fula and Ilamba nouns are structural series containing complementary morphemes.

Morphemes of the same order occur in the same relative order, counting from the nucleus, and are mutually exclusive. They usually belong to the same category.

Morphemes of the same category are mutually exclusive and of the same general meaning class. In Totonac the subject pronouns, including the first person singular prefixal pronoun ki- and the other, suffixal pronouns, are mutually exclusive and belong to the same general meaning class, i.e. 'subject indicator.'

---

[4] A "sequence series" is not a sequence class, unless it identifies sets of immediate constituents.

[5] Sentences may occur in certain wider distribution classes determined by the context. These may be called "context classes."

A <u>simple paradigm</u> consists of a series of forms which are identical except for one set of morphemes of the same category. For example, forms 1-3 and 6-8 of Problem 5 constitute a simple paradigm.

A <u>complex paradigm</u> consists of multiple simple paradigms (not always complete) with at least one morpheme in common between each set of simple paradigms. Complex paradigms are abundantly illustrated in the data of Chapters 2 and 3.

A <u>determiner</u> consists of a single morpheme, supplementary morphemes, or complementary morphemes, and constitutes the peripheral immediate constituent of a structural series.

<u>Subclasses of</u> determiners include allomorphic determiners, e.g. /-ǝz ∞ -ǝn/ in <u>boxes</u> and <u>oxen</u>, supplementary determiners, e.g. /-ǝd/ and /e ← iy/ in <u>faded</u>, <u>bred</u>, and <u>fled</u>, and complementary determiners.

A set of allomorphic, supplementary, or complementary determiners constitutes a <u>single determiner series</u>.

A <u>determined</u> is an immediate constituent occurring with a particular determiner. A <u>determined series</u> is a set of immediate constituents occurring with a single determiner series. For example, all the English singular nouns occurring with the plural determiner series constitute a determined series.[6]

5.13.2 <u>Types of Distributional Arrangements</u>

The types of distributional arrangements may be described most satisfactorily in terms of occurrence in single sequence classes and in multiple sequence classes.

5.13.21 <u>Distributional Arrangements in Single Sequence Classes</u>

There are two primary types of distribution in single sequence classes: (1) those in which there are determiner and determined immediate constituents and (2) those in which there is no such determiner-determined relationship. The first type includes structural series in which the determiner is a single morpheme or a set of supplementary or complementary morphemes. The members of the determiner immediate constituent are strictly limited in number, and the members of the determined immediate constituent are equal in number to the number of forms in the structural series. The second type of distributional arrangement involves compounds, in which there are approximately the same number of different members in each immediate-constituent series.

----

[6]It is possible to employ "determiner" and "determined" in another sense. For example, the forms of the stems may be considered determiners of the distribution of the alternants /-ǝz ~ -z ~ -s/ of the English plural morpheme. Here the stems may be said to be the determiner constituents and the particular form of the suffix is determined. In the series of allomorphs /wayf ∞ wayv-, θiyf ∞ θiyv-, layf ∞ layv-, riyθ ∞ riyd-, yuwθ ∞ yuwd-, haws ∞ hawz-/ <u>wife</u> ∞ <u>wiv(es)</u>, <u>thief</u> ∞ <u>thiev(es)</u>, <u>life</u> ∞ <u>liv(es)</u>, <u>wreath</u> ∞ <u>wreath(s)</u>, <u>youth</u> ∞ <u>youth(s)</u>, <u>house</u> ∞ <u>hous(es)</u>, there is a phonological similarity in the type of allomorphic development. The particular form of this change from voiceless to corresponding voiced continuants, i.e. /f/ to /v/, /θ/ to /d/, or /s/ to /z/, may be described as determined by the forms of the stems. Similarly, it may be said that the stems are the determiners of the distribution of the plural suffix allomorphs: /(-ǝz ~ -z ~ -s) ∞ -ǝn ∞ -0/. However, in the system employed in this text the peripheral elements are always treated as the determiners and the nuclear ones as the determined, since it is the peripheral constituent which determines the membership of any structural series. The limitations of distribution within any structural series are treated in terms of subclasses of determiner or determined constituents.

5.13.21.1 Forms Occurring in Determiner-Determined Series

There are four primary arrangements of determiner and determined constituents in single sequence classes:

1. With no subclasses of determiner and no subclasses of determined.

2. With subclasses of determiner and no subclasses of determined.

3. With no subclasses of determiner but subclasses of determined.

4. With subclasses of determiner and subclasses of determined.

All the following problems consist of single structural series, and some are simple internal distribution classes. The subclasses of determiner or determined constituents are based upon allomorphic contrasts, supplementary morphemes, or complementary morphemes.

5.13.21.11 Structural Series with No Subclasses of Determiner and No Subclasses of Determined

Structural series in which there are no subclasses of determiner or determined immediate constituents are very simple. In English there are two such formations: (1) the noun formation with agentive -er, e.g. dancer, player, walker, worker, flier, beginner, and (2) the verbal formation with -ing, e.g. dancing, playing, walking, working, flying, beginning. There are, of course, some verbs which do not occur with -er, e.g. seem, be, mean, and the so-called auxiliary verbs may, can, shall, will, must, and ought. Likewise, there are certain verbs which do not occur with -ing, namely, these same auxiliaries, may, can, shall, will, must, and ought.

These structural series may be described in terms of the distribution of the determiners. For example, in describing the noun derivatives of English we would list -er as one of the noun-forming suffixes, and under -er we would list all the forms which occur with -er. Since in this instance, however, almost all verbs are included, it is simpler to list the exceptions. Similarly, in discussing the inflection of verbs, we would list the suffix -ing and then note all the verbs with which this suffix occurs. But here, too, it is easier to list the exceptions.

Several fundamental principles of description should be noted:

1. A structural series is described on the basis of immediate constituents.

2. The determiner immediate constituent is noted first.

3. The distribution of the determiner immediate constituent is described in terms of the determined immediate constituent.

4. The determined immediate constituents may be identified as follows:

   a. By listing.

   b. By reference to a previously listed class, with or without exception.

5.13.21.12 Structural Series with Subclasses of Determiner and No Subclasses of Determined

Problem 77 (data from Huave, a language of Mexico)

Instructions: Describe the structural series in terms of the determiner constituents and their distribution.

1. andiomáac   'we (incl.) wish'

2. ačiatíac   'we (incl.) tear'

3. imboláac   'we (incl.) fear'

4. ahiráac   'we (incl.) have'

5. ačičíac   'we (incl.) suck'

6. əhəčíac   'we (incl.) give'

7. andokóoc   'we (incl.) fish'

8. iənáac   'we (incl.) come from'

9. acohóoc   'we (incl.) play a game'

10. uwíac   'we (incl.) borrow'

11. akoočíac   'we (incl.) cut'

12. auwáac   'we (incl.) go out'

13. anjialáac   'we (incl.) grind'

14. ašomáac   'we (incl.) find'

Supplementary information:

1. The determiner morpheme consists of the last three phonemes of each form.

2. The variant forms constitute allomorphs of this morpheme.

Discussion of Problem 77:

There are three allomorphs of the first person plural inclusive subject pronoun: -áac, -íac, and -óoc. There are no observable phonologically definable environments which could determine the distribution of these allomorphs. Accordingly, their distribution can only be described by listing the forms with which they occur. This structural series may be described as follows:

-áac ∞ -íac ∞ -óoc, first person plural inclusive subject pronoun, occurs with the following distribution:

-áac:

    andiom-   'to wish'

    imbol-   'to fear'

    ahir-   'to have'

    iən-   'to come from'

    auw-   'to go out'

    anjial-   'to grind'

    ašom-   'to find'

-íac:

    ačiat-   'to tear'

    ačič-   'to suck'

    əhəč-   'to give'

    uw-   'to borrow'

    akooč-   'to cut'

$-\acute{o}oc$:

andok-   'to fish'

acoh-   'to play a game'

The discussion of Problem 77 introduces two practical problems: (1) the form of the descriptive statement and (2) the amount of data which must be included. There are three essentials to the form: (1) that the structural series be introduced by identifying the determiner, (2) that the meaning or some identifier of the determiner be given, and (3) that the distribution of the subclasses of the determiner be indicated. Of course, it is not necessary to list forms in a column. This is simply easier in introductory analyses. It is also possible to give the full forms with the suffixes, but where there are no phonological changes involved, it is an economy to list only the stems.

It is possible to reduce the amount of data given in the solution of this problem by listing the two classes with $-\acute{i}ac$ and $-\acute{o}oc$, and then stating that all other stems occur with $-\acute{a}ac$. This is quite an acceptable procedure. For example, in describing the plural formations in English, we would list the exceptions in full under -en, -zero, -ren, -i (alumni), -a (criteria), and so on, and state that all other plurals occur with the productive formation /-əz ~ -z ~ -s/. For the limited problems which occur in this chapter, all the members of each distributional subdivision should be listed unless it is otherwise indicated in the instructions.

Problem 78 (data from Futa-Fula, a language of French Guinea)

Instructions:

   a. Isolate the suffixal morphemes by comparing the data given in Problem 39 with those below.

   b. Describe the structural series of noun formations.

1. a·deŋ   'person'

2. paikuŋ   'child'

3. gertogal   'chicken'

4. puttyu   'horse'

5. ŋgurndaŋ   'life'

6. fena·ndɛʔ   'lie'

7. d'yi·d'yaŋ   'food'

8. gomd'iŋd'oʔ   'believing'

9. nyala·ndɛʔ   'day'

10. d'oudi   'shadow'

11. di·niri   'bottle'

12. nya·wo·rɛʔ   'judgment'

13. yurmɛ·ndɛʔ   'mercy'

Supplementary information:

   1. Regard a·deŋ 'person' as having a zero noun-class suffix.

   2. Regard gomd'iŋd'oʔ 'believing' as occurring with the noun-class suffix -oʔ.

   3. In Futa-Fula there are many structural subclasses of determined immediate constituents, so that this problem is not typical.

Discussion of Problem 78:

   This structural series consists of complementary morphemes. The morphemic status of the morphemes is determined by their occurrence with the same attributives. Their meaning consists in their identification of grammatically significant classes. The structural series may be described as follows:

-uŋ, -al, -u, -aŋ, -ɛˀ, -oˀ, -i, and zero, complementary noun-class morphemes, occur in the following distribution:

   -uŋ: paik-   'child'

   -al: gertog-   'chicken'

    -u: putty-   'horse'

  -aŋ: ŋgurnd-   'life'

        d'yi·d'y-   'food'

  -ɛˀ: fena·nd-   'lie,'

        nyala·nd-   'day,'

        nya·wo·r-   'judgment,'

        yurmɛ·nd-   'mercy'

  -oˀ: gomd'iŋd'-   'believing'

   -i: d'oud-   'shadow'

       di·nir-   'bottle'

 zero: a·deŋ   'person'[7]

Problem 79

Instructions:

  a. Rewrite the forms phonemically.

  b. Describe the structural series, using only the forms listed here.

1. bridges	5. pits	9. sheep
2. roses	6. lips	10. grouse
3. bills	7. tricks	11. salmon
4. cows	8. oxen	12. deer

Supplementary information: All the allomorphs in this problem belong to a single morpheme.

Problem 80

Instructions:

  a. Rewrite the forms phonemically.

---

[7]It is customary to list a zero morpheme last. Overt forms have precedence over covert ones.

b. Describe the structural series, using <u>only</u> the forms listed here.

1. filled	5. pulled	9. cut	13. hurt
2. braided	6. slipped	10. hit	14. fled
3. towed	7. kicked	11. pled	15. felt
4. rented	8. beat	12. bled	16. meant

Supplementary information: All forms are past-tense forms.

Discussion of Problem 80:

The suffixal morpheme consists of /(-əd ~ -d ~ -t) ∞ -t ∞ -0/. The supplementary replacive morpheme consists of /e ← iy/. This structural series may be described as follows:

1. Past-tense forms with simple periphery:

a. /-əd/ (after dental-stop stems) ~ /-d/ (after non-dental-stop voiced stems) ~ /-t/ (after non-dental-stop voiceless stems): <u>braid</u>, <u>rent</u>, <u>fill</u>, <u>tow</u>, <u>pull</u>, <u>slip</u>, <u>kick</u>.

b. -0: <u>beat</u>, <u>cut</u>, <u>hit</u>, <u>hurt</u>

2. Past-tense forms with complex periphery:

a. /e ← iy/ + -0: <u>plead</u>, <u>bleed</u>[8]

b. /e ← iy/ + /-əd ~ -d ~ -t/: <u>flee</u>

c. /e ← iy/ + /-t/: <u>feel</u>, <u>mean</u>

Problem <u>81</u> (data from Tzeltal [cf. Problem 35])

Instructions: Describe this verb structural series in terms of allomorphic distribution.

1. -betan 'to loan'		1a. bet 'loan'	
2. -ʔipan 'to nourish'		2a. ʔip 'strength'	
3. -k'opan 'to speak with'		3a. k'op 'speech'	
4. -ʔabatin 'to serve'		4a. ʔabat 'servant'	
5. -mulin 'to commit sin'		5a. mul 'sin'	
6. -hawc'un 'to fall backwards'		6a. -hawc'- 'fall backwards'	

---

[8]The replacive attains morphemic status by the very fact that it occurs with zero. See Chapter 2, Principle 4.

Problem 82 (data from a Guerrero dialect of Aztec, a language of Mexico)

Instructions: Describe the plural structural series.

1. picomeh	'pigs'		1a. pico	'pig'
2. čičimeh	'dogs'		2a. čiči	'dog'
3. wakašti	'cows'		3a. wakaš	'cow'
4. nočimeh	'all'		4a. noči	'all'
5. kwečwahkeh	'rattlesnakes'		5a. kwečwa	'rattlesnake'

Supplementary information: Regard -meh and -hkeh as allomorphs.

Problem 83 (data from Spanish)[9]

Instructions: Describe the structural series consisting of the root and the stem formative which precedes the first person plural ending -mos.

1. sentímos	'we feel'		1a. sent-	'feel'
2. ablámos	'we speak'		2a. abl-	'speak'
3. kontámos	'we count'		3a. kont-	'count'
4. desímos	'we say'		4a. des-	'say'
5. kaémos	'we fall'		5a. ka-	'fall'
6. dolémos	'we grieve'		6a. dol-	'grieve'
7. mobémos	'we move'		7a. mob-	'move'
8. kebrámos	'we break'		8a. kebr-	'break'
9. andámos	'we walk'		9a. and-	'walk'
10. dámos	'we give'		10a. d-	'give'
11. tenémos	'we have'		11a. ten-	'have'
12. dormímos	'we sleep'		12a. dorm-	'sleep'
13. pedímos	'we ask for'		13a. ped-	'ask for'

Supplementary information: These should be construed as present-tense forms. The preterite is, of course, homophonous in most instances.

5.13.21.13 Structural Series with No Subclasses of Determiner but Subclasses of Determined

Problem 84

Instructions:

   a. Rewrite the forms phonemically.

---

[9]The phonemic notation follows usage in Mexico.

b. Determine the morphological classes of the nuclear immediate constituents.

c. Classify the phonological changes which have taken place in the determined immediate constituents by comparing them with corresponding free forms.

d. Describe the structural series on the basis of allomorphic contrasts in nuclears.

1. countess	6. governess	11. empress	16. negress
2. duchess	7. waitress	12. poetess	17. sorceress
3. princess	8. tigress	13. huntress	
4. goddess	9. lioness	14. hostess	
5. heiress	10. mistress	15. murderess	

Discussion of Problem 84:

There are a number of morphological classes represented by the nuclear immediate constituent. For example, there are single-morpheme nuclears, e.g. count, poet, god, heir, and multiple-morpheme nuclears, e.g. waiter, hunter. Also, there are noun nuclears, e.g. count, prince, god, and verb nuclears, e.g. govern, murder. Some nuclears are free forms, e.g. count, god, heir; others are bound alternants of free forms, e.g. duch-, tigr-, mistr-; and still others are always bound, e.g. sorcer- and negr-. Omitting, however, these problems of class, we may, in accordance with the instructions, describe this structural series as follows:

/-es/, formative of feminine nouns, occurring

       1. With free stems:

/káwnt/	/láyən/	/gə́vərn/
/príns/	/pówet/	/mə́rdər/
/gád/	/hówst/	/ér/

       2. With bound stems

          a. Exhibiting allomorphic alternation

             1'. In the root:

                 /də́č- (< dúwk)/

                 /émpr- (< émpayr)/

                 /táygr- (< táygər)/

                 /místr- (< místər)/

                 /níygr- (< nígər)/

             2'. In a nonroot morpheme:

                 /wéytr- (< wéytər)/

                 /hə́ntr- (< hə́ntər)/

b. Exhibiting no allomorphic alternation:

/sówrsər-/

This description of the distribution of -ess is in an outline form showing sub-classes. It would also be possible to list the four resultant classes as coördinate:

1. Free stems: /káwnt, príns, gád/, etc.

2. Bound stems exhibiting allomorphic alternation in the root: /dóč- (< dúwk), émpr- (< émpayr)/, etc.

3. Bound stems exhibiting allomorphic alternation in a nonroot morpheme: /wéytr- (< wéytər), héntr- (< hóntər)/.

4. Bound stems exhibiting no allomorphic alternation: /sówrsər-/.

The coördinate listing of classes has many advantages, and is frequently used, but for the sake of our analyses in this text, it is preferable to employ an outline form, unless otherwise directed. An outline form helps to emphasize the parallelisms and the contrasts.

Problem 85

Instructions:

a. Rewrite the forms phonemically.

b. Compare the related free forms of the nuclears.

c. Determine the number and relative size of the morphological classes of the nuclears.

d. Classify the nuclears in terms of allomorphic alternation.

e. Describe the structural series on the basis of allomorphic contrasts in the nuclears.

1. width	6. strength	11. depth
2. breadth	7. health	12. dearth
3. length	8. warmth	13. birth
4. death	9. stealth	14. truth
5. growth	10. filth	15. wealth

Supplementary information:

1. Regard die, foul, bear, and weal (cf. the public weal) as the related free forms of death, filth, birth, and wealth.

2. The basic forms of long and strong occur with final /g/; cf. longer /lóŋgər/ and stronger /stroŋgər/. The forms /lóŋ/ and /stróŋ/ are allomorphs occurring as morphologically free forms. The allomorphs /léŋk-/ and /stréŋk-/ involve assimilation, but this phonological process need not be considered when we treat the distribution in terms of allomorphs and when the pattern is as limited as in this instance.

Problem 86

Instructions:

a. Rewrite the forms phonemically.

b. Determine the subclasses of nuclears.

c. Describe the structural series.

1. reddish	6. old-maidish	11. Turkish	16. Irish
2. oldish	7. prudish	12. English	17. British
3. childish	8. selfish	13. foolish	18. thievish
4. boyish	9. doggish	14. purplish	19. flattish
5. Spanish	10. bookish	15. uppish	20. ticklish

Discussion of Problem 86:

There are four types of facts observable in this series: (1) some nuclears are bound and others free, (2) free nuclears are adjectives, nouns, or verbs, (3) some nuclears are bound allomorphs of free forms and others are not, (4) the resultant forms may be adjectives or (in some cases) nouns, but this last class is limited, since none of the nouns occur with plural formations.

As has been suggested in Problems 84, 85, and 86 there are a number of facts to be observed about any set of nuclears. The descriptive linguist must make two decisions about such facts: (1) what the relative importance of the various types of data is and (2) which facts are relevant to a particular description. Having made a decision, he must preserve the same perspective throughout the section of the grammar which treats similar structures.

There are five primary facts about any set of nuclear data, and they have the following priority of relevance: (1) the determiner (including its subclasses), which makes a set of forms a structural series, (2) the major[10] external distribution class or classes of the structural series, (3) the major external distribution class or classes of the nuclear constituents, (4) the morphologically defined allomorphs of the nuclear constituents, and (5) the phonologically defined allomorphs of the nuclear constituents. Every description must indicate the first and second types of data; the third and fourth are optional; and the fifth should be indicated in the listing of the morpheme. Priority is given to the determiner by making it the heading for the description of the structural series. The external distribution class of the structural series is indicated by (1) the placement of the description in the grammar (for example, such classes as derived nouns, inflected nouns, derived verbs, and inflected verbs are discussed in separate, labeled sections), and (2) by the identifying name given to the determiner, e.g. "noun-forming suffix," "noun-class suffix," "third person singular verb suffix."

When the nuclear constituents all belong to the same major external distribution class, this fact can be easily noted. For example, the agentive noun-forming suffix

---

[10]The major external distribution class membership, e.g. noun, adjective, verb, adverb, pronoun, must be distinguished from the limited external distribution class membership, since by occurrence with the same determiner any determined series constitutes a limited external distribution class.

-er occurs only with verb stems, e.g. <u>dancer</u>, <u>player</u>, <u>worker</u>, <u>contriver</u>, <u>formalizer</u>. This fact may be indicated when the determiner is listed, e.g. "-er, agentive noun-forming suffix occurring with verbs." However, the situation is not usually so simple, for there may be several different classes, including some bound stems (which may not be identifiable as belonging to a particular word class), and there is sometimes little or no correlation between the subdivisions of external distribution classes and differences of allomorphic alternation. If the facts of types 3 and 4 are to be indicated by some outline form, then separate outlines are usually needed, but this involves repetition. Accordingly, one is left with the alternative of systematic notation in a list. A partial statement of the structural series of Problem 86 will illustrate the procedure:

/-iš/, derivational formative of adjectives and of a few words belonging to adjective and noun classes, occurs with noun, adjective, adverb, and verb nuclears.

    1. Adjective resultants:

        /ówld/ adj.

        /čáyld/ n.

        /óp/ adv.

        /tíkl- (< tíkəl)/ v.

        /brít-/

    2. Adjective and noun (limited) resultants:

        /tórk/ n.

        /íŋgl-/

        /áyr-/

There are several significant features about this type of description:

1. The structural series is identified and described "under" the determiner.

2. The class of the determiner and the class of the resultant structural series are stated next.[11]

3. The classes of the resultant forms are specifically indicated by the subdivision in the listing.

4. The classes of the free nuclears are listed in the heading and noted by abbreviations postposed to each form.

5. The external distribution classes of nuclears are marked only in dealing with free forms or bound alternants of free forms. In some languages bound stems are class distinctive, but in others there is relatively little significance in listing their class memberships.

---

[11]In this series there is a special difficulty with the nouns having restricted distribution. A form such as British is not considered a noun, even though one may use it in such a construction as The <u>British</u> are ..., for almost all adjectives may occur in a similar environment, e.g. The <u>poor</u> are ..., The <u>intelligent</u> are .... Adjectives do not, however, occur as the final words in such expressions as <u>very poor</u> English and <u>rather good</u> Spanish.

6. It is possible, but cumbersome, to avoid the subdivision of data by a fuller notation of each form, e.g.

/ówldiš/ adj. (/ówld/ adj.)

/čáyldiš/ adj. (/čáyld/ n.)

/tíkliš/ adj. (/tíkl- < tíkəl/ v.)

/íŋgliš/ adj., n. (/íŋgl-/)

Problem 87

Instructions:

a. Rewrite the data phonemically.

b. Compare the forms with the corresponding free or bound nuclears.

c. Describe the structural series, following the form suggested for Problem 86.

1. cubic	7. demonic	13. atomic
2. nomadic	8. melodic	14. heroic
3. climatic	9. magic	15. oceanic
4. catholic	10. idiotic	16. lunatic
5. music	11. egoistic	17. catastrophic
6. angelic	12. metric	18. philanthropic

Supplementary information:

1. The differences in stress must be treated as characteristics of the allomorphs. Note that not all forms have presuffixal stress.

2. Certain nuclears consist of two morphemes, but the alternation is more conveniently described as belonging to a single unit rather than as consisting of separate changes occurring in each morpheme. For example, catastroph- (cf. catalogue, catabolic, strophe) consists of the two morphemes having the forms /kətǽ-/ and /strowf-/ in /kətǽstrowfiy/ catastrophy, but the forms /kæ̀tə-/ and /stróf-/ in /kæ̀təstrófik/ catastrophic. In recording these allomorphic contrasts it is not necessary to list each separately, for the combination may be treated as a whole. It then constitutes a complex allomorphic unit. In a series these forms would be listed as follows:

/kæ̀təstróf- (∞ kətǽstrowf-)/

This listing of entire allomorphic units is in keeping with the principle of treating immediate constituents as the significant combining units.[12]

---

[12]In describing the construction catastroph- (in another place in the grammar) it would be necessary to note that each morpheme has two allomorphs and that they occur in particular combinations. That is to say, /kətǽ-/ occurs only with /strowf-/ and /kæ̀tə-/ only with /stróf-/.

Problem 88

Instructions:

a. Rewrite the forms phonemically.

b. Describe the structural series, following the procedure suggested for Problem 86.

1. deaden	5. lengthen	9. threaten
2. gladden	6. strengthen	10. frighten
3. widen	7. sicken	11. open
4. harden	8. lessen	12. happen

Problem 89 (data from the Sierra dialect of Zapotec, a language of Mexico)

Instructions: Describe the structural series of the present progressive stem. This does not include the subject suffix.

1st Person Sg. Progressive Present		Basic Stems
1. rudibiciza$^{\text{?}}$ 'I am drying'		1a. udibici-
2. rekabiza$^{\text{?}}$ 'I am answering'		2a. ekabi-
3. riθellaza$^{\text{?}}$ 'I am sending'		3a. iθella-
4. rugalaza$^{\text{?}}$ 'I am setting fire'		4a. ugala-
5. rik^{w}anaza$^{\text{?}}$ 'I am robbing'		5a. ikwana-
6. rikiza$^{\text{?}}$ 'I am washing'		6a. ki-
7. rikiaza$^{\text{?}}$ 'I am sewing'		7a. kia-
8. rikuwaza$^{\text{?}}$ 'I am keeping'		8a. kuwa-
9. riduwaza$^{\text{?}}$ 'I am living'		9a. duwa-
10. riga$^{\text{?}}$aza$^{\text{?}}$ 'I am serving'		10a. ka$^{\text{?}}$a-
11. rigu$^{\text{?}}$uza$^{\text{?}}$ 'I am putting'		11a. ku$^{\text{?}}$u-
12. rigisieza$^{\text{?}}$ 'I am putting down'		12a. kisie-
13. rigilaza$^{\text{?}}$ 'I am watering'		13a. kila-
14. ribeciza$^{\text{?}}$ 'I am crying'		14a. k^{w}eci-
15. ribedaza$^{\text{?}}$ 'I am hoping'		15a. k^{w}eda-
16. ribieza$^{\text{?}}$ 'I am drying'		16a. k^{w}ie-
17. ribiazeciza$^{\text{?}}$ 'I am dividing'		17a. k^{w}iazeci-
18. runaza$^{\text{?}}$ 'I am knowing'		18a. guna-

(Continued on next page.)

19. ruʔnazaʔ	'I am throwing'	19a. čuʔna-
20. raʔazaʔ	'I am going'	20a. caʔa-
21. ritazaʔ	'I am coming'	21a. zita-
22. riʔazaʔ	'I am taking'	22a. siʔa-

Supplementary information:

1. The tones are not indicated.

2. The first person subject affix is -zaʔ.

3. The present progressive stems consist of the determiner ri- ~ r- plus the basic stem.

4. The basic stems may consist of one morpheme or more than one morpheme, but any internal construction is derivational.

5. The distribution of the allomorphs ri- ~ r- is determined by (1) whether or not the stem begins with a vowel or a consonant and (2) the particular consonant in question. Before certain consonants the form ri- occurs and before others r- occurs with the loss of the first consonant of the stem.

6. The allomorphs of stems undergoing loss may be listed as guna- ∞ -una-. This loss occurs only in certain combinations.

7. In describing this structural series, treat the distribution of ri- ~ r- in the heading to the section and the differences in nuclear allomorphic alternation under the following subdivisions: (1) stems exhibiting no allomorphic alternation, (2) stems exhibiting allomorphic alternation: (a) voiceless to voiced consonant and (b) loss of initial consonant of the stem.

Problem 90 (data from Spanish)

Instructions: Describe the structural series of the third person singular present indicative.

3d Person Sg. Present Ind.		Basic Stems
1. píde	'he asks for'	1a. ped-
2. síge	'he follows'	2a. seg-
3. sírbe	'he serves'	3a. serb-
4. bénde	'he sells'	4a. bend-
5. báře	'he sweeps'	5a. bař-
6. kóme	'he eats'	6a. kom-
7. krée	'he believes'	7a. kre-
8. aprénde	'he learns'	8a. aprend-
9. desíde	'he decides'	9a. desid-

(Continued on next page.)

10. lúse   'he (it) shines'   10a. lus-

11. siénte 'he feels'   11a. sent-

12. miénte 'he lies'   12a. ment-

13. duérme 'he sleeps'   13a. dorm-

14. piérde 'he loses'   14a. perd-

15. buélbe 'he returns'   15a. bolb-

16. múebe   'he moves'   16a. mob-

Supplementary information:

1. The placement of the accent need not be considered in this particular description.

2. Classify the nuclears on the basis of occurrence or nonoccurrence of allomorphic alternation.

3. The suffix -e is actually a stem formative, with the third person being indicated by zero, but for the sake of our analyses here it is more convenient to treat this morpheme as including the third person subject indicator.

5.13.21.14 Structural Series with Subclasses of Determiner and Subclasses of Determined

Problem 91 (data from Spanish)

Instructions:

a. Add the following forms to those of Problem 90.

b. Describe the total structural series.

17. ábla   'he speaks'   17a. abl-

18. kéma   'he (it) burns'   18a. kem-

19. síta   'he cites'   19a. sit-

20. gósa   'he enjoys'   20a. gos-

21. r̃óba   'he steals'   21a. rob-

22. piénsa 'he thinks'   22a. pens-

23. siér̃a 'he closes'   23a. ser̃-

24. kuésta 'he (it) costs'   24a. kost-

25. suéña 'he dreams'   25a. soñ-

26. dúda   'he doubts'   26a. dud-

Supplementary information:

1. The third person singular suffix may be construed as -a ∞ -e, but see supplementary information 3 under Problem 90.

2. The subclasses of the determiner constitute the primary division in the structural series. The allomorphic alternations are secondary.[13]

Problem 92 (data from Chichewa, a language of Nyasaland)[14]

Instructions: Describe the causative stem.

Causative Infinitive

1. kubúnt^hica   'to cause to become blunt'
2. kupézɛca   'to cause to find'
3. kugwádica   'to cause to kneel'
4. kukúmbica   'to cause to dig'
5. kufuɓírica   'to cause to become red'
6. kuzúzica   'to cause to make miserable'
7. kugúlica   'to sell'
8. kulavúlica   'to cause to spit'
9. kucɔkɔ́mɔlɛca   'to cause to cough'
10. kuwɔ́lɔvya   'to cause to become wet'
11. kuwɔ́fya   'to cause to fear'
12. kusɔ́ŋk^hɛca   'to cause to gather taxes'
13. kubwérɛza   'to repeat'
14. kukániza   'to cause to refuse'
15. kusúŋgiza   'to cause to protect'
16. kut^hávya   'to cause to run away'

Active Infinitive

1a. kubúnt^ha   'to become blunt'
2a. kupéza   'to find'
3a. kugwáda   'to kneel'
4a. kukúmba   'to dig'
5a. kufúɓira   'to become red'
6a. kuzúza   'to make miserable'
7a. kugúra   'to buy'
8a. kulávura   'to spit'
9a. kucɔkɔ́mɔra   'to cough'
10a. kuwɔ́lɔɓa   'to become wet'
11a. kuwɔ́pa   'to fear'
12a. kusɔ́ŋk^ha   'to gather taxes'
13a. kubwéra   'to return'
14a. kukána   'to refuse'
15a. kusúŋga   'to protect'
16a. kut^háɓa   'to run away'

Supplementary information:

1. The final -a in both series of forms is an indicative-mode morpheme.

2. The initial ku- is the infinitive-forming morpheme.

3. In phrase-final position all these forms occur with long vowels in the penultimate syllable. These long vowels have not been written, since they are not pertinent to this problem. The long vowels are essentially an intonational feature.

4. The changes in placement of the high tones should be included in the listing of nuclear allomorphs.

---

[13]This is in accordance with the discussion under Problem 86.

[14]Mark Hanna Watkins, A Grammar of Chichewa, Language Dissertation No. 24 (Baltimore: Linguistic Society of America, 1937), pp. 72-76.

5. Treat the causative stem as consisting of (1) basic stems, as they occur in the active infinitives (i.e. the forms of the second column minus ku- and -a) plus (2) the causative suffixal morpheme.

6. The distribution of the vocalic differences in the suffixal forms -ic, -ɛc, -iz, and -ɛz may be phonologically defined.

7. The allomorph -y occurs in a phonologically definable environment.

Problem 93 (data consist of the Tzeltal forms listed in Problem 35)

Instructions: Describe the verb structural series.

Problem 94 (data consist of the Shilluk forms listed in Problem 58)

Instructions:

a. Describe the plural forms as a structural series.

b. Describe the singular combinative forms as a structural series.

5.13.21.2 Forms Not Occurring in Determiner-Determined Series

Certain sequence classes do not exhibit determiner or determined constituents. These are compounds, i.e. combinations of nuclei. According to the terminology we are employing, such sequence classes do not constitute structural series, but they have structural similarities which make it possible and necessary to describe them by classes.

Constructions consisting of nuclei as immediate constituents may be classified on the basis of (1) the general external distribution class or classes of the resultant constructions and (2) the general external distribution class or classes of the immediate constituents. For example, millstone and catbird are considered to belong to the same class because they are both nouns and because the corresponding nuclei in each construction belong to the same classes. Similarly, greenhouse and redbird belong to the same class, since they are members of the same external distribution class and the corresponding nuclei in each are adjectives and nouns. On the other hand, pickpocket, which is also a noun and hence belongs to the same external distribution class as millstone, catbird, greenhouse, and redbird, differs in internal structure from all four, just as greenhouse and redbird differ in internal structure from millstone and catbird. The first task in a descriptive analysis of compounds is to determine the external distribution classes. Then the compounds are classified according to internal structure. The internal structure is analyzed first in terms of distribution classes and secondly in terms of allomorphic alternation.

Problem 95

Instructions:

a. Rewrite the following compounds phonemically.

b. Classify the forms according to external distribution classes.

c. Subdivide the classification according to sequence classes.

1. skinflint
2. figurehead
3. make-believe (n.)
4. wind-up
5. upset (v.)
6. know-it-all

(Continued on next page.)

7. state-wide

8. blue-pencil (v.)

9. hand-pick

10. bull's-eye

11. jew's-harp

12. jack-in-the-box

13. jack-o'-lantern

14. sea-adder

15. knife-edge

16. pickpocket

17. himself

18. herself

19. he-goat

20. she-goat

21. go-between

22. holdup

23. driveway

24. playground

25. mother-in-law

26. foot-pound-second

27. ton-mile-day

28. redbird

29. tut-tut (v.)

30. choo-choo (n.)

31. flip-flop (n.)

32. tiptop (adj.)

33. bittersweet (adj.)

34. queen-mother

35. overhead

36. carefree

37. purse-proud

38. greenhouse

39. everybody

40. nobody

41. breakwater

42. anyone

Problem 96

Instructions:

a. Rewrite the following noun compounds phonemically.

b. Classify the forms according to sequence classes.

1. cutthroat

2. kill-joy

3. spendthrift

4. turnkey

5. outcast

6. thoroughbred

7. hearsay

8. whatnot

9. overhead

10. afternoon

11. cure-all

12. dreadnought

13. giveaway

14. kickback

15. stopover

16. castaway

17. setback

18. grownup

19. once-over

20. crow's-foot

21. helmsman

22. blueblood

23. dry-bones

24. acre-foot

25. watt-hour

26. secretary-treasurer

27. bonbon

28. tom-tom

29. hodgepodge

30. riffraff

31. downpour

32. zigzag

33. backdrop

34. onrush

35. upstart

36. inlay

37. blowpipe

38. gocart

39. drawbar

(Continued on next page.)

40. chimney-sweep

41. sunup

42. sundown

43. cranberry

44. crayfish

45. aircraft

46. anthill

47. beeswax

48. bluebell

49. greyhound

50. bloodshed

51. hide-and-seek

52. thick-and-thin

53. hand-me-down

54. forget-me-not

55. stay-at-home

56. fly-by-night

57. free-for-all

58. son-in-law

59. man-of-war

60. cowboy

Problem 97 (data consist of the Tzeltal forms listed in Problem 70)

Instructions: Describe the noun compounds.

Discussion of Problem 97:

The Tzeltal forms may be described as follows:

Noun compounds in Tzeltal consist of the following sequence classes:

1. Noun (nuc.) plus noun (per.):[15]

  tomut   'egg' < ton   'stone' + mut   'hen'

  holwic   'summit' < hol   'head' + wic   'mountain'

  nič̌k'ahk'   'spark' < nič   'flower' + k'ahk'   'fire'

   haʔč'uht'   'diarrhea' < haʔ   'water' + č'uht'   'stomach'

2. Adjective (per.) plus noun (nuc.):

  panteʔ   'bridge' < pam   'flat' + teʔ   'wood'

  č'ultat   'god' < č'ul   'holy' + tat   'father'

  ʔancilʔal   'daughter' < ʔancil   'female' + ʔal   'child'

  muk'haʔ   'river' < muk'   'big' + haʔ   'water'

3. Verb (nuc.) plus noun (per.):

  k'atimbak   'hell' < k'atim   'to heat' + bak   'bone'

  čik'pom   'incense-burner' < čik'   'to burn' + pom   'incense'

---

[15]The abbreviations "nuc." and "per." identify the nuclear and peripheral immediate constituents. Both of the immediate constituents constitute nuclei, but by comparison with syntactic patterns in Tzeltal (which are reflected in the meaningful relationships of the forms), we may identify the nuclear and peripheral constituents of the endocentric constructions. It is also possible to employ certain symbols: a simple arrow to point to the nuclear constituent, an arrow pointing in both directions to mark coördinate endocentric constructions, and an x to mark exocentric constructions. It is not always necessary to indicate the relationships of peripheral to nuclear constituents, but there are some instances in which sequence classes differ only in this respect.

mel'ot'an   'sadness' < mel   'to explain' + ?ot'an   'heart'

k'anpatan   'tax-collector' < k'an   'to ask for' + patan   'tax'

Problem 98 (data consist of the Tonkawa forms of Problem 71)

Instructions: Describe the compounds on the basis of external distribution classes and internal structure. The Tonkawa classes may be identified from the classes of the English forms used in the translation.[16]

5.13.22 Distributional Arrangements in Multiple Sequence Classes

Distributions of determiners in related sequence classes (i.e. sequence classes having the same nuclears) tend to be similar. This means that if we distinguish subclasses of nuclears with one determiner, we may be able to use these same subclasses in describing the distributions of other determiners. If several determiners have similar distributions, we set up nuclear classes and describe the various structural series on the basis of these.

Problem 99 (data from Spanish)

Instructions:

a. Determine the number of parallel distributions.

b. Describe the major distribution classes of nuclear constituents.

I Infinitive	II 3d Sg. Pres. Ind.	III 3d Sg. Pres. Subj.	IV 3d Sg. Pret. Ind.	V 3d Sg. Imperf. Ind.	VI Past Part.
1. ablár 'to speak'	1a. ábla	1b. áble	1c. abló	1d. ablába	1e. abládo
2. sitár 'to cite'	2a. síta	2b. síte	2c. sitó	2d. sitába	2e. sitádo
3. dudár 'to doubt'	3a. dúda	3b. dúde	3c. dudó	3d. dudába	3e. dudádo
4. xugár 'to play'	4a. xuéga	4b. xuége	4c. xugó	4d. xugába	4e. xugádo
5. kemár 'to burn'	5a. kéma	5b. kéme	5c. kemó	5d. kemába	5e. kemádo
6. pensár 'to think'	6a. piénsa	6b. piénse	6c. pensó	6d. pensába	6e. pensádo
7. řobár 'to steal'	7a. řóba	7b. řóbe	7c. řobó	7d. řobába	7e. řobádo
8. kostár 'to cost'	8a. kuésta	8b. kuéste	8c. kostó	8d. kostába	8e. kostádo
9. bařér 'to sweep'	9a. báře	9b. bářa	9c. bařió	9d. bařía	9e. bařído
10. bendér 'to sell'	10a. bénde	10b. bénda	10c. bendió	10d. bendía	10e. bendído
11. perdér 'to lose'	11a. piérde	11b. piérda	11c. perdió	11d. perdía	11e. perdído
12. komér 'to eat'	12a. kóme	12b. kóma	12c. komió	12d. komía	12e. komído

(Continued on next page.)

---

[16]This practice is, of course, unreliable as an analytical procedure, but may be followed in this exercise in making a tentative description.

13. mobér 'to move'	13a. muébe	13b. muéba	13c. mobió	13d. mobía	13e. mobído
14. gañír 'to yelp'	14a. gáñe	14b. gáña	14c. gañió	14d. gañía	14e. gañído
15. admitír 'to admit'	15a. admíte	15b. admíta	15c. admitió	15d. admitía	15e. admitído
16. adkirír 'to acquire'	16a. adkiére	16b. adkiéra	16c. adkirió	16d. adkiría	16e. adkirído
17. sentír 'to feel'	17a. siénte	17b. siénta	17c. sintió	17d. sintía	17e. sentído
18. pedír 'to ask for'	18a. píde	18b. pída	18c. pidió	18d. pedía	18e. pedído
19. dormír 'to sleep'	19a. duérme	19b. duérma	19c. durmió	19d. dormía	19e. dormído
20. bruñír 'to burnish'	20a. brúñe	20b. brúña	20c. bruñió	20d. bruñía	20e. bruñído

Supplementary information:

1. The abbreviations in the headings may be explained as follows: II, third person singular present indicative; III, third person singular present subjunctive; IV, third person singular preterite indicative; V, third person singular imperfect indicative; and VI, past participle.

2. These forms include the major classes of the so-called regular and radical-changing verbs.

3. These sequence classes do not represent all the principal variants, but they are typical.

4. The final -o in the past participles is a separate morpheme.

Discussion of Problem 99:

In analyzing a series of related forms to determine whether there is any parallelism of distribution and hence any justification for setting up principal stem classes to which one may refer the distribution of more than one determiner, we check the data to discover (1) any distributional agreement between two or more determiners and (2) any similarities between allomorphs of the determined constituents. The following similarities of determiner distribution may be noted:

1. In series II the suffix -a has the same distribution as -ár in series I. Similarly, the suffix -e has the same distribution as the suffixes -ér and -ír combined.

2. In series III the suffix -e has the same distribution as the suffix -a of series II, and the suffix -a of series III has the same distribution as the suffix -e of series II.

3. In series IV the suffixes -ó and -ió have the same distribution as the set -a ∞ -e of series II and the set -e ∞ -a of series III.

4. In series V the suffixes -ába and -ía have the same distribution as the complementary sets noted in series II, III, and IV.

5. The distributional differences in series VI between -ád- and -íd- parallel those in the other series.

6. In describing all of the Spanish verb series it would be more economical to split some of these forms into two morphemes, e.g. the stem formative vowels -á ∞ -é ∞ -í plus -r, -áb ∞ -í plus -a, and -á ∞ -í plus -d. However, because

of the small amount of data and for the sake of greater simplicity in this particular problem, we are treating the suffixal elements as units, except the final -o of series VI.

To understand something of the structural parallelisms we may diagram the relationships as follows:

	I	II	III	IV	V	VI
Forms 1-8	-ár	-a	-e	-ó	-ába	-ád-
Forms 9-13	-ér	-e	-a	-ió	-ía	-íd-
Forms 14-20	-ír					

If we examine the allomorphs of the stems we find the following types:

1. Stems with two allomorphs[17]

   a. With no changes in segmental phonemes:

1	2		1	2	
abl- ~ ábl-	'to speak'		dud- ~ dúd-	'to doubt'	
sit- ~ sít-	'to cite'		kem- ~ kém-	'to burn'	
bar̃- ~ bár̃-	'to sweep'		řob- ~ řób-	'to steal'	
bruñ- ~ brúñ-	'to burnish'		bend- ~ bénd-	'to sell'	
gañ- ~ gáñ-	'to yelp'		kom- ~ kóm-	'to eat'	
admit- ~ admít-	'to admit'				

   b. With changes in segmental phonemes:

1	2		1	2	
xug- ~ xuég-	'to play'		adkir- ~ adkiér-	'to acquire'	
pens- ~ piéns-	'to think'		perd- ~ piérd-	'to lose'	
kost- ~ kuést-	'to cost'		mob- ~ muéb-	'to move'	

---

[17] The first allomorphs occur before a morpheme bearing a stress and the second allomorphs occur before a morpheme not bearing a stress.

2. Stems with three allomorphs:

$$1 \qquad 2 \qquad 3$$

(sent- ~ siént-) ∞ sint-   'to feel'

(dorm- ~ duérm-) ∞ durm-   'to sleep'

(ped- ~ píd-) ∞ pid-   'to ask for'

An examination of the distribution of the allomorphs shows that second allomorphs occur in series II and III and that where there is a third allomorph, it occurs in series IV.

There is certainly sufficient parallelism of distribution to warrant our setting up basic stem classes in order to simplify the total description. Of course, we could decide to list all the verb stems as we describe the distribution of each determiner, but this is uneconomical. Furthermore, it actually obscures the great amount of structural parallelism, which is an essential part of the language. The verb stems may be classified as follows:

A-class stems:[18]

abl_1 ~ $ábl_2$ 'to speak'[19] kem_1 ~ $kém_2$ 'to burn'

sit_1 ~ $sít_2$ 'to cite' $pens_1$ ~ $piéns_2$ 'to think'

dud_1 ~ $dúd_2$ 'to doubt' $ř\!ob_1$ ~ $ř\!ób_2$ 'to steal'

xug_1 ~ $xuég_2$ 'to play' $kost_1$ ~ $kuést_2$ 'to cost'

E-class stems:

$ba\tilde{r}_1$ ~ $bá\tilde{r}_2$ 'to sweep' kom_1 ~ $kóm_2$ 'to eat'

$bend_1$ ~ $bénd_2$ 'to sell' mob_1 ~ $muéb_2$ 'to move'

$perd_1$ ~ $piérd_2$ 'to lose'

I-class stems:

$admit_1$ ~ $admít_2$ 'to admit' $(sent_1$ ~ $siént_2)$ ∞ $sint_3$ 'to feel'

$adkir_1$ ~ $adkiér_2$ 'to acquire' $(ped_1$ ~ $píd_2)$ ∞ pid_3 'to ask for'

$bru\tilde{n}_1$ ~ $brú\tilde{n}_2$ 'to burnish' $(dorm_1$ ~ $duérm_2)$ ∞ $durm_3$ 'to sleep'

$ga\tilde{n}_1$ ~ $gá\tilde{n}_2$ 'to yelp'

---

[18] The classes are named by the characteristic vowel of the infinitive form. These stems could be called A, B, C; I, II, III; or 1, 2, 3, but there is a great convenience in being able to identify a series by some formal distinction. The division of stems is into three classes because the distribution of all the determiners may be made on the basis of three classes, whereas a division into two classes would necessitate a further subdivision to take care of certain forms in the distribution of the infinitive suffix.

[19] First, second, and third allomorphs are indicated by subscript numerals. For stems which exhibit no allomorphic alternation except loss of stress, we could cover all the

Having set up the basic stem forms, we have little difficulty in describing the distribution of the various suffixal morphemes:

1. -ar ∞ -er ∞ -ir infinitive formative, suffixed to the first allomorphs of the A-stems, E-stems, and I-stems respectively:

    ablár   'to speak'

    bendér   'to sell'

    dormír   'to sleep'

2. -a ∞ -e 'third person singular present indicative,' suffixed to the second allomorphs:

    -a suffixed to A-stems:

        ábla   'he speaks'

        dúda   'he doubts'

    -e suffixed to E-stems and I-stems:

        piérde   'he loses'

        duérme   'he sleeps'

3. -e ∞ -a 'third person singular present subjunctive,' suffixed to the second allomorphs:

    -e suffixed to A-stems:

        áble   '(that) he speak'

        dúde   '(that) he doubt'

    -a suffixed to E-stems and I-stems:

        piérda   '(that) he lose'

        duérma   '(that) he sleep'

4. -ó ∞ -ió 'third person singular preterite indicative,' suffixed to the third allomorphs (where they exist) or to first allomorphs:

    -ó suffixed to A-stems:

        abló   'he spoke'

        dudó   'he doubted'

    -ió suffixed to E-stems and I-stems:

        sintió   'he felt'

        bruñió   'he burnished'

---

allomorphs in a single statement, but for the sake of the structural parallelism we are employing a fuller notation.

5. -ába ∞ -ía 'third person singular imperfect indicative,' suffixed to the first allomorphs:

    -ába suffixed to A-stems:

        ablába   'he was speaking'

        dudába   'he was doubting'

    -ía suffixed to E-stems and I-stems:

        komía   'he was eating'

        dormía   'he was sleeping'

6. -ád- ∞ -íd- past participle formative, suffixed to the first allomorphs:

    -ád- suffixed to A-stems:

        ablád-   'spoken'

        dudád-   'doubted'

    -íd- suffixed to E-stems and I-stems:

        komíd-   'eaten'

        dormíd-   'slept'

If we should assign certain symbolic values to the various morphemes and their alternants, we could obtain an even more concise statement. If, for example, we identify the stems as A, E, and I, using subscript numerals to identify the allomorphs (e.g. abl- 'speak' would be A_1 and ábl- would be A_2), and if we identify the suffixes as I, II, III, IV, V, and VI, using similar subscript numerals to identify the allomorphs (e.g. -ár, -ér, and -ír would be I_1, I_2, and I_3, respectively), we could describe the structural series as follows:

    1. Infinitive:

        $A_1 + I_1$: ablár   'to speak'[20]

        $E_1 + I_2$: komér   'to eat'

        $I_1 + I_3$: dormír   'to sleep'[21]

    2. Third person singular present indicative:

        $A_2 + II_1$: ábla   'he speaks,'   piénsa   'he thinks'

        $E_2, I_2 + II_2$: piérde   'he loses,'   duérme   'he sleeps'

---

[20]In Chapter 8 a much more adequate system of symbolic notation will be introduced, but we are using the symbols indicated here in order to show the relationship to the preceding form and discussion of the problem.

[21]The typography results in an ambiguity because the capital letter I and the Roman numeral I are identical.

3. Third person singular present subjunctive:

A_2 + III_1: <u>áble</u>   '(that) he speak,'   <u>piénse</u>   '(that) he think'

E_2, I_2 + III_2: <u>piérda</u>   '(that) he lose,'   <u>duérma</u>   '(that) he sleep'

4. Third person singular preterite indicative:

A_1 + IV_1: <u>abló</u>   'he spoke,'   <u>pensó</u>   'he thought'

E_1, $I_{3,1}$ + IV_2:[22] <u>perdió</u>   'he lost,'   <u>durmió</u>   'he slept'

5. Third person singular imperfective indicative:

A_1 + V_1: <u>ablába</u>   'he was speaking,'   <u>pensába</u>   'he was thinking'

E_1, I_1 + V_2: <u>perdía</u>   'he was losing,'   <u>dormía</u>   'he was sleeping'

6. Past participle:

A_1 + VI_1: <u>abbád</u>-   'spoken,'   <u>pensád</u>-   'thought'

E_1, I_1 + VI_2: <u>perdíd</u>-   'lost,'   <u>dormíd</u>-   'slept'

Problem 100 (data from Spanish)

Instructions:

a. Add the following data to Problem 99.

b. List the additional allomorphs.

c. Describe the entire series of forms (those in Problems 99 and 100), using either an expanded form (like the first description given above) or a reduced form (like the second description).

21. uír 'to flee'	21a. úye	21b. úya	21c. uyó	21d. uía	21e. uído
22. lusír 'to shine'	22a. lúse	22b. lúska	22c. lusió	22d. lusía	22e. lusído
23. abér 'to have'	23a. á	23b. áya	23c. úbo	23d. abía	23e. abído
24. tenér 'to have, hold'	24a. tiéne	24b. ténga	24c. túbo	24d. tenía	24e. tenído
25. sér 'to be'	25a. és	25b. séa	25c. fué	25d. éra	25e. sído
26. ír 'to go'	26a. bá	26b. báya	26c. fué	26d. íba	26e. ído
27. benír 'to come'	27a. biéne	27b. bénga	27c. bíno	27d. benía	27e. benído
28. ponér 'to place'	28a. póne	28b. pónga	28c. púso	28d. ponía	28e. puésto
29. asér 'to make'	29a. áse	29b. ága	29c. íso	29d. asía	29e. éčo
30. desír 'to say'	30a. díse	30b. díga	30c. díxo	30d. desía	30e. díčo

---

[22] The order of the allomorphs indicates their distributional priority.

Supplementary information:

1. The forms of Problem 99 (1-20) represent the predominant, productive formations. The irregular forms (21-30) should be described in terms of the principal patterns.

2. One may describe subclasses of allomorphs. For example, in accordance with the system set forth under Problem 99, the verbs benír and sér could be listed as having the following allomorphs:

$$ben_1, \text{ } bién_2, \text{ } béng_{2a}, \text{ } bín_3$$

$$s_1, \text{ } ér_{1a}, \text{ } és_2, \text{ } sé_{2a}, \text{ } fu_3$$

The reason for setting up subclasses of the first and second allomorphs is that in the predominant patterns the first allomorph occurs in sequence classes I, V, and VI and the second allomorph usually occurs in sequence classes II and III. Where there is a third allomorph, it occurs in sequence class IV. If we follow this primary arrangement, we can simplify our statements by making subclasses of allomorphs, rather than continue to number them serially.

3. One of the allomorphs in form 26 is the stem i-, which contracts with an identical vowel.

4. There are four allomorphs in the determiner of IV: -ó, -ió, -o, and -é.[23]

5. This treatment of the data in Problems 99 and 100 is not supposed to constitute the basis of a structural statement for all the Spanish verbs. Some important adaptations of this must be made when considering all the tenses and all the persons.

---

[23]It is quite wrong to assume that our descriptive statements of the structure reflect altogether accurately the system of symbolics (the language as a whole) which we are describing. For example, we set up an allomorph in this series as -o, and describe the distribution of this morpheme in relation to its occurrence with certain allomorphs of the stem: túbo 'he had,' bíno 'he came,' púso 'he put,' díxo 'he said.' This allomorph -o is homophonous with the most common allomorph of the first person singular, e.g. kánto 'I sing,' áblo 'I speak,' téngo, 'I have,' béngo 'I come,' póngo 'I place,' dígo 'I say.' The way in which we usually describe these forms involves setting up kánt-, ábl-, téng-, béng-, póng-, and díg- as allomorphs of the particular stems, and we assign the "meaning" of person, tense, and number to the suffix. At such points our description of the structure does not always "square" with the semantic units.

It must be assumed that allomorphs whose distribution is not phonologically defined carry their share of the meaning in any combination. For example, in áblo 'I speak' and abló 'he spoke' we can describe the difference in terms of the suffixes -o 'first person singular present indicative' and -ó 'third person singular preterite indicative.' This seems perfectly sufficient, and the allomorphic contrast between ábl- and abl- may appear to be more or less meaningless. But, having set up such a distinction, we then assume that in forms such as túbo 'he had,' púso 'he put,' and díxo 'he said,' the tense-person-mood meaning can be assigned to the allomorph -o. This, of course, is not entirely true, for it is the entire composite form which provides the meaning. The allomorph díx-, stem of the preterite díxo 'he said,' does not bear the same relationship as a symbol to des-, the stem of the infinitive desír 'to say,' as abl-, stem of the preterite abló 'he spoke,' bears to the homophonous abl- stem of the infinitive ablár 'to speak.' Structurally the parallelism is exact, but we cannot assume ipso facto that this adequately describes the symbolic entities as reflected by the semantic distinctions.

There is much research which must be done on this phase of descriptive analysis. Nevertheless, sufficient data are in hand to allow us to realize that the "signaling

It is somewhat easier to understand the types of descriptions which may be made of any series of related sequence classes and the validity of combining descriptions of such classes, if certain hypothetical sets of data are employed.

Problem 101 (hypothetical data)

Instructions:

    a. Describe each structural series.

    b. Determine the degree of conformity.

    c. Describe all the structural series by means of basic stem classes.

    d. Make a composite statement of all structural series.

Present		Past	Future
1. minito	'eat'	1a. miŋki	1b. mimfo
2. samato	'go'	2a. saŋki	2b. samfo
3. lototo	'walk'	3a. lobki	3b. lobfo
4. tukuto	'jump'	4a. tuĥki	4b. tukzi
5. feseto	'cry'	5a. feski	5b. feszi
6. tabka	'wish'	6a. tabpu	6b. tabzi
7. reŋka	'think'	7a. rempu	7b. renzi
8. mapisa	'fall'	8a. mapu	8b. mapna
9. bogisa	'come'	9a. bogpu	9b. bogna

Supplementary information: The stems consist of CVC- patterns.

Discussion of Problem 101:

    In relating the structural series in Problem 101 we are confronted with two types of data: (1) the similarities in allomorphs, phonologically and morphologically defined, and (2) the structural parallelisms.

    An examination of the phonologically defined allomorphs reveals that (1) nasals assimilate to the point of articulation of the following consonant, (2) sequences of identical consonants reduce to a single consonant, and (3) the suffix -Vto assimilates the first vowel to the stem vowel. The first two facts apply to any morpheme, and the last fact refers only to one morpheme.

---

features" of a form include all the morphologically defined allomorphs. It is true that we find it "more convenient" and "structurally more valid" to describe the differences of meaning between digo and dixo in terms of different distributions of homophonous morphemes, i.e. -o 'first person present' vs. -o 'third person preterite,' but this does not mean that our structural analysis reflects adequately the symbolics of the language. The very fact that certain new analogical creations may arise means that symbolics and structure have not been identical, and when this happens the structure is reformed or extended to conform with the semantic symbolism.

The morphologically defined allomorphs of the present and past formations show partial parallelism in distribution, and the future series agrees to some extent with the present. This structural parallelism and nonconformity may be diagramed as follows:

Forms	Present	Past	Future
1	-Vto	-ki	-fo
2			
3			
4			-zi
5			
6	-ka	-pu	
7			
8	-isa		-na
9			

In any description it is advantageous to list allomorphic alternations which may be characteristic of all morphemes. For example, initial statements that nasals assimilate according to the point of articulation of the following consonant and that sequences of identical consonants reduce to a single consonant make it unnecessary to repeat these facts when the particular morphemes are being listed. The assimilation of -Vto cannot be described as applicable to the language as a whole, for the morpheme of similar shape -isa does not assimilate in the same way. Hence, the phonologically defined distribution of -Vto should be described when the morpheme is listed, rather than in any introductory morphophonemic statement.

The description of the structural series may be made in two ways: (1) by setting up stem classes and then describing the distribution of each morpheme on the basis of these classes or (2) by making a composite statement of the distribution of all the morphemes. We shall consider these two methods in order.

The three structural series subdivide the stems into four classes: I (stems 1-3), II (stems 4-5), III (stems 6-7), and IV (stems 8-9). On the assumption that this hypothetical problem represents the proportion of stems in the various classes of an actual language, several hundred stems would then be listed under each stem type. The distribution of the morphologically defined allomorphs of the present, past, and future series could then be described as follows:

1. Present formation:

   -Vto, with assimilation of V to the vowel of the stem, occurs with classes I and II:

   minito   'eat'

   tukuto   'jump'

-ka occurs with class III:

   tabka   'wish'

   reŋka   'think'

-isa occurs with class IV:

   mapisa   'fall'

   bogisa   'come'

2. Past formation:

   -ki occurs with classes I and II:

      miŋki   'ate'

      tuki   'jumped'

   -pu occurs with classes III and IV:

      tabpu   'wished'

      mapu   'fell'

3. Future formation:

   -fo occurs with class I:

      mimfo   'will eat'

      samfo   'will go'

   -zi occurs with classes II and III:

      tukzi   'will jump'

      tabzi   'will wish'

   -na occurs with class IV:

      mapna   'will fall'

      bogna   'will come'

This description presupposes, of course, some general morphophonemic statement about allomorphic alternations which occur throughout the series.

A composite statement could be made as follows:

Stems in Problem 101 occur with tense formatives in the following distributional arrangements:

   1. Stems suffixing -ki 'past tense' and -Vto 'present tense,' with V assimilating to the vowel of the stem

A. With -fo 'future tense':

    sam-   'go'

    lob-   'walk'

B. With -zi 'future tense':

    tuk-   'jump'

    fes-   'cry'

2. Stems suffixing -pu 'past tense'

A. With -ka 'present tense' and -zi 'future tense':

    tab-   'wish'

    ren-   'think'

B. With -isa 'present tense' and -na 'future tense':

    map-   'fall'

    bog-   'come'

    The composite statement has the advantage of combining a formational statement with a listing of stem classes. However, when there are many overlapping classes such a statement involves repeating determiner morphemes, and on the whole appears to be less valuable as a descriptive technique than the first method, which sets up stem classes.

    When there is perfect parallelism of distribution, the composite statement, whereby more than one determiner may be described at a time, is more economical, but it is less and less valuable the fewer the parallelisms. A description of stem classes, followed by individual treatment of the determiners, is more efficient in dealing with complex relationships and structural nonconformities.

Problem 102 (data from Chichewa, a language of Nyasaland)[24]

Instructions:

    a. Identify the two parallel structural series.

    b. Describe the forms (1) by setting up classes and describing each structural series and (2) by means of a composite statement.

    c. In listing the determiners, state the phonologically defined distributions of the allomorphs.

1. mu·nt^hu   'man'   4. ɓá·na   'children'

2. ɓa·nt^hu   'men'   5. mú·p^hwa   'man's sister's child'

3. mwá·na   'child'   6. ɓá·p^hwa   'man's sister's children'

(Continued on next page.)

---

[24] These data are from Watkins, op. cit., pp. 25-44.

7. ŋná·si   'neighbor'

8. aná·si   'neighbors'

9. ŋza·mba   'midwife'

10. aza·mba   'midwives'

11. dá·mbɔ   'marsh'

12. madá·mbɔ   'marshes'

13. fu·nɔ   'wish, need'

14. mafu·nɔ   'wishes, needs'

15. pɛmpʰɛ·rɔ   'prayer'

16. mapɛmpʰɛ·rɔ   'prayers'

17. bwɛ́·zi   'friend'

18. mabwɛ́·zi   'friends'

19. čá·ka   'year'

20. vyá·ka   'years'

21. čiɓá·lɛ   'coconut tree'

22. viɓá·lɛ   'coconut trees'

23. čipa·nda   'calabash'

24. vipa·nda   'calabashes'

25. čisɔ́·ŋga   'wooden arrow point'

26. visɔ́·ŋga   'wooden arrow points'

27. čićú·rɔ   'iron'

28. vicú·rɔ   'pieces of iron'

Supplementary information:

1. The differences of tone should not be considered in describing these structural series. The tones are basic to the stems.

2. The penultimate (next to the last) syllable is always long in these forms. This is true of these nouns in isolation, but not necessarily in context.

3. Certain phonologically defined allomorphs occur:

    a. mw- and vy- occur before vowels.

    b. ŋ- and a- occur before polysyllabic stems.

    c. The stem of form 3 and 4 is -ána.

4. The list of forms in Problem 102 is highly selective, so that many of the complications are not included.

Discussion of Problem 102:

There are six noun-class morphemes, of which one is zero. They comprise three distributional doublets in occurrence with noun stems, but they all occur with the same attributives or verbs. (Compare the forms in Ilamba, Problem 38.) These morphemes may be numbered 1s, 1p, 2s, 2p, 3s, 3p. The numerals stand for the three sets of forms; s stands for singular, and p for plural. Prefixes of classes 1, 2, and 3 are in complementation in this structural series and may be described as follows:

Nouns exhibit the following concordant-class formations:

1. mu- (preceding monosyllabic stems) ~ ŋ- (preceding polysyllabic consonant stems) ~ mw- (preceding polysyllabic vowel stems) 'singular concordant prefix' and ba- (preceding monosyllabic stems) ~ a- (preceding polysyllabic stems) 'plural concordant prefix';

-nt^hu   'man'25

-ána   'child'

ʹ-p^hwa   'man's sister's child'

etc.

2. Zero 'singular concordant prefix' and <u>ma-</u> 'plural concordant prefix':

fu·nɔ   'wish, need'

pɛmp^hɛ·rɔ   'prayer'

etc.

3, <u>či-</u> (preceding consonant stems) ~ <u>č-</u> (preceding vowel stems) 'singular concordant prefix' and <u>vi-</u> (preceding consonant stems) ~ <u>vy-</u> (preceding vowel stems) 'plural concordant prefix':

-áka   'year'

-bá·lɛ   'coconut tree'

etc.

This type of composite statement may be altered a little by listing the determiners first and assigning a number to each. Then the distribution may be described in a slightly more concise manner.

1s. <u>mu-</u> ~ <u>m̩-</u> ~ <u>mw-</u>   'singular concordant prefix'26

1p. <u>ba-</u> ~ <u>a-</u>   'plural concordant prefix'26

2s. Zero 'singular concordant prefix'

2p. <u>ma-</u>   'plural concordant prefix'

3s. <u>či-</u> ~ <u>č-</u> 'singular concordant prefix'26

3p. <u>vi-</u> ~ <u>vy-</u>   'plural concordant prefix'26

The distribution could then be described as follows:

1s and 1p:

-nt^hu   'man'

-ána   'child'

etc.

25The fact that penultimate vowels in phrase-final position are long would be indicated in the morphophonemic section of the morphology.

26Some statement as to the distribution of phonologically defined allomorphs would have to be made.

2s and 2p:

    fu·nɔ   'wish, need'

    pɛmpʰɛ·rɔ   'prayer'

    etc.

3s and 3p:

    -áka   'year'

    -bá·lɛ   'coconut tree'

    etc.

     The forms in Problem 102 exhibit two parallel structural series. Morphemes 1s, 2s, and 3s constitute complementary morphemes;[27] similarly, 1p, 2p, and 3p are complementary morphemes. Morphemes 1s and 1p occur in a simple paradigm; so do set 2s and 2p and set 3s and 3p. The parallelism of distribution warrants in this instance some type of composite statement.

Problem 103 (data from Loma, a language of Liberia)

    Instructions: Describe the structural series (1) by setting up stem classes and then describing the distribution of each determiner and (2) by a composite statement.

Indefinite Singular		Definite Singular		Indefinite Plural	
1. bálá	'bracelet'	1a. báláí		1b. báláá	
2. táá	'town'	2a. tááí		2b. táá	
3. súbù	'morning'	3a. súbùì		3b. súbùà	
4. náágɔ̀	'four'	4a. náágɔ̀ì		4b. náágɔ̀à	
5. kɔ̀fí	'coffee'	5a. kɔ̀fígí		5b. kɔ̀fígá	
6. ŋábú	'fire'	6a. ŋábúí		6b. ŋábúá	
7. míté	'spoon'	7a. mítéí		7b. mítéá	
8. bóá	'knife'	8a. bóáí		8b. bóáá	
9. kísì	'kitchen'	9a. kísìì		9b. kísìà	
10. kɔ̀pú	'cup'	10a. kɔ̀púí		10b. kɔ̀púá	
11. bílí	'goat'	11a. bílíí		11b. bílíá	
12. bété	'bed'	12a. bétéí		12b. bétéá	

(Continued on next page.)

---

   [27]Complementary morphemes must, of course, be distinguished from complementary allomorphs. Allomorphs are complementary in all occurrences, but morphemes may be complementary only in certain structural series.

13. bébè 'bag'	13a. bébègì	13b. bébègà
14. pétè 'mirror'	14a. pétègì	14b. pétègà
15. kpókpò 'chair'	15a. kpókpògì	15b. kpókpògà
16. tétè 'thatch'	16a. tétègì	16b. tétègà
17. másá 'chief'	17a. máságí	17b. máságá
18. wùò 'frog'	18a. wùògì	18b. wùògà
19. máázá 'banana'	19a. máázágí	19b. máázágá

Supplementary information:

1. A sequence of aaa reduces to aa.

2. Analyze the suffixal forms as consisting of two layers: (1) stem formatives -g ∞ -0 and (2) the suffixes -i and -a.

3. The tonal differences in the suffixes may be described in terms of phonological environment.

Problem 104 (data from Loma, a language of Liberia)

Instructions: Describe the structural series by setting up stem classes and then noting the distribution of each determiner.

Basic Stem	Progressive	Recent Past
1. lí 'go'	1a. líízú	1b. líá
2. pú 'pour'	2a. púúzú	2b. púá
3. bó 'tell'	3a. bósú	3b. bógá
4. tó 'build'	4a. tósú	4b. tógá
5. gílí 'cook'	5a. gílízù	5b. gílíá
6. dówá 'beat'	6a. dówázù	6b. dówáá
7. pétè 'see'	7a. pétèsù	7b. pétègà
8. láámì 'eat'	8a. láámìzù	8b. láámìà
9. ŋíí 'sleep'	9a. ŋíízú	9b. ŋííyá
10. wúdé 'jump'	10a. wúdésù	10b. wúdégà
11. dódó 'read'	11a. dódósù	11b. dódógà
12. záá 'die'	12a. záázú	12b. záá
13. kέ 'do'	13a. kέέzú	13b. kέέ
14. gúó 'wash'	14a. gúózú	14b. gúá

(Continued on next page.)

15. páá 'kill'	15a. páázú	15b. páá
16. tévé 'send'	16a. tévésù	16b. tévégà
17. tévé 'cut'	17a. tévézù	17b. tévéá
18. vá 'come'	18a. váázú	18b. váá

Supplementary information:

1. Monosyllabic short-vowel stems lengthen the vowel before the stem formative -z.

2. Identical vowel sequences of the type VVV reduce to VV.

3. Sequences of identical vowels are phonetically long without rearticulation.

4. The suffix -a assimilates to a preceding ɛ, and after monosyllabic stems ending in a long vowel ii it occurs in an allomorphic form -ya.

5. Form 9b contains a phonologically definable nasal assimilation.

6. The tones on these verbs are first person plural subject forms. They may be taken as constituting the basic tone patterns. The tones of the suffixes may be determined by the tones of the stems.

7. Stems 16 and 17 are homophonous but belong to two different basic classes.

8. Analyze the progressive and recent past forms as consisting of stem formatives plus the suffixes -u and -a.

Problem 105 (data from Loma, a language of Liberia)

Instructions: Describe the structural series by setting up stem classes.

Basic Stem		Singular Definite	Plural Indefinite	Recent Past	Progressive	Continuous State
1. kpádí	'hot'	1a. kpádíí	1b. kpádíá	1c. kpádíá	1d. kpádízù	1e. kpádívè
2. págɔ́	'good'	2a. págɔ́í	2b. págɔ́á	2c. págɔ́á	2d. págɔ́zù	2e. págɔ́vè
3. déí	'cold'	3a. déígì	3b. déígà	3c. déígà	3d. déísù	3e. déígè
4. gwálá	'large'	4a. gwáláí	4b. gwáláá	4c. gwáláá	4d. gwálázù	4e. gwálávè
5. téí	'black'	5a. téígì	5b. téígà	5c. téígà	5d. téísù	5e. téígè
6. kpákpá	'big'	6a. kpákpáí	6b. kpákpáá	6c. kpákpáá	6d. kpákpázù	6e. kpákpávè
7. kpáánà	'hard'	7a. kpáánàgì	7b. kpáánàgà	7c. kpáánàgà	7d. kpáánàsù	7e. kpáánàgè

Supplementary information:

1. These so-called adjectives may follow the noun which they modify, and any suffixes indicating definite or indefinite, singular or plural categories are added to the final adjective of the construction.

2. These same stems occur with all the tense forms of regular verbs as well as with the continuous state.

3. All inflected parts of speech are divided into two more or less equal classes.

4. The plural indefinite -a and the recent past -a are homophonous in these forms, but they never occur in the same syntactic constructions and they may differ in tone depending on different types of subjects and certain arbitrary classes of stems which perturbate the suffixal tone.

5. The verb tones are first person plural subject forms, but they do not follow the same patterns as do those in Problem 104.

5.2 Systems of Structural Classes

Languages differ greatly in number and types of structural classes. In the Indo-European languages we are accustomed to a great many major structural classes, which we call "parts of speech." These are nouns, verbs, adjectives, adverbs, prepositions, pronouns, conjunctions, and interjections. These parts of speech are sometimes formally distinguishable by their internal structure (this is particularly true in Greek and Latin), but in a language such as English the parts of speech are distinguished largely by their external distributions.

In Turkish there is no such elaborate set of word classes. Voegelin and Ellinghausen[28] have described Turkish on the basis of two principal word classes, nouns and verbs. There are also certain enclitic particles which are syntactically pertinent. Though, structurally, there are only two major classes, noun and verbs, this does not mean that there are no possessive pronominal relationships such as my houses; it is only that my is a suffix -im in such a form as evlerim 'my houses.' There are, as well, forms equivalent to English prepositions, but these, also, are suffixes, e.g. kaza?en 'by accident' (kaza 'accident') and kïsïn 'in winter' (kïs 'winter').

In Maya there are four principal word classes: nouns, verbs, attributives, and particles. In translating from Maya to English there is a certain amount of correspondence in word classes, but there are also many important exceptions. For example, ye·tel 'and' is according to its structure a possessed noun meaning 'his with-ness,' and uti?al, usually a conjunction translated 'in order that,' is a possessed noun meaning literally 'his for-ness' (compare inti'al 'for me' and ati'al 'for you'). In Tojolabal (a Mayan language) the indirect or benefactive object may be expressed by a possessed noun. For example, wa šk'ulan awi 'I make it for you' consists of a tense particle wa, the verb šk'ulan, and the benefactive object noun awi 'for you,' which is possessed like any other noun (compare ki 'for me' and yi 'for him'). In Kekchi (another Mayan language) certain forms translated by prepositional phrases in English have quite a different structure from what the translation would seem to imply. One might at first assume that the forms činben 'on me' and čaben 'on you (sg.)' consist of č...ben plus the pronominal infixes -in- 'me' and -a- 'you (sg.).' These forms are, however, prepositional noun phrases consisting of the prepositional particle č- (~ či-) 'at' or 'to' plus the possessive pronominal prefixes in- and a- and the noun -ben 'upper surface of.' The form čigwu, translated 'before me,' is literally 'at my face.'

Hall[29] describes Marshallese in terms of three principal structural classes, illustrated as follows:

28C. F. Voegelin and M. E. Ellinghausen, "Turkish Structure," Journal of the American Oriental Society, 63 (1943), 1: 54-56.

29Robert A. Hall, Jr., Leave Your Language Alone (Ithaca: Cornell University, 1948), pp. 62-63. This book provides an excellent orientation in scientific linguistics.

Class A

neǰü　'my child'

  neǰim　'your (sg.) child'

  neǰin　'his child'

bara　'my head'

  baram　'your (sg.) head'

  baran　'his head'

ainigiŏ　'my voice'

  ainigiŏm　'your (sg.) voice'

  ainigiŏn　'his voice'

aŏ　'my property'

  am　'your (sg.) property

  an　'his property'

ituru　'beside me'

  iturum　'beside you (sg.)'

  iturin　'beside him, her, it; beside ...'

ibba　'with me'

  ibbam　'with you (sg.)'

  ibben　'with him, her, it; with ...'

Class B

mɛdak　'pain, suffering; to suffer'

nuknuk　'clothing, clothes'

bŏk　'to take'

ǰudak　'to stand'

ǰerabal　'work, to work'

rik　'little, to be little'

bat　'slow, to be slow'

til　'to burn'

lang　'sky'

miǰ　'to die, be dead'

Class C

Alone	Before Type A or B	Forms of A or B
nga	i-	'I'
kwa	ko-	'you (sg.)'
e		'he, she, it'
ǰe		'we (you and I)'
kim		'we (he, she, it, or they and I)'
kom		'you (pl.)'
ir	re	'they'

The forms of class A all occur with a suffixal possessive pronoun, whereas those of classes B and C may not occur with such suffixes. If one wants to possess a form belonging to class B, it is necessary to use a combination such as aŏ mɛdak 'property-my suffering.' Similarly, 'your (sg.) clothing' is am nuknuk, literally 'property-your clothing,' and 'his work' is an ǰerabal, literally 'property-his work.' Forms in class B may combine with pro-nominal elements, e.g. iǰerabal 'I work' and ebat 'it is slow.' A typical Marshallese sentence is ebat am ǰerabal 'you (sg.) work slowly,' literally 'it-is-slow property-your work.'

In describing the morphology of a language we are concerned primarily with the morpho-logical classes as determined by their internal composition. These classes usually parallel quite closely the significant syntactically defined classes, but this is not always true. For example, in Maya there is a distinct break between those possessed nouns which may func-tion as conjunctives and those which may not. In a syntactic inventory of Maya, such noun formations would be divided.

The most frequently distinguished morphological classes are nouns, verbs, particles, and pronouns. It is quite impossible to predict what will occur in any one language or the characteristics which any class will have. For example, we generally associate tense with the verb, but in Mongbandi the tense may be indicated by the tone on the pronouns. The pronouns mbi 'I' and ʔe 'we' occur with low tone in the past, mid tone in the present, and high tone in the future. The tones on the Mongbandi verbs represent completive, continuative, and future tense-aspects. These two tonal systems are, however, independent, for ʔé, future tense of 'we,' occurs with gwé, completive of 'go,' in ʔé gwé 'we may go' or 'in order that we go,' in contrast with ʔè gwé 'we went' and ʔé gwē 'we will go.' Despite such very evident contradictions, there are some features which may profitably be noted about the morphological categories and the structure of the principal word classes.[30]

Nouns

1. Possessable by pronominal affixes.

2. Singular and plural contrasts.

3. Case relationships, e.g. subject, direct object, indirect object.

4. "Prepositional" relationships, e.g. in, by, for, through, with.

Verbs

1. Agreement with subject or object or inclusion of a subject or object pronoun.

2. Time and aspect of the action.

3. Voice, e.g. transitive, intransitive, active, and passive.[31]

4. Mode (the psychological background of the action as represented by the speaker), e.g. indicative, optative, conditional, interrogative, and potential.

Particles

1. Relatively shorter than other parts of speech.

2. Uninflected, and hence exhibit no formal categories.

3. Frequently clitic.

Pronouns

1. Relatively short.

2. Very irregular in derivation and inflection.

3. Affixal or clitic.

4. Grammatically related to classes of nouns.

---

[30]There are so many languages in which the following generalizations do not hold that one is tempted to avoid such statements altogether, and yet with proper caution and due reservations, there is something to be gained from a brief consideration of some of the primary formal and semantic characteristics of these word classes.

[31]The "voice" defines the relationship of the verb to the subject and object elements.

Many of these features have been illustrated a number of times in the data included in various problems, but it must not be assumed that we can classify a form of another language because it exhibits some of these characteristics or expresses one of these categories. Every language is a system within itself, and a morphological classification must be based upon the language in question.

C H A P T E R   6

THE MEANING OF MORPHEMES AND SEQUENCES OF MORPHEMES

In the preceding chapters on the development of methods of linguistic analysis we have assumed that morphemes have meanings, and in Chapter 2 we discussed the bases for deciding whether meanings are related or different. In describing only the structure of a language it is not necessary for us to do more than identify morphemes and state their distributions, but the structure of a language is not everything. Even though our techniques for treating the meaningful units of a language are much less adequate than those for discovering its structure, we must make some attempt to describe the ways in which a language may symbolize phenomena.

6.1 Semantic Principles

There are three principles which govern semantic analysis and classification; these principles are concerned with: (1) the nonexistence of real synonyms, (2) the definability of meaning by environment, and (3) the nonconformity between systems of symbolization.

6.11 Principle 1

No morphemes or combinations of morphemes are identical in meaning.

This principle means that there are no real synonyms, i.e. forms which have identical meanings. Words such as peace and tranquillity are ordinarily listed as synonyms, but they are far from being identical in meaning. One may speak of a peace conference, but the expression tranquillity conference is certainly no identical equivalent. Forms such as childish and puerile or truth and reality illustrate this same principle, namely, that there are no semantically equivalent terms. By equivalence we mean capacity for occurrence in precisely the same linguistic and contextual environments with the same meanings, both denotative and connotative.

This principle of semantic nonequivalence extends to optional allomorphs and morphologically defined allomorphs. For example, the alternant pronunciations of duty (1) /duwtiy/ and (2)/dyuwtiy/ carry certain distinct connotations. In some circumstances the form /dyuwtiy/ induces an unfavorable response from the listener, who interprets it as pedantic or associated with people whose culture he does not appreciate. On the other hand, among a certain small set of speakers of American English the form /duwtiy/ is a mark of educational and cultural inferiority. The alternant pronunciations of creek /kriyk/ and /krik/ bear similar distinctions, but to different types of speakers. If alternant pronunciations of morphemes do nothing more than identify the dialect area, they are to that extent nonequivalent.

We have already touched upon the problems of different meanings of morphologically defined allomorphs in section 2.23.1, H. Alternants such as shown and showed indicate that there is a meaningful difference between such allomorphs. The semantic differences which exist are subclass distinctions within the framework of the phonetic-semantic contrastiveness of the morpheme as a whole. The contrast in meaning between the allomorphs -en and -ed is primarily one of connotation. The productive suffix -ed, having an expanding distribution, is less acceptable in traditional contexts than the suffix -en. This is a matter of appropriateness and involves the reactions of the speakers and hearers. There is nothing intrinsic about the semantic values; they are dictated simply by the reactions of language-users to the sociolinguistic environment.

Phonetically defined allomorphs do not exhibit semantic differences, for the environment provides no basis for contrast, and without this contrast there can be no difference in meaning.

6.12 Principle 2

Meaning is definable by environment.

The significance of this principle is most vividly appreciated by those who have learned a foreign language in a purely monolingual situation. Having been suddenly thrust into a foreign-language community, they have been forced to learn a language by closely observing the environment in which certain forms are used. The meaning of every word and phrase had to be learned from its sociolinguistic setting.

Environment is very complex and includes several significant subdivisions. These are primarily (A) nonlinguistic and (B) linguistic. The nonlinguistic environment may be divided into (1) objective and (2) subjective, and the linguistic environment into (1) structural and (2) contextual.

A. Nonlinguistic Environments

1. Objective Environments

Morphemes and combinations of morphemes are definable in terms of the various phenomena for which they are symbols. For example, they may be symbols for (1) objects: horse, cow, sun, moon, tree, grass; (2) relationships: in, from, behind, high, low, one, two; (3) abstractions: good, bad, red, true; (4) processes: run, walk, speak, swim; and (5) states: sick, full, be. This is only a very general classification, and by no means all-inclusive or accurately restrictive. For example, the morpheme ouch does not fit any of these subdivisions accurately. It may be said, however, to symbolize a state, which results in a process of exclamation, because of a relationship to some irritating object. The objective environment of such an exclamatory term is very complex. There is no altogether satisfactory way to classify the various types of symbolization.

2. Subjective Environments

Almost as important as the objective symbolization of the various aspects of the environment is the subjective evaluation of these symbols. The objective part of symbolization we call the denotation and the subjective part we term the connotation. For example, the denotation of damn is a condemnatory imprecation, but the connotation of the word depends very largely on who is speaking and under what circumstances. Similarly, the word colonial produces one emotional response in an empire-worshiper and quite a different reaction in some downtrodden native. The word is objectively the same, but differences of environment provide a basis for different subjective reactions. A word may also carry a different connotation when used by the same person in varying circumstances. For example, there are probably no raised eyebrows when a minister uses damn in the pulpit, but if he used the same term in conversation about some uncoöperative neighbor, it would produce quite a different response.

Whether the meaning is denotative or connotative, however, it must still be referred to the environment for a definition. Regardless of whether we are analyzing a form as a symbol for something in the environment or in terms of its emotional overtones, we can only define its value in the light of the environment to which it refers and of which it is a part.

In every society there are certain taboo words. For example, in English there are the so-called four-letter words which designate various bodily functions, but their connotation is such that they cannot be used in most situations without loss of prestige among those whose conduct dictates the cultural norms. In many other societies the equivalent terms are not at all taboo, but the name of one's grandmother, for example, may never be uttered. These differences are the result of the cultural past of a people. In some cases, we may learn enough of the history of a people to know why, for example, they may name their children Peter or Paul, but not Nero or Judas, but in many instances there are few historical evidences of the reasons for such predispositions. However, knowledge of the history of a situation is not necessary in describing the present semantic value of the symbols.

Problem 106

Instructions:

a. Describe the intended connotations of the following words in a rabble-rousing American newspaper.

b. Describe the connotations which these terms have for you.

1. communism

2. America First

3. vivisection

4. socialism

5. imperialism

6. Wall Street

7. democracy

8. republican

9. England

10. Jap

B. Linguistic Environments[1]

1. Structural Environments

There are certain symbols which (1) stand for other symbols or (2) mark relationships between symbols. Pronouns illustrate the first type. The English word she is an obligatory substitute (a type of symbol) for feminine singular persons: Mrs. Jones, woman, girl; it is an optional one for (a) institutions: church, school, state, (b) countries: England, France, India, (c) ships: the President Harding, the Queen Mary, (d) fauna (particularly those which have sex-distinctive names): cow, ewe, doe, mare, sow, and (e) abstracts: art, science, beauty. The meaning of any pronoun must be defined in terms of the linguistic symbols for which it may substitute. Such an environment is strictly limited, though sometimes it is possible to provide nonlinguistic parallels from the practical world (as with English she); but in German the cognate sie is an obligatory substitute for Sprache 'language,' Sorge 'care,' and Frau 'woman,' whereas es (equivalent to English it) is the substitute for Fräulein 'young woman' and Schiff 'ship,' and er (equivalent to English he) is the substitute for Hut 'hat,' Grund 'ground,' and Freitag 'Friday.' The meaning of the German pronouns er, sie, and es must be defined in terms of the words for which they substitute, and this can be done only on the basis of the linguistic environment. The same is true of the Spanish pronouns él and ella and the Bantu pronominal substitutes with verbs (see Ilamba, Problem 38).

---

[1]There are a number of connotative differences which are defined primarily by the structural linguistic environment, but these are relatively insignificant, and hence they are not treated in a special section.

Problem 107

Instructions: Define the meanings of the following pronouns.

1. which   4. it

2. who   5. all

3. what

Some morphemes symbolize the relationships between linguistic symbols. For example, in the German sentence Der Knabe sah den Mann 'the boy saw the man' the suffix -r of der signals that der Knabe 'the boy' is the subject of the sentence, and the suffix -n of den signals that den Mann is the object of the verb. The meanings of -r and -n are definable in terms of the linguistic environment of German syntactic constructions.

In Chinese there is a particle ti which marks the end of an attributive expression just before the head word of the phrase. Note the following phrases:[2]

tiŋ xaw ti žen   'very good (particle) man'

wo çye tse ti pi   'I write (particle) brush,' that is, 'the brush I write with'

may ti šu   'buy (particle) book,' that is, 'the purchased book.'

The particle ti has a grammatical meaning which marks the relationship of the preceding to the following expression. This is a linguistic environment.

We may state that there are three functional types of symbolization: (1) signals for objects (this is in the broadest sense of the term), (2) signals for classes of signals (these are pronouns and other types of substitutes), and (3) signals for relationships between signals. To define the meaning of any of these types of symbols we must refer to the environment in which they are employed. In the first instance, we refer to the practical world and to the subjective reactions of speakers to the signals for practical-world objects. In the second two instances, we refer to the linguistic environment. There are some slight connotative differences perceptible in these second two types, but they are very minor in comparison with those conveyed by the first type. Subjective reactions are much more evident in matters involving human actions than in features of linguistic relationships. Nevertheless, morphemic differences which are primarily definable by linguistic environment, e.g. the difference between I and me, do take on connotative significance in the sociolinguistic environment which provides It's I vs. It's me.

2. Contextual Environments

The contextual environment of a form consists of the particular meaningful collocations in which it may occur. For example, we define out in terms of its general nonlinguistic environment, which indicates a relationship between the interior and the exterior of an object. However, this does not give all the meaning of out, for in the phrase Look out! the morpheme out may not preserve its usual meaning derived from the nonlinguistic environment. More than one joke has been constructed on this apparent contradiction, for look out may have precisely the opposite meaning from what one might be led to expect from the primary meanings of the morphemes in question. In the compound setup we have no difficulty deriving the meaning of the combination from the central, primary meanings of the constituent parts set and up. In the word upset this is not nearly so easy.

─────────────────

[2]Leonard Bloomfield, Language (New York: Henry Holt and Co., 1933), p. 199. Tone and stress markings are omitted.

There are two ways in which we can describe these types of problems. First, we may depict the meaning of any morpheme as an area, and plot the central (or primary) meaning and then describe various peripheral meanings; or, secondly, we may describe each morpheme as having a sememe (cf. the root sem- of semantics), and each sememe (the meaningful contrastiveness of any morpheme) would then be subdivided into allosemes. Though each morphologically defined allomorph would have a different alloseme, yet the primary divisions of allosemes might not parallel these allomorphic distinctions. Just as we describe the various allomorphs of the plural suffix in terms of their distribution, so we may describe the various allosemes of out in terms of their distribution. Some of these allosemes are:

1. Exterior to a delimitation: go out of the house, come out to see, look out of the door.

2. Result to a process: turn out (well), outcome.

3. Surpassing degree: to be out-and-out, outright, outwit.

4. Selectivity: to find out the answer, look out for trouble (he'll hit you).

Even these allosemes do not adequately treat all the circumstances, for the semantic function of an expression cannot be described purely in terms of the constituent morphemes. To know the meaning of Look out! in such a context as Look out! He'll hit you! we must consider the morphemes, the construction, the intonation, the voice quality, the linguistic context (that it occurs together with an expression of warning), the particular circumstance in which it is uttered, and the relationship of the persons speaking and hearing. Even when we have added all these factors together, we still do not have all the significance, for this totality of individual items occurs in a configuration which has a meaning of its own. Meanings of recurring complex items are more than the sum total of the parts, for such a combination has its own history and acquires its own set of associations.[3]

Problem 108

Instructions: Describe the allosemes of got in the following expressions.

1. He got caught by the cop.

2. He got a hundred dollars from the State.

3. He got silly before the evening was over.

4. He got him at the railroad station.

5. He got a beating at home.

6. It got him how she could find out so much.

7. He got cold in the hall.

8. He got a thrill.

9. It got him down.

10. He has got to go.

11. He got it in the neck.

In every language there are combinations of morphemes which do not seem to reflect the meaning of the individual morphemes. For example, in Loma the word tineb'ab'ai 'umbrella' is derived from tine 'rain' and b'ab'ai 'group of small thatch shelters.' Of course, it is

---

[3]There is nothing metaphysical about this meaning of the whole. The point is just that configurations and patterns acquire meaning as well as do individual units, and the combinations are not fully explicable in terms of the constituent parts. This is precisely what gives meaning to style, and such complex configurations must be treated as meaningful on the basis of their overall patterns. In the same way that a rain dance among the Hopi Indians has more cultural significance than the sum total of the paraphernalia, the participants, and the movements of the dancers, so constantly recurring conventional groupings of morphemes, whether in words, sentences, or discourses, have meanings which can only be understood in terms of their own environments.

possible to conceive of circumstances which would lead to this type of compound, but it is quite unnecessary to revert to the cultural history. We may set up allosemes for the sememes involved and include in our description (by implication) the fact that this combination has its own corporate semantic value.

In Spanish the pronoun se in se péga 'he hits himself' may be described as the reflexive goal of the action. But in se dise 'it is said' or 'they say' (literally, 'it says itself') the se is obviously not the goal of the action. The phrases se péga and se dise are formally identical, but the meanings of the constructions (wholly apart from the meanings of the verbs) are quite different. Part of this difference may be described by setting up two allosemes for se: (1) a reflexive alloseme with certain verbs and (2) a neutral-voice, indefinite-subject alloseme with other verbs.[4]

In the Zacapoaxtla dialect of Aztec there is an excellent example of allosemic contrast.

Problem 109 (data [restricted] from the Zacapoaxtla dialect of Aztec, a language of Mexico)

Instructions: Identify the morphemes, comparing the forms in Problem 2.

1. nikita   'I see it'   6. kitah   'they see it'

2. tikita   'you (sg.) see it'   7. tikitah   'we see it'

3. tikinita   'you (sg.) see them'   8. nankitah   'you (pl.) see it'

4. nikinita   'I see them'   9. tikinitah   'we see them'

5. kita   'he sees it'   10. kinitah   'they see them'

Supplementary information:

1. The morphemes are as follows: -ita stem of 'to see,' k- third person singular object, kin- third person plural object, ni- first person singular subject, nan- second person plural subject, -h plural subject, and ti- second person singular and first person plural.

2. The third person subject morpheme is zero.

The morpheme ti- indicates both second person singular and first person plural. When there is no plural subject suffix -h, the morpheme ti- means second person singular. When the suffix -h occurs, then the ti- denotes first person. This is, of course, not too much of a contradiction, for in the meaning of 'we' the second person may be included.[5] We may state that ti- has two allosemes: (1) second person singular and (2) first person plural in combination with -h. The distributional contrasts make this type of semantic alternation possible.

In Potawatomi[6] there is a basic distinction between animate and inanimate nouns. The

---

[4]This construction may often be translated in English by the so-called passive construction, and in French by the indefinite subject pronoun on (cf. French on parle français 'French is spoken' and Spanish se habla español 'Spanish is spoken'). These two Spanish constructions, however, do not exhaust all the allosemes of se.

[5]This is, however, true only of the inclusive first person plural, but this Aztec dialect makes no distinction between inclusive and exclusive first person.

[6]See Charles F. Hockett, "Potawatomi II: Derivation, Personal Prefixes, and Nouns," International Journal of American Linguistics, 14 (1948), 2: 69.

plural suffix for animates ends in -k[7] and for inanimates ends in -n.[7] In general, there is very little difficulty in describing these suffixes, for names of people, animals, and spirits are animate and nouns denoting things are inanimate. There are, however, some important exceptions. Though, for example, body parts are generally inanimate, the nouns meaning 'fur,' 'feather,' and 'hip' are animate. Similarly, though names of plants and parts of plants are usually inanimate, the nouns meaning 'log,' 'flat cedar,' 'bean,' and 'blackberry' are animate. There are also certain other exceptions such as 'bluff along a river,' 'big cooking spoon,' 'snow,' 'bucket,' 'ice,' 'bow,' 'kettle,' and 'clay,' which are all animate. We may describe the allosemes of the animate suffix -k as including (1) plural animate objects and (2) certain plural inanimate objects. The second class may be treated as exceptions, or, better, as subdivisions of the sememe of the morpheme. The meaning of -k is based essentially on the environment, and we are obliged to include all of the environment.

Problem 110 (data from a Veracruz dialect of Aztec, a language of Mexico)

Instructions:

a. Compare the forms cited in Problem 42.

b. Define the sememes of the morphemes in the following forms. This may be done by means of one definition to cover all the environments or by the use of allosemes.

1. nikwa·   'I eat'

2. tikwa·   'you (sg.) eat'

3. kwa·   'he eats'

4. nikwah   'we (excl.) eat'

5. tikwah   'we (incl.) eat'

6. aŋkwah   'you (pl.) eat'

7. kwah   'they eat'

8. nikwas   'I will eat'

9. tikwas   'you (sg.) will eat'

10. kwas   'he will eat'

11. nikwaske   'we (excl.) will eat'

12. tikwaske   'we (incl.) will eat'

13. aŋkwaske   'you (pl.) will eat'

14. kwaske   'they will eat'

15. nikwah   'I ate'

16. tikwah   'you (sg.) ate'

17. kwah   'he ate'

18. nikwake   'we (excl.) ate'

19. tikwake   'we (incl.) ate'

20. aŋkwake   'you (pl.) ate'

21. kwake   'they ate'

6.13 Principle 3

Systems of symbolization differ in the way in which they classify phenomena.

Not only are there no synonymns within languages, but no two languages agree completely in the manner in which they classify phenomena. In English, for example, we employ a number of words denoting color, e.g. red, white, blue, yellow, orange, purple, pink, vermilion, green, brown, black, gray, and tan. In Tarahumara there are only five primary words for color: sitákame, uráname, rosákame, siyóname, and čokame. Each of these words covers a much wider segment of the spectrum than any corresponding English term. For example, sitákame includes any bright pink, red, or orange, and uráname applies to the darker reds in the

---

[7]These suffixes have a variety of forms.

direction of brown. Rosákame means 'white,' though this may be a degree of whiteness in comparison with something·else, and čókame similarly denotes 'black, or objects comparatively blacker than something else.' The word siyóname covers 'blue, green, and purple.' Of course, in Tarahumara one may be more explicit about color by saying that some particular object has the same color as another object, but these five primary color words serve for the entire spectrum.

Other languages may make far more distinctions than does English. In Totonac, for example, there are eight basic stems for different varieties of smells, and these occur with a number of suffixal formatives. The principal words, grouped by stems, are as follows:

1. mú·kɫún, a pleasant smell, as of flowers or food

   mú·qšún, the smell of corn mush which has too much lime

   mú·ksún, the smell of mint, parsley, tobacco, Sloan's liniment

   mú·kún, the smell of raw beans and unripe fruit, with a related meaning of a puckery taste

2. púksa, the smell of a skunk, a dead dog, foul meat, manure

   púqša, the smell of mold or mushrooms

   pukɫa, the smell of human excrement and rotten things

3. haksa, the smell of alcohol, camphor, burnt chile, dust just settled by a rain

   haqɫa, the smell of urine, certain medicines, and ashes

   hakša, the smell of citrus fruits, especially the skins

4. cí·kí·n, the smell of perfume, scented soap, sometimes with the definite pejorative implication of a nice smell but in the wrong place, e.g. in speaking of effeminate men who use perfume

5. skunka, the smell of metals, mice, fish, and snakes

   squnqa, the smell of some fish and of dirty feet

   ɫkunka, the smell of grease and fat

6. šqúta, the smell of leather, sweat, an open sore, and walls that have been damp for a long time

   škúta, the smell of anything sour, e.g. vinegar

7. škíha, the smell of savory, tasty food

   šqáha, the smell of burnt gunpowder, firecrackers, and rockets

8. kinkalah, a smell, usually bad, which has permeated an area

Two features about the meanings of this series of Totonac stems are important: (1) the meanings can be defined only in terms of the local environment and (2) the system does not conform to any "logically" definable set of relationships. We may be assured that no other language would have precisely this type of classification, but this failure of agreement between languages does not destroy the validity of the classificatory system used by the

Totonacs. Sets of symbols have no more scientific validity than the styles of hats or the designs in neckties. Any apparent lack of logic in this Totonac series may be matched by the use of she in English to substitute for nouns denoting ships, countries, and institutions. Symbolic systems tend to reflect the relationships of things, but they are never exact, and are frequently quite contradictory.

There are some types of symbolic classification which we expect to find in certain classes of words, but not in others. For example, we frequently discover nouns classified as to form, e.g. round, long, flat, flexible, animate, and inanimate, but we do not expect to find these distinctions indicated in verbs. Some languages, however, do indicate such object-distinctive differences by means of verb forms. In Cherokee[8] these differences are expressed by different verb affixes.

1. ʔáàhhą̂   'it is lying (round object)'

2. čiíyą̂   'it is lying (long object)'

3. ka̧ʔną̂   'it is lying (flexible object)'

4. kàneehą̂   'it is lying (a liquid)'

5. ka̧hnką̂   'he is lying (living object)'

1a. čìʔahsį̂   'I gave ... (round object)'

2a. čiitíìsį̂   'I gave ... (long object)'

3a. čiiną́hsį̂   'I gave ... (flexible object)'

4a. čiinʔą́hsį̂ 'I gave ... (container with liquid contents)'

5a. čiiyáàkʰáàsį̂ 'I gave ... (living being, nonhuman)'

1b. čìkį̂   'I pick up ... (round object)'

2b. čìyą̂   'I pick up ... (long object)'

3b. čìnàkį̂   'I pick up ... (flexible object)'

4b. čineekį̂   'I pick up ... (container with liquid contents)'

5b. čɨ̧ɨnakį̂   'I pick up ... (living being, nonhuman)'

6b. čɨ̧ɨ́nakį̂   'I pick up ... (living being, human)'

Differences in number of the subject or the object may be indicated by the verb stem. For example, Muskogee[9] has some verbs of rather irregular formation which indicate differences of singular, dual, and plural subjects:

---

[8]Mary R. Haas, "Classificatory Verbs in Muskogee," International Journal of American Linguistics, 14 (1948), 4: 244.

[9]Haas, op. cit., p. 245.

Singular	Dual	Plural	
1. litkitá	1a. tukuɬkitá	1b. pifa·tkitá	'to run'
2. ayíta	2a. ahuyitá	2b. api·yitá	'to go'
3. leykitá	3a. ka·kitá	3b. apu·kitá	'to sit'
4. huyɬitá	4a. sihu·kitá	4b. sapaklitá	'to stand'
5. wakkitá	5a. wakhukíta	5b. lumhitá	'to lie'

In other constructions a difference in the number of the object may be indicated by the verb stems:

Singular Objects	Plural Objects	
1. apaykitá	1a. atihitá	'to put ... inside'
2. wakicitá	2a. lumheycitá	'to lay ... down'
3. isíta	3a. cawíta	'to grasp, hold ...'
4. halatitá	4a. halatheycitá	'to take hold of ...'

Navaho[10] also distinguishes certain classes of objects by means of the verb:

1. ʔááɬ[11] 'to handle one round or bulky object'

2. ģééɬ 'to handle a load or pack'

3. kááɬ 'to handle anything in a vessel'

4. lééɬ 'to handle a slender flexible object'

5. ǰoɬ 'to handle noncompact matter (wool)'

6. cos 'to handle a flat flexible object'

7. tɬoh 'to handle mushy matter'

8. ǰih 'to handle plural granular objects'

9. tééɬ 'to handle one animate object'

10. tį́į́ɬ 'to handle a slender stiff object'

11. ʔaɬ 'to eat a hard object'

12. ģaɬ 'to eat meat'

13. kiɬ 'to eat one round object'

---

[10] Robert W. Young and William Morgan, The Navaho Language (Phoenix, Arizona: United States Indian Service, 1943), p. 43.

[11] The stems are listed in the progressive form.

14. c'ah   'to eat mushy matter'

15. čoš   'to eat herbs'

16. ʔał   'to lose or toss a flat flexible object'

17. dił   'to lose or toss a slender flexible object'

18. niił   'to lose or toss a round or bulky object'

The illustrative data which have been cited from Totonac, Tarahumara, Cherokee, Muskogee, and Navaho demonstrate quite adequately the nonconformance of various systems. It is impossible to anticipate the types of semantic distinctions which will be found in any particular language. Such systems of symbols certainly differ as much as the cultures which they reflect, and their meaning can only be ascertained from their environmental distribution.

6.2 The Use of Symbols

Linguistic symbols are used in three different types of situations: (1) immediate, (2) displaced, and (3) transferred. Immediate symbolization occurs when the speaker employs a form in response to some factor in the immediate environment. For example, when a person spies a rat running across the floor and exclaims "Look! There's a rat!" the employment of symbols is in response to an immediate situation. When the same person speaks of his experience the next day, he uses displaced symbols, for the action to which he is referring is not in the immediate environment. The word rat may also be used in a transferred sense, as when someone says, "That gangster is a rat." Determining the meanings of forms occurring in an immediate context is comparatively easy. The meanings of forms in a displaced context demand fuller explanation. Forms used in transferred contexts are very difficult to define, for the subjective features of the environment are vitally important. If we set up immediate, displaced, and transferred contexts as representing three successive stages of symbolism, we may state that the number of allosemes and the degree of difference in allosemes increases proportionately as we pass from one stage to the next.

6.3 Definability of Meaning

Even at best, the meaning of any form is very difficult to define adequately. There are four principal methods employed by dictionaries: (1) the citation of so-called synonyms and antonyms (i.e. words with similar or contrastive meanings), (2) a description of the object or process, (3) indication of a corresponding word or phrase in a foreign language, and (4) the listing of expressions in which the form is employed.

None of these methods are entirely satisfactory, largely because of our insufficient knowledge of many features of the environment which we symbolize. In the meaning of words such as love and hate there are many emotional and cultural factors which we do not understand. We cannot expect to make completely satisfactory definitions of such terms without a great deal of help from other sciences.

Even in defining a word such as boy there are many complications. It would seem simple enough to define boy as an adolescent male homo sapiens, but this definition does not include all the situations in which boy is used, e.g. Boy! (used in addressing a male servant of any age),[12] Oh boy! (an exclamation of delight), and He's a grand old boy (usually applied to a rather old man).

---

[12]This usage is particularly frequent in the Orient and in Africa.

The meanings of bound forms are particularly difficult to describe. Even the meaning of a root such as -ceive (receive, deceive, perceive, conceive) cannot be easily defined. It is difficult to discover any common feature of meaning in all the occurrences of this stem, and even the allosemes are not easily related. Nevertheless, within the area of the phonetic-semantic contrastiveness of this morpheme to all other morphemes we can identify a semantic entity, though we may not be able to define it adequately or accurately.

Nonroots (e.g. -th: truth, growth; en-: enable, empower; and -ment: statement, equipment) are especially difficult to define, since they do not correspond to any features in the nonlinguistic world. In terms of our present techniques for treating such problems of meaning we usually can do little more than make the following types of statements:[13]

-th forms abstract nouns from character and process stems.

en- forms process verbs from character and object stems.

-ment forms concrete nouns from process stems.

These descriptions define the bound form by stating its semantic relationship to the resultant form in contrast with the stem.

The description of any language includes a grammar and a lexicon. The grammar should contain a description of the phonology, the morphology, and the syntax, and the lexicon should contain a description of the sememes of morphemes, the meanings of all constantly recurring combinations of morphemes (including words and phrases), and the meanings of all grammatical sequences. A lexicon would treat such morphemes as apple and sauce in terms of their individual meanings, noting that each morpheme has, among other allosemes, a particular alloseme in the combination applesauce. There would be one aspect of the meaning of applesauce which would not be explicable in terms of the constituent parts. Applesauce as an expression of rejection or contempt (roughly equivalent to bologna and horsefeathers) is a configuration, the meaning of which should be described in terms of the entire unit. In a similar way such expressions as flew the coop, between the devil and the deep blue sea, jeepers creepers, stood her up, and blow me down must be described as units. It would be hopeless to attempt to describe the meaning of the combinations from any set of allosemes. A form such as applesauce would also be described in terms of the meaning of the sequence class to which it, together with such other noun-noun combinations as goldfish, airplane, lampstand, and tabletop, belongs.

6.4 Procedures in Determining the Meanings of Morphemes

Despite the actual and theoretical difficulties involved in describing the meanings of morphemes, we are able, for all practical purposes, to arrive at fairly satisfactory working definitions. To do so, we may employ the following suggested steps in procedure:

1. Collect a number of occurrences of a morpheme. It is quite impossible to arrive at an adequate definition of a morpheme on the basis of two or three occurrences. Of course, one may make some tentative hypotheses about the meaning, but at least eight or ten occurrences should be checked.

2. Note carefully the context of the morpheme in each occurrence. The context includes the practical and the linguistic environment.

3. Attempt to find some striking minimal contrast or similarity in relation to this morpheme. This procedure was employed frequently in Chapter 2.

---

[13]These statements are only partly accurate.

4. Make some hypothesis as to meaning on the basis of one or more such contrasts or similarities.

5. Check all the forms, to confirm or destroy the hypothesis.

6. If the hypothesis proves correct in all the forms examined, the procedure is finished, but if the hypothesis is not correct, then

   a. Modify the hypothesis to include the contradictory data or

   b. Begin again with other contrasts or similarities and frame other hypotheses, testing them in all the data.

Problem 111 (data from the Sierra dialect of Zapotec, a language of Mexico)

Instructions:

   a. Identify the derivational morpheme which is common to most of the following words.

   b. Describe its meaning.

1. zu bici	'dry earth'	6. skalaciza?	'I want'
2. udibiciza?	'I am dry'	7. slalaciza?	'I am mad'
3. ibicilaciza?	'I am thirsty'	8. edalaciza?	'I remember'
4. rulabaza'	'I count'	9. ekalaciza?	'I am well'
5. rulabalaciza?	'I think, wonder'	10. edakalaciza?	'I am content'

Supplementary information:

   1. The suffix -za? indicates a first person singular subject.

   2. Tones are not written.

Discussion of Problem 111:

   The form which is common to most of the words is -laci-. If we follow the suggested steps in procedure, we will (1) note carefully all the words which contain this form, (2) attempt to find some striking contrasts or similarities in relation to this form, (3) frame a hypothesis, and (4) test the hypothesis with the other forms. We find a contrast in forms 2 and 3, and we might assume that the difference here is one of desire. Form 2 seems to indicate only a condition, whereas form 3 adds a possible desiderative aspect. This interpretation would apply very satisfactorily in form 6 skalaciza? 'I want,' but it does not seem to be supported by the differences in forms 4 and 5. In the rest of the words there is only a very remote connection to it.

   Since our initial hypothesis has not proved satisfactory, we should look for some other contrast. Forms 4 and 5 provide some basis for a contrast, and we could assume that the difference is one of continued mental activity vs. noncontinued activity. This, however, does not seem to be substantiated by the other words. But if we check forms 2 and 4 against the rest (except, of course, form 1) we do find some persistent contrast between emotional and nonemotional psychological response or activity. The action of 'counting' and the state of 'being dry' have no emotional content, but 'being thirsty' and 'thinking, wondering' do have such a content. Pending further corroboration by other forms we may assume that this meaning gives us some clue to the value of the morpheme -laci-.[14]

There is also an interesting connection between forms 8, 9, and 10, for the form edakalaciza? 'I am content' includes the morphemes meaning 'to remember,' and 'to be well,' and -laci-.

Problem 112 (data from Huichol, a language of Mexico)

Instructions:

    a. Identify the morphemes.

    b. Define the meanings.

1. nepinaneni   'I will buy it'

2. pepinaneni   'you (sg.) will buy it'

3. pe?enaneni   'you (sg.) will buy'

4. pepinanenike   'you (sg.) are about to buy it'

5. pinanenikekai   'he was going to buy it'

6. neptinaneni   'I will buy them'

7. zəka tinaneni   'if he buys them'

8. petinaneme   'after you (sg.) buy it, [you (sg.) ...]'

9. neptikwani   'I will eat them'

10. tepinaneni   'we will buy it'

11. te?inaneyu   'after we buy it, (I, you, he, they ...)'

Supplementary information:

    1. The third person singular subject is indicated by a zero prefix.

    2. The prefixal modal morpheme has the allomorphs p- ~ pe-.

Problem 113 (data from Mazatec, a language of Mexico)

Instructions:

    a. Identify as many morphemes as possible.

    b. Define the meanings.

1. šó?yá   'rose'   4. nā?yác?i̧   'stinger'

2. ší?yá   'flea'   5. ntīc?i̧   'tail'

3. nā?yá   'thorn'

---

[14]Further investigation in the language does substantiate this conclusion.

Supplementary information: There is a morpheme -ʔyá occurring in forms 1-4.

Problem 114 (data from Mazatec, a language of Mexico)

Instructions:

a. Identify as many morphemes as possible.

b. Define the meaning of the morpheme -hį̀ ~ -hį̄.

1. čāhį̄   'to forget'

2. čā   'to be missing'

3. thį́hį̀   'to remember'

4. thį́   'to have'

5. thį́hį̀kǫ̀ą̀   'I agree'

6. vìthòhį̄ą̀   'I go out from among'

7. vìthòà   'I go out'

8. sʔèhį̀kǫ̀ą̀   'I memorize'

9. fáʔà   'I pass'

10. fáʔàsʔę̄   'I go in'

11. fáʔàsʔęhį̄ą̀   'I go in among'

12. fáʔàhį̄ą̀   'I choose'

6.5 The Labeling of Morphemes

Definition of the meaning of morphemes belongs properly to the lexicon, but in the grammatical description of a language there is a certain amount of meaning indicated by the process of labeling morphemes. In the actual analysis of a language we first identify the morphemes, and then label them. This is to enable us to refer to them quickly and accurately. The labeling can be done in a number of different ways, but there are three principal methods: (1) by applying descriptive names, (2) by identifying the form, and (3) by using arbitrary symbols.

Descriptive names are drawn from (a) the meaning of the form, e.g. singular, plural, agentive, past tense, locative, instrumental, or (b) its relationship to other forms, e.g. subject, object, attributive, nuclear, first order, second order, peripheral. These names are valuable, for they may identify categories and structural features at the same time. They do, however, have two principal drawbacks: (1) the same words have different meanings in different languages (no two languages are identical in any part) and the reader may make the mistake of assuming structural similarities where they do not exist, and (2) there are not enough of these terms to cover all the features of a language accurately.

The second type of label consists of a formal identification. For example, the Spanish stems in Problem 99 were identified as A-stems, E-stems, and I-stems, because the characteristic vowels in the infinitive forms were a, e, and i. Similarly, the so-called present participle in English may be termed the -ing verbal and certain plurals may be called -s plurals. In Bantu the classes of nouns are referred to by such names as "the mu- ba- class," "the zero ma- class," and "the ci- vi- class" (see Problem 102).

The third type of label is an arbitrarily chosen symbol. These symbols are generally A, B, C; a, b, c; 1, 2, 3; or I, II, III, and so on. To these may be added superscript and subscript numerals and letters to indicate subclasses. Such symbols may be combined in a number of ways. Certain of these systems will be treated more extensively in Chapter 8.

It is possible to write an entire grammar employing only the last type of label, but though the statements are quite concise they are frequently very difficult to follow and the objectivity gained by arbitrary symbolization may not prove such an asset as it is reputed to be. Sometimes symbols of this sort fail to make fully evident many of the significant features of the language. For the most part, linguists employ all types of labels, using the first type for the larger classes of forms and the second and third types for those classes which are not so economically treated by the more easily remembered and understood symbols.

6.6 Grammatical Categories Expressed by Bound Forms

There are many grammatical categories which may be indicated by bound forms, e.g. tense, person, number, voice, mode. It is quite impossible to predict which part of speech will distinguish any particular category. For example, we normally expect tense indicators to be a part of the verb if they occur as bound forms, but in Hupa, a language of Northern California, tense may be indicated by nouns:[15]

xonta   'house now existing'

xontaneen   'house formerly existing, i.e. in ruins'

xontate   'house that will exist, i.e. not yet built'

The following list of categories is not complete, but it will provide some basis for understanding the range of meanings indicated by various grammatical forms. It may also serve as a set of convenient labels, if the corresponding grammatical forms are found in any language. One is not bound, of course, to employ the more or less technical terms given here. Any unambiguous terms are adequate, but these names have a certain conventional usage in descriptions of grammatical structure.

Some of the categories listed below are illustrated, either by references to previously cited data or by translations. For example, in describing the category of tense the English expressions 'had gone' and 'have gone' are used. This specific contrast between perfect and pluperfect is indicated in English by verb phrases, but in other languages it may be indicated by a bound form attached to the verb. It must be understood that in the following list the categories refer to the use of bound forms in various languages, even though the illustrations may be translation equivalents which are phrases.

1. Possession, e.g. Popoluca (Problem 28) ʔimo·ya 'his flower' (< ʔi- 'his,' mo·ya 'flower').

2. Tangibility, a contrast between objects which are touchable and those which are not.

3. Identification, a contrast between items which have been previously identified by the context and those which have not.

4. Definite vs. indefinite, e.g. Loma (Problem 103) bálá 'a bracelet' and báláí 'the bracelet.'

5. Proper vs. common, e.g. John, which normally occurs without a proclitic determiner in English, and boy, which normally occurs with some determiner: the boy, a boy, this boy.[16]

6. Number, e.g. English boys, oxen, alumni. Some languages distinguish singular, dual, and plural, and a few indicate singular, dual, trial, and plural. Number is frequently denoted in nouns, verbs, pronouns, and attributives.

---

[15]Robert A. Hall, Jr., Leave Your Language Alone (Ithaca: Cornell University, 1948), p. 154.

[16]This category in English is syntactically pertinent, but is indicated morphologically in many languages.

7. <u>Location</u>, e.g. Huichol <u>nepeinanai</u> 'I bought it in another place' (<u>ne-</u> 'I,' <u>p-</u> 'indicative mode,' <u>e-</u> 'action in another place,' <u>i-</u> 'third person object,' <u>-nanai</u> stem used in completive aspect). Languages may distinguish a position near the speaker (Spanish <u>éste</u> 'this'), near the hearer (Spanish <u>ése</u> 'that'), and away from either (Spanish <u>akél</u> 'that').

8. <u>Size</u>, e.g. Spanish <u>péřo</u> 'dog' vs. <u>peříto</u> 'little dog' and <u>níño</u> 'child' vs. <u>niñíto</u> 'little child.'

9. <u>Value</u>, a contrast between more valuable (i.e. socially honored) and less valuable objects or action. For example, the honorifics in Aztec[17] distinguish degrees of social value, e.g. <u>moma</u> 'your hand,' <u>moma·ci·</u> 'your honorable hand,' <u>moma·wa</u> 'your hands' and <u>moma·cici·wa</u> 'your honorable hands,' <u>koči</u> 'he sleeps' and <u>kočiwa</u> 'he (the honored one) sleeps.'[18]

10. <u>Causation</u>, classified as (a) <u>agentive</u>, if an animate object performs the action, e.g. English <u>dancer</u>, <u>painter</u>, <u>worker</u>, or (b) <u>instrumental</u>, if an inanimate object is responsible.

11. <u>Shape</u>. Nouns may be classified as to shape, e.g. long and slender, flat and round, angular,[19] and so on, and verbs may identify the different shapes of their so-called objects, e.g. Navaho verbs (section 6.13).

12. <u>Animateness</u>, e.g. Potawatomi nouns (section 6.12).

13. <u>Gender</u>, e.g. German masculine <u>der</u> 'the,' feminine <u>die</u>, and neuter <u>das</u>.

14. <u>Grammatical relationships</u>, e.g. Greek nominative (subject) /hippos/ 'horse,' genitive /hippou/ 'of a horse,' dative /hippo·i/ 'to a horse,' accusative (object) /hippon/ 'horse,' vocative (calling form) /hippe/ 'horse!' and Eskimo <u>avku</u> absolute or accusative 'the ones in the north' and <u>avkua</u> relative or nominative. Verbs may indicate grammatical relationships by forms which denote that one verb is subordinate to another verb. This occurs in Comanche.

15. <u>Tense</u>, e.g. Hupa nouns (see section 6.6), English <u>run</u>, <u>ran</u>; <u>walk</u>, <u>walked</u>. Tense is frequently divided into three primary classes: past, present, and future. Past tense may be divided into remote past, regular past, and near past (e.g. in many Bantu languages), and future time may be divided into near future, regular future, and remote future (e.g. in many Bantu languages). Relative tenses define time in terms of other times, e.g. perfect (past action in relationship to the present) 'have gone,' pluperfect (prior action in relationship to the past) 'had gone,' future perfect (prior action in relationship to the future). Tenses may be very closely associated with aspects.

16. <u>Aspect</u> (the kind of action):[20]

a. Punctiliar, action considered as a single temporal unit.

b. Momentaneous, action covering a short period of time.

---

[17]See Richard S. Pittman, "Nahuatl Honorifics," <u>International Journal of American Linguistics</u>, 14 (1948) 4: 236-39.

[18]The plural morpheme <u>-wa</u> and the honorific <u>-wa</u> are different morphemes.

[19]Such classifications occur in Tarascan, a language of Mexico.

[20]Aspect may also identify a type of process, a quality, or a state.

c. Continuative, action which continues.

d. Repetitive, repeated action.

e. Frequentative, action repeated frequently.

f. Habituative, a habitual action.

g. Customary, a customary action.

h. Simulfactive, an action occurring all at the same time.

i. Inchoative (or inceptive), an action beginning.

j. Cessative, an action ceasing.

k. Completive (or perfective), an action which is complete.

l. Incompletive (or imperfective), an action which is not complete.

m. Augmentative, an action increasing in volume.

n. Diminutive, an action decreasing in volume.

17. Voice (the relationship of the participants to the action):

a. Active. The subject performs the action, e.g. 'he went.'

b. Passive. The subject is the goal of the action, e.g. 'he was hit.'

c. Reflexive. The subject acts upon himself, e.g. 'he hit himself.'

d. Reciprocal. A plural subject acts reciprocally, e.g. 'they hit each other.'

e. Transitive. The action carries over to a goal, e.g. 'he hit the man.'

f. Intransitive. The action does not carry over to a goal, e.g. 'he hit.'

g. Causative. The actor causes an action, e.g. 'he caused him to go.'

h. Middle. The actor acts to or for himself.

i. Benefactive. The actor acts for the benefit of someone, e.g. Zoque suffix -hay in kyenhayu 'he looked for him.'

j. Impersonal. The subject is impersonal, e.g. 'it's raining.'

18. Mode (the psychological atmosphere of an action as interpreted by the speaker):

a. Indicative (or declarative), indicating a more or less neutral, objective attitude.

b. Narrative, indicating that one is relating past events.

c. Optative, indicating hope.

d. Desiderative, indicating desire.

e. Intentive, indicating intention.

f. Interrogative, indicating a question.

g. Negative.

h. Quotative, indicating that someone other than the speaker is originally responsible for the statement.

i. Dubitative, indicating doubt.

j. Potential, indicating that something may not exist at the time but that it might exist at some other time.

k. Conditional, indicating that an action is conditioned in its occurrence.

l. Subjunctive, indicating some contingent character of an action.

m. Obligatory, indicating obligation.

n. Imperative, indicating a command, e.g. 'Go!'

o. Permissive, indicating a permission granted.

19. Persons:

a. First person, relating to the speaker.

b. First person inclusive, relating to the speaker and the hearer.

c. First person exclusive, relating to the speaker and others, but specifically excluding the hearer.

d. Second person, relating to the hearer.

e. Third person, relating to someone spoken about.

f. Fourth person, relating to a second third person.[21]

20. Movement, e.g. Kekchi tolinbanu 'I will do it, coming from elsewhere' and tošinbanu 'I will do it, going elsewhere.'

Problem 115 (data from the Zacapoaxtla dialect of Aztec, a language of Mexico)

Instructions:

a. Identify the morphemes.

b. Assign meanings to the morphemes.

c. Classify the morphemes by categories.

---

[21]In translating the English expression the man struck John, but he hit him back, a language having both third- and fourth-person forms would employ a fourth person as an equivalent of he and a third person for him, since he is a substitute for John, the second third person introduced into the context.

1. ničoka   'I am crying'

2. ničokaya   'I was crying'

3. ničokas   'I will cry'

4. ničokak   'I cried'

5. ničokaka   'I had cried'

6. ničokani   '(if) I had cried'

7. ničokati   'I am going out to cry'

8. ničokato   'I went out to cry'

9. ničokaki   'I am coming in to cry'

10. ničokako   'I came in to cry'

11. ničokaskia   'I would cry'

12. ničokatok   'I keep crying'

13. ničokatos   'I will keep crying'

14. ničokatoskia   'I would keep crying'

15. ničokatoya   'I kept crying'

16. ničokatoni   '(if) I had kept crying'

17. ničokatoti   'I am going out and keep crying'

18. čoka   'he is crying'

19. čokah   'they are crying'

20. čokayah   'they were crying'

21. čokaya   'he was crying'

22. tičokaka   'you had cried'

23. čokaka   'he had cried'

24. tičokakah   'we had cried'

25. nančokakah   'you all had cried'

26. čokakah   'they had cried'

27. ničokatoya   'I kept crying'

28. tičokatoya   'you kept crying'

29. čokatoya   'she kept crying'

30. tičokatoyah   'we kept crying'

31. nančokatoyah   'you all kept crying'

32. čokatoyah   'they all kept crying'

33. tičokaskia   'ycu would cry'

34. čokaskia   'it would cry'

35. tičokaskiah   'we would cry'

36. nančokaskiah   'you all would cry'

37. čokaskiah   'they would cry'

38. tičokatok   'you keep crying'

39. čokatok   'she keeps crying'

40. tičokati   'you are going out to cry'

41. čokati   'she is going out to cry'

42. tičokatih   'we are going out to cry'

43. nančokatih   'you all are going out to cry'

44. čokatih   'they are going to cry'

45. tičokakih   'we are coming to cry'

46. tičokaki   'you are coming to cry'

47. čokaki   'she is coming to cry'

48. čokakih   'they are coming to cry'

49. tičokako   'you came to cry'

50. čokako   'she came to cry'

51. čokakoh   'they came to cry'

52. tičokakoh   'we came to cry'

53. nančokakoh   'you all came to cry'

54. tičokatoti   'you are going to keep crying'

55. čokatoti   'he is going to keep crying'

56. tičokatotih   'we are going to keep crying'

57. nančokatotih   'you all are going to keep crying'

58. čokani   '(if) he had cried'

(Continued on next page.)

59. čokatotih   'they are going to keep crying'

60. tičokani   '(if) you had cried'

61. tičokanih   '(if) we had cried'

62. nančokanih   '(if) you all had cried'

63. čokanih   '(if) they had cried'

64. tičokatos   'you will keep crying'

65. čokatos   'he will keep crying'

66. tičoka   'you are crying'

67. tičokah   'we are crying'

68. nančokah   'you all are crying'

69. tičokato   'you went out to cry'

70. čokato   'she went out to cry'

71. tičokatoh   'we went out to cry'

72. nančokatoh   'you all went out to cry'

73. čokatoh   'they went out to cry'

74. tičokas   'you will cry'

75. čokas   'he will cry'

76. tičokaya   'you were crying'

77. tičokayah   'we were crying'

78. nančokayah   'you all were crying'

79. tičokatoskiah   'we would keep crying'

80. nančokatoskiah   'you all would keep crying'

81. čokatiw   'he is going out to cry later'

82. čokakiw   'he is coming in to cry later'

Problem 116 (data from Zoque, a language of Mexico)

Instructions:

   a. Identify the morphemes.

   b. Assign meanings to the morphemes.

   c. Classify the morphemes by categories.

1. kenu   'he looked'

2. kenpa   'he looks, he will look'

3. kyenhayu   'he looked for him (i.e. on his behalf)'

4. kyenhapya   'he looks for him'

5. yahkenu   'he made him look'

6. keñahu   'they looked'

7. kyenhayahu   'they look for (on behalf of) him'

8. kyenhayto?yu   'he wanted to look on his behalf'

9. kento?yu   'he wanted to look'

10. kento?pya   'he wants to look'

11. kente?u   'he was going to look (but did not)'

12. kyenu   'he saw it'

(Continued on next page.)

13. kyenpa   'he sees it'

14. kyenhapya   'he sees it for him'

15. kyenhayṭoʔyu   'he wanted to see it for him'

16. keñahtəʔu   'they were going to look (but did not)'

17. kenkeʔtpa   'he is going to look too'

18. kenkeʔtu   'he looked again'

19. kyenhakyeʔtu   'he looked again for him'

20. kyenhayahtəʔkeʔtu   'they also were going to look on his behalf'

21. kenkeʔtpa   'he looks again'

22. kenkeʔtutih   'he looked again'

23. kenutih   'he just looked'

24. kyenhayutih   'he just looked on his behalf (did nothing else)'

25. yahkenatəhu   'he had someone look'

26. yahkenatəhyahu   'they had someone look'

27. nakyenatəhyahu   'they looked at each other'

28. nakyenatəhyahkeʔtutih   'they looked at each other again'

29. hakyena   'he did not look'

30. hakyenatih   'he just did not look'

31. hakyenkeʔtatih   'he did not look again; he did not look either'

32. kenwaʔa   'he already looked'

33. kenpaʔa   'he already looks'

34. keñahwaʔa   'they already looked'

35. kenkeʔtwaʔa   'he already looked again'

36. kenuʔk   'when he looked'

37. kenuʔka   'already when he looked'

38. keñahpaʔka   'already when they looked'

39. keñahpaməy   'where they looked'

40. kenušeh   'the way he looked'

41. kenpamah   'he still looks'

(Continued on next page.)

42. kenpahsə^ʔŋ   'perhaps he looks'

43. kyenhayahtə^ʔke^ʔtušehtih   'the way they were just going to look again on his behalf'

44. kyenu^ʔk   'when he saw it'

45. keñahke^ʔtuhsə^ʔŋ   'perhaps they also looked'

46. kenuha   'did he look?'

47. hakyenamah   'he did not still look'

48. hakyena^ʔa   'he no longer looked'

49. hakyenahsə^ʔŋtih   'perhaps he just did not look'

50. hakyenatih   'he has not looked yet'

51. kenhawya^ʔa   'he already looked on his behalf'

52. kenhakye^ʔtwa^ʔa   'he already looked again on his behalf'

53. kenpamaha   'does he still look?'

54. yahkenatəhyahtə^ʔutih   'they were just going to have someone look'

55. kyenwa^ʔa   'he already saw it'

56. kyenušeh   'the way he looked at it'

57. kyenke^ʔtpatih   'he looked at it again'

58. ke^ʔnaŋhehu   'he left off looking'

59. kye^ʔnaŋhehpa   'he leaves off looking at it'

60. kye^ʔnaŋhehwa^ʔa   'he already left off looking at it'

61. kye^ʔnaŋhehyahke^ʔtutih   'they again left off looking at it'

62. keñahṭo^ʔyu   'they wanted to look'

63. kenwa^ʔhsə^ʔŋ   'perhaps he already looked'

64. kenke^ʔtwa^ʔšeh   'the way he already looked again'

65. kyenuhsə^ʔŋmah   'perhaps he is still looking'

66. kyenke^ʔtwa^ʔtih   'he already looked at it again'

67. yahkenhayahke^ʔtu^ʔka   'already when they also caused him to look on his behalf'

68. keñahke^ʔtušehtih   'the way they looked again'

69. kyenke^ʔtpatiha   'will he look at it again?'

Supplementary information:

1. The morpheme y-, which metathesizes with the initial consonant of the stem, indicates a third person subject in transitive verb forms.

2. The suffix -a occurs instead of -u or -pa when the negative ha- is prefixed.

3. The perfective suffix (translated 'already') occurs in the forms -aʔa ∞ -ʔa ∞ -a.

6.7 The Meaning of Grammatical Sequences

Not only morphemes, but the grammatical arrangements of morphemes, also, have meaning. We are not discussing here the meaning of any particular sequence such as applesauce, but rather the meaning of the sequence class to which such forms as goldfish, tent-post, apple-sauce, and ax-handle belong. Such combinations of noun-plus-noun do have a meaning, which may be defined as A (the first noun) modifies B (the second noun). We could also state that B (the roots fish, post, sauce, and handle) are delimited in semantic area by A (the roots gold, tent, apple, and ax). Note that in Tzeltal the combinations of noun-plus-noun have exactly the opposite direction of attribution: tomut 'egg' (< ton 'stone' + mut 'hen') and ničk'ahk' 'spark' (< nič 'flower' + k'ahk' 'fire').

The meaning of grammatical sequences is far more important in the syntactic than in the morphological analysis. In the syntax the constituent elements have much greater freedom of occurrence, and hence we can contrast these positions. In the morphology the relation-ships are more or less fixed, and the lack of contrastive occurrences makes it difficult, if not impossible, to define adequately the grammatical meaning of the sequences. These complications do not mean, however, that morphological sequence classes consisting of bound forms have no grammatical meaning. It is only that the statement of such meanings is dif-ficult and for all practical purposes is usually unnecessary. On the other hand, when free forms are involved in morphological constructions, there are frequently important distinc-tions which are discoverable by checking the contrasts in the meanings of the sequences. For example, pickpocket, breakwater, cutthroat, playground, driveway, and gocart all consist of verb-plus-noun combinations. The immediate constituents belong to the same word classes, but the meanings of these grammatical arrangements are different. The first three pick-pocket, breakwater, and cutthroat constitute an action-goal relationship and playground, driveway, and gocart have an action—related-object meaning, i.e. a playground is 'a ground for playing,' a driveway is 'a way for driving,' and a gocart is 'a cart for going.'

There are a number of types of morphological constructions involving bound forms in which some meaning may be assigned to the sequence. For example, in Kekchi the subject-verb sequences (see Problem 37) šinkam 'I died' and šatkam 'you (sg.) died' contrast in meaning with the verb-subject sequences yašin 'I am sick' and yašat 'you (sg.) are sick.' The grammatical meaning of the subject-verb sequence is 'A indicates the subject of the action B' and the meaning of the verb-subject sequence is 'A indicates the state of the subject B.'

In the series ability, truth, and kindness we may state that 'B (the suffixes -ity, -th, and -ness) substantivizes the quality A.' This type of statement is, however, very little different from a description of the resultant noun word class as being derived from adjectives plus nominalizers. The fact that -ity, -th, and -ness are extremely restricted in distribution means that we have very little contrast to enable us to define the partic-ular semantic value of the grammatical sequence.

There is a definite parallelism between the subdivisions of structure and meaning. On the structural level we recognize allomorphs, morphemes, and grammatical sequences; on the semantic level we recognize allosemes, sememes, and episememes.[22] The episememes are the meanings of the grammatical sequences.

---

[22]See Bloomfield, op. cit., p. 166.

CHAPTER 7

FIELD PROCEDURES

Actual work in the field differs greatly from the analysis of nicely formulated problems. The paradigms which are cited in the previous chapters are not easily obtained from the informant, and psychological and cultural difficulties often beset him. To utter words out of their natural context may seem foolish and meaningless to him, and he may grasp their significance only with great effort. Furthermore, he may be under accusation by fellow tribesmen of betraying the linguistic secrets of the tribe.

Added to these practical complications is the fact that linguistic data cannot be neatly divided into phonological, morphological, and syntactic sections, each to be treated in turn after the preceding one has been fully analyzed. The linguist must, in a sense, operate a three-ring circus, and at the same time try to ascertain the meaning of all the contrasts in all these aspects of the language.

Proper field procedure is absolutely essential to any adequate analysis or description of a language, but frequently it is the most neglected aspect of the linguist's training. Too much is taken for granted, and the beginner fumbles needlessly because of lack of experience. He should have some understanding of the various approaches to collecting data, of the most successful ways of handling informants, and of the methods by which the field procedure may most advantageously supplement the analytical processes.

There are two principal methods of approach to the acquisition of language data: (1) the monolingual, in which there is no intermediate language used by the investigator and the informant, and (2) the bilingual, in which there is some intermediate language (or languages). The monolingual approach requires very special initial techniques, but as soon as the investigator can receive explanations of forms within the native language, then the two approaches coincide.

7.1 Monolingual Approach

Many missionaries and explorers have used the monolingual approach in learning the language of isolated peoples. Even today in some areas this method is required, since none of the members of a society may know any language known to the linguistic investigator.[1] Usually, however, some member of the society knows another language (at least in part), and by means of several informants one may learn a few words or phrases which will facilitate the initial contacts.

For a strictly monolingual situation, the following steps in procedure are recommended:[2]

1. Approach with a smile. A genuine smile has practically the same meaning in all cultures.

---

[1]Of course, there are instances in which investigators must work through more than one intermediate language, by means of several informants. This procedure is essentially a "bilingual" approach.

[2]These suggestions result from the experience of missionaries and the experiments of the writer and his colleagues of the Summer Institute of Linguistics.

2. Talk. It is essential to speak (English, French, Spanish, or anything). This lets the natives know that you want to communicate.[3]

3. Act out friendly gestures. The investigator should extend the hand or hands, meanwhile watching native actions carefully, so as to conform to them. For example, if the natives[4] offer to snap fingers (the practice of the Uduks near the Ethiopian border), the investigator must do the same. If they seize the thumb rather than the hand, he must do likewise.

4. Readily smile or laugh at your own mistakes. This will at least prevent misunderstanding arising from unwitting offense because of improper conduct. A smiling, cheerful manner is the best means of guaranteeing that you will not be suspected of bad motives.

5. Show interest in native objects. You should notice various things about the native dress and homes, and indicate admiration, but not covetousness.

6. Exhibit an equal interest in displaying your own possessions to the natives. Attempt to talk about these objects, even though you know that the people understand nothing of what you say.

7. Ask for the name of some object,[5] using appropriate gestures.[6] The natives will usually guess what is wanted and will reply with something.

8. Repeat this procedure for several objects. If you get the the same response each time, the likelihood is that the natives are commenting about your request. It is reported that in one instance the natives were giving the name of the finger with which the investigator was pointing. He should have stuck out his lower lip toward the objects.

9. If different responses are given for each object, then go back to them in a different order and repeat the words, noting carefully the natives' reaction. If the natives are at all friendly toward you, they will probably be delighted and amazed by this use of their words.

10. Continue to ask for the names of objects.

11. In order to pick up the phrase 'What is that?' pay very careful attention to natives speaking to one another about your paraphernalia. Once this phrase has been obtained, the process of word acquisition can be speeded up considerably.

12. Write down the words in a notebook. In doing this in a society which is not likely to know anything about writing, the investigator should be careful to show the natives precisely what he is doing, as any attempt to be secretive may be gravely

---

[3]There is, of course, also the possibility that the natives may catch on more quickly than the investigator.

[4]It must be understood that "native" is not employed here with any pejorative connotation. It is simply a convenient term to designate a native speaker of any language, regardless of the degree of complexity of the culture.

[5]Be sure to avoid the impression of asking for the names of people, for the knowledge of personal names is often guarded out of fear that they may be used in black magic.

[6]The investigator must attempt to employ the proper gestures. This he can usually do by carefully noting the behavior of the people. The gesture of pointing is accomplished in various ways, e.g. with the chin, the lower lip, the elbow, or a nod of the head.

misunderstood. After writing down a list of words, he should point to each word in turn (while the natives look on), pronounce it, and then identify the object. Complete openness about this writing procedure will alleviate possible suspicion and may indirectly enhance the investigator's prestige.

13. Use care in selecting words to be elicited. Certain types of words should be avoided at first: (1) names of people, (2) names of body parts, and (3) names of what may be religious objects, e.g. sacrifices, shrines, amulets, and fetishes.

14. Act out processes. For example, the investigator may walk around, and talk about himself, attempting to get some response from the natives to describe his action. All the time he must be alert to hear native comment about his activity and to apply it to himself, and if possible to someone else doing the same thing nearby. If the form selected is correct, there will inevitably be an assent on the part of the natives.

15. While acting out a process, attempt to catch the native phrase 'What is he doing?' This phrase may then be applied to someone performing some other type of action nearby.

16. Mimic other processes, e.g. jumping, running, eating, sleeping, and drinking.

17. Attempt, in good humor and fun, to get some native to participate in a mimic performance with you. If you succeed, try to talk to him about the action performed by the two of you. By this means the pronouns 'I' and 'you' will probably be elicited. By getting another person to act and by speaking about him to the first participant, the forms of 'he' may be elicited.

18. Try all the verbs with possible forms of 'I,' 'you,' and 'he.' The chances are that there will be a number of mistakes in forms uttered by an investigator, but the people will usually understand what is wanted and correct him.

19. Write down everything, together with possible meanings.

20. Analyze these forms as soon as you can, so as to isolate the morphemes.

21. Memorize everything, even if it appears to be wrong. The ability of the investigator to reproduce what he has heard on previous occasions is the best means of guaranteeing that the natives will be willing to continue helping him. Nothing stimulates a teacher like a smart student.

22. Enjoy being laughed at. The investigator's mistakes may provide a great deal of merriment for the native speakers, and his willingness to entertain others at his own expense may prove to be his greatest social asset.

23. Remain, if possible, in a place where you may hear the language constantly. It is very desirable to live in the village, even though this means a fish-bowl type of existence.

24. Use the language on every opportunity and repeatedly. This is particularly necessary during the first few days, for once the novelty of the experience wears off for the natives and they take the stranger as a matter of course, they may be much less willing to assist him in learning the language.

25. Listen to the language on every possible occasion. Though the native speech may mean absolutely nothing at first, you will gradually pick up recurring expressions. Listening is the all-important part of language learning which some people neglect.

The monolingual approach quickly becomes identical with the bilingual one, and hence we shall not describe the procedure in full under each type. Since the bilingual situation is the more common, the further developments of the field procedure will be treated in relation to it.

7.2 Bilingual Approach

There are three principal phases of the bilingual approach: (1) the nature of the data, (2) the methods of recording the data, and (3) the informant. During the discussion of the first two phases we must take for granted an average informant, who knows something of an intermediate language, though this knowledge may be, and frequently is, limited to a trade usage. For example, if he is an Indian in Latin America he may know some Spanish or Portuguese, but we cannot expect him to explain fine distinctions of tense or aspect in his own language or to provide equivalents for the numerous tense forms in Spanish or Portuguese. He probably does not use more than three or four tenses in the language foreign to him, maybe only one mode, and even these do not have any one-to-one correspondence with forms in his own language. These practical limitations must always be considered in a realistic field procedure.

7.21 The Data

There are six increasingly complex types of data which the investigator attempts to obtain: (1) simple object words, (2) object words in possible morphological categories, (3) simple process words, (4) process words in possible morphological categories, (5) object and process words in combinations, and (6) texts. The first five types of data are elicited from informants by direct questions, such as "How do you say 'so-and-so'?" The last type of data consists of expressions given in more or less normal contexts.

7.21.1 Simple Object Words

The investigator attempts at first to obtain the names of objects. These should be concrete things to which one may point, e.g. houses, trees, grass, sun, clouds, dogs, sticks. The names of such objects are generally as short as any nounlike words, but some compounds may be conspicuous exceptions. Long terms may be set aside for analysis after one has learned more of the language structure.

The investigator should ask at any one time for words with related semantic areas. For example, names of body parts, articles of clothing, objects about the house, industries, fauna, and flora should be asked for in their appropriate groupings, rather than jumbled in such sequences as 'head, pants, pot, plow.' Semantic grouping makes it easier for the informant, and morphological characteristics often parallel such semantic subdivisions.

It is absolutely essential that the words elicited be culturally pertinent. There is no point in asking for 'plow' in the rocky terrain of Yucatan, where people employ only a dibble stick. Where natives use grinding stones, one should ask for the term for these; there is no value in trying to obtain the names for mortar and pestle, if these utensils are unknown. Various peoples' manufactured articles, their relationships to one another, their domesticated animals, and the flora and fauna of the areas in which they live differ so greatly that one must be constantly aware of the local factors. This means that no list of words will be universally applicable, and hence that the investigator must make up his own list, preferably in advance of working with the informant.

One should exclude minute semantic subdivisions in the initial investigation. For example, in eliciting names of body parts one should not attempt to get further different words for the extremities than 'arm, hand, finger, leg, foot, toe.' Even in regard to these simple body parts, languages may not make the same distinctions, and a single native term may be used for arm and hand or hand and finger. To ask for such distinctions as 'upper arm, lower arm, elbow, thumb, palm, wrist, thigh, calf, knee, ankle, instep' may prove very confusing. Even though a language may make some of these distinctions, many of them will not correspond exactly, and the informant is not likely to know these less familiar terms in the intermediate language.

One must avoid terms possibly taboo, and in questioning the informant any sign of embarrassment about a particular question should be immediately passed over by asking for some other word.

The following groupings of words may provide some basis for selecting similar types of words for a particular culture:

A. Body parts: 'head, hair of the head, nose, eye, ear, neck, arm, hand, finger, stomach, heart, leg, foot, toe, bone, blood, flesh.'

B. Clothing: 'hat, shirt, pants, sandals, beads, face paint, body paint.'

C. Objects about the house: 'knife, spoon, ladle, water container, animal skin, bed, hammock, fire, mush, bread, flour, meal, grinding stone, mortar, pestle, bananas, oranges, meat.'

D. Relationships between people: 'father, mother, daughter, son, sister, brother, uncle, aunt, brother-in-law, sister-in-law.'[7]

E. Articles used in native occupations: 'machete, hoe, dibble stick, plow, seed, hammer, saw, forge, iron, ax, nails, planks, vines for tying, thatch, canoe, paddles, bow, arrow, spear, gun.'

F. Fauna: 'horse, cow, ox, pig, dog, cat, sheep, goat, ass, lion, tiger, jaguar, wildcat, elephant, buffalo, hippopotamus, rhinoceros, antelope, deer, monkey, snake, eagle, hawk, buzzard, sparrow, crane, fly, flea, louse, spider, ant.'

G. Geographical and astronomical objects: 'river, stream, rapids, lake, water hole, hill, mountain, valley, forest, planted field, cleared field, star, sun, moon, cloud.'

It is not only valuable to select words by semantic groups, but the order of these groups should be considered also. It has been found from experience that some of the easiest forms to obtain are names for body parts, since they can readily be pointed to. Next may come the names for clothing and objects about the house. But among the other semantic groups there is not much basis for preference. The one difficulty with the words for body parts is that they sometimes occur with obligatory possessive affixes, and this may greatly complicate the initial problems.

Problem 117

Instructions:

a. Select one of the following cultural areas:

---

[7]The system of such relationships between people may be extremely complex. For example, there may be different terms depending upon whether a man or a woman is speaking about a relative, whether the person is older or younger than someone else, or whether the person belongs to one's mother's or one's father's family line. These are only a few of the many possible complications. The investigator should try to obtain some knowledge of the kinship systems in the area beforehand, and then not attempt to work out too many of the details immediately. Many of the complexities can only be explained in the native language, for the intermediate language would fail to convey all the distinctions adequately.

1. Nilotic, in the southern Anglo-Egyptian Sudan

2. Bantu, central Belgian Congo

3. Marshall Islands

4. Aboriginal southwest China

5. Aboriginal central Australia

6. Eskimo, northern Canada

7. Hunting-fishing tribe in the Amazon jungle

b. Make out a culturally appropriate word list including 150 object words and 50 process words.

7.21.2 Object Words in Possible Morphological Categories

After obtaining the names of words for various objects, it is important to discover whether these words occur with certain additive, replacive, or subtractive formatives. The most important practical structure to elicit is the possessive formation. For example, having obtained the Kekchi words očoč 'house' and ci 'dog' (together with many others), we should proceed to elicit 'my house, your (sg.) house, his house,' and so on, and 'my dog, your (sg.) dog, his dog,' and so on. It is of course impossible to know at first whether the forms gwočoč 'my house' and inci 'my dog' are each two words or one, but we would not expect a nonsyllabic gw- to constitute a word by itself, and if we ask the informant the meaning of gw- he is quite incapable of explaining. These are both excellent bits of evidence that gwočoč is a single word and that we have here a morphological construction. Though in- is pronounceable in isolation, it nevertheless has no meaning in isolation, and can likewise be considered a prefix.[8]

In eliciting possessed forms one should obtain the equivalents of 'my, your (sg.), his, our, your (pl.), and their.' Further distinctions may also be attempted between dual and plural 'our, your, and their,' between 'his, her, and its,' and between 'our (inclusive)' and 'our (exclusive).'

At the beginning it is better to sample data rather than obtain comprehensive paradigms. For example, select one word from each of the semantic categories and elicit all the possible possessives with each of these words. If all these forms are perfectly regular in formation, the chances are that most of the other words will be regular. This can be investigated by chosing twenty more words at random and trying them with various personal formatives. It may be that certain persons fall into one class and others into another. For example, in Mongbandi it is necessary to know only the first person singular and plural forms of verbs, for all the other forms may be predicted on the basis of these.

There are two very important cautions in eliciting possessed forms: (1) be sure that the informant is clear as to the pronominal reference and (2) choose words that make sense. If the investigator asks for 'my house,' the informant is likely to reply with a form meaning 'your house.' With a little accommodation to the informant's difficulties, the investigator can easily avoid misunderstanding; but it is the investigator who must conform to the informant's understanding and not the reverse, if satisfactory results are to be obtained. Forms must also make sense. For example, one investigator began asking a Chipewyan Indian to give the paradigm 'my skunk, your skunk, his skunk,' and so on, and the

---

[8]These rules of thumb are by no means adequate for a final analysis, but they indicate some important features about the structure and provide clues to further investigation.

informant refused, saying that no Chipewyan owns a skunk. If for some special reason it is important to discover such possible though unused forms (as a practice, however, this is not recommended), one must make it perfectly clear to the informant that the forms are only "make-believe."

There are important reasons for eliciting the possessive forms with nouns early in the investigation:

1. They are often very irregular and reveal many basic morphological classes.

2. They are more easily elicited than many other categories, e.g. case, gender, and location.

3. They occur frequently in text and should be analyzed in anticipation of other more complex combinations.

4. They are important to the language-learning process since they are used in many practical situations.

5. They are often closely related in form to independent pronouns or to affixes used as subjects or objects of verbs.

The second morphological category which may be elicited is number. The same nouns used before should be tested for plural and, possibly, dual forms. In some languages there are no distinctions, e.g. Tarahumara towíki means 'boy' or 'boys.' In a great many languages, however, the distinction between singular and plural is highly important, and basic to the linguistic analysis. But one must not be blind to the many discrepancies between languages. In English, for example, there are no common plurals for mass nouns, e.g. flour, wheat, sand, except in the sense of different kinds of flour, wheat, and sand. The investigator must be fully aware of such problems and not attempt to force a language into an artificial mold.

Many other categories occur with nouns, e.g. definite vs. indefinite, case, identification, causation, and shape, but these formations are difficult to elicit by means of a paradigmatic approach. For example, once a form has been identified by the context, it is then generally treated as definite by the informant. It is extremely difficult for a more-or-less untrained informant to take a list of words and constantly shift back and forth between indefinite and definite forms. Case relationships are even more complicated to elicit, because in isolation the framework into which the words would normally fit is lacking. Frames are treated in section 7.12.15.

7.21.3 Simple Process Words

In eliciting simple process words one should observe the following principles:

1. Select easy demonstrable words. For example, 'walking, running, jumping, seeing, hitting' are more readily obtained than 'thinking, feeling, trying, becoming.'

2. Employ full sentences, e.g. 'he is walking, we are running, they are swimming.' One should avoid asking for infinitive or stem forms. Imperatives such as 'Go! Walk! Run!' often involve special inflectional and suprasegmental features which are not easily treated at first.

3. Use present continuous-action forms, e.g. 'he is walking, they are running.'

4. Begin by using third person singular or plural subjects. If one begins with 'I' or 'you,' the informant is very likely to be confused by the form of the question. After he becomes used to giving verb forms, however, and after the investigator is

somewhat acquainted with the stems and possible tense-mode-aspect indicators, there is less danger of misunderstanding about the persons.

5. Select first those processes which are not likely to require an object and secondly those which may require an object. This means that possible intransitive verbs, e.g. 'walk, run, fall, climb, jump, swim, sing, whistle, sleep, work, laugh, speak, write' should be elicited first, and then possible transitive verbs, e.g. 'see, hear, smell, feel, hit, hunt, hurt, kill, like, love, talk to, recognize, desire.' It is, of course, impossible to predict whether a particular verb in any language will be transitive or intransitive, but processes which normally involve a goal are often more complex in formation than those which do not require a goal.

7.21.4 Process Words in Possible Morphological Categories

Process words should be tested for four possible morphological categories: (1) person, (2) tense-aspect, (3) negation, and (4) interrogation. It is not particularly important whether the forms elicited prove to be morphological or syntactic constructions, except that as morphological constructions they are usually more complex and include more allomorphic alternation. These four types of formation are both practically and theoretically significant.

The various persons should be obtained for subjects of transitive and intransitive verbs. If the transitive verbs include a pronominal object, then all the possibilities of that relation must be discovered also. One may construct a frame for obtaining all the possible forms, e.g.

I ... myself _____

I ... you (sg.) _____

I ... him _____

I ... us[9] _____

I ... you (pl.) _____

I ... them _____

You (sg.) ... me _____

You (sg.) ... yourself _____

You (sg.) ... him _____

etc.

If there are differences of dual and plural, inclusive and exclusive, masculine, feminine, and neuter, animate and inanimate, or human and nonhuman, these add to the complications and the possible number of forms. In Barrow Eskimo, which distinguishes reflexives, and singular, dual, and plural (though dual and plural are not distinct throughout), there are fifty-seven forms for every subject-object paradigm of a transitive verb.

One should restrict the tense-aspect paradigms elicited from the informant to three: (1) a past or completive, (2) the present continuous (this has already been obtained under

---

[9]With many verbs, and in a number of languages, this form is not possible. For example, 'I spoke to us' does not make sense, but 'I involved us in trouble' is meaningful.

the preceding step in procedure), and (3) a future or intentive. It is quite difficult for an informant to provide more than this number of forms with any degree of consistency; and even in eliciting these there are often difficulties, for he may think first of one and then of another completive aspect or past tense. The same is true of the future forms. Many times the complications can be resolved only by examining text material.

The negative forms of some languages (e.g. many Bantu languages, cf. Problem 5) are extremely complicated; but whether they are complex or not, it is necessary for the sake of subsequent analysis to collect data on this important semantic and structural feature.

Samplings of just four types of formations--i.e. persons (subject and object), tense-aspects (past, present, and future), negation, and interrogation--often provide a good structural framework by means of which one may proceed rapidly with the analysis and, on the basis of the analysis, with the further probing of the language and the eliciting of other forms. Knowledge of these structures has, furthermore, practical importance for the investigator in helping him to learn the language as he proceeds with the analysis.[10]

The investigator must be warned against trying to gather all the data first and to analyze them later. This is a fatal mistake, for the nature and extent of the data gathered will be determined largely by the concurrent analysis. Field procedures and analytical procedures must go hand in hand.

7.21.5 Combinations of Object and Process Words

We have been assuming that the forms elicited in steps 1-4 (sections 7.21-7.24) would result in single words. This is, of course, not always true, for there are numerous important exceptions, depending upon the language. However, having elicited forms the majority of which contain only one root or one structurally primary root, we may combine these expressions in a number of ways by means of simple and complex[11] paradigmatic series.

Simple paradigms consist of a frame in which certain substitutions may be made. We may, for example, substitute different subjects, leaving the verb the same, e.g:

1. 'The boy runs.'

2. 'The man runs.'

3. 'The horse runs.'

4. 'The cow runs.'

5. 'The pig runs.'

    etc.

Such a frame seems perfectly fixed, but in another language it may be necessary to employ at least two different words for 'run,' one to denote the action of a two-legged runner

---

[10]Though it is frequently true that professional linguists are not able to acquire a facility in the speaking of the language during the limited time alloted for the structural analysis, yet it is essentially a mistake to believe that one can do a completely satisfactory job of analysis without actually learning to speak the language under investigation. There are many of its features which only a speaking knowledge will reveal.

[11]It must be remembered that simple and complex paradigms in the intermediate language may not correspond structurally with forms which are semantic equivalents in another language.

and the other of a four-legged runner. Frames which are constant in one language often undergo change in other languages.

Instead of making substitutions of subjects, we may substitute different verbs, e.g.:

1. 'The boy runs.'

2. 'The boy walks.'

3. 'The boy swims.'

4. 'The boy falls.'

5. 'The boy jumps.'

It is also possible to preserve the same roots and change the various number, tense, possessive, affirmative-negative, and declarative-interrogative formatives, e.g.:

1. 'The boy runs.'   7. 'His boy will not run.'

2. 'The boys run.'   8. 'His boys will not run.'

3. 'The boy ran.'   9. 'Will his boy run?'

4. 'The boys ran.'   10. 'Will his boys run?'

5. 'His boy will run.'   11. 'Will his boy not run?'[12]

6. 'His boys will run.'   etc.

Such structural frames may include objects, e.g.:

1. 'He hit the man.'

2. 'He hit the boy.'

3. 'He hit the girl.'

4. 'He hit the horse.'

5. 'He hit the post.'

    etc.

Or we may have different verbs with the same object, e.g.:

1. 'He hit the man.'   5. 'He hated the man.'

2. 'He saw the man.'   6. 'He killed the man.'

3. 'He beat the man.'   etc.

4. 'He addressed the man.'

It is by means of frames such as these that one may discover various case distinctions. For example, if there is a difference between the subject and the object form of a noun,

---

[12]This series is a restricted type of complex paradigm.

then all nouns can be placed in one or the other of the pertinent frames in order to elicit the proper forms. Generally, it is only in frames of this sort that the informant will provide the proper form of the word.

Complex paradigms consist of series in which a different member (or members, sometimes) is substituted in each successive expression. It is important to change the lexical elements in such a series just as little as possible, for the occurrence of similar elements in different combinations is the purpose of the series. There should also be some narrative continuity if possible. This will insure the informant's preserving some meaningful relationship between the various portions, and the series will more closely resemble actual text. The following is an illustrative series:

1. 'The boy heard a monkey in the forest.'[13]   6. 'The monkey screeched at the boy.'

2. 'The boy saw the monkey in the forest.'   7. 'The boy was afraid.'

3. 'The boy followed the monkey.'   8. 'The boy ran.'

4. 'The monkey saw the boy.'   9. 'The monkey chased the boy.'

5. 'The monkey stopped.'   10. 'The boy ran out of the forest.'

This same type of structural framework may be employed with different nouns, e.g.:

1. 'The man heard a buffalo in the tall grass.'

2. 'The man saw the buffalo in the tall grass.'

3. 'The man followed the buffalo.'

4. 'The buffalo saw the man.'

5. 'The buffalo stopped.'

6. 'The buffalo bellowed at the man.'

   etc.

The framework may also be expanded by including various attributives to the nounlike words, e.g.:

1. 'The little girl heard a large dog in the cotton field.'

2. 'The little girl saw the large dog in the cotton field.'

3. 'The little girl followed the dog.'

   etc.

This constant repetition of the same object and process words may seem unnecessarily tedious and appear to be practically useless. But no linguistic investigator beginning the analysis of a language can plunge immediately into the task of taking down text material. He must become familiar with the sounds, the morphological structure, the sentence forms, and the vocabulary. To be sure, he cannot do this all at once, but by employing successively more complex types of expression which contain already analyzed or recognized data, he

_____

[13]The words chosen for this type of series will, of course, depend upon the nonlinguistic environment.

can discover a great deal in regard to the structure. No satisfactory analysis can be made without using expressions containing a high percentage of recurring patterns. Rather than being obliged to hunt for such expressions in widely scattered portions of text material, the investigator may construct expressions which will serve something of the same purpose. The extent to which he employs this means of eliciting forms depends largely upon the informant's ability to respond in natural phraseology. There is a very strong tendency for informants to translate more or less word for word; and if this happens, the morphological forms may be more or less accurate, but the sentence structure may be badly distorted. Whether or not there is distortion can only be discovered later, when actual texts are obtained.

Even if the informant is quite exceptional, there are severe limitations to the paradigmatic approach:

1. The informant is often confused, for the context is not normal.

2. The form of the paradigms is necessarily based upon the intermediate language, and many distinctions in the informant's language cannot be adequately approximated in the intermediate language.

3. The paradigmatic approach will of necessity fail to discover many structural distinctions in the informant's language. No extent of probing can unearth all the significant structures.

4. The paradigmatic approach is especially inadequate in revealing the syntactic structure, since the form of the intermediate language determines so largely the form of the informant's response.

Despite these facts it is possible with alert and capable informants to expand the frames even more than we have in the preceding sentence types. For example, we may substitute different and larger units, e.g.:

1. 'When the old man came to the water hole he saw the fierce buffalo.'

2. 'Then he was very much afraid of the fierce buffalo.'

3. 'Because he was afraid of the buffalo, he ran back to the village.'

4. 'When he arrived at the village, he got his gun.'

   etc.

Theoretically there is no limit on the extent to which one may use such sentence frames, employing constant variations. However, by the time the investigator is able to take down rather complex sentences from dictation, he should be prepared to start writing text material. Paradigmatic data that one obtains by eliciting forms must be thoroughly checked and corroborated by actual text data, for one cannot be absolutely sure of forms which have been elicited. The meanings are particularly subject to question, and the order of words should be suspect until text material is found to exhibit the same characteristics.

7.21.6 Texts

Texts consist of anything uttered by a native speaker which is not in response to some such question as "How do you say 'so-and-so'?" There are six principal kinds of texts: (1) greetings, (2) conversation, (3) exposition and personal narrative, (4) traditional stories, (5) songs and poetic forms, and (6) proverbs.

Greetings tend to be stereotyped and clipped expressions with highly idiomatic usages. It is particularly important to note (1) the persons speaking, (2) the time of the day, and (3) the religious implications.

Conversational texts are extremely difficult to take down from dictation, for the speed is too great for them to be recorded by the conventional means. Some investigators have employed shorthand symbols, and others have made use of various mechanical recording devices. Such records are valuable, but they must be transcribed before they can be adequately studied. An electric recorder is extremely helpful for advanced study of a language, but it is of quite limited value for the investigator in the beginning stages of analysis. For matters of intonation, sentence sequence, and rapid conversational give-and-take these recordings are most important, but this type of study can be profitably undertaken only after much preliminary analysis and after a considerable practical facility in speaking and understanding the language has been acquired. Even where the investigator cannot record large sections of conversation in writing, it is very helpful to take down snatches of it. Forms are often phonologically reduced in conversation, and in the use of pronouns the syntax of conversation is frequently quite different from that of narrative or expository styles.

Expository and personal-narrative texts consist of explanations of activities or processes and descriptions of actual events. The investigator may ask the informant to describe a journey he has made, a hunting expedition, a severe illness, a period of famine, the clearing of fields in the jungle, the making of a canoe, or the building of a house. These texts are usually the easiest to take down from dictation and are likely to contain the least number of complications due to stylistically idiomatic forms.

Traditional stories are the most common type of text requested by investigators, and if the informant happens to be a famous storyteller, there may be an almost inexhaustible supply of these tales. Such stories are sometimes more difficult to analyze than straight expositions or personal narratives because the very familiarity of the story permits the informant to omit many syntactic devices employed in other types of discourse. For example, in personal narratives the informant may make the pronominal reference quite explicit or he may repeat nouns to make sure that the participants in the action are properly identified. In traditional stories there is a tendency to omit such explicit reference, since it is assumed that the hearers will understand perfectly well who is being talked about.

Songs and poetic forms are often very complicated, for they frequently contain archaic or pseudoarchaic forms, together with many allusions to historical and supernatural phenomena.

Proverbs are as difficult as songs, for in many instances the meaning of a proverb is intentionally obscure, and the significance may depend upon some play on words. The cultural features of proverbs are also highly complex. A language cannot be fully investigated without some analysis of songs and proverbs, but the investigator is urged to consider these forms only after rather thorough treatment of other types of texts. Furthermore, he will find it more efficient to describe these specialized forms in terms of the more standard data found in expository and narrative styles.

In writing down text it is important to space the material adequately. At least three blank lines should be left after each line of text. One should first write down all of the story without inquiring as to the meanings of the individual words and phrases. After the story has been dictated and transcribed, one should then go over it, trying to read it back from the transcription. Some errors will be picked up in this fashion. During this process, or subsequent to it, one may inquire as to the meanings of the individual words or phrases. It is important to select first for inquiry the units in the text marked by hesitation or pause, since pauses generally coincide with the borders of words or phrases. Frequently it is possible to break up such phonological phrase units and to obtain the meanings of individual items included within them. As long as the informant is responding readily and consistently to questions about the meanings of forms, it is profitable to pursue this inquiry as far as possible. The meanings may be indicated directly under each word. Often, however, the informant can give only the meaning of a phrase as a whole, and there are numerous instances in which the meaning of the phrase differs from the meaning of the constituent parts. This type of problem has already been treated in section 6.3. When the meaning of the phrase differs from that of the individual words, it is necessary to indicate this discrepancy in the space immediately below each line of text.

Where the word order and the syntactic structure of the native language is radically different from that of the intermediate language, one must write out a complete free translation in the intermediate language, in order that the meaningful arrangements of words may be known. A person beginning work in Quechua surely needs to construct a translation of the sentences as a whole, for the word order is conspicuously different from the intermediate language, Spanish.

The analysis of texts depends very largely on the proper elaboration of text data by a type of paradigmatic approach. This is, however, primarily an analytical procedure, and hence will be discussed in the following chapter.

7.22 Recording the Data

The following suggestions are important in recording the data:

1. Print each phonetic symbol. If symbols are connected as in traditional forms of writing, there is too much tendency to confuse them afterward.

2. Use pencil or permanent ink. Many investigators prefer pencils because they are more easily carried about than ink and because there is less danger of losing notes if the paper becomes watersoaked by accident.

3. Use unlined paper, preferably 8 1/2 by 11 inches. It is helpful to put a considerable amount of data on a single page, for it is then possible to discover relationships more easily. These data can later be transferred to small slips to be filed.

4. Record the data at the normal speed of utterance. It may be necessary to ask the informant to speak slowly, in order to pick up all the sounds, but the recording should be based upon the normal utterance, and not upon the unnaturally slowed-up speech.

5. Do not phonemicize too soon. The investigator inevitably commences to phonemicize the moment he begins to listen to a language, but it is a grave error to phonemicize the transcription immediately on the basis of more-or-less intuitive guesses as to the relationships of sounds. Later analysis may reveal that important phonetic distinctions have been neglected.

6. Mark all the phonetic features which can be readily detected. These should include pauses, the general intonational contour, and the segmental phonemes. Pauses prove to be very significant in distinguishing word and phrase boundaries, and intonational contours are basic to morphological and syntactic analysis. The intonational contour cannot be marked precisely, but a line indicating the general rise and fall of the syllables can be drawn right through the transcribed segmental phonemes.

The investigator should not be too meticulous and exacting about the first transcriptions. After the informant has pronounced the form three or four times and the investigator has become able to utter a fairly acceptable reproduction, the form should be written down. Some linguists prefer to write down the forms on the basis of the first utterance, and to employ repeated utterances to check this transcription. It is not a good practice to ask an informant to repeat an expression dozens of times in order to analyze some particularly difficult sound. Any special complication should be noted for further investigation, after the linguist has had more experience with the language. Subsequent data may clear up initial difficulties.

7. Be honest with the data. Some investigators are tempted to regularize and systematize the findings. Apparent discrepancies are as much a part of the language as the regular forms and must not be set aside.

8. Indicate the name of the informant providing the forms. Not all speakers, even within a comparatively compact ethnic group, use the same forms. Differences may represent two or more dialects, or optional variants within a single dialect. The source of each bit of datum should be noted.

9. Date the data. The investigator will find that recording improves with experience, and that sometimes a discrepancy in forms is due to his inexperience in the initial stages of the work.

10. Indicate all corrections plainly. When going over data at a later time to check for accuracy of recording, it is advisable to use pencil or ink of a different color in marking changes. This is a distinct aid in subsequent analysis of the materials.

7.23 The Informant

7.23.1 Dialect Differences among Informants

Any native speaker of a language is a potential informant. It makes no difference whether he is a poor peasant selling vegetables in the market place or a court scribe; he is still a speaker of the language. It is true, of course, that in every society there are differences of dialect depending upon many personal and cultural factors. These fall into three major classes:

1. Economic and social groups. These differences include dialect contrasts between outcasts and caste peoples, slaves and free men, and ignorant and traditionally educated persons. In some instances the dialect differences are so great that the various groups can scarcely understand each other when they employ the forms customarily used within their own social and economic units. The linguist must treat such differences in terms of dialectal contrasts, and certainly not as if one set of them were some "pure" form of the language in contrast with a "corrupted" variety.

2. Men vs. women. Men's and women's speech may differ in the words customarily used and the forms employed. In some languages the formal differences are quite extensive, e.g. in Koasati, Yana, and Chukchee.[14]

3. Young people vs. adults. The differences in speech between the younger generation and their parents may be quite extensive in some areas. This is particularly true where the native usage may be in a state of rapid transition because of the influence of some trade language. In a number of languages in Africa one finds the younger generation unfamiliar with many terms of religious and ethnic significance known by their parents. This is especially true in areas where the old cultural forms are rapidly dying out. Linguistic borrowings are usually greater among the younger generation, especially if there is some formal education in the trade

---

[14]Mary R. Haas, "Men's and Women's Speech in Koasati," Language, 20 (1944), 3: 142-49.

language. In regions where less and less emphasis is being placed upon village community life, one may also find that younger speakers employ fewer of the refinements of tense and aspect. Frequently this is because they receive less practice in using their own tongue and because the native language may have lost some of its prestige to the trade language of the area.

7.23.2 Qualifications of Informants

In selecting informants one should recognize the factors of dialect difference and consider certain personal matters as well. Linguists have found the following factors highly important:

1. Age. The informant should be over sixteen years of age. With very rare exceptions a person younger than this does not have sufficient language experience to qualify as an informant. Elderly people often make the best informants since they have a rich experience and are frequently more disposed to the sedentary type of work which is involved.

2. Sex. Men usually have broader social contacts and a wider tribal experience. As a group, they generally have a better grasp of the trade language which may constitute the intermediate language in the bilingual approach.

3. Intelligence. Mental alertness is extremely important in an informant.

4. Knowledge of the intermediate language. An adequate knowledge of the intermediate language is distinctly valuable, though much less so after the analyst progresses to the point where the investigation may be carried on within the framework of the native tongue.

5. Communicative personality. The reticent, taciturn person rarely qualifies as an informant. The more genuinely communicative the native speaker, the more helpful he is.

6. Acceptable social group. In some tribes only persons of a particular group are regarded as qualified to teach a foreigner the language. It is advisable to conform to this tradition in the beginning of the investigation. In certain areas the sex of the investigator determines the choice of the informant, since it may be considered quite improper for people of opposite sexes to be together under the circumstances of language study.

7.23.3 Handling of Informants

The success of field work depends largely upon the linguist's handling of his informants. The investigator must not exhibit a patronizing superiority, but, rather, a genuine appreciation of the informant's ability and his willingness to teach. The Golden Rule applies in this situation as well as in all others.

The following principles should assist the investigator to understand more fully the practical problems of dealing with informants.

1. Do not argue with the informant.

   This means that the investigator must assume as a basis of operation that the informant is always right. In reality, the informant may be wrong, but it rarely, if ever, does any good to argue. If the informant appears to be contradicting data previously given, it may be that there is an entirely different aspect involved. On one day the informant may give a past completive and on the next day a past incompletive for substantially the same action. The difference is essentially one of perspective, and quite without realizing it, the informant may have shifted his viewpoint. Such problems cannot be resolved by arguing; their solution depends primarily upon evidence acquired in other contexts.

2. Let the informant teach.

The investigator should pronounce each expression after the informant, insisting that the informant approve only when the forms are fully intelligible.

3. Do not ask the informant to repeat many times.

Dozens of repetitions are tedious and nonsensical. Furthermore, the linguist will profit by returning to a particularly difficult problem after he has examined more data.

4. Do not work too long at a stretch.

It has been found that forty-five minutes is usually long enough. Some type of intermission of ten or fifteen minutes before another session is important.

Usually an investigator will acquire sufficient data in three forty-five minute sessions to keep him busy for the rest of the day analyzing and memorizing the material. It is most essential that analysis keep up with acquisition, for otherwise a great deal of time is wasted. If the linguist is unable to take the time to memorize all the roots, he must, at any rate, be fully familiar with all the bound forms.

5. Do not inquire as to the "why's" of the language.

Questions as to why a language has certain allomorphs or why certain combinations occur rather than others should not be asked. If the informant is honest, he will probably not be able to answer; and if by such a question the investigator implies a lack of knowledge on the part of the informant or a deficiency in the language, then the question has done more harm than it could ever do good. It would be quite as ridiculous to ask the average speaker of English to define the meaning of -ceive in receive, deceive, perceive, and conceive, to explain why intolerable begins with in- and improbable begins with im-, or why I occurs with am and he with is, or how it is that mushroom looks as though it were derived from mush and room. The informant is the source of the data, but he is not the analyst.

6. Elicit meanings by asking how a form is used.

It is often difficult for informants to provide adequate meanings of forms (either bound or free), but they can usually offer illustrations of how a particular form would be used in various contexts.

7. Show genuine appreciation of the informant's help and ability.

The linguist's enthusiasm about the informant's language, about his assistance, and about his willingness to teach is often the most rewarding compensation for work which may be regarded by the informant's own tribesmen as socially degrading or suspect. Treating the informant as a person and a friend is the best guarantee of success.

C H A P T E R 8

ANALYTICAL PROCEDURES

The steps in the analysis of a language differ considerably from the order of exposition of linguistic techniques. In the process of working with an informant we cannot expect to receive neatly classified data and complete paradigmatic series. We are confronted with an interrelated mass of phonological, morphological, and syntactic materials. Furthermore, we must have all of these types of data, for problems of allophones and allomorphs are closely related to matters of juncture, and these in turn point to morphological and syntactic groupings. The sounds are, of course, primary and basic, but as a matter of practical procedure, we do not attempt to solve all the phonemic problems without considering the structural features.

8.1 Relationship of Analytical to Field Procedures

Analysis must go hand in hand with field work. In fact, it may be considered a large part of it. The person who expects to gather all the materials before beginning the analysis will find that many pertinent data have been neglected because no evaluation accompanied the collection. Furthermore, even the best phonetician will not detect all the significant features of any language without at the same time investigating the structural and semantic contrasts.

The analysis tells the investigator what to look for. As the data are analyzed he begins to realize which categories are expressed in the language and which not. In sampling the language material (practically all linguistic work consists to some degree of sampling) the linguist then knows what type of forms to elicit and which distinctions should be further investigated. To elicit paradigms without supplementing the process by analysis may be a sheer waste of time.

8.2 Steps in Analytical Procedure

It is impossible to keep all the details of a language in one's mind. This means that one must sort, classify, and file observations and the substantiating data. But one cannot afford to file blindly, or the materials will be classified in a more-or-less irrelevant manner and the investigator may be able to find what he wants only with great difficulty. It is necessary, therefore, to make some initial observations of the data, and on the basis of these to work out some practical format for a file in which data may be classified. After making the initial observations and planning the framework of classification, one begins the major task of filing and analysis.

8.21 Initial Observations

Morphological analysis entails three principal types of initial observations: (1) phonetic, (2) identificational, and (3) distributional.

8.21.1 Phonetic Observations

Certain phonetic facts are particularly pertinent to the morphological analysis. These include:

1. Pauses or breaks between intonational units. Intonational pauses and breaks usually occur between morphological constructions rather than within them and thus they provide important clues to the boundaries of such constructions.

2. The distribution of allophones. Certain contrasts of allophonic distribution provide valuable clues to word units. For example, phrase-initial and phrase-final forms tend to be extended by analogy to word-initial and word-final positions.

3. The distribution of clusters. The distribution of certain clusters is often found to coincide with the occurrence of certain morphological units, e.g. morphemes, compounds, and words.

4. Phonemic junctures. These junctures are based on phonetic features which may be included in the preceding types of phonetic data.

5. Position of the stress. The stress may be variable, as in Eskimo, or fixed, as in Kekchi (on the last syllable) and Quechua (for the most part, on the next to the last syllable). If there is only one stress for each word, then the stress may be very helpful in determining structural units. If the stress is always on a positionally fixed syllable, then the problem is simplified even more.

6. Phonological sequences. If there are patterns of vocalic or tone harmony which have a definitely restricted distribution, it usually happens that the boundaries of such formations coincide with some structurally pertinent groupings.

8.21.2 Identificational Observations

From the very beginning it is essential to identify as many morphemes as possible. There are two principal techniques:

1. Comparing partially similar forms to determine whether the formally similar portion reflects a corresponding semantic likeness. For example, we may compare the two Congo Swahili forms wunasema 'you (sg.) speak' and wutakapikiwa 'you (sg.) will be hit' and conclude, temporarily at least, that wu-, which is identical in the two forms, is probably the same morpheme, since there is a corresponding similarity in the meaning of the two forms.

2. Comparing partially similar forms to determine whether a formally contrastive portion reflects a corresponding semantic difference. For example, we may compare the Congo Swahili words ninasema 'I speak' and wunasema 'you (sg.) speak' and conclude that ni- must mean 'I' and wu- must mean 'you (sg.).'

These two techniques are just the converse of each other, but their employment is determined by the extent of conformity between the partially similar forms.

The investigator may, depending upon the ability of the informant and the structure of the language, ask the informant to identify the meanings of the forms. The chances are that the informant will be able to identify only full words (free or in morphological constructions) and some bound roots. If it is found that he can identify the meaning of almost every syllable-morpheme, then one may be comparatively certain that the language has a type of isolating structure, in which practically every syllable-morpheme is a syntactically pertinent unit. In such languages, however, there are usually a number of particles to which the native informant cannot readily assign a meaning.

The identificational techniques have been fully discussed in Chapter 2, but the solution of many difficulties listed there depends upon considerable knowledge of the language. The procedures indicated here are the initial techniques which enable one to get a quick, overall glance at the language structure.

8.21.3 Distributional Observations

Even in the very beginning of linguistic investigation there are some distributional facts which should be noted:

1. The classes of morphemes

    a. Do the roots and nonroots differ in size and shape?

    b. Are some nonroots inflectional and others derivational?

    c. Are there many root-plus-root combinations which seem to act like single words?

    d. Are there many nonroot morphemes?

2. The order of the classes of morphemes

    a. Do all roots occur in the same relative order as regards the nonroots?

    b. Is the relative order of morphemes fixed?

    c. Do apparent derivational and inflectional formations preserve a strict relative order?

3. Recurring combinations of morphemes

    a. Do some morphemes seem to be mutually obligatory?

    b. Do some morphemes seem to be mutually exclusive?

4. Degree of allomorphic alternation

    a. Do morphemes exhibit many allomorphs?

    b. Do the allomorphs appear to be phonologically conditioned in distribution? or

    c. Do the changes in phonological form appear to be completely arbitrary?

5. Separability of units

    a. Can the informant readily divide expressions into constituent parts and assign meanings?

    b. Are combinations readily split by what seem to be free forms?[1]

6. Sequences of morphemes

    a. Do some roots occur with certain nonroots and not with others?

    b. Do some roots act only as nounlike words and others only as verblike words? or

---

[1] If so, they are probably not morphological, but syntactic, constructions.

c. Are there many roots which seem to occur in both types of situations?[2]

It is quite impossible to give complete and final answers to all these questions, but they serve to direct the analysis and guide the formation of the file.

8.22 Filing of Data

8.22.1 Purpose of Filing Data

By the process of filing each bit of information on a separate slip of paper one is able to collect in one place a quantity of similar data. It is, of course, also possible to achieve the same result by making long lists of words on large sheets of paper; but this device proves very awkward, for in all linguistic analysis it is constantly necessary to reorganize data. As more data are gathered, the relevance of certain distinctions may be increased or diminished, and constant regroupings must be made. For example, in Maya one might conclude that there is a class of words which are conjunctions, and which are structurally entirely separate from other types of words. It is only after considerable study of the language that most of these so-called conjunctions turn out to be possessed nouns (see section 5.2). If the data are filed on separate slips, the entire sections can be easily shifted from one place to another; but if the data have been laboriously described on long sheets of paper, then the necessary recopying or repagination (or both) must be undertaken.

In addition to its flexibility one of the principal advantages of a filing method of this type is its expandibility. One cannot anticipate the size of certain classes of forms and only an expandible device can adequately meet the investigator's needs.

Such a file has a further advantage in that it may be organized along the lines of the ultimate grammatical description of the language. Theoretically, it should be possible to file the data in such a manner that in the final description of the structure one could proceed section by section through the file.

8.22.2 Form of the Filing Slip

The most convenient size for the filing slip is 3 by 5 inches.

The slip should contain the following information:

1. An identification of the form under which the slip is to be filed. The form may be entered in the upper left-hand corner, with or without the meaning, or may be underlined, with or without starring (see below).

2. An indication of the location of the form in the field notes from which it was copied. It is absolutely essential that one be able to refer to the context when necessary. This notation may be made in the upper right corner.

3. An expression which contains the form in question. At least one full morphological construction should be given. If the morpheme appears to be relational, then an entire phrase or sentence should be recorded, in order to illustrate the use.

4. The meaning of the entire expression.

---

[2]As, for example, man, hit, bull, roar, fish, jump, and run, which may be either nouns or verbs in English.

The following facsimiles (reduced) show the two types of file slips; they contain the data for form 25 of Problem 5:

A.

```
┌─────────────────────────────────────────────────┐
│                                                  │
│  -iz- 'causative'                        1-6     │
│                                                  │
│                                                  │
│                                                  │
│             wutakanipiki̲z̲wa                      │
│                                                  │
│                                                  │
│    'you (sg.) will cause me to be hit'           │
│                                                  │
│                                                  │
└─────────────────────────────────────────────────┘
```

B.

```
┌─────────────────────────────────────────────────┐
│                                          1-6     │
│                                                  │
│                                                  │
│                                                  │
│        w̲u̲t̲a̲k̲a̲n̲i̲p̲i̲k̲i̲z̲w̲a̲                          │
│                           *                      │
│                                                  │
│      'you (sg.) will cause me to be hit'         │
│                                                  │
└─────────────────────────────────────────────────┘
```

In facsimile A we assume that the morpheme has been fully identified and its meaning determined. In B the morpheme is identified, but no meaning is given, either because the morpheme is of frequent occurrence and this is simply a supplementary form illustrating its use, or because the meaning has not been properly identified and illustrative examples are being filed so that the meaning may be ascertained later, on the basis of the several occurrences. The star under the form -iz- indicates that the slip is to be filed under this particular morpheme.

There are, of course, a number of variations of such filing slips possible; but they must all contain (1) an indication of the morpheme under which the slip is to be filed, (2) the illustrative form which contains the morpheme, and (3) the reference. In the facsimiles above the numerals 1-6 stand for notebook 1, page six. The line, too, may be indicated.

8.22.3 Relationship of Filing to Analysis

The investigator has presumably collected or is in the process of collecting two types of data, paradigmatic and text. The analysis of the paradigmatic data should be comparatively easy, for the partially identical forms help to reveal the minimal recurring units. Once the morphemes are isolated, a separate slip should be made out for each, and then the slips should be filed under the individual morphemes. The place in which each morpheme is to be filed will be considered in section 8.22.6. There are, of course, many morphemes which are difficult to identify because of their ambiguous meanings, their relatively numerous allomorphs, or their shifting positions. It is particularly important to file data on as many instances of these forms as are recorded in the field notes; on the basis of a score or more of such occurrences it is often possible to determine the numerous allosemes, allomorphs, and the complex distribution. Only by collecting these examples in some form of file can one conveniently treat such difficult problems.

The analysis of texts is by no means so simple, for there are no such series of partially similar forms. For example, in a popular Comanche story one finds the following two lines of text:[3]

1. pa'ru·ku,   'hunu?ru   no'hini·nA.

   raccoon   creek-in   played-around.

2. 'surĭkĬse?   pi-'puiha   'cahto?i?etĬ,   'hu·-,ma-,tu ?uwih'?e·yU.[4]

   he   his-own-eye with-his-hand-takes-out tree-on-in   it-was-throwing.

A free translation of these sentences is: 'The raccoon played around in the creek. He took out his eye and was throwing it up into the tree.'

With no more information than is provided in these two sentences it is quite impossible to isolate the morphemes and to know how to classify and file them. There are two possible solutions: (1) to continue taking hundreds of pages of text until there will be a sufficient number of partially similar forms or (2) to supplement the text with a paradigmatic series of questions which will enable the investigator to isolate the morphemes and determine something about their distributions. This second method is adopted for the first sentence of text above in the following eight sentences:

1. wa'sape,   'hunu?ru   no'hini·nA.

   bear   creek-in   played-around.

2. pa'ru·ku,   'va·ru   no'hini·nA.

   raccoon   water-in   played-around.

3. pa'ru·ku,   'hunu?kuhpa·ikĬ   no'hini·nA.

   raccoon   creek-through   played-around.

4. pa'ru·ku,   'hunu?ru   poh'pini·nA.

   raccoon   creek-in   jumped-around.

5. pa'ru·ku,   'hunu?ru   nih'kani·nA.

   raccoon   creek-in   danced-around.

6. pa'ru·ku,   'hunu?ru   no'hini·yU.

   raccoon   creek-in   was-playing-around.

---

[3]Eugene Nida, "Field Techniques in Descriptive Linguistics," *International Journal of American Linguistics*, 13 (1947), 3: 138-46.

[4]Hyphens in the Comanche mark phonemic junctures which are phonologically identical with spaces, but structurally contrastive. Commas mark secondary pauses, and periods primary pauses. A raised vertical bar marks the onset of primary stress, and a lowered one the onset of secondary stress. Capitals indicate voiceless vowels. These data are not fully phonemicized, but they are admittedly more so than would be possible after only a week or two of work in the language.

7. pa'ru·ku,   'hunuʔru   no'hi·yU

   raccoon   creek-in   was-playing.

8. pa'ru·ku,   'hunuʔru   no'hinU.

   raccoon   creek-in   played.

By means of this series of paradigmatic forms we have succeeded in isolating the morphemes in the first sentence, as well as in discovering a number of others which are used in the supplementary sentences. The morphemes, in so far as our data reveal, consist of:

$$\underset{\text{raccoon}}{\underline{\text{pa'ru·ku,}}}^{1} \quad \underset{\text{creek-in}}{\underline{\text{'hunuʔ}}^{2} \;\; \underline{\text{ru}}^{3}} \quad \underset{\text{played-around.}}{\underline{\text{no'hi}}^{4} \;\; \underline{\text{ni·}}^{5} \;\; \underline{\text{nA.}}^{6}}$$

This means that we should file six different slips, one for each morpheme. We may not be able to assign the full meanings to the morphemes or state their distribution, but that is not necessary at this stage. In fact, the filing of the forms is precisely to enable us eventually to state the distribution on the basis of numerous instances of each morpheme in various combinations. From what we would already have learned about the structure of Comanche before reaching the stage of analyzing texts, we would know that pa'ru·ku 'raccoon' has the distribution of a noun in this sentence. Though it is rather long for a single morpheme, we are unable to analyze it into any smaller segments,[5] and hence we file it under simple nouns, but in a special subdivision composed of forms which may prove to be complex. The morpheme 'hunuʔ- 'creek' may be filed under noun stems. The morpheme -ru 'in' may be tentatively filed as a suffix occurring with nouns. However, if we filed a number of occurrences of -ru, we would discover that it has a very wide distribution and is postposed to a number of different types of expressions. As such, it would actually prove to be a clitic, and we would treat its distribution in the syntax and not in the morphology.

The fourth slip containing no'hi- 'play' would be filed under verb stems, and the fifth, with -ni· 'around,' under suffixes to verbs. Since -ni· does not appear to be inflectional either in meaning or distribution, we can treat it tentatively as derivational. The final suffix -nA should be filed as occurring with verbs and as probably inflectional.

We could then isolate the various additional morphemes occurring in the eight sentences of supplementary paradigmatic data and could file these forms, also; but if we did so, we should indicate on the slips that these data were not found in original texts, but in supplementary paradigmatic forms.

These two processes, of supplementing the text data by paradigmatic forms and of filing such data in order to collect the occurrences necessary for describing the distributions of forms, are the most essential features of the analytical procedures.

8.22.4 Nature and Quantity of the Data to be Filed

We are concerned in this chapter only with the data which are pertinent to the morphology. These include (1) the morphemes, including their allomorphs, (2) the meanings of the morphemes, and (3) the distributions of the morphemes. The data concerning the meanings of morphemes are only indirectly pertinent to the morphological structure, but one must know something of the meaning in order to isolate the morphemes. Furthermore, a complete statement of the distribution involves many features which require a more or less adequate

---

[5] Popular etymology connects the first syllable pa- with the morpheme pa- ∞ va- 'water' (cf. 'va·ru, second sentence of the supplementary paradigmatic data), but this connection is not certain.

semantic analysis. However, the meanings of the morphemes are primarily a problem of the lexicon and not of the structure.

All instances of morphophonemic contrasts should be listed under types of allomorphic alternation. Subdivisions based on phonologically and morphologically defined environments should be made.

In filing a morpheme to determine its meaning one should continue to make entries so long as there are occurrences with apparent allosemic differences.

In filing occurrences of a morpheme to determine its distribution, one should continue to list and file examples until in any new context the distribution can be accurately predicted. Linguists usually do not attempt to file all the occurrences of each morpheme in several hundred or a thousand pages of field notes, but in checking over text data one should record and file any previously unnoted type of distribution.

8.22.5 Number of Files

Whether one keeps a number of separate files on the data of a language or makes major subdivisions in a single file is unimportant. What does matter is the proper division of data. There are three principal subdivisions: (1) phonological (including data on phonetics and phonemics), (2) structural (including morphology and syntax), and (3) lexical. We are concerned here primarily with the structural, or grammatical, file and secondarily with the lexical one.

As noted in the previous section, the lexical file constitutes a type of supplementary aid to the structural analysis, for it proves valuable in the isolation and identification of morphemes.

The structural file, which may be called the "grammar file," includes the morphophonemic differences, the inventory of morphemic classes, and the distributions of these classes.

It is also convenient to have a reference, or discard, file, into which may be placed all slips which for one reason or another have been taken out of the regular structural file. In the process of working on the distribution of morphemes one frequently makes out several hundred slips for a particular morpheme, only to discover later that its distribution can be succinctly stated in terms of some other recognized class. These hundreds of slips may encumber the structural file, and it is advisable to remove them and to substitute a simple statement in their place. Such slips, however, should not be thrown away, for one may wish to refer to these illustrative data later. Furthermore, it may be that the restatement of the distribution will not be entirely correct. The slips will then be of great value in revision.

8.22.6 Form of the Structural File

The structural file contains three primary divisions: (1) morphophonemics (including all allomorphic alternations), (2) morphology, and (3) syntax. We are concerned here only with the first two divisions, but it has already been remarked that one cannot treat the morphology properly without at the same time analyzing the syntax. As we have noted in previous chapters, there is often no clearly marked distinction between morphological and syntactic structures; furthermore, at the beginning of one's filing and analysis there are always important structures which are not immediately classifiable as unmistakably morphological or unmistakably syntactic.

The illustrative data of the language are written on slips of paper, as described in section 8.22.2. Each division in the file should be marked by an index card, on which may be written the name of the division, e.g. Morphophonemics, Morphology, Syntax,

<u>Syntactophonemics</u>, <u>Nouns</u>, <u>Derivation</u>, <u>Inflection</u>, <u>Suffixes</u>, <u>Order 3</u>, -θε '1st pl.' The
number and variety of such index cards depends upon the structure of the language.

Some investigators have found it convenient to indicate the successive sets of primary coordinate divisions by different-colored tabs. These color distinctions make it possible to file the data more rapidly, and at the same time they serve to emphasize the structural divisions.

8.22.61 <u>Morphophonemic</u> <u>Section</u>

All allomorphic alternations should be filed in the morphophonemic section of the file.
Some of these changes may be morphologically pertinent and others syntactically so, but this
subdivision can be made only after considerable investigation of the structure. If the morphologically and syntactically significant allomorphic alternations are identical, and especially if they can be defined in terms of phonological environment, it is profitable to
classify them together; in the description of the grammar they may be treated in the same
section.

As soon as possible one should begin to subdivide allomorphic alternations on the basis
of phonologically vs. morphologically defined environments. This classification must be
constantly reexamined, for differences which are apparently definable in terms of phonological environment may prove to be morphologically conditioned, and vice versa.

Under the subdivisions of phonologically and morphologically definable environments
the different allomorphic alternations should be classified, in so far as they can be,
under phonological processes, e.g. assimilation, dissimilation, reduction of clusters, loss
of final vowels, palatalization, and nasalization. This is the most significant manner of
assembling possibly related changes. Such subdivisions will not include all the types of
allomorphic alternation, but they will account for a high percentage of the morphophonemics,
and the exceptions (most of which will be morphologically defined) can be listed as special
types.

It is important to file all the morphophonemic data in a single section, even though
in the ultimate description of the language one may not include all of these data in the
morphophonemic section of the grammar. As a rule, one does not include in the morphophonemic section of a grammar those allomorphic alternations which occur in only one morpheme.
Such matters affecting individual morphemes are discussed at the point where the distribution of the morpheme in question is described, but it is impossible to know the extent of
any one type of allomorphic alternation unless one lists all the examples of it in an
appropriate place in the file.

8.22.62 <u>Morphology</u> <u>Section</u>

Allomorphic alternation which occurs in morphological constructions is essentially a
part of the morphology of a language, in the same way that similar changes occurring in
syntactic constructions are actually a part of the syntax. If we find that the types and
occurrences of such changes are distinct, we may set up two sections, (1) morphophonemics
and (2) syntactophonemics, each of which would treat the allomorphic alternations occurring
within its province. In the beginning of our analysis of a language we cannot easily make
such distinctions, so we tend to group all these changes together in a single morphophonemic section. This does not mean, however, that we must follow this procedure in the ultimate organization of the grammar. On the other hand, if we do distinguish morphophonemic
and syntactophonemic changes, then we should file each of these under the proper headings
in the following type of arrangement:

A. Morphology

   1. Morphophonemics

   2. Morphology proper

B. Syntax

   1. Syntactophonemics

   2. Syntax proper

The morphology (or the morphology proper) includes the following primary divisions:
(1) the inventory of morphemes by classes, and (2) the distributions of morphemes.

The inventory of morphemes is divided between (a) roots and (b) nonroots. This is for
most languages the primary structural division. Certain isolating languages, in which each
morpheme is a root and has a syntactic type of distribution, would exhibit no such dichot-
omy.

Roots are divided on the basis of their major distributional environments, e.g. nouns,
verbs, pronouns, nouns and verbs, nouns and pronouns, particles. Further distinctions may
be made between free roots and bound roots, but this distinction is generally indicated by
the manner in which the morpheme is listed, i.e. with or without a structural hyphen.

Nonroots are divided on the basis of occurrence with various classes of roots, e.g.
nouns, verbs, nouns and verbs, pronouns. The divisions of roots and nonroots in the inventory of forms anticipates the distributional statements made later in the grammar.

In the inventory section of the file there must be a special division for unclassified
stems. There are always morphemes which do not seem to fit into any class, and the assigning of class membership to such morphemes must wait further examination of the distributions.

It is obvious that this section of the file reflects the data included in the following section, where the distribution of specific morphemes and classes of morphemes is listed. However, the grouping of classes of morphemes in this inventory section makes possible
more accurate and comprehensive descriptions of the particular distributions.

The section on the distribution of morphemes is subdivided according to the principal
word classes (and morphological-structure classes, or both) of the language as determined
by their internal distribution. The external distribution of such classes is a matter for
the syntax. In many instances, however, we need to recognize internal and external distributions in order to make a coherent description of the language as a whole. One will probably find it necessary to set up at least three principal classes: nouns, verbs, and particles. As the number of primary distributional distinctions increases, more principal
classes may be set up. Later such classes may be combined if the structure reveals important affinities not previously recognized. The value of the filing system lies precisely
in this flexibility.

If we set up nouns as the first principal structural class, we should then subdivide
this class into derivational and inflectional formations, provided, of course, that the
language exhibits such distinctions.[6] Under the derivation we distinguish (1) root-plus-
root (or nucleus-plus-nucleus) and (2) root-plus-nonroot formations. Nouns in the first
of these constructions we subdivide under their sequence classes and those in the second

---

[6]Many languages, among them Chinese and Burmese, exhibit only derivational formations.

we list under their determiners. The determiners may at first be subdivided purely on the basis of alphabetical listing, but later it may be convenient to classify them by relative orders, categories, or sets of mutually obligatory or mutually exclusive morphemes.

In actual practice the analysis of the derivational formations of any word class is undertaken rather late in the procedure. The usual reasons for this are:

1. The many complex allomorphic alternations.

2. The nonproductive character of many of the structures, which makes it difficult to isolate morphemes.

3. Complications due to borrowings from foreign languages. Portions of the borrowed words may show partial resemblances to nonborrowed ones, but they may be structurally and semantically very difficult to relate.

As a result of these complications, many descriptive grammars merely touch on the derivation, mentioning solely the very productive patterns.

The inflectional formations, as well as the derivational ones, should ultimately be treated in terms of immediate constituents, since they determine the pertinent environment of any morpheme. It is quite impossible, however, to know the immediate constituents of formations without a knowledge of all the patterns. Accordingly, in filing inflectional formations the determiners, which identify and define the extent of the structural pattern, may be filed (1) alphabetically, (2) by broad subdivisions of structure, e.g. prefixal, suffixal, suprafixal, (3) by categories, and (4) by relative orders. Whether one employs a subdivision by categories depends largely upon the relationship of categories to formal and distributional features. The significance of relative orders is likewise dependent upon their correlation with successive sets of immediate constituents. However, there tend to be many more relationships between relative orders and immediate constituents, than between categories and immediate constituents. Special attention must also be paid to mutually obligatory and mutually exclusive occurrences between different orders.

Having treated the nouns in accordance with derivational and inflectional formations, one then considers the other structural classes, e.g. verbs, pronouns, attributives, and particles. The term "particle" is usually not applied to a class of forms exhibiting inflectional formations; and so in this instance at least, one would describe only the derivation. Treatment of the derivation might consist solely in listing a few complex formations. All single root words serving as particles would be listed in the inventory section.

It is impossible to determine in advance of analysis what specific form a file should have. Nevertheless, the following outlines will be found to be broadly applicable in a number of situations.

Outline A

   I. Morphophonemics

      A. Phonologically defined distribution

         1. Classifiable by phonological processes

            a. Assimilation

            b. Nasalization

            c. Palatalization

            d. Reduction of clusters

               etc.

       2. Not classifiable by phonological processes

    B. Morphologically defined distribution

       1. Classifiable by phonological processes

          a. Assimilation

          b. Nasalization

             etc.

       2. Not classifiable by phonological processes

II. Morphology

    A. Inventory of morphemes

       1. Roots

          a. Noun[7]

          b. Verb

          c. Noun and verb

          d. Attributive

          e. Attributive and noun

          f. Particle

             etc.

       2. Nonroots

          a. Occurring with nouns[8]

          b. Occurring with verbs

          c. Occurring with nouns and verbs

             etc.

    B. Distribution of morphemes

       1. Nouns

          a. Derivational formations

             1'. Root plus root

                a'. Noun plus noun

---

[7]These classes may be subdivided to indicate any major distribution classes.

[8]These classes may be further subdivided to distinguish derivational and inflectional morphemes.

        b'. Noun plus verb

        c'. Noun plus attributive

          etc.

      2'. Root plus nonroot[9]

    b. Inflectional formations[10]

  2. Verbs

    a. Derivational formations

    b. Inflectional formations[10]

  3. Attributives

    a. Derivational formations

    b. Inflectional formations[10]

  4. Particles

    a. Derivational formations[11]

III. Syntax[12]

Whether any file has these particular divisions depends entirely upon the structure of the language; similarly, the number of subdivisions is dependent upon the complexity of the structure. In languages where the allomorphic alternation occurring in morphological constructions differs significantly from that occurring in syntactic constructions, it is advisable to employ a somewhat altered file outline:

Outline B[13]

  I. Morphology

---

[9]Subdivisions in this class are usually listed under specific determiners; but where successive layers occur, the subdivisions should reflect such sets of immediate constituents.

[10]Subdivisions should ultimately reflect successive sets of immediate constituents, beginning with the uninflected stem, but initial filing usually follows an alphabetical listing of morphemes.

[11]There are usually very few such formations; inflectional formations are rare in classes called particles.

[12]The construction of the syntax file does not come within the scope of this treatment, but the general pattern is the same. The primary division is between (1) inventory of syntactic word classes and (2) distribution of these classes. The second section is subdivided between (a) non-sentence-forming constructions and (b) sentence-forming constructions. The non-sentence-forming constructions may be subdivided in accordance with endocentric, exocentric, coördinate, and subordinate distinctions, and the sentence-forming constructions may be subdivided conveniently between principal and nonprincipal.

[13]This second outline does not attempt to include the detail of the first, since the differences are ones of primary, not secondary, divisions.

A. Morphophonemics

   1. Phonologically defined distributions

   2. Morphologically defined distributions

B. Morphology proper

   1. Inventory of morphemes

   2. Distribution of morphemes

II. Syntax

A. Syntactophonemics

B. Syntax proper

8.3 Determining the Relative Order of Morphemes

In determining the relative order of morphemes there are two steps in procedure: (1) plotting the actual positions as they occur in the recorded data and (2) determining the successive sequences.

We may illustrate the process of determining the relative order of morphemes by treating the suffixes of Zoque in the data of Problem 116. The procedure includes several steps:

1. List the morphemes in a column.

2. Rule off and number additional columns in which to indicate successive positions counting from the stem.

3. Indicate in these columns (by x) all the actual positions, counting from the stem, which are occupied by each morpheme.

4. List for one of the morphemes all the forms in which it occurs in its farthest position from the stem (or numerically highest position) according to step 3.

5. Now determine the farthest position from the stem (or numerically highest position) which may be occupied by each of the morphemes that immediately precedes the particular morpheme in the forms listed for it in step 4.

6. Assign the particular morpheme a relative order that is one number higher than the numerically highest position of any of the morphemes treated in step 5.

A chart of the actual positions of the Zoque suffixal morphemes would look like this:

Suffixes	Actual Position Counting from Stem											Forms Containing Suffix in Farthest or Highest Actual Position from Stem
	1	2	3	4	5	6	7	8	9	10	14	
1. -pa ~ -p	x	x										4, 10, 14, 17, 21, 38, 39, 57, 59, 69
2. -u ~ -w	x	x	x	x								20, 43
3. -hay[15]	x											3, 4, 7, 8, 14, 15, 19, 20, 24, 43, 51, 52, 67
4. -yah	x	x										7, 20, 26, 27, 28, 43, 54, 61, 67
5. -ṭoʔy	x	x										8, 15, 62
6. -teʔ	x	x	x									20, 43, 54
7. -keʔt	x	x	x	x								20, 43
8. -tih		x	x		x		x					43
9. -šeh		x		x		x						43

etc.

Having charted the actual positions of morphemes and listed the forms which exhibit the suffixes in their hightest actual positions, our next task is to determine the relative order of each morpheme by the fifth step in the procedure. To describe this process we may designate the morpheme whose relative order we wish to determine as **X** and all other morphemes as **Y**. Step 5 may be subdivided as follows:

1. List the Y morphemes immediately preceding **X** in those forms in which **X** occurs in its highest actual position. For the morpheme -pa ~ -p we must list all the morphemes occurring in forms 4, 10, 14, 17, 21, 38, 39, 57, 59, 69.

2. Determine which Y morpheme has the highest actual position. We will then know that the **X** morpheme has a relative order at least one number higher than the highest Y. In the case of -pa ~ -p we find that in forms 17, 21, 57, and 69 the Y morpheme immediately preceding **X** is -keʔt (morpheme 7), which occurs in a fourth actual position. This means that -pa ~ -p belongs to at least the fifth relative order.

3. Select the highest Y morpheme, and treat it as an **X** morpheme in determining its own relative order. This means that we shift our attention to -keʔt and consider its Y morphemes, which occur in forms 20 and 43. The Y morpheme in these forms is -teʔ, which never occurs in an actual position higher than 3.

4. Continue to select Y morphemes to establish successive series of **X** morphemes until all the relative orders are determined.

The test of mutually exclusive occurrence must be employed in dealing with morphemes listed as belonging to the same relative orders. For example, we may determine that -pa ~

---

[14] It is possible to treat morphemes in orders 8, 9, and 10 as clitics, but the evidence for this is not provided by the data of Problem 116.

[15] It is obvious that a form which is always juxtaposed to the root belongs to the first relative order.

-p and -u ~ -w both belong to the fifth relative order. We must then proceed to check through all the data to see whether any one form contains both morphemes. If it does, then we have made a mistake. If not, then our description of relative orders can stand until we discover contradictory evidence.

Problem 118 (data consisting of the Zoque forms listed in Problem 116)

    Instructions:

        a. Continue the charting of the actual positions of the suffixes.

        b. Determine the relative orders of all the suffixes.

Problem 119 (data consisting of the Congo Swahili forms listed in Problem 5)

    Instructions: Determine the relative orders of the morphemes in the verb forms.

Problem 120 (data consisting of the Aztec forms listed in Problem 115)

    Instructions: Determine the relative orders of the morphemes in the verb forms.

8.4 Use of Arbitrary[16] Symbols in Identifying Forms

    Just as the mathematician finds it convenient to employ symbols for various factors and to describe relationships by these, so the linguist uses symbols to simplify and clarify his statements about structure.[17]

    Symbols may be used in a number of different ways to identify forms and structure. For example, in describing the inflection of verbs, various classes of roots or stems may be identified as A, B, C, etc.; I, II, III, etc.; or 1, 2, 3, etc. In some analyses one may wish to distinguish verb, noun, attributive, and pronominal roots as V, N, A, and P, respectively. Then subclasses of verb stems may be indicated by subscript numerals, e.g. V_1, V_2, V_3, etc.; or if the subclasses are related to such distinctions as transitive and intransitive, then the classes may be indicated as V_t and V_i or, somewhat more conveniently, as Vt and Vi. Noun stems may be distinguished as Np^t 'possessed noun stems' and Nu 'unpossessed noun stems.' Or one may want to distinguish masculine, feminine, and neuter stems by Nm, Nf, Nn. There are no limits, except practical ones, to the extent to which one may employ such symbols, and there is no fixed manner in which this symbolization must be carried out.

    In symbolizing inflectional formations it has been found convenient to use series of numerals which indicate the various features of the structure. For example, the Zoque inflectional affixes in Problem 116 may be symbolized by numerals arranged according to the following system:

---

[16]The term "arbitrary" does not apply to the system employed, but to the fact that the symbols chosen are not related to the forms of the morpheme. In this sense, all mathematical symbols, also, are arbitrary.

[17]The following articles indicate how structural statements may employ arbitrary symbolization: C. F. Voegelin, "A Problem in Morpheme Alternants and Their Distribution," Language, 23 (1947), 3: 245-54; Zellig S. Harris, "Structural Restatements II," International Journal of American Linguistics, 13,(1947), 3: 175-86; and Paul L. Garvin, "Kutenai III: Morpheme Distributions (Prefix, Theme, Suffix)," International Journal of American Linguistics, 14 (1948) 3: 171-87.

1. Successive positions counting to the left from a decimal point.

   a. The number of the morpheme within a relative order.

   b. The relative order counting from the stem.

   c. The relationship of the affix to the form as a whole, i.e. suffixal or prefixal.

2. Successive positions counting to the right of the decimal point.

   a. The morphologically defined allomorphs.

   b. The phonologically defined allomorphs.

In the Zoque data there are three suffixes in the fifth order: -pa ~ -p 'incompletive,' -u ~ -w 'completive,' and -a 'neutral aspect,' occurring in forms with ha-, negative prefix. We may list these as follows:

-pa 251.01

-p 251.02

-u 252.01

-w 252.02

-a 253.

When there is no need of distinguishing phonologically defined alternants then the numerals 251. and 252. suffice. To identify all of this series we may employ 250.

The prefixal morpheme y- 'third person subject in the transitive verb' could be symbolized as 111., and yah- 'causative' as 112.

The first numeral indicates whether the form is prefixal or suffixal. Prefixes are 100., and suffixes 200.

The perfective morpheme -a?a ∞ -?a ∞ -a constitutes a set of morphologically defined allomorphs:[18] -a?a occurs in forms 32, 33, 34, 35, 51, 52, 55, and 60; -?a occurs in form 48; and -a occurs in forms 37, 38, and 67. These may be listed as 271.1, 271.2, and 271.3. There are no other morphemes of the seventh order.

Having determined a numerical value for all the morphemes, we may describe the forms by their symbols, e.g.:

1. kenu V + 252.01[19]

2. kenpa V + 251.01

3. kyenhayu 111.± V ± 211. + 252.01

---

[18] In the restricted data treated here it would be possible to describe these allomorphs as having phonologically defined distributions, but because of the nature of the environments given in this problem, it is "safer" to consider them morphologically defined.

[19] One does not normally indicate phonologically defined allomorphs, particularly if some comprehensive statement may be made in the morphophonemics covering all such phonological alternants.

43. <u>kyenhayahteʔkeʔtušehtih</u> 111. ± V ± 211. ± 221.± 231.± 241.+ 252.± 281.± 291.[20]

There are some statements which may be simplified by the use of such symbols. For example, we may say that the basic requirements of any verb are V + 250. These are the only required constituents. All the others are optional. Furthermore, we can easily state the types of sequences which occur, and may even determine something in regard to their frequency.

<u>Problem 121</u> (data consisting of the Zoque forms listed in Problem 116)

Instructions: Write out the formulas for the following forms: 10, 16, 19, 36, 49, 55, and 62.

<u>Problem 122</u> (data consisting of the Ilamba forms listed in Problem 38)

Instructions:

a. Set up three major classes of stems: nouns, adjectives, and verbs.

b. Subdivide the adjectives into A1, e.g. <u>-ko·lu</u> 'big,' and A2, e.g. <u>-akoe</u> 'his,' <u>-moe</u> 'one,' and <u>-bele</u> 'two.'

c. Subdivide the noun stems into eight classes, e.g. N1, N2, N3, etc.

d. Treat only the prefixal forms of the first five words in each sentence.

e. Do not attempt to indicate the different relative orders in the verbs.

f. Describe the distributions which occur.

Certain important cautions must be indicated in the use of arbitrary symbols to identify morphemes and classes of morphemes:

1. Symbolization should simplify. The difficulty with any system of symbolization is the tendency to be exceedingly complicated. The economy enjoyed as a result of neater statements does not always compensate for the space occupied in the listing and defining of the symbols.

2. Symbols must be adapted to the language. It is impossible to adopt one type of symbolization and employ it for all types of languages.

3. Symbols should be used only when the structure of the language is so complicated that it can be much more easily described in this fashion.

4. The construction of symbolic formulas cannot substitute for description by immediate constituents. The mechanical listing of sequences without indicating the layers of formation and the successive sets of immediate constituents is entirely inadequate.[21]

---

[20] The symbol ± means "plus or minus" and denotes that a form is not obligatory. Note that order 5 is always marked by the symbol +.

[21] It should be noted in this connection that Garvin's treatment of Kutenai (<u>op. cit.</u>) is an excellent listing of the sequences, and indirectly indicates the main outlines of the sets of immediate constituents; but it is essentially a step (though a very important one) in the analytical procedure, rather than a final description of structure.

Problem 123 (data [restricted] from the Isthmus dialect of Zapotec, a language of Mexico)

Instructions:

    a. Identify the morphemes.

    b. File the data in accordance with the proper outline.

1. baʔdu   'child'

2. nawiʔini   'is small'

3. nabiǰi   'is dry'

4. bibiǰini   'it dried'

5. baʔdu-wiʔini   'baby'

6. ma biǰagaaʔ   'I'm already tired'

7. bikičini   'it became white'

8. giči   'paper'

9. giči-kiči   'white paper'

10. nanaaʔ   'I know'

11. nakaaʔ   'I am'

12. nanalu   'you (sg.) know'

13. nakabe la   'is he?'

14. naroʔ   'is big'

15. yoʔo   'house'

16. yoʔo-roʔ   'big house'

17. -ǰapa   'feminine person'

18. baʔdu-ǰapa   'girl'

19. ngiʔiu   'man'

20. baʔdu-ngiʔiu   'boy'

21. nakiči   'is white'

22. kayoʔo   'houses'

23. yoʔoka   'that house'

24. ngiʔiuka   'that man'

25. kangiʔiuka   'those men'

26. baʔdu-wiʔinika   'that baby'

27. kabaʔdu-ǰapa   'girls'

28. baʔduka   'that child'

29. nabaaninu   'we live'

30. nabaanitu   'you (pl.) live'

31. zabaanipe   'they will live'

32. bikaʔaʔ   'I wrote'

33. bikaʔnu   'we wrote'

34. zabiʔitu   'you (pl.) will go home'

35. zabiʔilu   'you (sg.) will go home'

36. ma   'already'

37. iǯiʔ   'tomorrow'

38. yanna   'now'

39. tobi   'one'

40. tapa   'four'

41. gaʔayu   'five'

42. skiči   'paper (someone's)'

43. spaʔdu   'child (someone's)'

44. geta   'corncake'

45. sketa   'corncake (someone's)'

46. diʔiǰa   'word'

47. stiʔiǰa   'word (someone's)'

48. doʔo   'rope'

49. stoʔo   'rope (someone's)'

50. stoʔo la   'rope? (someone's)'

51. nabiʔilu la   'are you (sg.) going home?'

Problem 124 (hypothetical data)[22]

Instructions:

    a. Phonemicize the following data.

    b. Identify the morphemes.

    c. File the data in accordance with the proper outline.

1. [linaa]　'his hand'

2. [ndiiˀ linaa]　'this is his hand'

3. [panda lopaluˀ]　'how many sticks do you have?'

4. [lᴐnaalaˀ]　'your hands'

5. [lanÑ̃ñaˀa]　'our mother'

6. [lonnaalaˀ]　'your (pl.) hands'

7. [naŋgakiˀ linaalaˀ]　'look at his hands!'

8. [naŋgawaˀ elbaˀdu]　'they are looking at the boy'

9. [naŋgawa elbaˀdu]　'the boy is looking'

10. [beendawaˀ enbaˀaldu]　'the boys are coming'

11. [beendapaˀ enbaˀaldu]　'the boys came'

12. [mualamaˀ eŋkiišalaˀ]　'the girls will return'

13. [ñenepa elkiiša]　'the girl thought'

14. [elbere ganupama]　'you saw the chicken'

15. [linlayalaˀ]　'their teeth'

16. [ᴍanisa elbeendaˀ]　'the fish is in the water'

17. [maniiza enberelaˀ]　'the chickens are in the corn'

18. [ganukiˀ ᴇnnaažaˀ]　'see the twins!'

19. [zendata niiza]　'he will gather corn'

20. [kanulaˀ]　'listen!'

21. [ganupaˀ biisi toobi]　'they saw one ghost'

(Continued on next page.)

---

[22]The stems and phonemic problems are from Zapotec of the Isthmus, while the affixes and the manner in which they occur with the stems reflect the usage in Chontal of Oaxaca, Mexico.

22. [sanisa winiwa elbeʔenda]   'the snake lives under water'

23. [ndiiʔ beʔenda toobi]   'this is one snake'

24. [gasetaʔ džiʔiña]   'they will look for sugar'

25. [zendapaʔ eldžiʔiña]   'they gathered the sugar'

26. [nuuma]   'he will start'

27. [rienemama]   'you will say'

28. [rawawaya]   'I am calling'

29. [rienepayaʔ]   'we said'

30. [beñe rawapayaʔ]   'we called it clay'

31. [ŋgaa]   'that?'

32. [sapalu elnisa]   'the water is under the stick'

33. [madžiʔiña niiza]   'there is corn in the sugar'

34. [paraʔa zialawamaʔ]   'where are you (pl.) going?'

35. [paraʔa enbeendalaʔ tšona]   'where are the three fish?'

36. [ganuwaya]   'I am seeing'

37. [panda džuuʔ gaseʔwaʔ]   'how many soldiers are they looking for?'

38. [ganaya]   'I have seen'

39. [šoono paluʔ]   'eight sticks'

40. [gaša endžuuʔ Mmaa]   'more soldiers are near'

41. [ndiiʔ beñe Mmaa]   'this is more clay'

42. [tšona džiiʔ zialamaʔ]   'they will go for three days'

43. [yaana zialamayaʔ]   'now we will go'

44. [starama]   'he will go home'

45. [štarapaʔ]   'they hit'

46. [waraatayaʔ]   'we will ask it'

47. [gaša winipaʔ]   'they lived nearby'

48. [winaʔ]   'they died'

49. [tapa Ññaʔalaʔ]   'four mothers'

50. [nažakiʔ]   'try it!'

(Continued on next page.)

51. [nažawaya^ɂ]　'we are trying'

52. [laaduwaya^ɂ]　'we are singing'

53. [laadula^ɂ]　'sing!'

54. [laada]　'he finished singing'

55. [laatula^ɂ]　'run!'

56. [para^ɂa laatuwa^ɂ]　'where are they running?'

57. [zialama]　'you have gone?'

58. [ŋgaa liniiza]　'that is his corn'

59. [para^ɂa loberela^ɂ]　'where are your chickens?'

60. [ganupa elÑña^ɂa elkiiša]　'the mother saw the girl'

61. [lanlayala^ɂ]　'our teeth'

62. [toobi laya]　'one tooth'

63. [tšona biišali]　'three ghosts'

64. [rienaya^ɂ]　'we finished saying'

65. [rienewaya^ɂ]　'we are saying'

66. [gaša be^ɂendala^ɂ]　'there are snakes nearby'

67. [zialamaya^ɂ]　'let's go'

68. [ñene^ɂmaya^ɂ]　'let's think'

69. [haa naaža^ɂ]　'imagine that! they are twins'

70. [tšu^ɂu]　'let's go!'

71. [hana]　'let's'

72. [neše elbeenda^ɂ]　'the fish is ready'

73. [neše elniiza]　'the corn is ready'

74. [haa rawawa]　'imagine that! he is calling'

75. [ŋgaa palu]　'that is a stick'

76. [kanuwama]　'are you listening?'

77. [para^ɂa winipa]　'where did he live?'

78. [mualapaya^ɂ]　'we returned'

79. [ñene^ɂaya^ɂ]　'we finished thinking'

(Continued on next page.)

80. [naaža elkiiša]   'the girl is a twin'

81. [beendawaya]   'I am coming'

82. [gasepamaʔ elbaʔdu ŋgaa]   'you (pl.) looked for that boy'

83. [elstala]   'the house'

84. [lanstalaʔ]   'our houses'

85. [lastala]   'my house'

Problem 125 (hypothetical data)

Instructions:

    a. Identify the morphemes.

    b. File the data in accordance with the proper outline.

1. minak   'I hunt'

2. mitonak   'we hunt'

3. mitonaket   'we hunted'

4. mitonaks   'we will hunt'

5. tinaket   'you (sg.) hunted'

6. tidilet   'you (sg.) climbed'

7. titodils   'you (pl.) will climb'

8. kadils   'he will climb'

9. kalams   'he will see'

10. katolam   'they see'

11. katolamet   'they saw'

12. titolam   'you (pl.) see'

13. titodilu   'you (pl.) begin to climb'

14. tidiletu   'you (sg.) began to climb'

15. titodilsu   'you (pl.) will begin to climb'

16. kanaku   'he begins to hunt'

17. kanaksu   'he will begin to hunt'

18. nilamu   'I begin to see'

19. nilametu   'I began to see'

20. somi   'my blanket'

21. somito   'our blanket'

22. sosomito   'our blankets'

23. sosoti   'your (sg.) blankets'

24. sosoka   'his blankets'

25. nuka   'his horse'

26. nunuka   'his horses'

27. nunukato   'their horses'

28. smoti   'your (sg.) grandfather'

29. smosmotito   'your (pl.) grandfathers'

30. smosmomi   'my grandfathers'

31. ksami   'my house'

32. ksaksaka   'his houses'

33. ksaksamito   'our houses'

Problem 126 (data from Tojolabal, a language of Mexico)

Instructions:

    a. Identify the morphemes.

b. File the data on verb inflection in accordance with the proper outline.

c. Work out a system of numerical symbolization for the inflectional affixes.

1. hman   'I buy'

2. ak'an   'you (sg.) want'

3. slap   'he dresses'

4. kil   'I see'

5. awal   'you (sg.) say'

6. yuʔ   'he drinks'

7. -man   'buy'

8. -k'an   'want'

9. -lap   'dress'

10. -il   'see'

11. -al   'say'

12. -uʔ   'drink'

13. sk'elawa   'he looks at you (sg.)'

14. sk'elawon   'he looks at me'

15. atup   'you (sg.) pay'

16. atupuwon   'you (sg.) pay me'

17. atupu   'you (sg.) see it'

18. hčono   'I sell it'

19. ačonowon   'you (sg.) sell me'

20. hk'elawa   'I look at you (sg.)'

21. smak'awon   'he hits me'

22. awila   'you (sg.) see him'

23. stupuwotik   'he pays us (incl.)'

24. spayaweš   'he calls you (pl.)'

25. sk'ušu   'he bites him, them'

26. hmahatik   'we (incl.) loan it'

27. ak'ep'awoneš   'you (pl.) give it to me'

28. smukuweʔ   'they conceal it'

29. hlik'atikon   'we (excl.) lift it'

30. swetawotikon   'he kicks us (excl.)'

31. hmak'awatikon   'we (excl.) hit you (sg.)'

32. hmesuneh   'I have swept it'

33. atuluneh   'you (sg.) have gathered it'

34. sk'anuneh   'he has asked for it'

35. hmanuneh   'I have bought it'

36. hsihpunehtikon   'we (excl.) have dropped it'

37. amahluneheš   'you (pl.) have waited for it'

38. sk'uluneheʔ   'they have made it'

39. sk'ep'unehotikon   'he has given us (excl.) a gift'

40. smak'uneheš   'he has hit you (pl.)'

41. slik'unehon   'he has lifted me'

42. hmak'unehestik   'we have hit you (pl.)'

43. ahekunehoneš   'you (pl.) have sent me'

44. slik'unehoneʔ   'they have lifted me'

Supplementary information:

1. The first-order suffixal morpheme -a ~ -aw ~ -o ~ -ow ~ -u ~ -uw, exhibiting vocalic harmony with the stem vowel, indicates that an object follows.

2. Third person singular and plural objects are indicated by zero.

3. Third person subjects are overtly plural only when the suffix -eʔ occurs. Otherwise, third person subject forms may be singular or plural depending upon the context.

4. Certain of the suffixal morphemes are structurally combined prior to their addition to the stem, e.g. -otik, -tikon, and -otikon.

<u>Problem 127</u> (data from the Tetelcingo dialect of Aztec, a language of Mexico)

Instructions:

    a. Identify the morphemes.

    b. List the types of pronouns.

1. itlak   'near him'

2. kotlaha   'which one?'

3. tlininu   'what is that?'

4. ɔki   'who?'

5. ɔkɪnu   'who is that?'

6. wɛlaha   'the very one'

7. yaha inu   'that one'

8. nokniwa   'my brothers'

9. ikniwa   'his brothers'

10. tokni   'our brother'

11. mokni   'your brother'

12. ɔki mɛhwa   'who are they?'

13. tlɪ   'what?'

14. tɛhwa tɪmɪcmaka   'we give it to you (sg.)'

15. yaha nɛmɛčmaka   'he gives it to you'

16. šinɛčmaka   'give it to me'

17. šɪkmaka   'give it to him'

18. yɛhwa nɛmɛčmaka   'they give it to you (pl.)'

19. yɛhwa tɛčmaka   'they give it to us'

20. nɛmɛhwa nɛnɛčmaka   'you (pl.) give it to me'

21. yaha kimaka   'he gives it to him'

22. šitɛčmaka   'give it to us'

23. yaha nɛčmaka   'he gives it to me'

24. taha tɪkmaka   'you (sg.) give it to him'

25. nɛmɛhwa nɛnkimaka   'you (pl.) give it to him'

26. naha tɪmɪcmaka   'I give it to you (sg.)'

27. tɛhwa tɪkmaka   'we give it to him'

28. taha titɛčmaka   'you (sg.) give it to us'

29. naha ninɛmɛčmaka   'I give it to you (pl.)'

30. ika   'with him'

31. totlak   'near us'

32. noka   'with me'

<u>Problem 128</u> (data from Pame-Chichimeca, a language of Mexico)

Instructions:

    a. Identify the morphemes.

    b. Determine the relative orders.

    c. Describe the future conditional (1-20) and the completive (21-40) series. Combine these descriptions in so far as possible.

1. lóhwę̨ʔʉkʔ   'I will pay you (sg.)'

2. lóhwę̨ʔʉik̓y   'I will pay you (du.)'

3. lóhwę̨ʔʉkŋ   'I will pay you (pl.)'

4. lóhwę̨ʔę̨p   'I will pay him'

(<u>Continued</u> <u>on</u> <u>next</u> <u>page</u>.)

5. lóhwę́ʔu̧i̧   'I will pay them (du.)'   23. nóhwę́ʔu̧kŋ   'I paid you (pl.)'

6. lóhwę́ʔu̧t   'I will pay them (pl.)'   24. nóhwę́ʔ ę̧p   'I paid him'

7. kíhyę́ʔu̧k   'You will pay me, us (du. excl.)'   25. nóhwę́ʔu̧i̧   'I paid them (du.)'

8. kíhyę́ʔu̧kŋ 'You will pay us (pl. incl. and excl.)'   26. nóhwę́ʔu̧t   'I paid them (pl.)'

9. kíhyę́ʔ ę̧p 'You will pay him'   27. níhyę́ʔu̧k   'You paid me, us (du. excl.)'

10. kíhyę́ʔu̧i̧ 'You will pay them (du.)'   28. níhyę́ʔu̧kŋ 'You paid us (pl. incl. and excl.)'

11. kíhyę́ʔu̧t 'You will pay them (pl.)'   29. níhyę́ʔ ę̧p 'You paid him'

12. láhę́ʔu̧k   'He will pay me, us (du. excl.)'   30. níhyę́ʔu̧i̧ 'You paid them (du.)'

13. láhę́ʔu̧i̧ky 'He will pay us (du. incl.)'   31. níhyę́ʔu̧t 'You paid them (pl.)'

14. láhę́ʔu̧kŋ 'He will pay us (pl. incl. and excl.)'   32. ndóhwę́ʔu̧k 'He paid me, us (du. excl.)'

15. láhę́ʔu̧kʔ 'He will pay you (sg.)'   33. ndóhwę́ʔu̧i̧ky 'He paid us (du. incl.)'

16. láhę́ʔu̧i̧kʔy 'He will pay you (du.)'   34. ndóhwę́ʔu̧kŋ 'He paid us (pl. incl. and excl.)'

17. láhę́ʔu̧kŋ 'He will pay you (pl.)'   35. ndóhwę́ʔu̧kʔ 'He paid you (sg.)'

18. láhę́ʔ ę̧p 'He will pay him'   36. ndóhwę́ʔu̧i̧kʔy 'He paid you (du.)'

19. láhę́ʔu̧i̧ 'He will pay them (du.)'   37. ndóhwę́ʔu̧kŋ 'He paid you (pl.)'

20. láhę́ʔu̧t   'He will pay them (pl.)'   38. ndóhwę́ʔ ę̧p 'He paid him'

21. nóhwę́ʔu̧kʔ 'I paid you (sg.)'   39. ndóhwę́ʔu̧i̧ 'He paid them (du.)'

22. nóhwę́ʔu̧i̧kʔy 'I paid you (du.)'   40. ndóhwę́ʔu̧t 'He will pay them (pl.)'

Supplementary information:

1. Postconsonantal y and w are conditioned by the occurrence of a preceding i or o.

2. The cluster Cʔŋ reduces to Cŋ.

3. The sequence V̧V becomes V̧V̧.

4. The prefixal portion of the future conditional series should be regarded as consisting of two sets of morphemes. Describe the alternation l- ∞ k- in terms of the following morphemes.

5. Forms 14 and 17 and forms 34 and 37 are homophonous as the result of the reduction in consonant cluster described in supplementary information 2.

Problem 129 (data from Pame-Chichimeca, a language of Mexico)

Instructions:

a. Identify the morphemes.

b. Describe the distributions. This may be done most conveniently by symbolizing the morphemes and allomorphs by some numerical or alphabetical device.

1. laháoʔ   'I drink, am drinking'

2. kihyáoʔ   'you (sg.) drink'

3. waháoʔ   'he drinks'

4. taháoiʔ   'we (du. incl.) drink'

5. kihyáoiʔ   'you (du.) drink'

6. waháoiʔ   'they (du.) drink'

7. tahábmʔ   'we (du. and pl. excl.) drink'

8. taháodnʔ   'we (pl. incl.) drink'

9. kihyáodnʔ   'you (pl.) drink'

10. lháoʔ   'they drink'

11. laháoʔ   'I will drink'

12. kiŋhyáoʔ   'you (sg.) will drink'

13. lanháoʔ   'he will drink'

14. laháoiʔ   'we (du. incl.) will drink'

15. kiŋhyáoiʔ   'you (du.) will drink'

16. lanháoiʔ   'they (du.) will drink'

17. lahábmʔ   'we (du. and pl. excl.) will drink'

18. laháodnʔ   'we (pl. incl.) will drink'

19. kiŋhyáodnʔ   'you (pl.) will drink'

20. lalháoʔ   'they will drink'

21. nohwáoʔ   'I drank'

22. niŋhyáoʔ   'you (sg.) drank'

23. ndohwáoʔ   'he drank'

24. nohwáoiʔ   'we (du. incl.) drank'

25. niŋhyáoiʔ   'you (du.) drank'

26. ndohwáoiʔ   'they (du.) drank'

27. nohwábmʔ   'we (du. and pl. excl.) drank'

28. nohwáodnʔ   'we (pl. incl.) drank'

29. niŋhyáodnʔ   'you (pl.) drank'

30. ndolháoʔ   'they drank'

31. ndaháoʔ   '(if) I had drunk'

32. ŋgiŋhyáoʔ   '(if) you (sg.) had drunk'

33. ndanháoʔ   '(if) he had drunk'

34. ndaháoiʔ   '(if) we (du. incl.) had drunk'

35. ŋgiŋhyáoiʔ   '(if) you (du.) had drunk'

36. ndanháoiʔ   '(if) they (du.) had drunk'

37. ndahábmʔ   '(if) we (du. and pl. excl.) had drunk'

38. ndaháodnʔ   '(if) we (pl. incl.) had drunk'

39. ŋgiŋhyáodnʔ   '(if) you (pl.) had drunk'

40. ndalháoʔ   '(if) they had drunk'

Supplementary information:

1. Forms 1–10 are progressive (past or present), forms 11–20 are future conditional, forms 21–30 are completive (past or present), and forms 31–40 are present or past conditional.

2. The stem is -háoʔ.

3. The form iŋ- (an allomorph of the second person subject prefix) occurs in certain tense-aspects and before a restricted number of stems beginning with h and ʔ.

4. See Problem 128 for additional morphophonemic data.

5. The morphemes -nd- (plural with certain persons) and -i- (dual with most persons) are infixes.

6. The morpheme -mbʔ replaces -oʔ of the stem.

Problem 130 (data from the Mesquital dialect of Otomi, a language of Mexico)

Instructions:

a. Identify the morphemes and determine the meaning of each.

b. Describe the relative orders.

1. ʔę̌hę́   'to come, he comes'

2. díʔę̌hę́   'I am coming'

3. gíʔę̌hę́   'you (sg.) are coming'

4. dáʔę̌hę́   'I came'

5. gáʔę̌hę́   'you (sg.) came'

6. biʔñ̌ę̌hę́   'he came'

7. ndíʔę̌hę́   'I was coming'

8. ngíʔę̌hę́   'you were coming'

9. mbíʔę̌hę́   'he was coming'

10. štáʔę̌hę́   'I have come'

11. škáʔę̌hę́   'you (sg.) have come'

12. šáʔñ̌ę̌hę́   'he has come'

13. gaʔę̌hę́   'I will come'

14. giʔę̌hę́   'you (sg.) will come'

15. daʔñ̌ę̌hę́   'he will come'

16. bíʔę̌hę́   'he is coming (from a distance)'

17. diñṹrí   'he·eats'

18. híndíʔę̌hę́ 'I am not coming'

19. škíʔñ̌ę̌hę́   'he had come'

20. hókí   'to make, he makes'

21. bihyókí   'he made'

22. díʔútí   'I teach'

23. diʔútʔí   'I teach you (sg.)'

24. díʔútaʔí   'I am teaching you (sg.)'

25. díhókaʔí   'I am making for you (sg.)'

26. bithókí   'it was made, someone made'

27. bitʔútí   'he was taught, someone taught'

28. díʔñ̌útíhṹ 'we (incl.) teach'

29. díʔñ̌útíhě̌ 'we (excl.) teach'

30. díʔñ̌útísě̌hṹ 'we (incl.) alone teach'

31. díʔñ̌útísě̌hé 'we (excl.) alone teach'

32. díʔñ̌útwíhṹ 'we (incl.) teach them'

33. díʔñ̌útwábíhṹ 'we (incl.) teach it to them'

34. híndiʔñ̌útwábíhṹ 'we (incl.) do not teach it to them'

35. hadíʔñ̌útwábíhṹ 'do we (incl.) teach it to them?'

36. ndíʔútí   'I was teaching'

37. ndíʔútíhmą̌hą́ 'I was teaching but not now'

38. ndíʔútíthohmą̌hą́ 'formerly I was teaching, nothing more'

39. ndíʔútíthowáhmą̌hą́ 'formerly I was teaching here, nothing more'

40. ndíʔútwithowáhmą̌hą́ 'formerly I was teaching him here, nothing more'

41. ndíʔútíthohě̌ 'we (excl.) were teaching, nothing more'

42. ndíʔútíthohě̌wá 'we (excl.) were teaching here, nothing more'

43. ndíʔútithohě̌wáhmą̌hą́ 'formerly we (excl.) were teaching here, nothing more'

44. ndíʔútwábíhě̌ 'we (excl.) were teaching it to him'

45. ndíʔútwábíhě̌ʔá 'we (excl.) were teaching it to them'

46. ndíʔútwábíhě̌thoʔáhmą̌hą́ 'we (excl.) were teaching it to them, nothing more'

Problem 131 (data from Tarascan, a language of Mexico)

Instructions:

    a. Identify the morphemes.

    b. Determine the meaning of each.

    c. Classify the postposed morphemes on the basis of three principal distribution and order classes.

1. t'iréni   'to eat'

2. t'iréšakani   'I am actually eating'

3. t'iréšakari   'you (sg.) are actually eating'

4. t'iréšati   'he is actually eating'

5. t'iréšakači   'we are actually eating'

6. t'iréšakaxcə   'you (pl.) are actually eating'

7. t'iréšatiksə   'they are actually eating'

8. t'irĕsəŋgani   'I eat as a custom'

9. t'irésəŋgari   'you (sg.) eat as a custom'

10. t'irésəndi   'he eats as a custom'

11. t'irésəŋgači   'we eat as a custom'

12. t'irésəŋgaxcə   'you (pl.) eat as a custom'

13. t'irésəndiksə   'they eat as a custom'

14. terékwaṛiati   'he will laugh'

15. terékwaṛixti   'he laughed'

16. terékwaṛišati   'he is actually laughing'

17. terékwarikwekasəndi   'he wants to laugh'

18. terékwaṛišamti   'he is about to laugh'

19. terékwaṛisəramti   'he used to laugh'

20. terékwaṛisəndi   'he laughs habitually'

21. terékwaṛintaxti   'he laughed again'

22. terékwaṛintati   'he will laugh again'

23. terékwaṛixperaxtiksə   'they laughed at each other'

(Continued on next page.)

24. terékwaṛinčaseramti   'he was wanting to laugh'

25. terékwaṛitišamu   'he laughed, I think'

26. terékwaṛixtiŋa   'he laughed, it is said'

27. terékwaṛitarati   'he will cause to laugh'

28. terékwaṛixtixku   'he laughed only'

29. terékwaṛipirindi   'he would laugh'

30. terékwaṛixtindaru   'he laughed then'

31. terékwaṛiseramtimindu   'he used to laugh indeed'

32. terékwaṛixtiru   'he laughed of course'

Supplementary information:

1. Morphemes which follow the personal pronouns are enclitics.

2. All bound forms in Tarascan are suffixal.

3. The stems of the verbs are t'iré- 'eat' and terékwaṛi- 'laugh.'

CHAPTER 9

THE DESCRIPTIVE STATEMENT OF THE MORPHOLOGY

The final stage in treating the morphology of a language consists in writing up a description. The problems may be classified as structural and technical. The structural difficulties involve the order in which the data are to be described, the relative importance assigned to the various parts, and the manner in which the sections of the description are related to each other. The technical problems include the methods of outlining, the terminology, and the types of statements one may employ.

9.1 Structural Difficulties

The formal description of the morphology should reflect as accurately as possible the structure of the language. By the structure we mean the morphemes and combinations of morphemes described according to their classes and in terms of their pertinent environments, i.e. by immediate constituents.

Many of these structural problems have already been anticipated in the previous chapter on analytical procedures, for the construction of a file necessitates organizing the structural features. There are, of course, a number of different ways in which the description of a language may be organized. The structural outlines in the following section help to point out the contrasts.

9.11 Illustrative Outlines

Certain features of the following outlines on Chichewa, Chiricahua Apache, Delaware, French, Hebrew, Potawatomie, Southern Paiute, Tzeltal, and Yuma should be noted:

1. Only the morphological sections are described in any detail. Phonological and syntactic sections are listed, however, where they occur.

2. The place where morphophonemic problems are treated is indicated, even though there is no special section.

3. All the outlines are given with the same set of symbols. This is designed to make comparison easier.

4. Explanations of content or criticisms are contained in brackets.

5. The outlines given may differ in the following ways from the outlines employed by the writers:

   a. Introductory and general explanatory information is sometimes omitted if it is not particularly pertinent to the structural development of the description.

   b. A good deal of minor detail is not listed.

   c. More subdivisions may be made here than in the originals. Where the headings and the description of the data indicate very clearly that there are subdivisions

or larger groupings not specifically indicated in the outline, these have been
introduced in order to point out more clearly the structural relationships.
Too many subdivisions in an outline make a system of notation very difficult to
follow and cross references are accordingly more complicated. Hence there is a
tendency to treat some sections as coördinate even though they are logically
subordinate. Accordingly, criticisms based upon the "illogical" coördinating
of items are applicable only in a very special sense.

   The following descriptions have been chosen because of the differences in language
structure and in the manner of treating those differences. They are by no means exhaustive
of the possibilities, but they serve to point out some of the more important features of
structural organization.

9.11.1 Chichewa, by Mark Hanna Watkins[1]

Outline

   I. Phonology
   [Certain phonologically defined allomorphic alternations are treated under the
   phonology.]

   II. Morphology

      A. Nouns
         1. Class 1
         2. Class 1a
         3. Class 2
         4. Class 2a
         5. Class 3
         6. Class 4
            etc.
            [The outline includes ten classes of nouns plus an indication of all the
            concordant prefixes which show agreement with each class.]

      B. Verbs
         1. Structure of the verb
         [This is an introductory statement of the structure, primarily from the
         phonological standpoint.]
         2. General survey of verb forms
         [This is an introductory statement of the inflectional structure.]
         3. Verb concordances
         [This deals with the use of subject and object prefixal pronouns with the
         verb.]
         4. Indicative mood
         [All the tenses occurring with this mood are also discussed.]
         5. Imperative mood
         6. Support of reference
         [This is a detailed analysis of the difference between the modal suffixes
         -a and -ε, noted in section B.4 of this outline. It amounts to a descrip-
         tion of the contingent mode form -ε.]
         7. Voice
         8. Radical descriptives
         [These are the independent ideophones, which denote various types of action.
         They are, however, free particles and not verbs. Their inclusion here is

---

[1]Mark Hanna Watkins, A Grammar of Chichewa, Language Dissertation No. 24 (Baltimore:
Linguistic Society of America, 1937).

based upon the fact that they frequently occur together with verbs and in some instances may take the place of verbs.]

   9. Auxiliary verbs
     [These are auxiliary in terms of the syntax.]
  10. Affixes of negation
  11. Auxiliary and subordinating elements

C. Copula
[This form has the function of a verb, but it consists of a stem plus postposed concordant affixes. In all other words the concordant affixes are preposed.]

D. Qualificative constructions
[The concords of adjective-like words are listed.]

E. Numerals

F. Pronouns
   1. Independent personal pronouns
   2. Pronominal concordances
   3. Enumerative pronouns
   4. Possessive pronouns
   5. The relative pronoun

G. Demonstratives
[These are a subclass of pronouns.]

H. Interrogatives
[These are types of pronouns and qualificatives.]

I. Locatives
[These are a subclass of concordant prefixes.]

J. Words with temporal significance
[These are words having a special syntactic usage. They actually form no primary morphological class.]

K. Conjunctions
[Some of these are particles, but a number belong to other morphological classes.]

L. Interjections
[These are primarily particles.]

Discussion:

This grammar of Chichewa contains a vast amount of important information and excellent, acute observations about many features of Bantu structure, but it is somewhat lacking in structural organization:

1. The sections under the verb are not coördinate.

  a. The "radical descriptives" are a separate class of words, and should not be treated along with mood and voice.

  b. All the moods should be grouped together.

  c. Tenses should be treated as a separate feature, coördinate with mood and voice, rather than subordinated to the indicative mood.

    d. Auxiliary verbs are structurally limited, but they conform to the same general morphological patterns.

2. The sections under the verb should be grouped either by categories (which is done in part) or, preferably, by layers of immediate constituents.

3. Entirely too many principal types of words are listed. Structurally there are many fewer types. The divisions are made on the basis of semantic differences or syntactic usage, neither of which criteria is valid for morphological analysis.

There is no section on syntax, but a short text reveals some of the syntactic structure. Furthermore, a number of the illustrations employed in the morphological section consist of entire sentences and so indicate the manner in which morphological constructions combine.

9.11.2 <u>Chiricahua Apache</u>, by Harry Hoijer[2]

<u>Outline:</u>

I. Phonology

II. Morphophonemics
[This section treats the various types of allomorphic alternation in terms of reduced, augmented, contracted, and internally modified syllables. The morphophonemics of Chiricahua Apache is very complex.]

III. Morphology

    A. Nouns
        1. Derivation
            a. Monosyllabic nouns
            b. Nouns requiring a constant possessive prefix
            c. Thematic nouns
            d. Nouns formed from verbs
            e. Compound nouns
        2. Inflection[3]
        [By possessive pronoun prefixes]

    B. Verbs
    [The twelve orders of preposed morphemes are divided into the following structural groupings, since their distribution is closely related. Order 1, consisting of proclitics and order 6, consisting of a distributive prefix, are only mentioned in an introductory statement and are not described.]
        1. Adverbial prefixes
        [Positions 2, 4, and 9]
        2. Object pronoun prefixes
        [Positions 3 and 7]
        3. Subject pronouns and deictic prefixes
        [Positions 8 and 11]
        4. Tense-modal prefixes
        [Positions 5 and 10]

---

[2]Harry Hoijer, "Chiricahua Apache" in <u>Linguistic Structures of Native America</u> (Viking Fund Publications in Anthropology, Vol. 6) (New York, 1946), pp. 55-84.

[3]This section is not labeled, but is clearly distinguished.

5. Classifiers
   [Position 12]

C. Particles
   1. Pronouns
      a. Independent personal pronouns
      b. Demonstratives
      c. Interrogatives

   2. Particles which function as numerals, connectives, adverbs, and adjectives.
      a. Free
      b. Clitic

Discussion:

   The structure of Chiricahua Apache is very complex. This complexity necessitates a rather extensive treatment of the morphophonemics of the language. The highly irregular verb-stem formations require a listing of forms rather than a dissecting of the formal contrasts into possible types of suprafixes and replacives.

   The treatment of the verb prefixes on the basis of categories rather than of relative order is a distinct advantage, since the distribution of the prefixes may be described much more economically in this way. There is some attempt to treat these formations in terms of immediate constituents, but in Chiricahua Apache (and all Athapaskan languages) the sets of immediate constituents are not easily distinguished.

   This grammar is an excellent example of making the framework of the description conform to the structure of the language.

9.11.3 Delaware, by C. F. Voegelin[4]

Outline:

   I. Sounds and phonemes

  II. Phonology
      [This is generally called "morphophonemics."]

      A. Morpheme alternants: in suffixation
         [The allomorphs of all inflectional suffixes are listed here.]

      B. Morpheme alternants: in prefixation
         [The allomorphs of all inflectional prefixes are listed here.]

 III. Prefix paradigms
      [All personal prefixes are treated in this section, whether they are possessives with nouns or subject indicators with verbs. Because of the particular structure of Algonquian languages this section makes constant reference to suffixes.]

  IV. Suffix paradigms
      [This section is subdivided according to various combinations of mode, voice, and person.]

---

[4]C. F. Voegelin, "Delaware, An Eastern Algonquian Language" in Linguistic Structures of Native America (Viking Fund Publications in Anthropology, Vol. 6) (New York, 1946), pp. 130-57.

V. Supplementary paradigms
[These include other affixes occurring with various word classes. Their precise relationship to the prefixal and suffixal paradigms is not stated.]

VI. Themes
[The derivation of various verb, noun, and particle stems is sketchily treated here.]

Discussion:

This grammar attempts to describe structure primarily in terms of distributions. In doing so, it avoids almost completely the divisions into primary word classes and does not follow any system of immediate constituents. This procedure results in considerable obscurity, for Algonquian prefixal and suffixal formations are such that a description based upon sets of immediate constituents is essential if their structure is to be adequately understood.

It is true that this grammar is only a sketch, but the grammar of Chiricahua, which treats an even more complicated type of structure, succeeds in revealing the major outlines of the classes of forms.

9.11.4 French, by Robert A. Hall, Jr.[5]

Outline:

I. Phonology
[One part of this section treats morphophonemic alternations.]

II. Inflection
[An introductory statement lists the various word classes and treats the sandhi, i.e. morphophonemic changes which occur when words are combined into phrases.]

    A. Substantives
       1. Gender relation
         a. Adjectives
         b. Nouns
       2. Number relation
       3. Substantive prefixes
         a. Definite article
         b. Possessive prefixes
         c. Demonstrative prefix

    B. Pronouns
       1. Personal pronouns
       2. Interrogative-relative pronouns
       3. Demonstrative pronouns
       4. Quasi pronouns
         a. Possessive
         b. Indefinite

    C. Verbs
    [An introductory statement treats the categories, the general verb structure, and the classes of verbs.]
       1. Relation of stems to root

---

[5]Robert A. Hall, Jr., French, Language Monograph No. 24, Structural Sketches 1 (1948).

        2. Tense signs
            a. Finite forms
            b. Nonfinite forms
        3. Personal endings
        4. Liaison suffixes

    D. Indeclinables
        1. Adverbs
        2. Prepositions
        3. Conjunctions

    E. Minor-clause forms
       [These are interjections.]

III. Derivation

    A. Alternations in bases
        1. Alternations of vowels
        2. Alternations of consonants
        3. Extended bases
        4. Zero bases

    B. Affixation
        1. Suffixation
            a. Noun-forming suffixes
            b. Adjective-forming suffixes
            c. Pronoun-forming suffixes
            d. Verb-forming suffixes
            e. Adverb-forming suffixes
        2. Prefixation
            a. Endocentric
            b. Exocentric

IV. Phrase structure
    [These are non-sentence-forming constructions.]

V. Clause structure
   [These are sentence-forming constructions.]

    A. Major clauses

    B. Minor clauses

Discussion:

    Rather than distinguish morphology and syntax, Hall has set up inflection and der-
ivation as morphology, and phrase structure and clause structure as syntax. This has
some advantages in dealing with a structure such as French, but it does not represent
a wholly logical type of division. In the first place, these four structural divisions are not coördinate with the phonology, and the order of the four does not follow a systematic development. After treating the more inclusive morphological constructions in the inflection, Hall takes up the less inclusive derivational formations. He follows this immediately with a discussion of the less inclusive syntactic
constructions and finally describes the more inclusive syntactic constructions. To
be perfectly logical one should either begin with the most restricted formations and
work outward, or begin with the most inclusive formations of each level and work toward the more restricted formations. In describing French, however, there are some
practical considerations which help to determine Hall's choice of sequence.

Hall's outline distinguishes levels of formation as primary and subsumes classes of formations under these. This approach has many advantages to recommend it, especially in a language such as French, where many derivational features of the roots and stems exhibit great similarity, regardless of the word class to which they belong.

9.11.5 Hebrew, by Zellig S. Harris[6]

Outline:

I. The phonemes

II. The distribution of the phonemes

III. Morphemes

    A. The morpheme list
    [This section describes the canonical types of morphemes.]

    B. The morpheme variants
    [These are the allomorphs, phonologically and morphologically defined.]

IV. Distribution of morphemes in the word.
[Harris takes as a definition of "word," a phonemically (i.e. orthographically) definable unit between certain types of junctures. Since this type of word does not always conform to sets of immediate constituents, a number of problems result.]

    A. Relative order of morphemes

    B. Coexistence of morphemes
    [This section lists those classes of morphemes which may occur within the same word.]

    C. Structure of the word
    [This section summarizes the preceding two.]

V. Successive inclusive constructions
[This is the syntax.]

    A. Distribution of the word within the phrase

    B. Distribution of phrases within the clause

    C. Note on the construction-initials
    [These are conjunctions.]

    D. Construction of the utterance
    [This section treats some of the types of sequence of clauses within the discourse.]

Discussion:

Sections I and II constitute the phonology. Sections III and IV the morphology, and V the syntax. Section III is essentially the inventory of morphemes, and IV the distribution of the morphemes.

---

[6] Zelliz S. Harris, "Linguistic Structure of Hebrew," Journal of the American Oriental Society, 61 (1941): 143-67.

Though this grammar indicates carefully the relative order of morphemes in section IV and the patterns of inclusion in section V, the primary difficulties lie in the fact that (1) the phonologically defined "word" is not adequately treated in terms of its sets of immediate constituents and (2) the various principal morphological formations, i.e. the word classes, are not sufficiently recognized.

9.11.6 Potawatomi, by Charles F. Hockett[7]

Outline:

   I. Phonemes

   II. Morphophonemics

   III. Morphological survey
   [This section sketches the principal features of the structure.]

      A. Participation of morphemes in bound forms
      [This section deals with root classes and derivational formations.]

      B. Participation of bound forms in free forms
      [This section deals with inflectional formations and some syntactic relation-
      ships.]

   IV. Derivation of nouns and verbs
   [Subdivision A treats various classes of roots; B, the derivation of nouns; and
   C-G, the derivation of verbs.]

      A. Roots, medials, and monomorphemic stems

      B. Noun-forming finals

      C. Intransitive finals

      D. Intransitive finals: reciprocals

      E. Intransitive finals: reflexives

      F. Intransitive finals: passives

      G. Transitive finals

   V. Personal prefixes
   [These occur with both nouns and verbs.]

   VI. Nouns
   [Sections A-D describe classes of stems, and E-I inflectional formations.]

      A. Gender

      B. Dependency

      C. Noun compounds

---

[7]Charles F. Hockett, "Potawatomi [Parts I-IV]," International Journal of American Linguistics, 14 (1948), 1-4: 1-10, 63-73, 139-49, 213-25.

   D. Classification of noun stems for suffixation

   E. Diminutives and pejoratives

   F. Possessed themes

   G. Plural, obviative, and vocatives

   H. Locatives

   I. Preterit

VII. Verbs
   [An introductory section describes the various structures.]

   A. Elements before the stem

   B. Suffixation for indicative and negative

   C. Suffixation for imperative and prohibitive

   D. Suffixation for conjunct and participial

VIII. Particles

   A. Numeral stems

   B. Substitutive particles

   C. Other particles

Discussion:

   The morphological survey consists of an inventory of morphemes and a helpful description of some of the more important structures. This type of orientation is valuable, even though it is not structurally coördinate with the other sections.

   Rather than discuss each word class, first as to derivation and secondly as to inflection, Hockett has chosen to describe the derivation of nouns and verbs in a single section. There is justification for this in the parallel derivational structures exhibited by the nouns and the verbs.

   The personal prefixes are treated as a separate class since they occur with both nouns and verbs. It would also be possible to consider these as inflectional elements under one class and, under the other classes, to make a cross reference to this description. They could also be treated as a special class of morphemes in the inventory.

9.11.7 Southern Paiute, by Edward Sapir[8]

Outline:

   I. Phonology
   [This includes a description of the phonetics and of the important morphophonemic

_____

   [8]Edward Sapir, "The Southern Paiute Language," Proceedings of the American Academy of Arts and Sciences, 65 (1930), 1: 1-296.

changes.   The transcription is not phonemicized, but all the data are given to permit phonemicization.]

II. Morphology

    A. Grammatical processes
       [This is a résumé of the processes of compounding, enclisis, prefixation, suf-
       fixation, reduplication, consonant change, and vowel change.]

    B. Compounding of stems
       [This includes all classes of words, considered according to sequence classes.]

    C. Enclitics
       [These are structurally bound particles, which have syntactically pertinent
       distributions.]

    D. Prefixes
       1. Adverbial prefixes
       2. Instrumental prefixes
       3. Reflexive and reciprocal na-

    E. Derivative and formal suffixes
       [The term "formal" is used for "inflectional."]
       1. Noun suffixes
          [These include derivative and inflectional formations.]
       2. Nominalizing suffixes
       3. Verbalizing suffixes
       4. Verb suffixes
          [These are inflectional.]
          a. Suffixes of movement
          b. Suffixes of voice
          c. Suffixes of verbal aspect
          d. Suffixes of number
          e. Temporal suffixes
          f. Modal suffixes
          g. Order of verbal elements
             [This section states the relative orders of all the preceding formations.]
       5. The diminutive
          [The diminutive suffixes are derivational with both nouns and verbs.]
       6. Numeral suffixes
          [These are derivational affixes in verb and attributive word classes.]
       7. Suffixes of quasi-pronominal force
          [These are derivative elements with very limited distribution.]

    F. Pronouns
       [This section is introduced by a general classification of the following types.]
       1. Personal pronouns
          a. Independent personal pronouns
          b. Enclitic personal pronouns
          c. Combinations of enclitic pronouns
       2. Postnominal pronouns
       3. Demonstrative pronouns
       4. Interrogative pronouns
       5. The relative pronoun
       6. Reflexive pronouns

    G. Noun morphology
       1. Noun and verb stem
          [This section deals with the canonicity of roots and the fact that some roots

> may occur in either noun or verb morphological constructions.]
> 2. Plurality of nouns
> 3. Syntactic cases
> 4. Postpositions
> [These are a special type of suffix, distributionally and structurally between the regular inflectional suffixes and the enclitics.]

  H. Verb morphology
[This section is introduced by a general statement about the following structures.]
> 1. The imperative
> 2. Internal stem changes
> 3. Singular and plural stems
> 4. Verb syntax
> [This section treats the affixes and clitics which indicate various types of subordination of the verb to other structures.]
> 5. Substantive verbs
> [This section treats the formation of a special type of verb roughly equivalent to English 'be.']

  I. Negation
[This section treats negative affixes and particles, which occur with several different classes of words.]

  J. Reduplication
[This section treats derivational and inflectional reduplication in both nouns and verbs.]

  K. Numerals
[This section treats the derivation of numerals.]

  L. Adverbs
[This section treats the derivation of adverbs.]

  M. Interjections
[This is a listing of the interjections.]

  N. Idiomatic usages
[This section treats special semantic problems relating to the use of verbs meaning 'to do' and 'to say.']

Discussion:

This grammar is exceedingly accurate and detailed. At first glance the structural divisions seem to be quite illogical, but the distinctions are much more valid than they appear. The morphological section of the grammar is divided into two principal divisions: (1) grammatical processes (section A-E and J) and (2) word classes (sections F-H and K-M). The contents of section I belong in various sections of F-H and K-M. Section N is a matter for the lexicon.

The difficulty with distinguishing grammatical processes and word classes is that it requires a double listing. The same morphemes must be treated under processes and also under the word class.

The grammar contains no syntactic section, but a great many syntactic facts are noted throughout the morphological sections. The copious texts also supplement this syntactic deficiency to some extent.

9.11.8 Tzeltal, by Marianna C. Slocum[9]

Outline:
[The following outline of Tzeltal structure includes only the noun and verb morphology.]

I. Nouns

    A. Derivation of nouns
       1. Simple stems
       2. Complex stems
          a. Prefixation
             [There is only one order.]
          b. Suffixation
             1'. First order
             2'. Second order
          c. Compounding

    B. Inflection of nouns
       1. Prefixation
          [There is only one order.]
       2. Suffixation
          a. First order
          b. Second order
          c. Third order
          d. Fourth order

II. Verbs

    A. Derivation of verbs
       1. Simple stems
       2. Complex stems
          a. Transitive verbs
             1'. First-order suffixes
             2'. Second-order suffixes
             3'. Third-order suffixes
             4'. Fourth-order suffixes
          b. Intransitive verbs
             1'. Infixation
             2'. Suffixation
                a'. First order
                b'. Second order
                c'. Third order

    B. Inflection of verbs
       1. Transitive verbs
          a. Prefixation
             [There is only one order.]
          b. Suffixation
             1'. First order
             2'. Second order
             3'. Third order
             4'. Fourth order
             5'. Fifth order
             6'. Sixth order

---

    [9]Marianna C. Slocum, "Tzeltal (Mayan) Noun and Verb Morphology," International Journal of American Linguistics, 14 (1948), 2: 77-86.

      2. Intransitive verbs
        a. Active
          1'. First order of suffixes
          2'. Second order of suffixes
          3'. Third order of suffixes
        b. Passive
          1'. First order of suffixes
          2'. Second order of suffixes
          3'. Third order of suffixes
      3. Stative verbs
        a. First order of suffixes
        b. Second order of suffixes

Discussion:

This description of noun and verb structure consists of a very systematic and formal arrangement of data. In treating prefixation before suffixation throughout the writer does not follow the succession of immediate constituents, but within the prefixal or suffixal series the orders and sets of immediate constituents coincide and the description indicates this fact.

The treatment could be improved by introducing a section on inventory, where morpheme classes could be described. In such a section the reduplicated intransitive verb stems, which occur with certain sets of suffixes, could be handled more advantageously than they are at present.

9.11.9 Yuma, by A. M. Halpern[10]

Outline:

  I. Phonology
    [A number of morphophonemic changes are discussed, but are not distinguished by a principal subdivision.]

  II. Morphology

    A. Grammatical processes
      [The following sections describe various general features of the language.]
      1. Word classes
      2. Word formation
      3. Formation of nonthematic elements
      4. Theme formation

    B. Nouns
      1. The noun theme
        a. Simple
        b. Reduplicated
        c. Compounded
      2. Pronominal prefixes
      [These are inflectional possessive prefixes.]
      3. Nonthematic nominal suffixes
      [These are inflectional case suffixes.]
      4. Demonstratives, pronouns, and adverbs
      [This section describes the limited number of case suffixes (section B,

---

  [10] A. M. Halpern, "Yuma" in Linguistic Structures of Native America (Viking Fund Publications in Anthropology, Vol. 6) (New York, 1946), pp. 249-88.

3, above) which may occur with demonstratives, pronouns, and adverbs.]
  5. Derivation of verb themes from noun themes.
   [This section belongs under C, 1, below.]

 C. Verbs
  1. Types of verb theme
   a. Themes based on stem alone
    1'. Simple-stem theme
    2'. Reduplicated-stem theme
   b. Prefix-stem themes
    1'. Single prefix plus simple or reduplicated stem
    2'. Two prefixes plus stem
   c. Developed themes, consisting of themes of type _a_ or _b_ plus thematic infix-suffix complex.
  2. Reduction of the theme
   [This is a type of allomorphic alternation.]
  3. Plural forms of the verb theme
  4. Distributive object conjugation
  5. Plurals of simple-stem themes
  6. Plurals of prefix-stem themes
  7. Plurals of themes indicating position
  8. Plurals of reduced themes
  9. Nonthematic prefixes of the verb
   a. First-position prefixes
   b. Second-position prefixes
   c. Third-position prefixes
   d. Fourth-position prefixes
  10. Nonthematic suffixes of the verb
   a. First-position suffixes
   b. Second-position suffixes
   c. Third-position suffixes
   d. Fourth-position suffixes
   e. Fifth-position suffixes
  11. Derivation of noun themes from verb themes
   [This section belongs under B, 1, above.]

Discussion:

  This grammar follows the obsolescent practice of introducing a section on grammatical processes. Ordinarily such a section is structurally superfluous. Halpern, however, makes very good use of this device to include some general comments about the following structure.

  The noun structure should be divided between (1) the noun theme and (2) the inflection of nouns. The second section should then be subdivided into (a) prefixation (section B, 2) and (b) suffixation (sections B, 3 and 4). The derivation of verb themes from noun themes belongs under the description of verb themes, just as the derivation of noun themes from verb themes belongs under the description of noun themes. Neither of these features should be treated after the inflection.

  The verb structure should be divided into (1) the verb theme and (2) the inflection of the verb theme. The inflection would include (a) pluralizing formatives, (b) nonpluralizing prefixal formatives, and (c) nonpluralizing suffixal formatives.

  In this brief sketch Halpern does not include a special section for particles.

  On the whole, this treatment of Yuma follows quite closely the principle of immediate constituents; and though the actual outline does not indicate all the structural groupings, the order of material brings out these relationships quite clearly.

9.12 Discussion of Illustrative Outlines

Certain features of the outlines in the preceding sections are very significant:

1. Variety of organization. The differences in the structural organization are due to (1) differences in the structures of the languages in question and (2) different methods of description. There is no agreement among linguists today that certain types of structure must be treated in a particular way.

2. Preservation of the same structural perspective. Though the different grammars have quite different outlines, yet it can be readily seen that the same structural perspective is preserved. For example, if the linguist sets up "inflectional formations" as a primary division, this is generally coördinated with "derivational formations." One does not find such a series as:

      A. Inflectional formations
        1. Nouns
        2. Derivational formations

      B. Verbs

On the other hand, one does find:

      A. Derivational formations
        1. Nouns
        2. Verbs

      B. Inflectional formations
        1. Nouns
        2. Verbs

and:

      A. Nouns
        1. Derivational formations
        2. Inflectional formations

      B. Verbs
        1. Derivational formations
        2. Inflectional formations

3. Parallelism of treatment. For the most part subclass distinctions are treated in parallel arrangements. For example, one may find:

      A. Nouns
        1. Derivational formations
        2. Inflectional formations

      B. Verbs
        1. Derivational formations
        2. Inflectional formations

but not:

      A. Nouns
        1. Derivational formations
        2. Inflectional formations

       B. Verbs
          1. Inflectional formations
          2. Derivational formations

4. Substantial agreement on the major divisions. In general there are three primary
   divisions: phonology, morphology, and syntax. In some descriptions the morphology
   and the syntax are not recognized as such, but the order and arrangement of subdivisions indicate these three principal structural units.

5. Contrast in the choice of secondary destinctions. There are three sets of secondary
   distinctions:

       a. Inventory and distribution
       b. Nouns, verbs, particles, and so on
       c. Inflection and derivation

Depending upon the choice of one of these sets as secondary, then the other two
become tertiary and quaternary. In most instances, the distinction between inventory and distribution is implied in the organization, though not overtly recognized
by any headings. The choice of secondary distinctions is dependent primarily upon
the structure of the language. It would seem, however, that the primary distinction should be made between inventory and distribution. Whether one selects one or
the other of the following two outlines of tertiary and quaternary divisions depends
upon the degree to which the inflectional and derivational formations overlap the
word classes:

       Outline A

          A. Nouns
             1. Derivation
             2. Inflection

          B. Verbs
             1. Derivation
             2. Inflection

          C. Particles

       Outline B

          A. Derivation
             1. Nouns
             2. Verbs
             3. Nouns and verbs[11]
             4. Particles

          B. Inflection
             1. Nouns
             2. Verbs
             3. Noun and verbs[11]

6. Wide variation in the treatment of morphophonemics. The morphophonemic alternations
   are treated (1) under the phonology, (2) in a separate section, or (3) under the

---

   [11]The use of outline B would involve situations in which a number of derivational or
inflectional formatives, or both, occur with more than one primary class of stems. If such
formatives are strictly limited in number, it would be easier to describe the distribution
of the particular formatives in two different places.

morphology. Fundamentally, such matters are more closely related to the morphemes than they are to the phonemes. Hence it is preferable to treat them either in a separate section or under the morphology.

7. Progression from smaller to larger units. On the whole, the grammars take up the less inclusive formations first and progress toward the more inclusive. It is theoretically possible to employ the reverse procedure, beginning with the more inclusive types of expressions and working down to the morphemes. This approach is not recommended, however, since the description of one of the immediate constituents is constantly left for a later section. By beginning with small units and working toward larger ones, it is possible to add new forms to those already identified and described.

8. Use of explanatory sections. The use of explanatory sections to outline the main features of the language is quite common. In some instances they are set up as separate parts of the grammar, but more frequently they are included at the beginning of major sections. In this position they are helpful to the reader, though they may not be necessary theoretically.

9. Lack of detailed subdivision. In many instances the outlines do not indicate the degree of subdivision which the various sections actually describe. This keeps the outline from becoming unwieldy, but at the same time it obscures many important relationships. Where possible, one should indicate clearly all the subdivisions of the description.

9.2 Technical Difficulties

9.21 Systems of Outlining

There are two principal systems of outlining. The first employs the traditional sequences:

```
I.
  A.
    1.
      a.
        1'.
          a'.
```

The second type of outline consists of numerals with periods. There are three principal varieties:

Type A	Type B	Type C
1.	1.	1.
1.1	1.1	1.1
1.1.1	1.11	1.11
1.1.1.1	1.11.1	1.111

Type A employs a period after the first numeral and between every succeeding numeral. Type B requires a period after the first numeral and after each set of two succeeding numerals. Type C requires a period only after the first numeral.

A zero may be used to indicate an introductory section, as in the following outline:

         0.
         1.0
         1.1
         1.11

The first 0. would mark an introduction to the entire description, and section 1.0 would be
introductory to the sections beginning with 1.

In general the numerical type of outline is used to mark the principal sections of the
grammar, and any minor patterns are distinguished by the more conventional type of outline
using I, A, 1, a, and so on. The traditional outline, which requires indentation, is uneconomical for lengthy sections, since it necessitates much blank space.

9.22 Terminology

There is considerable agreement among descriptive linguists as to terminology; this
may be readily seen by reading various articles in Language and the International Journal
of American Linguistics. On the other hand, the use of terms is not absolutely fixed, and
a linguist often employs a known term in a different sense or adopts a hitherto unused term
for some feature which has been previously identified by a traditional expression. There is
no justification for novelty purely for the sake of novelty, but there are many situations
in which new terms help to point out significant features of structure. The important considerations in the use of such new words are (1) that they be clearly defined and (2) that
they be used consistently.

Though a great many terms have been used in this book, the linguistic investigator will
find that these do not cover all the features of language which he wishes to describe. It
is therefore essential that he read extensively in various linguistic journals and become
thoroughly acquainted with the many descriptive grammars published in recent years.

Whether one employs one or another type of terminology is dependent very largely upon
the prospective readers of any grammar. If one is writing for a scientific journal read by
professional linguists, then the terminology may be as technical as the subject matter war-
rants. On the other hand, if one's description of the language is intended for people who
have had only the traditional orientation to grammar, then it is essential that the technical vocabulary be reduced to a minimum. Furthermore, for such readers it is impossible
to rely entirely upon the concise descriptions of morpheme distribution by classes. One
must cite numerous paradigms. Despite the fact that traditional grammars have many uneconomical ways of describing features, there are certain pedagogical features which must not
be overlooked. The type of scientific description which we have been studying in this book
is not designed to be applied to constructing a textbook to be used by people learning a
language. It is the type of organization of data which should underlie the construction of
a good pedagogical grammar, but it is no substitute for one. The contrast between types of
grammars is vividly illustrated by Hall's monograph on French, cited in section 9.11.4, and
Spoken and Written French, by Denoeu and Hall.[12] Each of these treatments is an excellent
example of its particular type, but one is not a substitute for the other.

9.23 Types of Descriptive Statements

It is quite impossible to consider all the types of descriptive statements, but there
are certain expressions which one should avoid and others which one may conveniently employ
to describe various types of relationships.

---

[12]François Denoeu and Robert A. Hall, Jr., Spoken and Written French (Boston: D. C.
Heath and Co., 1946).

One should carefully avoid the following types of statements:

1. Mentalistic

In place of the statement:

"Because the suffix -ik has the idea of 'bad,' it naturally does not go with words expressing good ideas."

Use:

"The pejorative suffix -ik occurs with the following words: .... Its distribution appears to reflect a cultural evaluation."

We seek to avoid any statements about suffixes "having ideas." They may "have meanings," "indicate relationships," and "reflect concepts," but they do not "have ideas." Furthermore, it does not "naturally" follow that pejorative affixes fail to occur with words indicating features meeting with cultural approval. The statement that the distribution of -ik reflects a cultural evaluation is not necessary in a purely structural analysis, but it may have value in determining the allosemes of this morpheme. The proper place for such a statement is in the lexicon.

2. Historical

In place of the statement:

"Since -ik is derived from ikak 'bad,' it adds an unfavorable idea to the stem with which it occurs."

Use:

"ikak ∞ -ik 'bad.'"

From the standpoint of the descriptive analysis of the language, we are not interested in the fact that -ik is derived from ikak. The allomorphic relationship of these morphemes should be stated without reference to the history. If the meaning is 'bad,' we assume that this sememe will be a part of any expression containing the morpheme.

3. Subjective

In place of the statements:

a. "We add -l to the root."

b. "You can see the suffix in the past-tense forms."

Use:

a. "-l is added to the root."

b. "The suffix occurs in the past-tense forms" or "The past-tense forms contain the suffix."

In so far as possible, the linguist should be completely objective about descriptive statements. The relationship of the speaker, the hearer, or the learner to the language is irrelevant.

4. Imperative

In place of the statement:

"To form the past tense, drop the infinitive -l and add -t."

Use:

"The infinitive suffix -l and the past-tense suffix -t are added to the stem."

It is the traditional practice in textbooks to use imperative expressions in the form of "rules" to describe the structure of a language. These are to be avoided completely.

There are certain types of expressions which linguists employ constantly in describing the relationships of forms. We cannot list all of these or indicate all the alternative expressions,[13] but the following are the ones most frequently recurring:

1. For describing the distribution of a morpheme:

"-ka occurs with the following stems: ..."

"-ka is suffixed to the following stems: ..."

"-ka is added to the following stems: ..."

"-ka is found with the following stems: ..."

2. For describing features of a class:

"Nouns exhibit the following features: ..."

"Nouns have the following features: ..."

"Nouns are characterized by the following features: ..."

3. For describing the composition of a form:

"kanatka consists of the stem kanat- and the suffix -ka."

"kanatka contains the stem kanat- and the suffix -ka."

"kanatka is composed of the stem kanat- and the suffix -ka."

4. For describing the constituency of a class:

a. "Class A consists of the following forms: ..."

"Class A includes the following forms: ..."

"Class A comprises the following forms: ..."

"Class A is composed of the following forms: ..."

---

[13]These alternative expressions are not, however, synonymous.

b. "Forms 1, 2, and 3 constitute Class A."

"Forms 1, 2, and 3 comprise Class A."

"Forms 1, 2, and 3 form Class A."

"Forms 1, 2, and 3 are included in Class A."

A typical descriptive statement consists of four parts: (1) the item being described, (2) the defined relationship, (3) the item or items to which it is related, and (4) the circumstances which govern or accompany the occurrence. Parts 3 and 4 are optional. Note the following illustrative statements:

1. "-ka is suffixed to verbs of class C with loss of the final consonant of the stem."

2. "Suffixes of class A occur with transitive verbs under the following circumstances: ...."

3. "Replacives occur with the following stems: ...."

4. "Assimilation is found under the following circumstances: ...."

In nontechnical writing one is supposed to vary expressions and sentence structure so as to avoid repetition of particular words and monotony of sentence form. In technical writing, however, this is not always possible; in such writing words are used in very specialized senses and we cannot be as free in the substitution of lexically similar forms. In Roget's Thesaurus, for example, the words repetitive, reduplicative, and recurring are are listed as synonyms, but in linguistic terminology these words have very different specialized meanings and cannot be substituted for each other.

Rather than vary the sentence structure to avoid monotony, we make use of similarities of sentence structure to emphasize similarities of linguistic structure. For example, in place of the sentence:

"Prefixes in- and ab- occur with stem classes A, B, and C; and stem classes D, E, and F occur with prefixes as- and ul-."

we should write:

"Prefixes -in and -ab occur with stem classes A, B, and C; and prefixes as- and ul- occur with stem classes D, E, and F."

The use of chiasm may be rhetorically pleasing, but parallel sentence structure is more valuable in indicating parallel structural relationships.

9.3 Illustrative Language Problems

Problem 132 (hypothetical data)[14]

Instructions:

---

[14]In order to appreciate adequately the way in which the grammatical statement may be made, it is helpful to consider a very limited amount of data which are carefully controlled. Problems 134 and 135 are even more limited than Problem 132, but they provide essential practical experience in the organization of linguistic statements. The other problems in the chapter are based on actual-language materials.

a. Analyze the following data.

b. Study carefully the form of the description which follows.

Paradigmatic data:

1. -tis   'to walk'

1a. uθtis   'there is walking'

1b. iktis   'walks'

1c. ikantis   'walk all of a sudden'

1d. ikeθtis   'walk continuously'

2. -tus   'to enter'

2a. uθtus   'entering occurs'

2b. iktus   'enters'

2c. ikantus   'enter suddenly'

2d. ikeθtus   'enter continually'

3. -kinsen   'to grieve'

3a. uxkinsen   'there was grief'

3b. ikkinsen   'grieved'

3c. ikaŋkinsen   'grieved suddenly'

3d. ikeθkinsen   'grieved constantly'

3e. otkinsen   'become grief-stricken'

3f. otaŋkinsen   'become grief-stricken suddenly'

3g. oteθkinsen   'become grief-stricken constantly'

4. -pam   'to hit'

4a. uxpam   'there is hitting'

4b. ikpam   'hit once'

4c. ikampam   'hit instantly'

4d. ikeθpam   'hit and hit'

4e. otpam   'is hit once'

4f. otampam   'be hit instantaneously'

4g. oteθpam   'is hit and hit'

4h. ampam   'hit (him)self once'

4i. amampam   'hit (one)self all of a sudden'

4j. emeθpam   'hit (them)selves continually'

5. -sil   'to see'

5a. uxsil   'there is seeing'

5b. iksil   'see once'

5c. ikansil   'see all of a sudden'

5d. ikeθsil   'looks and looks'

5e. otsil   'is seen once'

5f. otansil   'is seen suddenly'

5g. oteθsil   'is seen continuously'

5h. insil   'to see (one)self once'

5i. amansil   'saw (him)self suddenly'

5j. emeθsil   'sees (him)self continuously'

6. -kuk   'to be sick'

6a. uxkuk   'there was sickness'

6b. ikkuk   'was sick once'

6c. ikaŋkuk   'was sick all of a sudden'

6d. ikeθkuk   'is continuously sick'

6e. otkuk   'will be made sick'

6f. otaŋkuk   'is made sick suddenly'

6g. oteθkuk   'is made sick for some time'

7. -sen   'to be sad'

(Continued on next page.)

7a. uθsen   'there is sadness'

7b. iksen   'is sad'

7c. ikansen   'will be sad all at once'

7d. ikeθsen   'is always sad'

7e. otsen   'is made sad'

7f. otansen   'is made sad suddenly'

7g. oteθsen   'is always made sad'

8. -lol   'to become'

8a. uxlol   'there is change'

8b. iklol   'become once'

8c. ikanlol   'will become all at once'

8d. ikeθlol   'is constantly becoming'

8e. otlol   'is made'

8f. otanlol   'was made instantly'

8g. oteθlol   'will be always made'

9. -kamis   'to fish'

9a. uxkamis   'there is fishing going on'

9b. ikkamis   'fished once'

9c. ikaŋkamis   'will fish all of a sudden'

9d. ikexkamis   'fishes continually'

10. -karit   'to be a man'

10a. uxkarit   'men were coming into existence'

10b. ikkarit   'is a man'

10c. ikaŋkarit   'was a man all of a sudden'

10d. ikexkarit   'will always be a man'

10e. otkarit   'be made a man once'

10f. otaŋkarit   'will be made a man suddenly'

10g. otexkarit   'will always be made a man'

11. -pik   'to kill'

11a. ufpik   'there is killing going on'

11b. ikpik   'killed once'

11c. ikampik   'killed instantly'

11d. ikefpik   'killed continually'

11e. otpik   'was murdered'

11f. otampik   'was killed instantly'

11g. otefpik   'will be killed continually'

11h. impik   'committed suicide'

11i. amampik   'killed (him)self instantly'

11j. emefpik   'will kill (him)self over a period of time'

12. -tot   'to call'

12a. uxtot   'there is calling going on'

12b. iktot   'call once'

12c. ikantot   'called instantly'

12d. ikeθtot   'was continually calling'

12e. ottot   'will be given a name'

12f. otantot   'was called suddenly'

12g. oteθtot   'will always be called'

12h. ontot   'gave (him)self a name'

12i. amantot   'suddenly gave (him)self a name'

12j. emeθtot   'is continually calling (him)self'

13. -mus   'to hear'

13a. ufmus   'there is listening going on'

13b. ikmus   'heard once'

13c. ikammus   'hear all of a sudden'

13d. ikefmus   'listen and listen'

(Continued on next page.)

13e. otmus   'is heard'

13f. otammus   'is heard instantly'

13g. otefmus   'is heard continually'

13h. ummus 'heard (him)self'

13i. amammus   'hear (him)self suddenly'

13j. emefmus   'hear (your)self continually'

14. -kan   'to run'

14a. uxkan   'there is a race'

14b. ikkan   'runs'

14c. ikaŋkan   'run suddenly'

14d. ikeθkan   'ran continuously'

15. -pir   'to knife'

15a. ufpir   'there is a knifing going on'

15b. ikpir   'knifed (cut)'

15c. ikampir   'knifed instantly'

15d. ikefpir   'knifed continually'

15e. otpir   'were knifed'

15f. otampir   'were knifed instantly'

15g. otefpir   'were knifed continually'

15h. impir   'knife (one)self'

15i. amampir   'knife (one)self instantly'

15j. emefpir   'will knife (one)self
                              continually'

16. -tinlol   'to rise'

16a. uθtinlol   'rising occurs'

16b. iktinlol   'rises'

16c. ikantinlol   'rise suddenly'

16d. ikeθtinlol   'rise continually'

17. mis-   'fish'

17a. imisat ac. p.15

17b. imison g. p.

17c. imisu at. p.

17d. misat ac. u.

17e. mison g. u.

17f. misu at. u.

18. rit-   'man'

18a. iritat ac. p.

18b. iriton g. p.

18c. iritu at. p.

18d. ritat ac. u.

18e. riton g. u.

18f. ritu at. u.

19. -kel-   'friend'

19a. ikelat   ac. p.

19b. ikelon g. p.

19c. ikelu at. p.

20. -pir-   'knife'

20a. ampirat ac. p.

20b. ampiron g. p.

20c. ampiru at. p.

21. pas- '   'instrument'

(Continued on next page.)

15The abbreviations are: ac. 'actor,' p. 'possessed,' g. 'goal,' at. 'attributive,' and u. 'unpossessed.'

21a. ampasat ac. p.

21b. ampason g. p.

21c. ampasu at. p.

21d. pasat ac. u.

21e. pason g. u.

21f. pasu at. u.

22. -tus-   'interior'

22a. itusat ac. p.

22b. ituson g. p.

22c. itusu at. p.

23. -nom-   'house'

23a. annomat ac. p.

23b. annomon g. p.

23c. annomu at. p.

24. -sur-   'wife'

24a. ansurat ac. p.

24b. ansuron g. p.

24c. ansuru at. p.

25. -mek-   'eye'

25a. ammekat ac. p.

25b. ammekon g. p.

25c. ammeku at. p.

26. -kim-   'heart'

26a. aŋkimat ac. p.

26b. aŋkimon g. p.

26c. aŋkimu at. p.

27. ton-   'woman'

27a. antonat ac. p.

27b. antonon g. p.

27c. antonu at. p.

27d. tonat ac. u.

27e. tonon g. u.

27f. tonu at. u.

28. -mak-   'husband'

28a. imakat ac. p.

28b. imakon g. p.

28c. imaku at. p.

29. -tin-   'top'

29a. antinat ac. p.

29b. antinon g. p.

29c. antinu at. p.

30. mor-   'I, we'

30a. omorat ac. p.

30b. omoron g. p.

30c. omoru at. p.

30d. morat ac. u.

30e. moron g. u.

30f. moru at. u.

31. pim-   'you (sg., pl.)'

31a. opimat ac. p.

31b. opimon g. p.

31c. opimu at. p.

31d. pimat ac. u.

31e. pimon g. u.

(Continued on next page.)

31f. pimu at. u.

32. kos-   'he, she, it, they'

32a. okosat ac. p.

32b. okoson g. p.

32c. okosu at. p.

32d. kosat ac. u.

32e. koson g. u.

32f. kosu at. u.

33. rak-   'all'

33a. orakat ac. p.

33b. orakon g. p.

33c. oraku at. p.

33d. rakat ac. u.

33e. rakon g. u.

33f. raku at. u.

34. kot-   'few'

34a. okotat ac. p.

34b. okoton g. p.

34c. okotu at. p.

34d. kotat ac. u.

34e. koton g. u.

34f. kotu at. u.

35. map-   'one'

35a. omapat ac. p.

35b. omapon g. p.

35c. omapu at. p.

35d. mapat ac. u.

35e. mapon g. u.

35f. mapu at. u.

36. tok-   'two'

36a. otokat ac. p.

36b. otokon g. p.

36c. otoku at. p.

36d. tokat ac. u.

36e. tokon g. u.

36f. toku at. u.

37. -tisor-   'walk'

37a. antisorat ac. p.

37b. antisoron g. p.

37c. antisoru at. p.

38. silor-   'view'

38a. isilorat ac. p.

38b. isiloron g. p.

38c. isiloru at. p.

38d. silorat ac. u.

38e. siloron g. u.

38f. siloru at. u.

39. -kukor-   'sickness'

39a. ikukorat ac. p.

39b. ikukoron g. p.

39c. ikukoru at. p.

40. pikor-   'murder'

40a. ampikorat ac. p.

40b. ampikoron g. p.

(Continued on next page.)

40c. ampikoru at. p.

40d. pikorat ac. u.

40e. pikoron g. u.

40f. pikoru at. u.

41. sen-   'sadness'

41a. isenat ac. p.

41b. isenon g. p.

41c. isenu at. p.

42. pam- 'strife'

42a. opamat ac. p.

42b. opamon g. p.

42c. opamu at. p.

42d. pamat ac. u.

42e. pamon g. u.

42f. pamu at. u.

43. ritmis-   'fisherman'

43a. iritmisat ac. p.

43b. iritmison g. p.

43c. iritmisu at. p.

43d. ritmisat ac. u.

43e. ritmison g. u.

43f. ritmisu at. u.

44. tonnom-   'maid'

44a. antonnamat ac. p.

44b. antonnomon g. p.

44c. antonnomu at. p.

44d. tonnomat ac. u.

44e. tonnomon g. u.

44f. tonnomu at. u.

45. tam   'and'

46. rismut   'if'

47. ris   'when'

48. rat   'suddenly'

49. mut   'possibly'

50. nan   'prior time'

51. kor   'now'

52. mur   'future time'

53. sum   'not'

54. kot   'again'

55. mutsum   'impossibly'

56. bat   'by, with'

(Text data on next page.)

Text data:[16]

ritat· (1)   ikelon (2)   moru (3)   nan (4)   ikampik. (5)   morat (6)
Man   friend   my   (past time)   killed instantly.   I

ikelon (2)   moru (3)   ris (7)   ikeθtot (8)   ikelat (9)   sum (10)   moron (11)
friend   my   when   called continually   friend   not   me

ikmus. (12)   morat (6)   ikeθtis (13)   tam (14)   kot (15)   kot (15)
hear.   I   walked and walked   and   again   again

ikeθtot. (8)   morat (6)   okoson (16)   rat (17)   ikansil. (18)   ampikorat (19)
called continually.   I   him   suddenly   saw.   Murderer

kosu (20)   ikelon (2)   moru (3)   bat (21)   ampiru (2)   kot (15)   kot (15)
his   friend   my   with   knife   again   again

ikeθpam. (23)   morat (6)   ituson (24)   annomu (25)   iktis. (26)   uθsen. (27)
hit repeatedly.   I   interior   house   walked   There is sadness.

aŋkimon (28)   moru (3)   oteθkinsen, (29)   ris (7)   ufpik. (30)   ikelat (9)
Heart   my   is continually grieved,   when   there is killing.   Friend

moru (3)   sum (10)   kot (15)   otkarit. (31)
my   not   again   will be a man.

Free translation:

A man killed my friend instantly. When I continually called for my friend, the
friend did not hear me. I walked and walked and called again and again. I suddenly
saw him. His murderer had stabbed him again and again with a knife. I walked into
the house. There was sadness. My heart is continually grieved when there is a murder. My friend will never again live.

Notes on the text:[17]

1. rit- 'man' + -at suffix. This form serves as subject of an active verb.

2. i- possessive prefix + -kel- 'friend' + -on goal suffix. This form serves as object of a transitive verb and subject of a passive verb. See note 28, below.

3. mor- first-person stem + -u attributivizing suffix.

4. nan uninflected particle indicating past time. All other temporal relationships
   are supplied by the context.

5. ik- active-voice prefix + am- prefix of instantaneous aspect + -pik 'to kill.'

6. mor- first-person stem + -at actor suffix.

7. ris uninflected particle 'when.'

---

[16]The text is given in order to indicate more clearly the use of the relational suffixes. The numbers in parentheses in the text refer to the explanatory notes that follow
the free translation.

[17]Zero morphemes are not listed.

8. ik- active-voice prefix + eθ- prefix of continuative aspect + -tot 'to call.'

9. i- possessive prefix + -kel- 'friend' + -at actor suffix.

10. sum uninflected particle 'not.'

11. mor- first-person stem + -on goal suffix.

12. ik- active-voice prefix + -mus 'to hear.'

13. ik- active-voice prefix + eθ- prefix of continuative aspect + -tis 'to walk.'

14. tam uninflected particle 'and.'

15. kot uninflected particle 'again.'

16. o- possessive prefix + kos- third-person pronoun + -on goal suffix.

17. rat uninflected particle 'suddenly.'

18. ik- active-voice prefix + an- prefix of instantaneous aspect + -sil 'to see.'

19. am- possessive prefix + -pik- verb stem 'to kill' + -or nominalizing suffix + -at actor suffix.

20. kos- third-person stem + -u attributivizing suffix.

21. bat uninflected particle 'by, with.'

22. am- possessive prefix + -pir- 'knife' + -u attributivizing suffix.

23. ik- active-voice prefix + eθ- prefix of continuative aspect + -pam 'to hit.'

24. i- possessive prefix + -tus- 'interior' + -on goal suffix.

25. an- possessive prefix + -nom- 'house' + -u attributivizing suffix.

26. ik- active-voice prefix + -tis 'to walk.'

27. uθ- impersonal-voice prefix + -sen 'to be sad.'

28. aŋ- possessive prefix + -kim- 'heart' + -on goal suffix.

29. ot- passive-voice prefix + eθ- prefix of instantaneous aspect + -kin- 'heart' + -sen 'to be sad.'

30. uf- impersonal-voice prefix + -pik 'to kill.'

31. ot- passive-voice prefix + ka- verbalizing prefix + -rit 'man.'

Supplementary information:

1. The translations of the verb forms reflect the types of responses obtained from informants. Note that tense is indicated by particles and aspect by verb affixes.

2. Number is indicated by separate words or is implicit in the context.

Discussion of the data:

1. There are three structural classes: verbs, nouns, and particles.

2. Stems may be classified as verbs, nouns, verbs and nouns, and particles.

3. Verbs have inflectional prefixes; nouns have inflectional prefixes and suffixes; particles have neither.

4. Verb stems differ in the number of paradigmatic forms in which they occur: 4, 7, or 10. All verbs occur with impersonal and active-voice prefixes. But some do not occur in the passive, and a few have no reflexive formations. This means that there are three inflectional classes of stems.

5. Noun stems exhibit two major inflection classes: (1) those which may occur without possessive prefixes and (2) those which never occur without possessive prefixes.

6. Nouns, verbs, and particles exhibit derivational formations. Compounding occurs with all classes, and affixation with nouns and verbs.

Solution of Problem 132:

1. <u>Morphology</u>

1.1 <u>Morphophonemics</u>

1.11 <u>Phonologically Defined Allomorphic Alternations</u>

Nasal continuants <u>m</u>, <u>n</u>, and <u>ŋ</u> are assimilated according to point of articulation of the following consonant.

1.12 <u>Morphologically Defined Allomorphic Alternations</u>

The morphemes <u>ux-</u> ∞ (<u>uf-</u> ~ <u>uθ-</u>) 'impersonal voice' and <u>eθ-</u> ∞ (<u>ef-</u> ~ <u>ex-</u>) 'instantaneous aspect' occur in phonologically assimilated patterns according to the point of articulation of the following consonant when prefixed to the stems: <u>-kamis</u> 'to fish,' <u>-karit</u> 'to be a man,' <u>-mus</u> 'to hear,' <u>-pik</u> 'to kill,' <u>-sen</u> 'to be sad,' <u>-pir</u> 'to knife,' and <u>-tis</u> 'to walk.'

1.2 <u>Morphology Proper</u>

1.21 <u>Inventory of Morphemes</u>

1.21.1 <u>Root Morphemes</u>

A. Verb roots, e.g. <u>-tis</u> 'to walk,' <u>-tot</u> 'to call,' and <u>-sil</u> 'to see'

B. Noun roots, e.g. <u>mis-</u> 'fish,' <u>-kel-</u> 'friend,' and <u>mor-</u> 'I'

C. Verb and noun roots, e.g. <u>-sen</u> 'to be sad, sadness,' <u>-tus</u> 'to enter, interior,' and <u>-pir</u> 'to knife, knife'

D. Particles: <u>tam</u> 'and,' <u>ris</u> 'when,' <u>sum</u> 'not,' <u>rat</u> 'suddenly,' <u>mut</u> 'possibly,' <u>nan</u> 'prior time,' <u>kor</u> 'now,' <u>mur</u> 'future time,' and <u>kot</u> 'again'

1.21.2 <u>Nonroot Morphemes</u>

A. Derivational affixes

    1. Verbalizing: ka-

    2. Nominalizing: -or

B. Inflectional affixes

    1. Occurring with verbs

       a. First order:[18] eθ- ∞ (ef- ~ ex-) continuous aspect,' am- 'instantaneous aspect,' and zero 'punctiliar aspect'

       b. Second order: ik- 'active voice,' ot- 'passive voice,' am- ~ em- ~ um- ~ im- ~ om- 'reflexive voice,' and ux- ∞ (uf- ~ uθ-) 'impersonal voice'

    2. Occurring with nouns

       a. Prefixal: i- ∞ am- ∞ o- 'possessive'

       b. Suffixal: -at 'actor,' -on 'goal,' -u 'attributive'

1.22 Distribution of Morphemes

The distribution of morphemes distinguishes three principal word classes: verbs, nouns, and particles. Verbs occur with inflectional prefixes, nouns with inflectional prefixes and suffixes, and particles are not inflected.

1.22.1 Verbs

Verbs exhibit derivational and inflectional formations.

1.22.11 Derivation of Verbs

Verbs are derived by prefixation and compounding.

1.22.11.1 Prefixation

The verbalizing prefix ka- occurs in the following constructions: -karit 'to be a man' (< rit- 'man') and -kamis 'to fish' (< mis- 'fish').

1.22.11.2 Compounding

The following verb compounds occur: -kinsen 'to grieve' (< -kin- 'heart' + -sen 'to be sad') and -tinlol 'to rise' (< -tin- 'top' + -lol 'to become'). All compounds consist of noun-verb sequences.

1.22.12 Inflection of Verbs

Verbs are inflected for aspect by prefixes of the first order, and for voice by prefixes of the second order.

1.22.12.1 First-Order Prefixes

Prefixes of aspect: eθ- ∞ (ef- ~ ex-) 'continuative,' am- 'instantaneous,' and zero 'punctiliar' occur with all verbs, e.g. -efpik 'kill continually,' -eθtot 'continually call,' -ampik 'kill instantly,' -antot 'called instantly,' (ik)pik 'killed once.'

---

[18] That is, counting from the stem.

1.22.12.2 Second-Order Prefixes

1.22.12.21 Verb Classes

The distribution of second-order prefixes distinguishes three classes of verb stems: Vt 'transitive,' Vs 'intransitive state,' Vp 'intransitive process.'

Class Vt: -mus 'to hear,' -pam 'to hit,' -pik 'to kill,' -sil 'to see,' -tot 'to call,' -pir 'to knife'

Class Vs: -karit 'to be a man,' -kuk 'to be sick,' -lol 'to become,' -sen 'to be sad,' -kinsen 'to grieve'

Class Vp: -kamis 'to fish,' -kan 'to run,' -tis 'to walk,' -tinlol 'to rise,' -tus 'to enter'

1.22.12.22 Distribution

ux- ∞ (uf-.~ eθ-) 'impersonal' and ik- 'active' occur with verb classes Vt, Vs, and Vp, e.g. uxpam 'there is hitting,' uxkuk 'there was sickness,' uθtis 'there is walking,' ikmus 'heard once,' ikaŋkarit 'was a man all of a sudden,' ikexkamis 'fishes continually.'

ot- 'passive' occurs with verb classes Vt and Vs, e.g. otammus 'is heard instantly,' and otexkarit 'will always be made a man.'

am- ~ em- ~ im- ~ om- ~ um- exhibiting vocalic harmony with the vowel immediately following, occurs with verb class Vt, e.g. ummus 'heard (him)self,' amampam 'hit (one)self all of a sudden,' emefpik 'will kill (him)self over a period of time.'

1.22.2 Nouns

Nouns exhibit derivational and inflectional formations.

1.22.21 Derivation of Nouns

Nouns are derived by suffixation and compounding.

1.22.21.1 Suffixation

The nominalizing suffix -or occurs in the following constructions: -tisor- 'walk' (< -tis 'to walk'), silor- 'view' (< -sil 'to see'), -kukor- 'sickness' (< -kuk 'to be sick'), and pikor- 'murder' (< -pik 'to kill').

1.22.21.2 Compounding

The following noun compounds occur: ritmis- 'fisherman' (< rit- 'man' + mis- 'fish') and tonnom- 'maid' (< ton- 'woman' + -nom- 'house').

1.22.22 Inflection of Nouns

Nouns are inflected for possession by prefixes and for case by suffixes.

1.22.22.1 Prefixation

The possessive prefixal morpheme i- ∞ an- ∞ o- occurs optionally with stems having no initial hyphens, and is obligatory with those having hyphens.

i-: -kel- 'friend,' -kukor- 'sickness,' -mak- 'husband,' mis- 'fish,' rit- 'man,' silor- 'view,' -tus- 'interior,' -sen- 'sadness,' ritmis- 'fisherman'

an-: -kim- 'heart,' -mek- 'eye,' -nom- 'house,' pas- 'instrument,' pikor- 'murder,' -pir- 'knife,' -wur- 'wife,' -tin- 'top,' -tisor- 'walk,' ton- 'woman,' tonnom- 'maid'

o-: kos- 'he, she, it, they,' kot- 'few,' map- 'one,' mor- 'I, we,' pim- 'you (sg., pl.),' rak- 'all,' tok- 'two'

1.22.22.2 Suffixation

-at 'actor,' -on 'goal,' and -u 'attributive' occur with all nouns, e.g. imisat 'fish' (possessed, actor), riton 'man' (unpossessed, goal), ikelu 'friend' (possessed, attributive).

1.22.3 Particles

Particles exhibit no inflection and only two instances of compounding derivation: rismut 'if' (< ris 'when' + mut 'possibly') and mutsum 'impossibly' (< mut 'possible' + sum 'not').

Discussion of the solution to Problem 132:

1. It would have been just as logical to treat nouns before verbs. There is in these data no morphological dependence as there is in Bantu, where some parts of the verb reflect noun classes, but where the reverse is not true.

2. It is necessary to use actor and goal instead of subject and object, because the subject of passive verbs (semantically a goal) has the same form as the object of transitive verbs.

3. The morphophonemic alternations are treated under the morphology, since such changes are not exhibited by the syntactic constructions.

4. The meanings of verbs are cited in the English infinitive-phrase form. This is a convenient device to prevent misunderstanding of class memberships.

5. The occurrence or nonoccurrence of hypnens before the nouns makes it possible to distinguish two important distribution classes without resorting to listing.

6. A colon introduces a list of all the members of a class, and the abbreviation e.g. indicates that only illustrative data follow.

7. This description is so limited that the summary statements made at the beginning of some sections seem completely superfluous, considering the fact that the data immediately following indicate all the relationships. In describing an actual language, such subordinate sections might cover eight or ten pages, so that general, explanatory statements are necessary. One must not expect the reader to finish all of a major section before he realizes the relevance of the first subdivisions to those that follow.

8. It is convenient to treat the punctiliar aspect as being indicated by a zero morpheme. This permits a structurally neater type of statement than if one assumes that the stem is basically punctiliar and modified by the various first-order prefixes.

9. In section 1.22.12.1 it is not really necessary to list the aspectual prefixes again, since they have been listed in the inventory under nonroot morphemes, but for the sake of the reader such double listing is valuable.

10. In describing the inflection of the verb for voice, it would be possible to list the various classes under each set of prefixes. It is more economical, however, to set up the classes distinguished by the inflectional formations and then describe the distributions on the basis of these.

11. The allomorph o- may distinguish a syntactically pertinent class of pronouns, but this fact is not significant on a morphological level.

Problem 133 (data consisting of Zapotec forms of Problem 123)

Instructions: Describe the morphology.

Problem 134 (hypothetical data)

Instructions:

a. Analyze the data.

b. Describe the morphology.

1. p^{y}at	'boy'		20. tupaso·ra	'he loves you (sg.)'
2. lap^{y}ip	'little girl'		21. pisita	'I run'
3. na·kip	'little dog'		22. pinaniri	'we go'
4. si·s	'cat'		23. pisitari	'we run'
5. runi·	'house'		24. lap	'girl'
6. na·k	'dog'		25. na·kipsu	'doggies'
7. si·s^{y}ip	'kitten'		26. si·ssu	'cats'
8. p^{y}atsu	'boys'		27. runi·psu	'little houses'
9. runi·su	'houses'		28. si·s^{y}ipsu	'kittens'
10. pinani	'I go'		29. tunaniri	'they go'
11. pilipapi	'I wash myself'		30. pilipara	'I wash you (sg.)'
12. rasita	'you (sg.) run'		31. ralipatu	'you (sg.) wash him'
13. tunani	'he goes'		32. pipaso·tu	'I love it'
14. na·ksu	'dogs'		33. pipasa·ptu	'we love it'
15. lap^{y}ipsu	'little girls'		34. tulipa·ppi	'they wash me'
16. p^{y}atip	'little boy'		35. rapasa·ptu	'you (pl.) love it'
17. runi·p	'little house'		36. ralipara	'you (sg.) wash yourself (sg.)'
18. p^{y}atipsu	'little boys'		37. tulipa·ptu	'they wash themselves'
19. lapsu	'girls'		38. tusitari	'they run'

(Continued on next page.)

39. tupasa·pra   'they are loving you'

40. tulipasappi   'they begin to wash me'

41. pipaso·saptu   'we begin to love it'

42. rasitasri   'you (pl) begin to run'

43. pibodi   'I hit'

44. pibodiri   'we hit'

45. pibodira   'I hit you (sg.)'

46. piboda·pra   'we hit you (sg.)'

Problem 135 (hypothetical data)

Instructions:

    a. Analyze the data.

    b. Describe the morphology.

1. soparu   'children'

2. paru   'child'

3. kataake   'he is, was small'

4. katigili   'it is, was dry'

5. ritigili   'it dried'

6. parutaa   'baby'

7. soparutaa   'babies'

8. rixikili   'it became white'

9. rataxikipa   'that European'

10. kanaa?   'I know'

11. kakaa?   'I am'

12. kanaaru   'you (sg.) know'

13. kakaake   'he is, was'

14. kareoke   'she is, was big'

15. yaka   'house'

16. yakareo   'palace'

17. kasa   'woman'

18. kasataapa   'that girl'

19. rata   'man'

20. ratataa   'boy'

21. toratataa   'boys'

22. kaxiki?   'I am white'

23. toyaka   'houses'

24. yakapa   'that house'

25. ratapa   'that man'

26. toratapa   'those men'

27. parutaapa   'that baby'

28. tokasataa   'girls'

29. parupa   'that child'

30. kaloepo   'we live'

31. kaloeta   'you (pl.) live'

32. saloezi   'they will live'

33. ritia?   'I wrote'

34. ritiapo   'we wrote'

35. sapixita   'you (pl.) will go home'

36. sapixiru   'you (sg.) will go home'

37. ma   'already'

38. ora   'when'

39. izi   'tomorrow'

40. aye   'yesterday'

41. xa   'now'

42. ata   'one'

(Continued on next page.)

43. axa   'four'

44. iki   'five'

45. paruʔ   'my child'

46. tega   'ear of corn'

47. sotegapo   'our cornfield'

48. diga   'word'

49. sodigake   'his words'

50. xaka   'dress'

51. taparu   'your (sg.) hat'

52. xakake   'her dress'

53. totapa   'hats'

54. kaleazi   'they are, were red'

55. rileake   'he, she blushed'

56. parutaazi   'their baby'

57. yakareopo   'our palace'

58. torataxiki   'Europeans'

59. tapaʔ   'my hat'

60. tokasa   'women'

61. torata   'men'

62. ma rilixaʔ   'I'm already tired'

63. kakaake la   'is he?'

64. tegata la   '(is this) your (pl.) corn?'

65. kaleazi soxakapa   'those dresses are red'

66. kaxikili tapapa   'that hat is white'

67. aye kareoli   'yesterday it was big'

68. ora ritigili, ritaali   'when it dried, it shrank'

69. xa kataali   'now it is little'

70. kaleali   'it is, was red'

Problem 136 (data from Mam [restricted], a language of Guatemala)

Instructions:

    a. Isolate the morphemes.

    b. File the data

    c. Describe the morphology.

1. xun šxal   'a person'

2. ošeʔ tšex   'three horses'

3. ntšexeʔ   'my horse'

4. qtšexeʔ   'our (excl.) horse'

5. qtšex   'our (incl.) horse'

6. qšxalil   'our (incl.) own people'

7. tts'umal nq'obeʔ   'the skin of my arm'

8. xun ts'uʔn   'a piece of leather'

9. tts'umal tšex   'the horse's hide'

10. tbe tšex   'the horse trail'

11. tbeyil tnam   'the road to town'

12. tbeyil ntanameʔ   'the road to my town'

13. txa tšex   'the stable'

14. nxayeʔ   'my house'

15. kxa šxal   'the people's home'

16. kšaxab tšex   'the horses' shoes'

17. kšaxabeʔ   'your (pl.) sandals'

18. tšaxaba   'your (sg.) sandals'

19. ošeʔ šxab   'three sandals'

20. ati itš ke šxal   'there is chile for the people'

21. ati itš weyeʔ   'there is chile for me'

(Continued on next page.)

22. witše^ʔ 'my chile'

23. itš te wanabe^ʔ   'chile for my sister'

24. tox kxa tanaba   'in your (sg.) sisters' house'

25. inbet šxal tox pts'an   'the man is walking in the cane'

26. intše^ʔbet tox tpats'ana   'they are walking in your cane'

27. intšinbete^ʔ twits xa   'I am walking in front of the house'

28. twits ntsike^ʔ   'the face of my older brother'

29. twits xa   'in front of the house'

30. tsikbax   'older brother'

31. mambax   'father'

32. mišti^ʔ nmane^ʔ   'I have no father'

33. mišti^ʔ a^ʔ   'there is no water'

34. qambax   'foot'

35. q'eq tqan šxal   'the man' foot is black'

36. q'eqaš   'it became black'

37. maq'eqaš   'it has become black'

38. xun k'wal kuw   'a strong child'

39. makuwiš k'wal   'the child has become strong'

40. tq'eqal kwitse^ʔ   'the pupil of your (pl.) eyes'

41. tsaqal xos   'the white of an egg'

42. saqlo   'it is probably white'

43. ttseyil xa   'the wood (e.g. rafters) of the house'

44. nim nwaye^ʔ ati   'I have a lot of food'

45. tnimal šxal oxetše^ʔtsax   'most of the people have already come'

46. mišti^ʔ wabx te kanab   'there is no food for their sister'

47. maq'anaš lo^ʔbx   'the fruit has ripened'

48. tša^ʔšlo tlo^ʔya   'no doubt your (sg.) fruit is green'

49. tša^ʔš ttši^ʔ   'his meat is raw'

50. ma ati tši^ʔbx teva   'is there meat for you (sg.)?'

51. pin twi^ʔ xa   'the roof of the house is thick'

52. tpimal kwi^ʔ k'wal   'the thickness of the children's heads'

53. twi^ʔ mes   'on the table'

54. inbeta tuk'il ttsika   'you (sg.) are walking with your older brother'

55. xata^ʔ tuk'ila   'where is your companion?'

56. nim tkuwal tuk'ila   'your (sg.) companion is very strong'

57. ši^ʔ txunal   'he went by himself'

58. oxetsaj koš   'the lame man has already come'

59. nim tkošil tqan   'his leg is very lame'

60. qošil inqo^ʔšob   'the three of us are afraid'

61. koš   'he is lame'

62. košiš tu^ʔn tyabil   'he got lame because of his sickness'

63. nim tše^ʔw xa^ʔlo   'it is very cold today'

64. matšewiš twaya   'your (sg.) food has become cold'

65. ta^ʔl lo^ʔbx   'the juice of the fruit'

66. nimin   'rather big'

67. tša^ʔšin   'a bit green'

68. q'eqin   'blackish'

69. ewilo kim   'she must have died yesterday'

70. malotše^ʔkim   'they have probably died'

71. kimlo   'no doubt he died'

72. oq'ši^ʔšlo   'no doubt she cried a lot'

73. makim tšex xa^ʔlo   'the horse died today'

74. mats'oq'ši^ʔš tu^ʔn   'he cried much because of it'

75. tkimsa   'he killed it'

76. tšobsa   'he made him afraid'

77. manoxši^ʔšlo tu^ʔn a^ʔ   'it has probably become very full of water'

78. tnoxsaya ewi   'you (sg.) filled it yesterday'

(Continued on next page.)

79. oknoxel   'it will get full'

80. oklokimel   'he will probably die'

81. oknoxsetel wuʔneʔ   'it will be filled by me'

82. ma oxenoxset   'was it filled?'

83. oxenaʔnoxset   'of course it was filled'

84. oxenaʔ   'of course it was'

85. noxsama   'fill it (sg. subject)!'

86. oxenaʔtšeʔkim   'yes, they died long ago'

87. tšʼiysama   'make it grow (sg. subject)!'

88. lwi matšʼiy kkʼwaleʔ   'your (pl.) child has grown fast'

89. kutsaxa   'come (sg. subject)!'

90. tsaxtsun   'then he came'

91. kuʔtsa   'you (sg.) came down'

92. oʔkuʔtseʔ   'we (excl.) came down'

93. eʔkuʔtstsuneʔ   'then you (pl.) came down'

94. oʔkuʔš   'we (incl.) went down'

95. qatsun matšeʔkuʔšeʔ   'if then you (pl.) go down'

96. šiʔ txa   'he went home'

97. kutšiʔya txaya   'go home (sg. subject)!'

98. kutkuʔtstsuna nman   'come down then, my father!'

99. etsa   'you came out (yesterday)'

100. matsʼets tox ttsi   'it came out of his mouth (today)'

101. kuteša ttsi xa   'go out the door (sg. subject)!'

102. inešeʔ   'I went out'

103. intšinetseʔ   'I am coming out'

104. eʔetslo   'no doubt they came out'

105. intšintsʼibaneʔ   'I am writing'

106. yabtoq   'he was sick'

107. intšeʔtsʼibantoq   'they were writing'

108. matoqtšintsʼibaneʔ   'I was about to write (but didn't)'

109. oxetoqttsʼiba   'he had already written it'

110. inntsʼibaʔneʔ   'I am writing it'

111. ttsʼiba   'he wrote it'

112. tsʼibbil   'a pencil'

113. intšeʔntsʼibaʔneʔ   'I am writing them (words)'

114. intšeʔktsʼibaʔneʔ   'we (excl.) are writing them'

115. intšeʔnkloʔneʔ   'I am defending them'

116. kolbil   'deliverance'

117. misbil   'a broom'

118. inmson   'he is sweeping'

119. intkʼmoʔn   'he is receiving it'

120. eš msol   'he went out to sweep'

121. misli   'it was swept'

122. kʼamli   'it was received'

123. tuʔn kkʼmet   'that they be received'

124. oktšinkʼmeteleʔ   'I will be received'

125. oʔšobseteʔ   'we (excl.) were threatened'

126. šobsbil   'a threatening'

127. tsuybil   'a holder'

128. ttsuy   'he held it'

129. oktsyetel   'it will be caught'

130. buybil   'a gathering'

131. tbuyi   'he gathered it'

132. oklotšeʔbuyitel   'possibly they will be gathered'

133. awbil   'a garden'

134. awama   'plant it (sg. subject)!'

135. tuʔn tawet   'that it be planted'

136. qʼoma   'give it (sg. subject)!'

137. qʼontsa   'give it this way (to me) (sg. subject)!'

(Continued on next page.)

138. q'onša   'give it that way (to him) (sg. subject)!'

139. ši?tq'o?n   'he gave it to him'

140. tsaxkq'o?n   'they gave it to me'

141. aq'li   'given'

142. taq'   'he gave it'

143. tunli   'hanging'

144. kušli   'lying down'

145. ku?kše   'he lay down'

146. kušbama   'lay it down (sg. subject)!'

147. ku?tkušba?na   'you (sg.) caused him to lie down'

148. okkbelqkušba?n   'we (incl.) will lay it down'

149. kšeku?ya   'lie down (sg. subject)!'

150. tsipeku?ya   'bow your head!'

151. tsipli   'with bowed head'

152. mexli   'kneeling'

153. tše?mxeku?ye?   'you (pl.) kneel down!'

154. xuntl   'another one'

155. oxetsuntšinkubtmexba?ntle?   'then he made me kneel down again'

156. el   'he left'

157. okkbeltune   'it will hang down'

Supplementary information:

1. The sequences tš and ts constitute single phonemes, but they are written here as digraphs for the sake of convenience in isolating morphemes.

2. Many relationships are expressed by series of possessives. For example, tox kxa tanaba 'in your (sg.) sisters' house' (24) is literally 'its-in(-ness) their-house your-sister(s).' The final morpheme -a goes with the prefix t- to constitute a discontinuous immediate constituent t-...-a meaning 'your (sg.).' Similarly, tts'umal nq'obe? 'the skin of my arm' (7) is literally 'its-skin my-arm.' The first person pronominal substitute consists of a prefix n- and an enclitic -e?. This clitic also occurs in other forms with other pronominal prefixes, cf. 4 and 17.

3. The bound forms occurring with nouns and verbs are of two different structural types: (1) those closely joined to the stem in fixed orders (i.e. affixes) and (2) those which occur in more than one relative position and whose grammatical attachment may be to the expression as a whole(i.e. clitics). All the data which would be required to differentiate these classes are not included. Hence, we are listing the following types of clitics: (1) tense particles, (2) definitive particles: -e? ~ -ye? and -a ~ -ya, and (3) certain aspect-mode particles: lo, na?, tsun, toq, and tl. These lists are not complete.

4. There are certain verbs of movement: tsax (45), ši? (57), kub (155), and el (156), which may also occur as preposed auxiliary verbs. The following are the principal morphophonemic reductions which take place: kub + tsax > ku?ts (91), kub + ši? > ku?š (94), el + tsax > ets (99), and el + ši? > eš (120). The morpheme kub also occurs as kb in certain combinations.

5. The prefixal indicators of persons are the same in the second and third persons singular and plural. Distinctions between these persons are made by enclitics.

6. There are two principal sets of prefixal pronouns, with certain allomorphic distinctions depending upon following consonant or vowel stems. Compare the system in Kekchi, a related language. The following forms indicate more fully some of the contrasts:

intše°bet   'they are walking'

tu°n kbet   'in order that they walk'

tex kbet   'when they walked'

intšints'ibane°   'I am writing'

intse°nts'iba°ne°   'I am writing them'

intse°kubnts'iba°ne°   'I am writing them down'

tu°n kkubnts'iba°ne°   'in order that I write them down'

7. The forms ati (20), mišti° (32), and -ta (55) constitute a subclass of verbs. Compare the following forms:

atine°   'I am (somewhere)'

atiya   'you (sg.) are'

ati   'he is'

ato°   'we (incl.) are'

ato°ye°   'we (excl.) are'

ate°ye°   'you (pl.) are'

ate°   'they are'

Problem 137 (data from the Isthmus dialect of Zapotec, a language of Mexico)

Instructions:

a. Isolate the morphemes.

b. File the data.

c. Describe the morphology.

1. stiné°   'mine'

2. stílu° ~ stíú°   'yours (sg.)'

3. stíbĕ·   'hers, his'

4. stímĕ·   'hers, his (of an animal)'

5. stíni·   'its'

6. stídŭ·   'ours (excl.)'

7. stínŭ· ~ stíkanŭ·   'ours (incl.)'

8. stítŭ·   'yours (pl.)'

9. stíkabĕ·   'theirs (of people)'

10. stíkamĕ·   'theirs (of animals)'

11. stíkani·   'theirs (of things)'

12. ñe°e   'foot'

13. ñe°é°   'my foot'

14. nǎ·°   'hand'

15. na·yá°   'my hand'

16. ži·gi   'chin'

17. ži·gilu°   'your chin'

(Continued on next page.)

18. ži·géʔ   'my chin'

19. ruaʔa   'mouth'

20. ruaʔáʔ   'my mouth'

21. ruaʔa giʔiguʔ   'the mouth of the river'

22. ike   'head'

23. ike-yóʔo   'roof'

24. ikéʔ   'my head'

25. ikebě·   'his head'

26. ike ma·níʔ   'the horse's head'

27. giña   'trunk'

28. škiñáʔ   'my trunk'

29. škiñabě·   'her trunk'

30. ti lubaʔ   'a vine'

31. hlubáʔ   'my vine'

32. hlubadǔ·   'our (excl.) vine'

33. hma·néʔ   'my horse'

34. hma·ninǔ·   'our (incl.) horse'

35. giča-ikéʔ   'my hair'

36. giča-iketǔ·   'your (pl.) hair'

37. luʔunaʔ   'bed'

38. hluʔúnáʔ   'my bed'

39. hluʔunakabě·   'their bed'

40. ne·za   'road'

41. hne·záʔ   'my road'

42. hne·zaluʔ   'your (sg.) way'

43. ǰum·i   'basket'

44. kašum·éʔ   'my baskets'

45. šum·ibě·   'her basket'

46. riʔi   'water jug'

47. stiʔibě·   'her water jug'

48. buʔú   'charcoal'

49. buʔú stíbě·   'her charcoal'

50. yoʔo   'house'

51. li·ǰéʔ   'my house'

52. li·ǰibě·   'his house'

53. rali·ǰitǔ·   'at your (pl.) house'

54. beúʔ stinéʔ   'my cherry'

55. kabeúʔ stídǔ·   'our (excl.) cherries'

56. čupa géta   'two corn cakes'

57. šketáʔ   'my corn cake'

58. šketaluʔ   'your (sg.) corn cake'

59. ti biʔkuʔ   'a dog'

60. špiʔkuáʔ   'my dog'

61. kabiʔkuʔ   'dogs'

62. kabiʔkukǎ·   'those dogs'

63. biʔkukǎ·   'that dog'

64. biʔkuríʔ   'this dog'

65. kabiʔkuríʔ   'these dogs'

66. biʔkukě·   'that dog (far away)'

67. kabiʔkukě·   'those dogs (far away)'

68. doʔo ziuʔulakǎ·   'that long rope'

69. štuaʔáʔ   'my rope'

70. štoʔobě·   'her rope'

71. ǰi·kě·   'that day (long ago)'

72. nase   'day before yesterday'

73. nasekǎ·   'several days ago'

74. ši·bě·   'his day'

75. zi·diríʔ   'this salt'

76. siidéʔ   'my salt'

(Continued on next page.)

77. bišo·zéʔ   'my father'

78. bišo·zeluʔ   'your (sg.) father'

79. hña·áʔ   'my mother'

80. hñaʔabě· 'her mother'

81. hñaʔa maría   'Mary's mother'

82. bendabě· 'her sister'

83. bizaʔanabě· 'his sister'

84. bizaʔanabě· her brother'

85. bičibě· 'his brother'

86. ragiʔiguʔ 'at the river'

87. iropákabě· 'both of them'

88. gionákabě· 'the three of them'

89. gidapákabě· 'the four of them'

90. to·bi 'one'

91. čupǎ· 'two'

92. čon·ǎ· 'three'

93. ta·pa 'four'

94. gaʔayuʔ 'five'

95. šupǎ· 'two more'

96. šon·ǎ· 'three more'

97. šta·pa 'four more'

98. nagáʔ 'green'

99. kaʔaǰi 'some'

100. škaʔaǰi 'a bit more'

101. ně· 'and, with'

102. naʔa 'I, me'

103. liʔi 'you (sg.)'

104. laʔadǔ· 'we, us (excl.)'

105. laʔanǔ· 'we, us (incl.)'

106. laʔatǔ· 'you (pl.)'

107. laʔakabě· 'they, them (persons)'

108. kanɪ̌· or laʔakanɪ̌· 'they, them (things)'

109. kahmósobě· 'his servants'

110. biaʔaniʔ 'light'

111. gendarati 'death'

112. nuʔú špiaʔanibě· 'he is intelligent'

113. gendašpiaʔaniʔ 'intelligence'

114. gendašeʔelaʔ 'wedding'

115. šeʔelaʔ 'wife, husband'

116. rane·za 'on the road'

117. rarí nuʔúnɪ̌· 'here it is'

118. rakǎ· 'there'

119. rakě· 'there (farther)'

120. rarikáʔ 'there (farther still)'

121. ndɪ̌·ʔ 'this'

122. kandɪ̌·ʔ 'these'

123. ngǎ· 'that'

124. ngě· 'that (farther)'

125. kangǎ· 'those'

126. rarípeʔ 'right here'

127. nga ngapeʔ 'that's exactly it'

128.

129. nuʔú lá 'is there?'

130.

131. tǔ· 'who?'

132. ndí lá 'this?'

133. ya· 'yes'

134. koʔ 'no'

135. paráʔa 'where'

(Continued on next page.)

136. guna·   'which one?'

137. guna'a   'woman'

138. ngi'iu   'man'

139. ba'du'   'child'

140. ti ba'du-wi'ini   'a baby'

141. stí ba'du-ngi'iu   'another boy'

142. kaba'du-ǰa'apa   'girls'

143. nawi'ini   'little'

144. nawi'inibě·   'he is little'

145. ta·pa ngi'iu   'four men'

146. ška'aǰi   'a bit more'

147. pandǎ·   'how many?'

148. pagála   'how much?'

149. ria·ndani nágeʔendǎ·   'it heals quickly'

150. má bia·ndabě·   'she's all well now'

151. či giá·ndá giú·ba   'I'm going to get well soon'

152. kaya·ndanǔ·   'we (incl.) are getting better'

153. ké zia·ndabě·   'he will not get well'

154. ké ñá·ndakabě·   'they did not get well'

155. ké wayá·ndakabě·   'they have not recovered'

156. doktor rí'ʔ, rusia·nda bin·Ɣ·   'this doctor cures people'

157. bisia·ndabe ná'a nage'éndǎ·   'he cured me quickly'

158. zusia·ndabe lí'i la'akǎ·   'he will cure you (sg.) too'

159. kusia·ndabe bíšó·zé'   'he is curing my father'

160. čí gusia·ndabé hña'abě·   'he is going to cure her mother'

161. ké nusiá·ndabe bíšo·zekabě·   'he did not cure their father'

162. la'aka ké wasiá·ndabé hña'akabě·   'he has not cured their mother either'

163. ručuʔúné ča'awi be'elǎ·   'I fry the meat well'

164. bičuʔunibe ni né'ege'   'she fried it yesterday'

(Continued on next page.)

165. zučúʔninu bê·re lá   'shall we (incl.) fry the chicken?'

166. kučúʔnirúdu bízaʔa   'we (excl.) are still frying beans'

167. čí gučúʔunilu stiúʔ lá   'are you (sg.) going to fry yours (sg.)?'

168. laʔakabe ké nučúʔunikabe stíkabě·   'they (emphatic) did not fry theirs'

169. wačúʔunilu ni čaʔawi lá   'have you (sg.) fried them well?'

170. riǰuʔuni bizaʔa ne zá· lá   'does one fry beans in pork grease?'

171. má biǰuʔunikani ne áséite   'they are already fried in oil'

172. zaǰuʔunikani nágeʔéndá lá   'will they fry quickly?'

173. kaǰúʔunikani náne·ne né beʔélǎ·   'they are frying slowly with the meat'

174. čí giǰuʔuni beʔelaka yán·aǰi·   'the meat is going to be fried today'

175. ké niǰúʔunini néʔegeʔ   'it was not fried yesterday'

176. ké waǰuʔuninǐ·   'it has not been fried'

177. ye gučúʔuni nǐ·   'go fry it (sg. subject)!'

178. riziʔídé diʔiǰaza nageʔéndǎ·   'I learn Zapotec rapidly'

179. biziʔidilu kadiʔiǰake lá   'did you (sg.) learn those words?'

180. biziʔidi kanǐ·   'learn them (sg. subject)!'

181. lagíziʔidi kani, báʔdukaʔ   'learn them, children!'

182. zaziʔídé čiʔi lá   'shall I learn ten?'

183. kazíʔidibe hmá ke čiʔi   'she is learning more than ten'

184. či gizíʔidinu gándé, háʔ   'we (incl.) are going to learn twenty, are we not?'

185. ke nizíʔidikabe gástíʔ   'they did not learn anything'

186. ké wazíʔidilu gástíʔ   'you (sg.) have not learned anything'

187. ké rusiʔídé liʔi gástíʔ   'I do not teach you (sg.) anything'

188. bisiʔidibe láʔa saʔa   'she taught her music'

189. bisiʔidi naʔa   'teach me (sg. subject)!'

190. lagúsiʔidi naʔa   'teach me (pl. subject)!'

191. zusiʔidilu laʔa lá   'will you teach him?'

192. kusíʔidikabe láʔatǔ·   'they are teaching you (pl.)'

193. ké gusíʔidilu laʔadǔ·   'do not teach us (excl.) (sg. subject)!'

(Continued on next page.)

194. ké nusíʔidu laʔakabě. 'you (sg.) did not teach them'

195. nábéˑ wasiʔídé laʔakamě.   'I have taught them (dogs) much'

196. rusíndáʔdu nísa   'we heat the water'

197. nandáʔnĭ·   'it (the water) is hot'

198. bisíndáʔya gendaroʔ   'I heated the dinner'

199. bisindáʔ léče kǎ·   'heat the milk (sg. subject)!'

200. zusíndaʔya ndií lá   'shall I heat this?'

201. kusíndáʔkabe káfé   'they are heating the coffee'

202. kádi gúsíndóú bizaʔa nagasĭ·   'do not heat the beans now (sg. subject)!'

203. ke núsíndáʔya nĭ·   'I did not heat it'

204. rindáʔni nágeʔéndă.   'it gets hot quickly'

205. čaʔawi bindáʔnĭ·   'it heated up slowly'

206. zandáʔ ndií nageʔéndá lá   'will this heat quickly?'

207. nisaríʔ, kándáʔ   'this water is getting hot'

208. gendaroríʔ, ké nindáʔ   'this dinner did not get hot'

209. gendaroríʔ, kádi wandáʔ   'this dinner has not heated up'

210. riʝiʔičibě·   'she gets angry'

211. biʝiʔíčéʔ stí tíru   'I got angry again'

212. zaʝiʔičirubé lá   'will he still be angry?'

213. žiñéʔe kaʝiʔíčitŭ·   'why are you getting mad?'

214. kádi (~ ke) giʝiʔíčú   'do not be mad (sg. subject)!'

215. ké niʝiʔíčínú háʔ   'we did not get mad, did we?'

216. ké waʝiʔíčéʔ   'I have not been angry'

217. ručiʔičime náʔa   'he (the dog) makes me angry'

218. bičiʔíčídú laʔame čúpá tíru   'we made him mad twice'

219. zučiʔíčé laʔakamě.   'will we anger them (the chickens)?'

220. kúčiʔíčé laʔakamě·   'I am making them angry'

221. ké gučiʔíčílú laʔakamě·   'do not make them angry (sg. subject)!'

222. ké nučiʔíčídú láʔamě·   'we (excl.) did not make her angry'

(Continued on next page.)

223. nábé· rušalébé puértá?   'he always opens the door'

224. bišalébé nǐ·   'she opened it'

225. zusǎlé nǐ lá   'shall I open it?'

226. bišalé nǐ·   'open it (sg. subject)!'

227. lagúšálé bentána kǎ·   'open that window (pl. subject)!'

228. kúšálédú nǐ·   'we (excl.) are opening it'

229. čigušalédú nǐ·   'we (excl.) are going to open it'

230. ké nušalétú nǐ·   'you (pl.) did not open it'

231. wašalé ní čúpá tíru   'I have opened it twice'

232. nábé· rižalénǐ·   'it always comes open'

233. zažalé stubini lá   'will it open by itself?'

234. bižalénǐ·   'it came open'

235. kážálení yán·a   'it is coming open now'

236. puertáká čí gižalé?   'that door is going to come open'

237. ndií ké nižalé?   'this one did not open'

238. stóbi kǎ· wažalé čon·a tíru   'that other one has opened three times'

239. rijiñ·abe ná?a idúbi óra   'he comes near me every few minutes'

240. bijiñ·á?, peru ké nuni?íbé nǐ·   'I went close but I did not move it'

241. bijiñ·a   'come over here (sg. subject)!'

242. lagíjiñ·a, bá?duka?   'come over here, children'

243. zajíñ·adu lá   'shall we (excl.) go closer?'

244. kajíñ·abe rálijinǔ·   'he is approaching our (incl.) house'

245. čígijiñ·abě·   'she is going to come near'

246. ké nijíñ·adǔ·   'we (excl.) did not go near'

247. žiñé?e nábé· ručíñ·alu nǐ·   'why do you always bring it so close?'

248. ké nučiñ·á ní né?ege?   'I did not take it close yesterday.'

249. bičiñ·a nǐ·   'bring it here (sg. subject)!'

250. lagúčiñ·a nǐ·   'bring it here (pl. subject)!'

251. zučiñ·alu gi?či ká lá   'will you (sg.) bring that paper here?'

(Continued on next page.)

252. kúčíñ·á nǐ·   'I am bringing it'

253. ke nučíñ·abe nǐ·   'she did not bring it here'

254. biʔkuka čí gučíñ·a ǰitakǎ·   'the dog is going to bring the bone here'

255. ručuʔuguá beʔelǎ·   'I cut the meat'

256. má bičuʔugulu ni lá   'did you (sg.) already cut it?'

257. zúčúʔugube nǎ·bě·   'she will cut her hand'

258. kučúʔugube pán kǎ·   'she is cutting the bread'

259. čí gučuʔugube žándié·kǎ·   'he is going to cut the watermelon'

260. laʔabe núčuʔugube nǐ·   'she (emphatic) should have cut it'

261. má biruʔugunǐ·   'it is already cut'

262. nábě· riruʔugubě·   'she always cuts herself'

263. záruʔugunǐ·   'it will get cut'

264. karúʔugunǐ·   'it is being cut'

265. pa gíruʔugu bikwin·i nóúʔ   '(careful lest) your (sg.) finger get cut'

266. nigúʔugunǐ·   'it might have been cut'

267. riče·zá ni dérěču   'I tear it straight'

268. gučeʔzu špéstídúáʔ   'you (sg.) tore my dress'

269. kádi gičéʔzu stíúʔ   'do not tear yours (sg.)'

270. zače·zá nǐ·   'I will tear it'

271. kádi káčé·zá nǐ·   'I am not tearing it'

272. guče·za ni ráríʔ   'tear it here (sg. subject)!'

273. ké ničé·zalu nǐ·   'you (sg.) ought not to tear it'

274. rire·zaka nageʔéndǎ·   'they tear quickly'

275. nare·zanǐ·   'it is torn'

276. gure·zani neʔegeʔ   'it got torn yesterday'

277. zare·zani lá   'will it tear?'

278. kare·za nǐ·   'it is tearing'

279. giré·zanǐ·   '(if you are not careful) it will tear'

280. ké niré·zanǐ·   'it did not tear'

(Continued on next page.)

281. nábé· riku'ušu la·rirí'   'this cloth always wrinkles'

282. biku'ušunǐ·   'it wrinkled'

283. zaku'ušunǐ·   'it will wrinkle'

284. kakú'ušu špízu'údé'   'my skirt is getting wrinkled'

285. čí giku'ušunǐ·   'it is going to wrinkle'

286. ke niku'ušunǐ·   'it did not wrinkle'

287. rusíkú'ušua nǐ·   'I always wrinkle it'

288. bisiku'ušulu špida'áné'   'you (sg.) wrinkled my blouse'

289. zusiku'ušube nǐ·   'he will wrinkle it'

290. kusiku'ušube špída'anibě·   'she is wrinkling her blouse'

291. bi'iyaga· ké gusiku'ušulu nǐ·   'look out that you (sg.) do not wrinkle it'

292. ké núsikú'ušua nǐ·   'I did not wrinkle it'

293. naku'ušunǐ·   'it is wrinkled'

294. runi'íbé nǐ·   'I move it'

295. žiñé'e bini'ibú gi'čikǎ·   'why did you (sg.) move the paper?'

296. zuni'ibilú ndǐ· lá   'will you (sg.) move this?'

297. bini'ibe mežákǎ·   'move the table (sg. subject)!'

298. lagúni'ibi mežákǎ·   'move the table (pl. subject)!'

299. kúní'íbídú nǐ·   'we (excl.) are moving it'

300. čé guni'ibíkabe lá'a   'they are going to move him (change his work)'

301. má wani'ibibe nǐ·   'he has already moved it'

302. má bini'ibibě·   'he already moved'

303. képe rini'ibibě·   'she does not move (works very slowly)'

304. zani'ibimě·   'it (a scorpion) will move'

305. kani'íbíkame stí tíru   'they are moving again'

306. má wani'íbíkamě·   'they have moved already'

307. kádi gini'íbú'   'do not move (sg. subject)!'

308. bini'ibǐ·   'do move (sg. subject)'

309. lagíni'ibǐ·   'do move (pl. subject)'

(Continued on next page.)

310. naya'ase' 'black'

311. riya'asé' 'I get black'

312. biya'asekabě· 'they turned black'

313. zaya'aselu' 'you (sg.) will get black'

314. kádi kaya'asedíbě· 'she is not getting black'

315. niyá'asedǔ· 'we (excl.) would get black'

316. rúziya'ase nǐ· 'I make it black'

317. biziya'aselu nǐ· 'you (sg.) got it black'

318. zuziya'asebe nǐ· 'she will get it black'

319. kuzíya'aserúlu nǐ· lá 'are you (sg.) still making it black?'

320. ké gúzia'aselu nǐ· 'do not make it black (sg. subject)!'

321. nuziya'aselu kanǐ 'you (sg.) should have made them black'

322. ké waya'aseruá nǐ· 'I have not yet gotten it black'

323. naya· 'clean'

324. biǎ·nǐ· 'it was cleaned'

325. rusia·yá nǐ· 'I clean it'

326. bisia· nǐ· 'clean it (sg. subject)!'

327. rinda'a nǐ· 'I break it'

328. binda'akabe nǐ· 'they broke it'

329. zanda'abe bladú lá 'will she break the plate?'

330. kando'oú nǐ· 'you (sg.) are breaking it'

331. gunda'a nǐ· 'break it (sg. subject)!'

332. ké gándá gínda'á nǐ· 'I can not break it'

333. ké ñándá nínda'á nǐ· 'I could not break it'

334. ké wanda'á ní ti bladú' 'I have not broken even one plate'

335. rila'ákani náge'endǎ· 'they break easily'

336. má gula'anǐ· 'it already broke'

337. zala'ani lá 'will it break?'

338. řéha kala'á 'the gate is breaking'

(Continued on next page.)

339. ke čí ndaʔatu r̃éhakǎ· 'do not break the fence (pl. subject)!'

340. ridiʔdibe rárí·irǎ· ʝi· 'he goes by here every day'

341. gudi·dé čupa tíru 'I went by twice'

342. gudíʔdiʔ 'go ahead (sg. subject)!'

343. zadiʔdu nageʔendá lá 'will you (sg.) be going by soon?'

344. kadíʔdibe yán·a 'she is going by now'

345. kartéro ké nidíʔdi yan·aʝi· 'the mailman did not come by today'

346. wadiʔdibe stálé tíru 'he has gone by many times'

347. rutiʔidilu kóče rakě· lá 'do you take the car through there?'

348. ké nutiʔídéní rákě· 'I did not take it there'

349. bitiʔidibe ní ráke· néʔegeʔ 'he took it there yesterday'

350. ke zutiʔidibe ni ráke· íꞳɪꞳ·ʔ 'he will not take it there tomorrow'

351. kútíʔídé laʔame čéríʔ 'I am putting him (the rooster) through here'

352. ke (~ kádi) gutiʔidu laʔame čéríʔ 'do not put him through here (sg. subject)!'

353. bitiʔidi laʔame čéríʔ 'put him through there (sg. subject)!'

354. ke nutíʔdidu láʔa čéríʔ 'we did not take her through there'

355. iza gudíʔdiʔ 'last year'

356. ži tál Ꭓǎ· 'how are you?'

357. galán purtí nábá·néʔ 'fine, because I'm alive'

358. baʔdu-wiʔinike čúpásí gúbi·ʝǎ·biba·nɪ̌· 'the baby lived just two days'

359. ndɪ̌· zaba·ni lá 'will this one live?'

360. ké nibá·ní místú wiʔini kě· 'the kitten did not live'

361. ríčésáʔ 'I jump'

362. gučeʔsuʔ 'you (sg.) jumped'

363. začesǎ· 'he will jump'

364. čí gičesabě· 'she is going to jump'

365. kanačesakamě· 'they (animals) go around jumping'

366. gučesa 'jump (sg. subject)!'

367. lagíčesa 'jump (pl. subject)!'

(Continued on next page.)

368. ké gičéʔsuʔ   'do not jump (sg. subject)!'

369. ké ničésadŭ·   'we (excl.) did not jump'

370. nábé· wačesatu lá   'have you (pl.) jumped much?'

371. natoʔope íkebĕ·   'she has gray hair'

372. nageʔéndá rítoʔope íkedŭ·   'we (my family) gray early'

373. bitoʔope iké ʔ   'I turned gray'

374. zatoʔope íkenŭ·   'we all will turn gray'

375. katoʔópé íkeluʔ   'you (sg.) are turning gray'

376. či gitoʔope íkekabĕ·   'they are going to turn gray'

377. ké nitoʔópé íketŭ·   'you (pl.) did not turn gray'

378. ike toʔopĕ·   'gray hair'

379. ngiʔiu ike toʔopekă·   'that gray-headed man'

380. riba·ba žieʔéʔ   'my nose always itches'

381. biba·ba ñeʔebĕ·   'her foot itched'

382. kabá·ba ikebĕ·   'his head is itching'

383. ké nibá·ba iké ʔ   'my head did not itch'

384. ruʔundáruá diʔiǰaza.   'I still study Zapotec'

385. kayúʔundaróu diʔiǰastia· lá   'are you (sg.) still studying Spanish?'

386. ké ñuʔundabĕ·   'he did not sing'

387. nase ruʔundabe iră· ǰi·   'she used to read every day'

388. biʔindaʔ   'sing (sg. subject)!'

389. lagúʔundaʔ   'sing (pl. subject)!'

390. či dúʔundanédú laʔabĕ·   'we (excl.) are going to study with her'

391. ké ñuʔundatu diʔiǰaza· nučíʔ   'you (pl.) did not study Zapotec last night'

392. idúbi ǰi· wayuʔúndáʔ   'I have read all day'

393. ruɥu·bé irá ládu   'I look everywhere'

394. biɥu·bu ni lá   'did you (sg.) look for it?'

395. biɥú·bi nĭ·   'look for it (sg. subject)!'

396. čí guɥu·bibe nĭ·   'he is going to look for it'

(Continued on next page.)

397. kuyú·bítú ní lá   'are you (pl.) looking for it?'

398. ké nuyu·bí ča·awikabe nǐ·   'they did not look well for it'

399. lagúyu·bi čá·awi   'look well (pl. subject)!'

400. kánáyú·bídǔ·   'we (excl.) were going around looking'

401. na·a ru·né nǐ·   'I (emphatic) do it'

402. bi·inilu ni lá   'did you (sg.) do it?'

403. la·abe gú·nibe nǐ·   'he (emphatic) will do it'

404. bi·ni nǐ·   'do it (sg. subject)!'

405. lagú·ni nǐ·   'do it (pl. subject)!'

406. ži káyú·ninelú ngǎ·   'what were you (sg.) doing with that?'

407. ži káyú·ninétu ngǎ·   'what are you (pl.) doing with that?'

408. ži gu·né ya·   'what shall I do?'

409. ži·í ngá ya·   'what's that?'

410. ké ñú·né nǐ·   'I did not do it'

411. ñu·né nǐ· peru ké ñándǎ·   'I was going to do it, but I could not'

412. ruto·okabe kwánanaši   'they sell fruit'

413. lu·be bítuá·á lí·ǰé·   'I sold her my horse'

414. lu·kabe   'their faces'

415. zuto·olo sta·alu luǎ·· lá   'will you (sg.) sell me your (sg.) mat?'

416. luǎ··   'my face'

417. kúto·obe géta   'she is selling corn cakes'

418. kádi gutó·olo nǐ·   'do not sell it (sg. subject)!'

419. ké nutó·odo nǐ·   'we (excl.) did not sell it'

420. wato·olo čon·a lá o ga·ayu·   'have you (sg.) sold three, or five?'

421. de yan·a rido·o bidua·a rarǐ· lá   'do they still sell bananas here?'

422. yo·oká bido·o ne·ege·   'the house was sold yesterday'

423. zado·oni náge·éndǎ·   'it will sell quickly'

424. mehór gidó·oni yán·a   'better it be sold now!'

425. ké wadó·onǐ·   'it has not sold'

(Continued on next page.)

426. nábé· riro'obe yán·a   'she is very fat now'

427. biro'obě·   'he got fat'

428. kádi zaro'olo stal·ě·   'you (sg.) will not get very fat'

429. kárua'á'   'I am getting fat'

430. čí giró'nǒ·   'we (incl.) are going to get fat'

431. ké niró'okamě·   'they (pigs) did not get fat'

432. ké waró'o yǔ·zekǎ·   'the cattle have not gotten fat'

433. geta rusiro'o na'a   'corn cakes make me fat'

434. la'aka bísiro'okani lá'abě·   'they made her fat too'

435. la'aka zúsiro'okani lí'i   'they will make you (sg.) fat too'

436. ndí kúsíro'o la'adǔ·   'this is making us (excl.) fat'

437. čí gúsíro'oni lá'atǔ·   'it is going to make you (pl.) fat'

438. ké nusiro'oni ná'a   'it did not make me fat'

439. ké wásíro'oni ná'a   'it has not made me fat'

440. ké nila'ánǐ·   'it did not break'

441. nala'a yá·gakǎ·   'that wood is broken'

442. ži ráku'   'what is the matter with you (sg.)?'

443. ži gúka   'what happened?'

444. zaka sa'a ižǐ·'   'there will be music tomorrow'

445. kayáka sa'a   'there is a fiesta going on'

446. ži čígaka ižǐ·'   'what is going to go on tomorrow?'

447. nábé· nandá'   'it is very hot (weather)'

448. nábé· káyákánándá'ya'   'I am very hot'

449. rakala·ǰé nǐ·   'I want it'

450. **rakala'ǰu na'a lá**   'do you (sg.) want me?'

451. zakala'ǰibe ndǐ· lá   'will she want this?'

452. kayákala·ǰé nǐ·   'I was wanting it'

453. ké ñákála'ǰidǔ·   'we (excl.) did not want to'

454. ra·zé irǎ· ǰi·   'I bathe daily'

(Continued on next page.)

455. má gu·zelu lá   'did you (sg.) already bathe?'

456. zázelu lá   'will you (sg.) bathe?'

457. ye ga·zebĕ·   'she went to bathe'

458. kaya·zekabĕ·   'they were bathing'

459. gu·ze   'bathe (sg. subject)!'

460. riga·zebe rági?igu?   'she goes to the river to bathe'

461. ké ñázelu hǎ?   'you (sg.) did not bathe, did you?'

462. wárá?ya?, ké waya·zé mǎ raka tapa gubi·ǰa   'I am sick; I have not bathed for four days'

463. ga?ayu gubi·ǰa   'five days'

464. má raka šo?opa gubi·ǰa   'six days ago'

465. ruga·zé ba?du-wi?ini stiné? irǎ· ǰi·   'I bathe my baby daily'

466. biga·zelu la?abe yán·aǰi lá   'did you (sg.) bathe him today?'

467. hña?abe zúga·ze la?abĕ·   'her mother will bathe her'

468. biga·ze bendalú?   'bathe your (sg.) sister!'

469. kúgázé la?abĕ·   'I am bathing her'

470. tu če guga·ze la?abĕ·   'who is going to bathe him?'

471. tǔ·   'who?'

472. tu?ú ngá   'who is that?'

473. ké nugáze ča?awilu la?abĕ·   'you (sg.) did not bathe him well'

474. ribe?ebe nǐ·   'she takes it out'

475. má gule?é nǐ·   'I already got it out'

476. zabe?elu pánká lá   'will you (sg.) take out the bread?'

477. la?abe kábe?ébé nǐ·   'she is taking it out'

478. ké nibe?é nǐ·   'I did not take it out'

479. ké gándá kue?é nǐ·   'I can not get it out'

480. kádi kue?eú nǐ·   'do not take it out (sg. subject)!'

481. ye nde?e nǐ·   'go take it out (sg. subject)!'

482. nábé· rire?ebe káǰi·rí?   'she goes out a lot these days'

483. bire?ɛ rarǐ·?   'get out of here (sg. subject)!'

(Continued on next page.)

484. lagíreʔe rarǐ·ʔ   'get out of here (pl. subject)!'

485. nagasi bíreʔebě·   'he just left'

486. čí gireʔelu yan·a geʔela lá   'are you (sg.) going out tonight?'

487. kareʔe mánčaka lá   'is the stain coming out?'

488. koʔ, ké zareʔenǐ·   'no, it will not come out'

489. r̃etrátoka ké nireʔe čaʔawi   'the picture did not come out good'

490. ribi·jíkabe náʔa síádoʔroʔ   'they call me early in the morning'

491. čupa tíru guri·jé liʔi   'I called you (sg.) twice'

492. zabi·jíkabe láʔanǔ·   'they will call us (incl.)'

493. kabí·jíbé láʔabě·   'he is calling her'

494. **ké kwí·jílú naʔa**   'do not call me (sg. subject)!'

495. ké ñándá níbí·jé liʔi   'I could not call you (sg.)'

496. rítí·jé laʔakabě·   'I always go to call them'

497. **rukwaʔáné laʔabě.**   'I regularly wake her up'

498. neʔege bikwaʔanibe náʔa   'yesterday she awakened me'

499. zukwáʔanu naʔa lá   'will you (sg.) awaken me?'

500. kwkwáʔanu baʔdu-wiʔinikǎ·   'you (sg.) are awakening the baby'

501. čé gukwaʔanilu laʔabě·   'you (sg.) are going to awaken him'

502. **ké nukwáʔanikabe láʔabě.**   'they did not awaken him'

503. biba·ni baʔduka lá   'did the child awaken?'

504. zaba·nibe nágasǐ·   'he will awaken soon'

505. má kabá·nibě·   'she is already awakening'

506. ké randa ríba·nibe témpráno   'she can not awaken early'

507. ké zanda gíba·nibe témpráno   'she will not be able to awaken early'

508. ké nibá·nikabě·   'they did not awaken'

509. nãbé· rusáʔbilu pelóta   'you (sg.) always drop the ball'

510. bisaʔbibe búñé·gáʔ   'she knocked over the doll'

511. zusáʔbilu ni lá   'will you (sg.) drop it?'

512. kusáʔbibe nǐ·   'she is dropping it'

(Continued on next page.)

513. čé gusáʔbibe nǐ·   'she is going to let it fall'

514. ké nusáʔbilu ni háʔ   'you (sg.) did not throw it down, did you?'

515. ria·ba baʔdu-wiʔini   'the baby falls'

516. bia·babe láyu·   'he fell on the ground'

517. zia·baluʔ   'you (sg.) will fall'

518. káyá·báʔ   'I am falling'

519. pa giá·baluʔ   'and what if you (sg.) fall?'

520. ké ñá·báʔ   'I did not fall'

521. ria·žabe štál·ě·   'he gets good pay'

522. bia·žá neʔegeʔ   'I was paid yesterday'

523. zia·žabe ížíʔ   'he will be paid tomorrow'

524. káyá·žáʔ   'I am getting my pay'

525. zé gia·žabě·   'he went to collect his pay'

526. ké ñá·žabě·   'they did not pay her'

527. má bia·žanǐ·   'it is already paid'

528. rigi·žéʔ   'I always pay'

529. má gudi·žéʔ   'I already paid'

530. zagi·žebe náʔa ížǐ·ʔ   'she will pay me tomorrow'

531. kagí·žebe láʔabě·   'he is paying her'

532. diuš ki·žepe liʔi   'thank you! (lit. God pay you)'

533. ké nigí·žedí·dǔ·   'we (excl.) did not pay it'

534. ké zándá kí·žebe nǐ·   'she cannot pay it'

535. ye ti·žebě·   'he went to pay'

536. kádi kiʔžu nǐ·   'do not pay it (sg. subject)!'

537. ruʔuti bínǐ·   'it kills people'

538. biʔitibe bíʔčibě·   'he killed his brother'

539. zuʔutibe béndábě·   'she will kill her sister'

540. biʔiti láʔamě·   'kill it (sg. subject)!'

541. kayuʔítíbé láʔamě·   'he is killing it'

(Continued on next page.)

542. čí guʔútídú tí biuwi   'we (excl.) are going to kill a hog'

543. ké ñúʔútíkabe néʔegeʔ   'they did not kill yesterday'

544. stal·e bín·í ráti de šinǰáʔ   'many people die of fever'

545. gu·tibě.   'he died'

546. za·téʔ   'I will die'

547. káyá·té nisa   'I am thirsty'

548. čí ga·tibě.   'she is going to die'

549. ké ñá·téʔ   'I did not die'

550. nábé· ruzaʔaké gendaroʔ   'I always burn the dinner'

551. peru ro·be nǐ·   'but he eats it'

552. nageʔéndá riaʔkinǐ·   'it burns quickly'

553. bizaʔakibe ǰúládi   'he burned the chocolate'

554. zuzaʔakilu ni záká·   'you (sg.) will burn it that way'

555. kuzáʔakilu nǐ·   'you (sg.) are burning it'

556. kádi guzaʔakilu nǐ·   'do not burn it (sg. subject)!'

557. ké nuzaʔáké nǐ·   'I did not burn it'

558. nuzʔakilu nisa   'you (sg.) would even burn water!'

559. guyaʔkinǐ·   'it burned'

560. ziaʔkiʔ   'it will burn'

561. káyáʔkiʔ   'it is burning'

562. pa čaʔkí ndǐ·ʔ   'what if this burns?'

563. ké ñaʔkiʔ   'it did not burn'

564. reʔeda ngíʔiuróʔka lá   'does that big man come regularly?'

565. naseke réndáʔ peru maʹkoʔ   'I used to come but do not any more'

566. má bendáʔ   'I already came'

567. ǰi· beʔédálú kě·   'that day (when) you came'

568. ké gándá geʔédábě·   'she cannot come'

569. ké ñeʔédatǔ·   'you (pl.) did not come'

570. zeʔédákabě·   'they will come'

(Continued on next page.)

571. biʔiya mistúróʔkǎ·   'look at that big cat'

572. nígutoʔobe ni péru ké ñándǎ·   'he was going to sell it but could not'

573. zíguʔundabě·   'she is going to go read'

574. zígá·zéʔ   'I am going to go to bathe'

575. nigi·žé laʔa peru beʔedabe rárí·   'I was going to go pay her but she came here'

576. laʔjibě·   'his liver'

577. gukwaʔaláʔjibě·   'he sighed'

578. rakalaʔjibě·   'he wants'

579. riuʔulaʔjibě·   'he likes'

580. nanalaʔjibě·   'he hates'

581. gukwaʔabě·   'he received, took, got'

Text:

1. <u>lu</u> <u>ti</u> <u>ya·ga</u> <u>gitu</u> <u>žiga</u> <u>nagáʔ</u> <u>kanagite</u> <u>lé·žu</u> <u>ti</u> <u>waji·</u>
   On a tree squash gourd green went playing Rabbit one afternoon.

2. <u>ngatí</u> <u>mál·á</u> <u>gúlúʔubeʔeje ʔ</u> <u>ma·níkě·</u>   3. <u>skasi</u> <u>níbičâ·</u> <u>ti</u> <u>žiga</u>
   In that moment roared animal-that.   Like had filled a gourd

   <u>nisa</u> <u>guka</u> <u>lé·žu</u> 4. <u>yan·a</u> <u>waža</u> <u>zauá</u> <u>liʔi</u> <u>ne</u> <u>zauá</u>
   water happened to Rabbit. "Now yes I will eat you, and I will eat

   <u>liʔi.</u> 5. <u>paráʔa</u> <u>či</u> <u>tóló</u> <u>naʔa</u> <u>yaʔ</u> <u>bíči.</u> 6. <u>de</u>
   you." "Where going to eat-you me (interrogative), brother. Since

   <u>numbápe</u> <u>ngá</u> <u>rá·béʔ</u> <u>paráʔa</u> <u>nuʔú</u> <u>ruáʔa</u> <u>geúʔ</u> <u>bičé</u> <u>rari·</u>
   before that was saying-I 'Where is mouth of Coyote, brother-my here

   <u>yaʔ.</u> 7. <u>biʔiya</u> <u>girǎ·</u> <u>biaʔawi</u> <u>ríʔ</u> <u>dedepe</u> <u>zitu</u> <u>kandáʔ</u>
   (inter.)?' Look all zapote fruit this; from far smelling

   <u>našikaʔ.</u> 8. <u>bišelé</u> <u>ruaʔaluʔ</u> <u>gusa·bá</u> <u>čupa</u> <u>gó·loʔ.</u> 9. <u>háho··</u>
   sweet-they. Open mouth-your knock down two that eat-you." "Hmmm!"

10. <u>bišelé</u> <u>ndaganda</u> <u>geú</u> <u>ruaʔa</u> <u>dedepe</u> <u>gučeyúʔubaʔ</u> <u>jitalaya.</u> 11. <u>čon·a</u>
    Opened very wide Coyote mouth until thundered jaw. Three

    <u>gídúbi</u> <u>gitužígakě·</u> <u>bisindaʔa</u> <u>léžu</u> <u>ndaʔani</u> <u>yan·i.</u> 12. <u>bizulunda</u>
    whole gourds-those threw Rabbit inside throat. Began

    <u>kaká·bieke</u> <u>kayáʔgaʔ</u> <u>yan·i.</u> 13. <u>rakéká</u> <u>nuʔú</u> <u>gúritaʔ.</u> 14. <u>duʔubitika</u>
    squirming, choking throat. Right there was sat down. Feathers

    <u>gúka</u> <u>lé·žu</u> <u>bieteti·</u> <u>zí</u> <u>gužoʔoñeʔ.</u>
    became Rabbit, went down, went running.

Free translation:

1. One afternoon Rabbit went playing on a leafy squash tree.   2. At that moment that animal roared.   3. Rabbit felt as if he had had a gourd of water dashed on him.   4. "Now, now, I'm going to eat you," [said the Coyote].   5. "What do you mean you're going to eat me, Brother?   6. Since earlier today I've been saying, 'Wonder where my brother Coyote is showing his face.'   7. Look at all of this zapote fruit. It smells sweet even at a distance.   8. Open your mouth and knock down a couple for you to eat."   9. "Hmmm."   10. Coyote opened his mouth so wide that his jaw popped.   11. Rabbit threw into his throat three whole gourds.   12. He began squirming and choking,   13. and sat down right there, unable to move.   14. Rabbit made himself like feathers; going down from the tree, he went running.

Supplementary information:

1. Some morphemes have alternative forms in identical environments, e.g. či (390) and čí (396).

2. Certain particles may be either clitic or nonclitic.

3. Zapotec of the Isthmus has two tones, high and low. The low is unmarked except in the case of glides on long vowels.

4. There are a number of tonal perturbations based upon the types of tonal sequences.

APPENDIX

Part I: Supplementary Problems

A. Problems Supplementary to Section 2.22.2

The problems in this section are arranged according to the phonological processes which they illustrate. Where necessary, a short statement about each process precedes the problems. All problems in the Appendix consist of hypothetical data.

A.1 Assimilation and Dissimilation

There are four factors involved in assimilation and dissimilation:

1. Progressive vs. regressive changes

2. Contiguous vs. noncontiguous phonemes

3. Type of articulation

4. Partial vs. complete assimilation

The change of np to mp is regressive, since the second phoneme has influenced the first. The change of np to nt is progressive, since the first phoneme has influenced the second.

Contiguous phonemes are juxtaposed to each other. The changes of np to mp and np to nt involve contiguous phonemes. Noncontiguous phonemes are not juxtaposed. A change of napi to nipi involves noncontiguous vowel phonemes.

In describing the assimilation and dissimilation of consonants, we generally distinguish the point of articulation and the manner of articulation. This is not always wholly satisfactory, but it enables us to describe and classify certain types of allomorphic alternation. The changes of np to mp and np to nt involve the points of articulation, i.e. dental + bilabial becomes bilabial + bilabial, and dental + bilabial becomes dental + dental. A change of np to nm would involve no change in the point of articulation, but rather a change from stop to continuant. This modification involves the manner of articulation.

Changes of np to mp, np to nt, and np to nm are all partial changes. A change of np to nn or to pp would constitute a complete assimilation. Completely assimilated phonemes are always identical.

Dissimilations are much rarer than assimilations and usually involve noncontiguous phonemes. Any dissimilation may be regarded as complete, though one may desire to indicate degrees of dissimilation.

Problem 138

Instructions:

a. Describe the following assimilations in terms of the four factors:

283

1. Progressive vs. regressive changes

2. Contiguous vs. noncontiguous phonemes

3. Point of articulation vs. manner of articulation

4. Partial vs. complete assimilation

b. Regard n, y, l, and r as having the same point of articulation, but as differing in manner.

c. Regard f, m, w, p, and b as having the same point of articulation.

1. an- 'I' + -xi 'to go' > aŋxi 'I go'

2. ib- 'we' + -to 'to come' > idto 'we come'

3. mak- 'boy' + -mi (pl. suf.) > mapmi 'boys'

4. tit- 'girl' + -ŋi (poss. suf.) > tikŋl 'girl's'

5. en- 'you' + -pi 'to ride' > empi 'you ride'

6. ap- 'they' + -go 'to move' > abgo 'they move'

7. as- 'she' + -di 'to show' > azdi 'she shows'

8. ap- 'they' + -θi 'to fall' > afθi 'they fall'

9. bed- 'man' + -ki (pl. suf.) > betki 'men'

10. on- 'it' + -θi 'to see' > oNθi 'it sees'

11. tip- 'ship' + -ko (pl. suf.) > tikko 'ships'

12. is- 'he' + -šo 'to drink' > iššo 'he drinks'

13. aθ- 'house' + -kin 'to fly' > akkin 'airplane'

14. am- 'noise' + -ni 'wheels' > anni 'bus'

15. ad- 'jump' + -pi 'song' > appi 'dance'

16. fol- 'field' + -ra (pl. suf.) > forra 'fields'

17. is- 'he' + -ri 'to leave' > irri 'he leaves'

18. ib- 'bee' + -to 'juice' > itto 'honey'

19. al- 'rock' + -yi 'dust' > alli 'chalk'

20. ar- 'tree' + -ni 'water' > arri 'canoe'

21. tiš- 'wrapping' + -ti 'leg' > tisti 'leggings'

22. bix- 'leather' + -bo 'foot' > bibbo 'shoes'

(Continued on next page.)

23. tag- 'wool' + -ri 'to twist' > tadri 'spindle'

24. am- 'knife' + -yo 'to kill' > aňyo 'sword'

25. ar- 'wood' + -to 'to write' > arro 'pencil'

26. up- 'iron' + -ki 'fish' > uppi 'fishhook'

27. tas- 'coffee' + -go 'juice' > tasdo 'coffee extract'

28. mič- 'man' + -si 'large' > mičši 'giant'

29. im- 'man' + -go 'to jump' > imbo 'dancer'

30. il- 'feather' + -no 'tail' > illo 'headdress'

31. pιn- 'lion' + -ko 'spotted' > kinko 'tiger'

32. sal- 'animal' + -ši 'to grin' > šalši 'chipmunk'

33. ɟa- 'tail' + -či 'to stink' > čači 'skunk'

34. ti- 'father' + -go 'sun' > tido 'god'

35. pin- 'mother' + -go 'sun' > pinpo 'moon'

36. li- 'wool' + -ro 'woven' > lilo 'blanket'

37. ras- 'fish' + -aš 'snake' > rašaš 'eel'

38. avi- 'bird' + -bi 'to catch' > avivi 'bird trap'

39. ol- 'fish' + -ar 'net' > orar 'fish net'

40. im- 'cow' + -in 'small' > inin 'calf'

Problem 139

Instructions: Describe the following dissimilations in terms of three factors:

    1. Progressive vs. regressive changes

    2. Contiguous vs. noncontiguous phonemes

    3. Point of articulation vs. manner of articulation

1. k^win- 'hut' + -k^wo 'many' > kink^{w}o 'villages'

2. pari- 'old man' + -gro 'big' > paligro 'chief'

3. t^{h}i- 'ring' + -t^{h}o 'arm' > tit^{h}o 'bracelet'

4. ma- 'white' + -mo 'stone' > namo 'quartz'

5. fi- 'yellow' + -fi 'metal' > pifi 'gold'

6. xa- 'green' + -xo 'stone' > kaxo 'turqoise'

(Continued on next page.)

7. argo- 'baby' + -ri 'toy' > algori 'doll'

8. zi- 'to hit' + -zi 'to hit' > rizi 'to fight'

9. θa- 'to jump' + -θa 'to jump' > θata 'to dance'

10. bo- 'money' + -bu 'much' > bopu 'rich'

Problem 140

Instructions:

    a. List the allomorphs of the negative morpheme.

    b. Describe the phonologically defined distribution.

    c. Determine the basic allomorph. (See section 2.23.2, D.)

1. ontini	'unhappy'		9. ompanu	'uncomfortable'
2. omali	'disagreeable'		10. omfura	'displeased'
3. onsamu	'untrue'		11. ommane	'disappointed'
4. omika	'unfinished'		12. orrika	'unpleasant'
5. ollika	'bad'		13. ončana	'worthless'
6. oŋkiri	'loose'		14. omwiki	'crazy'
7. oŋxitu	'small'		15. onθusi	'uncertain'
8. onnipa	'stingy'			

Problem 141

Instructions:

    a. Determine the allomorphs of the prefixal morpheme.

    b. Describe the phonologically defined distributions.

    c. Determine the basic allomorph. (See section 2.23.2, D)

1. iθim	'I ran'		6. ixko	'I yelled'
2. ifpik	'I jumped'		7. issat	'I stopped'
3. iθosi	'I ate'		8. ifman	'I slept'
4. iθris	'I sank'		9. iθθik	'I danced'
5. iθtan	'I talked'			

Problem 142

Instructions: Describe the distribution of the allomorphs of the reduplicative morpheme.

1. pampano   'talks incessantly'   5. tirtiri   'falls repeatedly'

2. setseti   'walks and walks'   6. kekkepo   'sleeps frequently'

3. mammaŋi   'cries continuously   7. tintimi   'laughs continuously'

4. rerrele   'dances continuously'   8. xekxeti   'has a bad cough'

Problem 143

Instructions: Describe the distribution of the allomorphs of the reduplicative morpheme.

1. pan   'to go'   1a. aampan   'to be going'

2. kis   'to work'   2a. iiskis   'to be working'

3. xam   'to run'   3a. aaŋxam   'to be running'

4. bol   'to stop'   4a. oolbol   'to be stopping'

5. dir   'to dance'   5a. iirdir   'to be dancing'

6. tuŋ   'to drink'   6a. uuntuŋ   'to be drinking'

7. šis   'to rise'   7a. iiššis   'to be rising'

8. mot   'to fly'   8a. oopmot   'to be flying'

9. kip   'to fall'   9a. iikkip   'to be falling'

Problem 144

Instructions: Describe the distribution of the allomorphs of the infixal morpheme.

1. toraθim   'she is going'   6. pumatko   'she is writing'

2. sulaθθi   'she is rising'   7. miraθxa   'she is small'

3. pasaθfi   'she is sick'   8. teratpu   'she is beginning'

4. tunadgi   'she is pretty'   9. munadri   'she is brown'

5. kinaθus   'she is good'

Vowels may assimilate and dissimilate, just as consonants do; but the manner of describing the changes in type of articulation differs. The contrasts in such changes are: high, mid, low; front, central, back; rounded, unrounded; nasal, nonnasal; tense, lax; breathy, nonbreathy; glottalized, nonglottalized; or any other qualitative contrast occurring in the particular language.

A change of sotim to setim is regressive (the second phoneme affects the first), noncontiguous, partial, and involves fronting. The o and e remain on the same level, but the e is a front vowel and the o is a back one. The change of kiu to kii is progressive, contiguous, complete, and involves fronting. The change of gati to geti is regressive, noncontiguous, partial, and involves fronting and raising.

Whether one describes a change as fronting, raising, backing, or lowering, depends entirely upon the morphophonemic structure of the language in question. Vowels may have a number of such structural relationships. The following are some of the more common symmetrical types of configuration:

```
A.  i        u           E.  i   ə   u

        a                       e   a   o


B.  i        u           F.  i       u

    e        o               e   ə   o

        a                       ɛ   a   ɔ


C.  i        u           G.  i ü     u

    e    a   o               e ŏ     o

                               ɛ æ a   ɔ

D.  i        u

    e        o

    a        ɔ           H.  i ü ɨ u

                            e ö a o
```

The manner in which we describe assimilative changes depends upon the way in which we set up these morphophonemic relationships.

Problem 145

Instructions:

    a. Describe the process of assimilation.

    b. Describe the phonological distribution of the allomorphs.[1]

1. kanot	'he thinks'	1a. kene	'I think'
2. pinot	'he learns'	2a. pine	'I learn'
3. čerot	'he forgets'	3a. čere	'I forget'
4. monot	'he remembers'	4a. meme	'I remember'
5. bakot	'he sees'	5a. beke	'I see'
6. furot	'he tastes'	6a. fire	'I taste'
7. molot	'he hears'	7a. mele	'I hear'
8. kumot	'he feels'	8a. kime	'I feel'

---

[1]This anticipates somewhat Chapter 4, but it is most important that one understand thoroughly the relationship of phonological changes to distribution of allomorphs.

Solution of Problem 145:[2]

a. On the basis of the following diagrammatic arrangement of vowels:

    i   u

              it may be said that back vowels preceding a low front vowel

  e   a   o

assimilate to front vowels of their own level.

b. Front-vowel allomorphs of bi-allomorphic stems precede the front-vowel morpheme. All other allomorphs precede -ot.

Problem 146

Instructions:

a. Describe the assimilative changes.

b. Describe the phonological distribution of the allomorphs of the stems.

1. sïtuk 'I fall'	1a. sitit 'he falls'	1b. sitem 'we fall'	1c. sitat 'you fall'
2. asukuk 'I run'	2a. asükit 'he runs'	2b. asükem 'we run'	2c. asukat 'you run'
3. məkuk 'I talk'	3a. mekit 'he talks'	3b. mekem 'we talk'	3c. mekat 'you talk'
4. namuk 'I hear'	4a. namit 'he hears'	4b. namem 'we hear'	4c. namat 'you hear'
5. futuk 'I call'	5a. fütit 'he calls'	5b. fütem 'we call'	5c. futat 'you call'
6. somuk 'I fish'	6a. sömit 'he fishes'	6b. sömem 'we fish'	6c. somat 'you fish'
7. ranuk 'I hunt'	7a. ranit 'he hunts'	7b. ranem 'we hunt'	7c. ranat 'you hunt'
8. imasuk 'I go'	8a. imasit 'he goes'	8b. imasem 'we go'	8c. imasat 'you go'
9. unətuk 'I feast'	9a. unetit 'he feasts'	9b. unetem 'we feast'	9c. unetat 'you feast'
10. rïkuk 'I dance'	10a. rükit 'he dances'	10b. rükem 'we dance'	10c. rükat 'you dance'
11. səkuk 'I skip'	11a. sökit 'he skips'	11b. sökem 'we skip'	11c. sökat 'you skip'
12. mïguk 'I dream'	12a. mügit 'he dreams'	12b. mügem 'we dream'	12c. mïgat 'you dream'
13. rəsuk 'I awake'	13a. rösit 'he awakes'	13b. rösem 'we awake'	13c. rəsat 'you awake'
14. mïruk 'I smoke'	14a. mirit 'he smokes'	14b. mirem 'we smoke'	14c. mirat 'you smoke'

Patterns of vocalic assimilation may be very widespread in morphological structures. Such forms are said to exhibit vocalic harmony. This is a predominant characteristic of the Ural-Altaic languages.

---

[2]This solution is given so as to indicate the manner in which such features may be described.

Problem 147

Instructions:

    a. Diagram the morphophonemic relationships of vowels.

    b. Describe the assimilative changes.

    c. State the phonological distribution of the allomorphs.

1. sirenkirmeni   'they may not be working'

2. benenkirmeni   'they may not be running'

3. parankirmani   'they may not be helping'

4. kusonkurmonu   'they may not be fishing'

5. sütönkürmönü   'they may not be hunting'

A.2 Medial Voicing

    Voiceless consonants tend to become voiced between vowels. This may be described as a kind of assimilation between the voiced and the voiceless segments of the continuum.

Problem 148

Instructions:

    a. Describe the phonological process.

    b. State the phonological distribution of the allomorphs.

1. maduk	'going'	1a. adtuk	'went'
2. mabis	'running'	2a. adpis	'ran'
3. magon	'sliding'	3a. adkon	'slid'
4. magar	'falling'	4a. adgar	'fell'
5. mavit	'trying'	5a. adfit	'tried'
6. magum	'coughing'	6a. adxum	'coughed'
7. mažas	'spitting'	7a. adšas	'spit'
8. mabul	'begging'	8a. adbul	'begged'

A.3 Final Unvoicing

    In word-final position there is a tendency for phonemes to become voiceless.

Problem 149

Instructions:

a. Determine the allomorphs of the morphemes.

b. Describe the phonological distributions.

1. tabek	'eating'	1a. tabegat	'I eat'
2. fasip	'riding'	2a. fasipat	'I ride'
3. nitit	'spitting'	3a. nititat	'I spit'
4. opat	'hunting'	4a. opadat	'I hunt'
5. osan	'tracking'	5a. osanat	'I track'
6. ramuk	'dancing'	6a. ramukat	'I dance'
7. simiθ	'smoking'	7a. simiθat	'I smoke'
8. rikap	'moving'	8a. rikabat	'I move'
9. samus	'trying'	9a. samuzat	'I try'
10. okaš	'loaning'	10a. okašat	'I loan'

A.4 Assimilation and Dissimilation of Tonemes

Problem 150

Instructions:

a. Reconstruct the unmodified forms.

b. List the types of allomorphic changes.

c. Describe the phonological distribution of the allomorphs exhibiting such changes.

1. tánúsí	'I go'	1a. tánúsabá	'we go'	1b. tánúki	'he goes'
2. ásansí	'I run'	2a. ásansábá	'we run'	2b. ásanki	'he runs'
3. mókisí	'I walk'	3a. mókisábá	'we walk'	3b. mókìki	'he walks'
4. ortasí	'I ride'	4a. ortasábá	'we ride'	4b. ortaki	'he rides'
5. musúsí	'I sleep'	5a. musúsábá	'we sleep'	5b. musúki	'he sleeps'
6. kanìsí	'I swim'	6a. kanìsábá	'we swim'	6b. kanìki	'he swims'
7. òtánsí	'I sneeze'	7a. òtánsábá	'we sneeze'	7b. òtánki	'he sneezes'
8. rànisí	'I carry'	8a. rànisábá	'we carry'	8b. ràniki	'he carries'
9. kùtusí	'I bring'	9a. kùtusábá	'we bring'	9b. kùtùki	'he brings'

(Continued on next page.)

1c. tánúgitu	'they go'	1d. tánukàfà	'you go'	1e. tánusù	'she goes'
2c. ásangitu	'they run'	2d. ásankàfà	'you run'	2e. ásansù	'she runs'
3c. mókìgitu	'they walk'	3d. mókìkàfà	'you walk'	3e. mókìsù	'she walks'
4c. ortagìtu	'they ride'	4d. ortakàfà	'you ride'	4e. ortasù	'she rides'
5c. musúgitu	'they sleep'	5d. musúkàfà	'you sleep'	5e. musúsù	'she sleeps'
6c. kanìgitu	'they swim'	6d. kanìkàfà	'you swim'	6e. kanìsù	'she swims'
7c. òtángitu	'they sneeze'	7d. òtankàfà	'you sneeze'	7e. òtansù	'she sneezes'
8c. rànigitu	'they carry'	8d. rànikàfà	'you carry'	8e. rànisù	'she carries'
9c. kùtùgitu	'they bring'	9d. kùtùkafà	'you bring'	9e. kùtùsù	'she brings'

Supplementary information:

1. Mid tones are unmarked.

2. There are dissimilative as well as assimilative changes.

Problem 151

Instructions:

a. Reconstruct the unmodified forms.

b. List the types of allomorphic changes.

c. Describe the phonological distribution of the allomorphs exhibiting such changes.

1. mósámo	'I walk'	1a. sánásamó	'we walk'	1b. kisámó	'you walk'
2. mókíta	'I hunt'	2a. sánakíta	'we hunt'	2b. kikíta	'you hunt'
3. mómátà	'I skate'	3a. sánamátà	'we skate'	3b. kimátà	'you skate'
4. móró	'I slip'	4a. sánáro	'we slip'	4b. kiró	'you slip'
5. móbimi	'I dance'	5a. sánábimi	'we dance'	5b. kibimì	'you dance'
6. mómará	'I kill'	6a. sánámará	'we kill'	6b. kimará	'you kill'
7. mórasò	'I shoot'	7a. sánárasò	'we shoot'	7b. kirasò	'you shoot'
8. mófi	'I ride'	8a. sánáfi	'we ride'	8b. kifi	'you ride'
9. móberì	'I bread'	9a. sánáberì	'we break'	9b. kibèrì	'you break'
10. mósokú	'I burst'	10a. sánásokú	'we burst'	10b. kisòkú	'you burst'
11. mómànu	'I thrust'	11a. sánámànu	'we thrust'	11b. kimànu	'you thrust'
12. mópà	'I push'	12a. sánápà	'we push'	12b. kipà	'you push'

(Continued on next page.)

1c. tokosámó	'they walk'	1d. rìsamó	'he walks'	1e. bìràsamó	'she walks'
2c. tokokíta	'they hunt'	2d. rìkíta	'he hunts'	2e. bìràkíta	'she hunts'
3c. tokomátà	'they skate'	3d. rìmatà	'he skates'	3e. bìràmatà	'she skates'
4c. tokoró	'they slip'	4d. rìró	'he slips'	4e. bìràró	'she slips'
5c. tokobìmi	'they dance'	5d. rìbimi	'he dances'	5e. bìràbimi	'she dances'
6c. tokòmará	'they kill'	6d. rìmará	'he kills'	6e. bìràmará	'she kills'
7c. tokòrasò	'they shoot'	7d. rìrasò	'he shoots'	7e. bìràrasò	'she shoots'
8c. tokofì	'they ride'	8d. rìfi	'he rides'	8e. bìràfi	'she rides'
9c. tokobèrì	'they break'	9d. rìbèri	'he breaks'	9e. bìràberì	'she breaks'
10c. tokosòkú	'they burst'	10d. rìsòkú	'he bursts'	10e. bìrasòkú	'she bursts'
11c. tokomànu	'they thrust'	11d. rìmànu	'he thrusts'	11e. bìramànu	'she thrusts'
12c. tokopà	'they push'	12d. rìpà	'he pushes'	12e. bìràpa	'she pushes'

A.5 Reduction of Word-Medial Consonant Clusters

Problem 152

Instructions:

a. Reconstruct the fuller, unmodified forms.

b. State the types of reductions which occur.

c. Describe the phonological distribution of the allomorphs.

1. kiko	'I see'	1a. piko	'you see'	1b. atniko	'he sees'
2. kate	'I go'	2a. pate	'you go'	2b. atmate	'he goes'
3. kuta	'I hear'	3a. puta	'you hear'	3b. atuta	'he hears'
4. koka	'I smell'	4a. poka	'you smell'	4b. atŋoka	'he smells'
5. kisu	'I cough'	5a. pisu	'you cough'	5b. atisu	'he coughs'
6. kliti	'I spit'	6a. pliti	'you spit'	6b. atliti	'he spits'
7. krapo	'I chew'	7a. prapo	'you chew'	7b. atrapo	'he chews'

Discussion of Problem 152:

1. The stems in series 1b-7b are the basic forms. They lose their initial consonant, unless this consonant is l or r, when preceded by the prefixes k- and p-. It can also be stated that this loss occurs when the prefix has the form C-, but not when it has the form VC-.

2. The phonological distribution of the resultant allomorphs may be stated as: Allomorphs beginning with vowels, r, and l follow prefixes of the type C-. Such a statement presupposes the listing of two types of allomorphs: (1) those beginning with vowels and (2) those beginning with consonants.

Problem 153

Instructions:

a. Reconstruct the fuller, unmodified forms.

b. State the types of reduction which occur.

1. tip	'will be going'		1a. ftip	'is going'
2. tsak	'will be riding'		2a. fsak	'is riding'
3. tlop	'will be walking'		3a. flop	'is walking'
4. tnut	'will be talking'		4a. fmut	'is talking'
5. tkus	'will be calling'		5a. fnus	'is calling'
6. tpit	'will be crying'		6a. fmit	'is crying'
7. tkrus	'will be dripping'		7a. frus	'is dripping'
8. tfat	'will be trying'		8a. fat	'is trying'
9. tut	'will be buying'		9a. fut	'is buying'

1b. ndip	'was going'		1c. atip	'has been going'
2b. nzak	'was riding'		2c. asak	'has been riding'
3b. nlop	'was walking'		3c. alop	'has been walking'
4b. mut	'was talking'		4c. amut	'has been talking'
5b. ŋgus	'was calling'		5c. aknus	'has been calling'
6b. mbit	'was crying'		6c. aprit	'has been crying'
7b. ŋgrus	'was dripping'		7c. agrus	'has been dripping'
8b. mvat	'was trying'		8c. afat	'has been trying'
9b. nut	'was buying'		9c. aut	'has been buying'

Problem 154

Instructions:

a. Reconstruct the fuller, unmodified forms.

b. Describe the types of consonant reduction.

c. Describe the types of assimilation.

1. satu	'to a man'	1a. katu	'for a man'	1b. natu	'from a man'
2. skoru	'to a boy'	2a. koru	'for a boy'	2b. ŋkoru	'from a boy'
3. sbisu	'to a girl'	3a. kpisu	'for a girl'	3b. mbisu	'from a girl'
4. sana	'to a lady'	4a. ksana	'for a lady'	4b. nsana	'from a lady'
5. spita	'to a cow'	5a. kpita	'for a cow'	5b. mpita	'from a cow'
6. sθira	'to a horse'	6a. kθira	'for a horse'	6b. nθira	'from a horse'
7. sama	'to a pig'	7a. ksama	'for a pig'	7b. nsama	'from a pig'
8. snofi	'to a goat'	8a. knofi	'for a goat'	8b. nofi	'from a goat'
9. sŋiru	'to a chicken'	9a. kŋiru	'for a chicken'	9b. ŋiru	'from a chicken'
10. suti	'to a snake'	10a. kuti	'for a snake'	10b. nuti	'from a snake'
11. sdoma	'to a bird'	11a. ktoma	'for a bird'	11b. ndoma	'from a bird'

Problem 155

Instructions:

a. Reconstruct the fuller, unmodified forms.

b. Describe the types of consonant reduction by the use of formulas.

c. Describe the assimilations.

1. sako	'of a man'	1a. saka	'in a man'
2. amaŋko	'of a girl'	2a. amaŋka	'in a girl'
3. tanto	'of a dog'	3a. taŋka	'in a dog'
4. hohpo	'of a house'	4a. hohka	'in a house'
5. agto	'of a soldier'	5a. agka	'in a soldier'
6. safθo	'of a chief'	6a. safka	'in a chief'
7. mampo	'of a box'	7a. maŋka	'in a box'
8. sando	'of a basket'	8a. saŋka	'in a basket'
9. reklo	'of a tent'	9a. reka	'in a tent'
10. salko	'of a tree'	10a. salka	'in a tree'
11. rarto	'of a lake'	11a. rarka	'in a lake'
12. manlo	'of a bridge'	12a. maŋka	'in a bridge'
13. sampo	'of a leaf'	13a. saŋka	'in a leaf'

(Continued on next page.)

| 14. fakto | 'of a hill' | 14a. faka | 'in a hill' |
| 15. mapto | 'of a hole' | 15a. mapka | 'in a hole' |

1b. saktu	'behind a man'	1c. sakpri	'for a man'
2b. amantu	'behind a girl'	2c. amampri	'for a girl'
3b. tantu	'behind a dog'	3c. tampri	'for a dog'
4b. hohtu	'behind a house'	4c. hohpri	'for a house'
5b. agtu	'behind a soldier'	5c. agpri	'for a soldier'
6b. saftu	'behind a chief'	6c. safpri	'for a chief'
7b. mantu	'behind a box'	7c. mampri	'for a box'
8b. santu	'behind a basket'	8c. sampri	'for a basket'
9b. rektu	'behind a tent'	9c. rekpri	'for a tent'
10b. saltu	'behind a tree'	10c. salpri	'for a tree'
11b. rartu	'behind a lake'	11c. rarpri	'for a lake'
12b. mantu	'behind a bridge'	12c. mampri	'for a bridge'
13b. santu	'behind a leaf'	13c. sampri	'for a leaf'
14b. faktu	'behind a hill'	14c. fakpri	'for a hill'
15b. maptu	'behind a hole'	15c. mapri	'for a hole'

Supplementary information:

1. Symbolize the consonants as C.

2. Distinguish between sequences of identical and nonidentical consonants.

3. Distinguish between sequences in which the final C of a cluster CCC is an l or an r and those in which it is not.

A.6 Reduction of Word-Final Consonant Clusters

Problem 156

Instructions:

a. Determine the basic allomorphs of the stem morphemes.

b. Describe the type of consonant-cluster reduction.

c. State the phonological distribution of the basic and the nonbasic allomorphs.

1. laŋ	'house'	1a. laŋgil	'in a house'
2. bim	'boat'	2a. bimpil	'in a boat'
3. kor	'temple'	3a. kortil	'in a temple'
4. bik	'tree'	4a. bikril	'in a tree'
5. pin	'lake'	5a. pinθil	'in a lake'
6. roh	'jar'	6a. rohkil	'in a jar'

Problem 157

Instructions:

a. Determine the basic allomorphs of the stem morphemes.

b. State the phonological distribution of the basic and the nonbasic allomorphs.

1. sak	'to go'	1a. saktup	'I go'	1b. saktlis	'we go'
2. boh	'to leave'	2a. bohtup	'I leave'	2b. bohtlis	'we leave'
3. mart	'to sweep'	3a. martup	'I sweep'	3b. martlis	'we sweep'
4. bis	'to drop'	4a. bisup	'I drop'	4b. bislis	'we drop'
5. tam	'to pick up'	5a. tamup	'I pick up'	5b. tamlis	'we pick up'
6. nimp	'to shave'	6a. nimpup	'I shave'	6b. nimplis	'we shave'
7. folt	'to cut'	7a. foltup	'I cut'	7b. foltlis	'we cut'
8. sas	'to see'	8a. sastup	'I see'	8b. sastlis	'we see'
9. rix	'to sit'	9a. rixkup	'I sit'	9b. rixklis	'we sit'
10. tiθ	'to fall'	10a. tiθkup	'I fall'	10b. tiθklis	'we fall'

A.7 Reduction of Vowel Sequences

Problem 158

Instructions:

a. Reconstruct the fuller, unmodified forms.

b. List all the types of changes in terms of raising, lowering, backing, and fronting.

c. List the various sets of allomorphs.

d. Describe the phonological distribution of the allomorphs.

1. me·r	'I am walking'	1a. maut	'you are walking'	1b. mo·n	'he is walking'
2. te·r	'I am talking'	2a. teut	'you are talking'	2b. teon	'he is talking'
3. ti·r	'I am looking'	3a. tiut	'you are looking'	3b. tion	'he is looking'
4. ruer	'I am dancing'	4a. ru·t	'you are dancing'	4b. ru·n	'he is dancing'
5. koer	'I am leaving'	5a. ko·t	'you are leaving'	5b. ko·n	'he is leaving'

Discussion of Problem 153:

The contracted vowels illustrate partially simultaneous morphemes (see section 3.32). It is possible, however, to describe the phonological distributions by referring only to the basic forms of the various allomorphs. The allomorphs of the stems may be listed as: ma- ~ me·- ~ mo· 'is walking,' te- ~ te·- 'is talking,' ti- ~ ti·- 'is looking,' ru- ~ ru·- 'is dancing,' ko- ~ ko·- 'is leaving.' The allomorphs of the suffixes may be listed as -er ~ -r 'I,' -ut ~ -t 'you,' and -on ~ -n 'he.'

The phonological distribution of the morphemes may be described as follows:

1. A suffix with a front vowel in the basic allomorph occurs in the form -C after front- and central-vowel stems and in the form -VC after back-vowel stems.

2. A suffix with a low back vowel in the basic allomorph occurs in the form -C after back- and central-vowel stems and in the form -VC after front-vowel stems.

3. A suffix with a high back vowel occurs in the form -C after back vowels and in the form -VC after front- and central-vowel stems.

4. Front-vowel stems occur in the long-vowel alternant preceding front-vowel suffixes and in the short-vowel alternant preceding back-vowel suffixes.

5. Back-vowel stems occur in the long-vowel alternant preceding back-vowel suffixes and in the short-vowel alternant preceding front-vowel suffixes.

6. A mid-vowel stem occurs with a long low front vowel before a front-vowel suffix, with a long low back vowel before a suffix with a low back vowel, and with a short central vowel before a high back suffix.

It is considerably simpler, however, to state these allomorphic modifications and distributions by describing the phonological changes. This may be done by three simple statements:

1. Sequences of front vowels and sequences of back vowels reduce to long vowels of the quality of the first vowel.

2. Sequences of a mid vowel plus a low front or a low back vowel reduce to a long vowel of the quality of the second vowel.

3. All other sequences are unchanged.

In describing the phonologically defined environments of allomorphs, we frequently employ statements based upon the phonological processes rather than upon the actual forms of the resultant allomorphs, since in many instances the descriptions of phonological processes are simpler and clearer.

Problem 159

Instructions:

    a. Describe the types of allomorphic alternation in terms of the phonological process.

    b. Describe the phonological distribution of the allomorphs.

1. sa·m	'in the house'	1a. saum	'before the house'	1b. sair	'behind the house'
2. na·m	'in the garden'	2a. neum	'before the garden'	2b. ne·r	'behind the garden'
3. tiam	'in the tree'	3a. tium	'before the tree'	3b. ti·r	'behind the tree'
4. kuam	'in the box'	4a. ku·m	'before the box'	4b. kuir	'behind the box'
5. ba·m	'in the temple'	5a. bu·m	'before the temple'	5b. boir	'behind the temple'

Problem 160

Instructions: Describe the types of allomorphic alternation in terms of the phonological process.

1. si·t	'by the house'	1a. si·m	'in the house'	1b. si·k	'through the house'
2. te·t	'by the hut'	2a. te·m	'in the hut'	2b. te·k	'through the hut'
3. lɛ·t	'by the bag'	3a. lɛ·m	'in the bag'	3b. lɛ·k	'through the bag'
4. kait	'by the cave'	4a. kaem	'in the cave'	4b. ka·k	'through the cave'
5. toit	'by the hole'	5a. toem	'in the hole'	5b. ta·k	'through the hole'
6. ruit	'by the tree'	6a. ruem	'in the tree'	6b. ruɛk	'through the tree'

1c. siam	'around the house'	1d. siom	'over the house'	1e. sius	'behind the house'
2c. tɛ·m	'around the hut'	2d. teom	'over the hut'	2e. teus	'behind the hut'
3c. lɛ·m	'around the bag'	3d. lɛom	'over the bag'	3e. lɛus	'behind the bag'
4c. ka·m	'around the cave'	4d. ka·m	'over the cave'	4e. ka·s	'behind the cave'
5c. to·m	'around the hole'	5d. to·m	'over the hole'	5e. to·s	'behind the hole'
6c. ru·m	'around the tree'	6d. ru·m	'over the tree'	6e. ru·s	'behind the tree'

    The reduction of vowel sequences may involve the change of some vowels to consonants, e.g. i to y and u to w.

Problem 161

Instructions: Describe the types of allomorphic alternation in terms of the phonological processes.

1. sanita	'to work'	1a. sani·s	'working'	1b. sani·t	'worked'
2. oneta	'to go'	2a. one·s	'going'	2b. oneut	'went'
3. kanɛta	'to sneeze'	3a. kanɛ·s	'sneezing'	3b. kanɛut	'sneezed'
4. ogata	'to show'	4a. ogais	'showing'	4b. oga·t	'showed'
5. fanota	'to cough'	5a. fanois	'coughing'	5b. fano·t	'coughed'
6. kanuta	'to hunt'	6a. kanu·s	'hunting'	6b. kanu·t	'hunted'
7. koti·ta	'to fish'	7a. koti·s	'fishing'	7b. koti·t	'fished'
8. kage·ta	'to spin'	8a. kage·s	'spinning'	8b. kageut	'spun'
9. monɛ·ta	'to weave'	9a. monɛ·s	'weaving'	9b. monɛut	'wove'
10. sisa·ta	'to beat'	10a. sisais	'beating'	10b. sisa·t	'beat'
11. sito·ta	'to drum'	11a. sitois	'drumming'	11b. sito·t	'drummed'
12. reku·ta	'to whistle'	12a. reku·s	'whistling'	12b. reku·t	'whistled'
13. mekta	'to call'	13a. mekis	'calling'	13b. meku·t	'called'
14. tanta	'to yell'	14a. tanis	'yelling'	14b. tanu·t	'yelled'
15. onta	'to cry'	15a. onis	'crying'	15b. onu·t	'cried'

1c. sanyo·n	'was working'	1d. sanyɛ·t	'has worked'
2c. oneon	'was going'	2d. oneɛt	'has gone'
3c. kanɛon	'was sneezing'	3d. kanɛ·t	'has sneezed'
4c. ogaon	'was showing'	4d. ogaɛt	'has shown'
5c. fano·n	'was coughing'	5d. fanoɛt	'has coughed'
6c. kanwo·n	'was hunting'	6d. kanwɛ·t	'has hunted'
7c. kotyo·n	'was fishing'	7d. kotyɛ·t	'has fished'
8c. kageon	'was spinning'	8d. kageet	'has spun'
9c. monɛon	'was weaving'	9d. monɛ·t	'has woven'
10c. sisaon	'was beating'	10d. sisaɛt	'has beaten'
11c. sito·n	'was drumming'	11d. sitoɛt	'has drummed'
12c. rekwo·n	'was whistling'	12d. rekwɛ·t	'has whistled'
13c. mekon	'was calling'	13d. mekɛ·t	'has called'
14c. tanon	'was yelling'	14d. tanɛ·t	'has yelled'
15c. onon	'was crying'	15d. onɛ·t	'has cried'

A.8 "Weakening" of Consonants

In intervocalic positions consonants tend to "weaken" from voiceless stops to voiced continuants. This change may be interpreted as a type of "leveling" of the voiceless stop "obstructions" in the voiced continuum.

Problem 162

Instructions:

a. State the types of changes.

b. Describe the phonological distributions of the allomorphs.

1.	ripka	'in the house'	1a.	riva	'of the house'
2.	tatka	'in the man'	2a.	tada	'of the man'
3.	sikka	'in the boy'	3a.	siga	'of the boy'
4.	biška	'in the town'	4a.	biža	'of the town'
5.	tabka	'in the hole'	5a.	tava	'of the hole'
6.	bodka	'in the well'	6a.	boda	'of the well'
7.	razka	'in the ocean'	7a.	raza	'of the ocean'

Problem 163

Instructions:

a. List the types of allomorphic alternations.

b. Describe the phonological distribution of these types.

1.	panra	'I chew'	1a.	paŋko	'you chew'	1b.	panata	'he chews'
2.	ti·mra	'I spit'	2a.	ti·ŋko	'you spit'	2b.	ti·mata	'he spits'
3.	lakra	'I lick'	3a.	lako	'you lick'	3b.	lakata	'he licks'
4.	to·tkra	'I taste'	4a.	to·tko	'you taste'	4b.	to·tkata	'he tastes'
5.	lapkra	'I blow'	5a.	lapko	'you blow'	5b.	lapkata	'he blows'
6.	fobra	'I suck'	6a.	fopko	'you suck'	6b.	fobata	'he sucks'
7.	tapra	'I swallow'	7a.	tapko	'you swallow'	7b.	tapata	'he swallows'
8.	ri·gra	'I point'	8a.	ri·ko	'you point'	8b.	ri·gata	'he points'
9.	togira	'I laugh'	9a.	togiko	'you laugh'	9b.	togieta	'he laughs'
10.	bana·ra	'I cough'	10a.	bana·ko	'you cough'	10b.	bana·ta	'he coughs'
11.	fanura	'I choke'	11a.	fanuko	'you choke'	11b.	fanuota	'he chokes'
12.	sote·ra	'I vomit'	12a.	sote·ko	'you vomit'	12b.	sote·ata	'he vomits'

(Continued on next page.)

1c.	panti	'she chews'	1d.	pano·ra	'they chew'
2c.	ti·nti	'she spits'	2d.	ti·mo·ra	'they spit'
3c.	lakti	'she licks'	3d.	lako·ra	'they lick'
4c.	to·kti	'she tastes'	4d.	to·tko·ra	'they taste'
5c.	lakti	'she blows'	5d.	lapko·ra	'they blow'
6c.	fopti	'she sucks'	6d.	foɓo·ra	'they suck'
7c.	tapti	'she swallows'	7d.	tapo·ra	'they swallow'
8c.	ri·kti	'she points'	8d.	ri·go·ra	'they point'
9c.	togiti	'she laughs'	9d.	togio·ra	'they laugh'
10c.	bana·ti	'she coughs'	10d.	bana·ora	'they cough'
11c.	fanuti	'she chokes'	11d.	fanuo·ra	'they choke'
12c.	sote·ti	'she vomits'	12d.	sote·ora	'they vomit'

A.9 "Weakening" of Vowels in Unstressed Syllables

Long vowels tend to be reduced to short vowels and short vowels frequently change to mid central vowels in unstressed positions.

Problem 164

Instructions:

   a. Reconstruct the basic stem forms.

   b. Determine the types of phonological change.

   c. Describe the phonological distribution of the allomorphs.

1.	'sokəli	'I am working'	1a.	sə'karə	'you are working'
2.	'bi·gəli	'I am reading'	2a.	bi'gorə	'you are reading'
3.	'ma·kili	'I am writing'	3a.	ma'ki·rə	'you are writing'
4.	'petəli	'I am drawing'	4a.	pə'terə	'you are drawing'
5.	'sɛməli	'I am cutting'	5a.	sə'marə	'you are cutting'

Supplementary information:

   a. The basic stem forms contain the first vowel of series 1-5 and the second vowel of series 1a-5a.

   b. Regard the nonroot morpheme as consisting of a stress and a suffix. These morphemes may be symbolized as '....-li and ..'..-rə. (See section 3.11.3.)

A.10 Loss of Vowels in Unstressed Syllables

Vowels tend to be lost in unstressed syllables.

Problem 165

Instructions:

a. List the allomorphs.

b. Describe the differences in the allomorphs in terms of the position of stress.

1. 'ta·kma   'he is hunting'   1a. ta·ko'to·ru   'they are hunting'

2. ma'ni·ma   'he is fishing'   2a. mani·'to·ru   'they are fishing'

3. sa·'go·ma   'he is stalking'   3a. sago·'to·ru   'they are stalking'

4. 'tirma   'he is ambushing'   4a. tiri'to·ru   'they are ambushing'

5. 'mi·bma   'he is shooting'   5a. mi·bo'to·ru   'they are shooting'

6. to'ri·ma   'he is fleeing'   6a. tori·'to·ru   'they are fleeing'

1b. 'ta·kko·   'I am hunting'   1c. ta·'kosga   'we are hunting'

2b. ma'ni·ko·   'I am fishing'   2c. ma'ni·sga   'we are fishing'

3b. sa·'go·ko·   'I am stalking'   3c. sa·'go·sga   'we are stalking'

4b. 'tirko·   'I am ambushing'   4c. ti'risga   'we are ambushing'

5b. 'mi·bko·   'I am shooting'   5c. mi·'bosga   'we are shooting'

6b. to'ri·ko·   'I am fleeing'   6c. to'ri·sga   'we are fleeing'

Problem 166

Instructions:

a. List the allomorphs.

b. Describe the differences in the allomorphs in terms of the position of stress.

1. pan'ti   'the man'   1a. panit'ko·   'a man'

2. soga·'ti   'the boy'   2a. soga·t'ko·   'a boy'

3. ri·t'ti   'the dog'   3a. ri·tut'ko·   'a dog'

4. ma·nu·'ti   'the house'   4a. ma·nu·t'ko·   'a house'

5. finu·'ti   'the sled'   5a. finu·t'ko·   'a sled'

6. kap'ti   'the canoe'   6a. kapat'ko·   'a canoe'

(Continued on next page.)

1b. panit'ma   'the men'   1c. panitoko·'ma   'some men'

2b. soga·t'ma   'the boys'   2c. soga·toko·'ma   'some boys'

3b. ri·tut'ma   'the dogs'   3c. ri·tutoko·'ma   'some dogs'

4b. ma·nu't'ma   'the houses'   4c. ma·nu·toko·'ma   'some houses'

5b. finu·t'ma   'the sleds'   5c. finu·toko·'ma   'some sleds'

6b. kapat'ma   'the canoes'   6c. kapatoko·'ma   'some canoes'

In some instances the forms occurring in a language have only one stress, and yet the ways in which certain vowels are lost reflect a situation involving alternate stressed and unstressed syllables (see the Tonkawa data of Problem 25). The procedure in such problems is as follows:

1. Reconstruct the longer, fuller forms.

2. Set up various hypothetical patterns of alternating stressed and unstressed syllables.

3. Test such patterns with all the forms to determine whether the changes are predictable on the basis of such alternating stresses.

Problem 167

Instructions:

a. Reconstruct the longer, fuller forms.

b. Determine the relationship of the allomorphs to the position of stress.

1. 'atkito 'I love'   1a. 'roktakto 'we love'   1b. me'nutkito 'they love'

2. 'amsuka 'I hate'   2a. 'rokmaska 'we hate'   2b. me'numsuka 'they hate'

3. 'afruga 'I quarrel'   3a. 'rokfarga 'we quarrel'   3b. me'nufruga 'they quarrel'

4. 'alsutka 'I scream'   4a. 'roklosutka 'we scream' 4b. me'nulsutka 'they scream'

5. 'atratkina 'I kiss'   5a. 'rokatratkna 'we kiss'   5b. me'nutratkina 'they kiss'

6. 'amantakti 'I hug'   6a. 'rokmantakti 'we hug'   6b. me'numantakti 'they hug'

7. 'asniko 'I leave'   7a. 'roksanko 'we leave'   7b. me'nusniko 'they leave'

Supplementary information:

1. The fuller forms are found by comparing the differences in the various sets. The reconstructed forms of 1-1b are as follows:

   1. *'atakito   1a. *'rokatakito   1b. *me'nutakito

2. A distinction must be made between syllables ending in a consonant and those ending in a vowel. In this problem the first syllable of a sequence VCCV is regarded as ending in a consonant unless the second consonant is r.

Problem 168

Instructions:

a. Reconstruct the longer, fuller forms.

b. Determine the relationship of the allomorphs to the position of stress.

1. appa·'tikno·	'going'		1a. apmut'pono·	'have gone'
2. a·mupa·t'kano·	'washing'		2a. a·mum'tapno·	'have washed'
3. i·tu·pa·'tikno·	'cleaning'		3a. i·tu·mut'pono·	'have cleaned'
4. eti·pa·t'kano·	'wiping'		4a. eti·m'tapno·	'have wiped'
1b. apia'ri·tpa	'may go'		1c. apmun'kari	'must go'
2b. a·muari·'tipa	'may wash'		2c. a·mum'nukri	'must wash'
3b. i·tu·a'ri·tpa	'may clean'		3c. i·ti·mun'kari	'must clean'
4b. eti·ari·'tipa	'may wipe'		4c. eti·m'nukri	'must wipe'

Supplementary information:

1. In some instances it is not the syllable unit itself but the length of the syllabic which determines the alternating stress patterns. In this problem a long-vowel
syllable counts as though it were two syllables and a short-vowel syllable counts
as a single syllable. Each unit of syllabic length may be called a mora.

2. Some vowels are lost entirely and others are reduced.

Problem 169

Instructions:

a. Reconstruct the longer, fuller forms.

b. Determine the relationship of the allomorphs to the position of stress.

1. rasitnaktma	'my hunting'		1a. rsitnaktaru·	'your hunting'
2. pri·ttakma	'my seeing'		2a. piri·ttkiru·	'your seeing'
3. ma·tnuga·natma	'my killing'		3a. ma·tnga·natru·	'your killing'
4. o·ri·kdatpma	'my resisting'		4a. o·ri·kdatpiru·	'your resisting'
5. riktigko·ru·fma	'my entreating'		5a. riktigko·ru·fru·	'your entreating'
6. mugi·ka·gma	'my persuading'		6a. mgi·ka·guru·	'your persuading'

(Continued on next page.

1b. rsitnaktanga   'our hunting'   1c. rasitnaktri·ga   'their hunting'

2b. piri·ttkinga   'our seeing'   2c. pri·ttakri·ga   'their seeing'

3b. ma·tnga·natnga 'our killing'   3c. ma·tnuga·natri·ga 'their killing'

4b. o·ri·kdatpinga 'our resisting'   4c. o·ri·kdatpri·ga   'their resisting'

5b. riktigko·ru·fnga 'our entreating'   5c. riktigko·ru·fri·ga 'their entreating'

6b. mgi·ka·gunga   'our persuading'   6c. mugi·ka·gri·ga   'their persuading'

Supplementary information:

1. The underlined vowels are voiceless.

2. Vowels in unstressed syllables may become voiceless. This happens extensively in Southern Paiute and Comanche.

A.11 Differences of Vowel Length Due to Open and Closed Syllables

There is a tendency for vowels in open syllables (those ending in a vowel) to be long and those in closed syllables (those ending in a consonant) to be short. Whether a syllable is open or closed depends upon the phonological facts of the particular language, but generally a sequence of CVCVCVCV consists of open syllables and a sequence of CVCCVCCVCCVC consists of closed syllables, though it may be that sequences of Cr, Cl, Cw, Cy, nC, and mC, are syllabified with the following vowel, and hence the preceding syllables are open.

Problem 170

Instructions: Describe the phonological distribution of the allomorphs.

1. sot 'bow'   1a. arsot 'my bow'   1b. otsot 'his bow'   1c. u·sot 'our bow'

2. ba·k 'arrow'   2a. arba·k 'my arrow'   2b. odba·k 'his arrow'   2c. u·ba·k 'our arrow'

3. ir 'string'   3a. a·rir 'my string'   3b. o·tir 'his string'   3c. wi·r 'our string'

4. kat 'sandal'   4a. arkat 'my sandal'   4b. otkat 'his sandal'   4c. u·kat 'our sandal'

5. o·r 'feather' 5a. a·ro·r 'my feather' 5b. o·to·r 'his feather' 5c. wo·r 'our feather'

6. tris 'mask'   6a. artris 'my mask'   6b. otris 'his mask'   6c. utris 'our mask'

Supplementary information: The prefix of series 1c-6c becomes a consonant before a vowel-initial stem. A following short vowel is lengthened. This is called compensatory lengthening. The allomorph may be symbolized as wV·-.

A.12 Compensatory Lengthening

When a consonant or a vowel is lost, a contiguous vowel (rarely a consonant) may be lengthened in a type of compensation for the loss of the segmental unit.

Problem 171

Instructions: Describe the phonological distribution of the prefixal allomorphs.

1. a·sono·	'my horse'	1a. i·sono·	'his horse'	1b. iksono·	'our horse'
2. araga	'my cow'	2a. ilaga	'his cow'	2b. ikaga	'our cow'
3. arbo·nu	'my dog'	3a. ilbo·nu	'his dog'	3b. igbo·nu	'our dog'
4. arkaga	'my bow'	4a. ilkaga	'his bow'	4b. ikkaga	'our bow'
5. a·liru	'my blowgun'	5a. i·liru	'his blowgun'	5b. ikliru	'our blowgun'
6. a·ratki	'my harpoon'	6a. i·ratki	'his harpoon'	6b. ikratki	'our harpoon'
7. arpirto·	'my lamp'	7a. ilpirto·	'his lamp'	7b. ikpirto·	'our lamp'
8. a·nomu	'my net'	8a. i·nomu	'his net'	8b. iknomu	'our net'
9. a·mikti	'my poison'	9a. i·mikti	'his poison'	9b. ikmikti	'our poison'

Supplementary information:

1. There is one instance of regressive assimilation according to manner of articulation.

2. This problem appears to be very similar to Problem 165, and the resultant alternations are indeed very much alike. However, the phonological processes underlying the changes are different. In Problem 165 the changes are dependent entirely upon the form of the syllable. In Problem 166 certain consonant clusters reduce, with compensatory lengthening of the preceding vowel.

A.13 Developed Phonemes

In certain clusters of consonants there tend to develop other consonants. These are sometimes called "transition" consonants, for they arise from the articulatory transitions from one to another position or type of combination. The following are some of the more common types: mr > mbr, mk > mpk, ŋr > ŋgr, nr > ndr, ns > nts, ŋt > ŋkt, sr > str, zr > zdr, lr > ldr. Developed consonants are, however, quite rare.

In sequences of consonants transition vowels sometimes develop. These tend to be short and to have mid and central quality. Such vowels are comparatively rare.

Problem 172

Instructions:

a. Determine the phonological distributions of the suffixes -po ~ -ǝpo and -sǝtu ~ -ǝstu.

b. Correlate these distributions with the types of consonant clusters.

c. Compare these consonant clusters with those occurring in series 1a-12a.

d. Make a general statement to cover all situations in which the vowel ǝ occurs in a nonroot syllable.

e. List two instances of developed consonants.

1. partpo	'by a wall'	1a. partri	'above a wall'	1b. partsetu	'on a wall'
2. kiktepo	'by a bag'	2a. kiktri	'above a bag'	2b. kiktestu	'on a bag'
3. goxkepo	'by a house'	3a. goxkri	'above a house'	3b. goxkestu	'on a house'
4. talmpo	'by a rock'	4a. talmri	'above a rock'	4b. talmsetu	'on a rock'
5. sospo	'by a tower'	5a. sostri	'above a tower'	5b. sossetu	'on a tower'
6. dišpepo	'by a lake'	6a. dišpri	'above a lake'	6b. dišpestu	'on a lake'
7. lartpo	'by a puddle'	7a. lardri	'above a puddle'	7b. lardsetu	'on a puddle'
8. kelppo	'by a mule'	8a. kelbri	'above a mule'	8b. kelbsetu	'on a mule'
9. torpo	'by a man'	9a. torri	'above a man'	9b. torstu	'on a man'
10. bokpo	'by a tree'	10a. bogri	'above a tree'	10b. bogsetu	'on a tree'
11. milpo	'by a box'	11a. milri	'above a box'	11b. milstu	'on a box'
12. tampo	'by a tree'	12a. tambri	'above a tree'	12b. tamsetu	'on a tree'

Problem 173

Instructions: Determine the phonological circumstances in which the transition vowel ǝ occurs.

1. eptoru	'my door'	1a. otoru	'his door'	1b. artoru	'your door'
2. eptrosa	'my room'	2a. otrosa	'his room'	2b. artrosa	'your room'
3. epektima	'my mantle'	3a. oktima	'his mantle'	3b. artektima	'your mantle'
4. eblagu	'my loom'	4a. oblagu	'his loom'	4b. ardblagu	'your loom'
5. epfroni	'my knife'	5a. ofroni	'his knife'	5b. artfroni	'your knife'
6. ependaga	'my belt'	6a. ondaga	'his belt'	6b. artendaga	'your belt'
7. epembrusi	'my rope'	7a. ombrusi	'his rope'	7b. artembrusi	'your rope'
8. episo	'my canoe'	8a. opiso	'his canoe'	8b. artpiso	'your canoe'
9. epestusa	'my raft'	9a. ostusa	'his raft'	9b. artestusa	'your raft'

A.14 Palatalization

For a discussion of palatalization see section 2.22.2, G, 6.

Problem 174

Instructions:

a. List the types of palatalization.

b. Describe the phonological distribution of the prefixal allomorphs.

1. ičeka 'my horse'   1a. ačeka 'your horse'   1b. ošeka 'his horse'   1c. ameka 'their horse'

2. ikɛči 'my shoe'   2a. atɛči 'your shoe'   2b. osɛči 'his shoe'   2c. amɛči 'their shoe'

3. ičimu 'my pants'   3a. ačimu 'your pants'   3b. ošimu 'his pants'   3c. amimu 'their pants'

4. ikaso 'my hat'   4a. ataso 'your hat'   4b. osaso 'his hat'   4c. amaso 'their hat'

5. ikuta 'my shirt'   5a. atuta 'your shirt'   5b. osuta 'his shirt'   5c. amuta 'their shirt'

Problem 175

Instructions:

a. List the types of palatalization.

b. Describe the types of vocalic assimilation.

c. Describe the phonological distribution of the stem allomorphs.

1. ukotos	'I returned'		1a. učeȼet	'we returned'
2. oganos	'I saw'		2a. oǰɛnet	'we saw'
3. itusos	'I fled'		3a. itušet	'we fled'
4. imonos	'I escaped'		4a. imenet	'we escaped'
5. apitos	'I fell'		5a. apiȼet	'we fell'
6. asagos	'I stumbled'		6a. ašɛǰet	'we stumbled'
7. orɛkos	'I collapsed'		7a. orɛčet	'we collapsed'

Problem 176

Instructions:

a. List the allomorphs of the infix.

b. List the types of palatalization.

c. Describe the phonological distribution of all allomorphic alternations.

1. tomas	'to beat'		1a. tominas	'beaten'
2. katom	'to strike'		2a. kaȼnom	'struck'
3. sokas	'to burn'		3a. sočnas	'burned'
4. fasak	'to fall'		4a. fašnak	'fallen'
5. tapan	'to shave'		5a. tapʸnan	'shaven'
6. toxur	'to pierce'		6a. toxinur	'pierced'
7. sark	'to shape'		7a. sariŋk	'shaped'

(Continued on next page.)

8. pump   'to saw'   8a. puṁimp   'sawed'

9. tetk   'to see'   9a. teȼiŋk   'seen'

10. razd   'to understand'   10a. ražind   'understood'

Problem 177

Instructions:

  a. List the types of palatalization.

  b. List the types of assimilation.

  c. Describe the phonological distribution of the prefixal allomorphs.

1. aȼito	'my net'	1a. išito	'your net'	1b. uǰito	'his net'
2. atomu	'my boat'	2a. isomu	'your boat'	2b. ugómu	'his boat'
3. aǰeǰa	'my fish'	3a. išeǰa	'your fish'	3b. uǰeǰa	'his fish'
4. aȼama	'my spear'	4a. išama	'your spear'	4b. uǰama	'his spear'
5. atwotu	'my food'	5a. iswotu	'your food'	5b. ugwotu	'his food'
6. atuma	'my paddle'	6a. isuma	'your paddle'	6b. uguma	'his paddle'
7. adgoma	'my canoe'	7a. izgoma	'your canoe'	7b. ugoma	'his canoe'
8. adbunu	'my float'	8a. izbunu	'your float'	8b. ugbunu	'his float'
9. atčari	'my rope'	9a. isčari	'your rope'	9b. ukčari	'his rope'

A.15   Nasalization

Nasalization is of two types: (1) assimilation of nonnasal vowels to nasal vowels, e.g. ko̧da > ko̧da̧ and toi̧ > to̧i̧, and (2) nasalization of a vowel because of a nasal consonant, which either remains or is lost, e.g. tin > ti̧n or ti̧. The loss of a nasal consonant is frequently accompanied by a compensatory lengthening, e.g. tin > ti̧·.

Problem 178

Instructions:

  a. Reconstruct the unmodified forms of series 1-7 and 1a-7a.

  b. Determine the phonological circumstances under which nasalization occurs.

  c. Determine the types of consonant cluster reduction.

  d. Describe the phonological distribution of the allomorphs.

1. sa·nima   'cutting'   1a. sa·ni̧·ta   'cut'

2. koraŋa   'falling'   2a. kora̧·ta   'fell'

(Continued on next page.)

3. bonana	'slipping'		3a. bonạ·ta	'slipped'
4. fa·tįka	'chopping'		4a. fa·tįkta	'chopped'
5. konapa	'driving'		5a. konapta	'drove'
6. kǫrara	'beating'		6a. kǫra·ta	'beat'
7. barila	'calling'		7a. bari·ta	'called'

Problem 179

Instructions:

    a. Describe all the phonological processes.

    b. Describe the phonological distribution of these processes.

1. ǫ·timo·	'my sister'		1a. taktimo·	'your sister'
2. ǫ·siga	'my daughter'		2a. taksiga	'your daughter'
3. ona·nu	'my cousin'		3a. taga·nu	'your cousin'
4. ollaga	'my uncle'		4a. taglaga	'your uncle'
5. oñi·gy	'my aunt'		5a. taji·gy	'your aunt'
6. olliñi	'my father'		6a. tagliñi	'your father'
7. orraga·	'my mother'		7a. tagraga·	'your mother'
8. ǫ·koni	'my brother'		8a. takkoni	'your brother'

A.16 Verner's Phenomenon

    Voiceless fortis consonants tend to occur after stressed syllabics and voiced lenis consonants tend to occur after unstressed syllabics. Compare the English exit /éksit/ and exact /egzǽkt/ in which the morpheme ex- occurs in two forms /éks- ~ egz-/.

    This phonological process is named after Karl Verner, the scholar who first noted the pattern in the historical and comparative study of Indo-European languages.

Problem 180

Instructions:

    a. List the types of suffixal allomorphs.

    b. Describe their phonological distributions.

1. ka'na·sanu	'we march'		1a. ka'na·firi·	'they march'
2. si·to'zanu	'we fight'		2a. si·to'viri·	'they fight'
3. ka·'di·sanu	'we kill'		3a. ka·'di·firi·	'they kill'
4. sa·pa'zanu	'we slaughter'		4a. sa·pa'viri·	'they slaughter'
5. bo'pu·sanu	'we flee'		5a. bo'pu·firi·	'they flee'

Problem 181

Instructions: Describe the phonological distribution of the stem allomorphs.

1. 'poti	'foot'	1a. po'dis	'a pair of feet'	1b. 'potina	'feet'
2. ni'do	'hand'	2a. ni'dos	'a pair of hands'	2b. 'nitona	'hands'
3. 'saxi	'eye'	3a. sa'gis	'a pair of eyes'	3b. 'saxina	'eyes'
4. 'bipi	'ear'	4a. bi'bis	'a pair of ears'	4b. 'bipina	'ears'
5. 'miθa	'shoe'	5a. mi'das	'a pair of shoes'	5b. 'miθana	'shoes'
6. go'gu	'glove'	6a. go'gus	'a pair of gloves'	6b. 'gokuna	'gloves'

Supplementary information: Treat the nonroot morphemes as having the structures ..'..-s '....-na.

A.17[3] Metathesis

Metathesis involves the changing of position of phonemes. The phonemes may be contiguous, e.g. tapya > taypa, or noncontiguous, e.g. arela > alera.

Problem 182

Instructions:

a. Describe the type of metathesis.

b. State the phonological distribution of the metathesis.

1. akkoti	'my bird'	1a. eksoti	'his bird'
2. amkaru	'my rattle'	2a. emsaru	'his rattle'
3. akkraka	'my toy'	3a. eksraka	'his toy'
4. apkligu	'my stick'	4a. epsligu	'his stick'
5. apktuma	'my box'	5a. epstuma	'his box'
6. arkasa	'my blowgun'	6a. ersasa	'his blowgun'
7. akoma	'my fish'	7a. esoma	'his fish'
8. akiso	'my bone'	8a. esiso	'his bone'

Problem 183

Instructions: Describe the phonological distribution of the metathesis.

---

[3]This list of phonological processes does not exhaust all the possibilities. Some of the other types are: (1) haplology, the reduction of two identical or similar succeeding syllables to one, e.g. shapapaʔ > shapaʔ, (2) rhotocism, the change of a phoneme to r, e.g. eza > era, (3) interchange of flap phonemes, the morphophonemic fluctuation between d, l, and r, and (4) development of labiovelars, e.g. g^w > w, b, or g; k^w > f, p, or k. Labiovelars may have a number of different developments, depending upon the following consonants and vowels.

1. togayk	'I spit'	1a. togaŋk	'you spit'	1b. togaksa	'we spit'
2. simuyt	'I cough'	2a. simunt	'you cough'	2b. simutsa	'we cough'
3. boniys	'I sneeze'	3a. bonins	'you sneeze'	3b. bonissa	'we sneeze'
4. baray	'I choke'	4a. baram	'you choke'	4b. barasa	'we choke'
5. tokoy	'I chew'	5a. tokom	'you chew'	5b. tokosa	'we chew'
6. midey	'I talk'	6a. midem	'you talk'	6b. midesa	'we talk'

B. Problems Supplementary to Section 2.23.2

Problem 184

Instructions: List the allomorphs of the morpheme occurring in series 1a-18a.

1. laθo	'going'	1a. lanθo	'went'
2. ramo	'working'	2a. rammo	'worked'
3. ŋapi	'falling'	3a. ŋampi	'fell'
4. sakto	'seeing'	4a. saŋkto	'saw'
5. siri	'speaking'	5a. sinri	'spoke'
6. atim	'carrying'	6a. antim	'carried'
7. fanan	'arriving'	7a. fapinan	'arrived'
8. čakit	'calling'	8a. čapikit	'called'
9. kunir	'swimming'	9a. kupinir	'swam'
10. marus	'diving'	10a. mapirus	'dove'
11. ramik	'floating'	11a. ramabik	'floated'
12. fusit	'sinking'	12a. fusabit	'sank'
13. kamok	'rising'	13a. kamabok	'rose'
14. petir	'climbing'	14a. petabir	'climbed'
15. fusim	'grasping'	15a. fusrim	'grasped'
16. kanit	'holding'	16a. kanrit	'held'
17. marer	'pushing'	17a. marrer	'pushed'
18. fustim	'grabbing'	18a. fustrim	'grabbed'

Problem 185

Instructions:

a. Describe the alternations in the stems in terms of Verner's phenomenon.

b. Determine the allomorphs of the suffixal morpheme in series 1a-9a.

1.	ba'daku	'to go'		1a.	'batakmi	'going'
2.	mi'riku	'to sleep'		2a.	'mirikmi	'sleeping'
3.	'sonugu	'to try'		3a.	'sonugmi	'trying'
4.	'bakiru	'to work'		4a.	'bakirmi	'working'
5.	mo'dusu	'to be lazy'		5a.	'motuso	'being lazy'
6.	me'gumu	'to eat'		6a.	'mekumo	'eating'
7.	'fasimu	'to die'		7a.	'fasimo	'dying'
8.	'resusu	'to return'		8a.	'resuso	'returning'
9.	bo'lipu	'to scare'		9a.	'bolipo	'scaring'

Problem 186

Instructions: List the allomorphs of the morpheme occurring in series 1a-21a.

1.	kogar	'gone'		1a.	kokogar	'going'
2.	utaŋ	'done'		2a.	uʔutaŋ	'doing'
3.	ktano	'finished'		3a.	kiktano	'finishing'
4.	matin	'continued'		4a.	mamatin	'continuing'
5.	tastan	'run'		5a.	tastastan	'running'
6.	ŋartil	'beaten'		6a.	ŋarŋartil	'beating'
7.	amtak	'worked'		7a.	amamtak	'working'
8.	xupit	'followed'		8a.	xuxupit	'following'
9.	tanris	'tried'		9a.	tantanris	'trying'
10.	assin	'woven'		10a.	asassin	'weaving'
11.	afit	'curved'		11a.	aʔafit	'curving'
12.	ačtin	'risen'		12a.	ačačtin	'rising'
13.	magir	'fallen'		13a.	mamagir	'falling'
14.	kranis	'proven'		14a.	kikranis	'proving'
15.	finis	'shaven'		15a.	amfinis	'shaving'
16.	ptilus	'come'		16a.	piptilus	'coming'
17.	sanik	'arrived'		17a.	ansanik	'arriving'

(Continued on next page.)

18. util   'written'   18a. aŋutil   'writing'

19. masič   'ridden'   19a. ammasič   'riding'

20. fisir   'arrived'   20a. amfisir   'arriving'

21. asam   'asleep'   21a. aŋasam   'sleeping'

Problem 187

Instructions: List the allomorphs of the pluralizing morpheme.

1. baka   'house'   1a. bakan   'houses'

2. bila   'tree'   2a. bilan   'trees'

3. mura   'boy'   3a. muran   'boys'

4. marka   'market'   4a. markan   'markets'

5. pilka   'fish'   5a. pilkis   'fish'

6. rika   'clam'   6a. rikis   'clams'

7. nopa   'worm'   7a. nopis   'worms'

8. sisa   'eel'   8a. sisis   'eels'

9. buza   'snake'   9a. bauzis   'snakes'

10. rama   'insect'   10a. remis   'insects'

11. mena   'fly'   11a. minis   'flies'

12. lola   'bird'   12a. lulis   'birds'

13. mira   'robin'   13a. mir   'robins'

14. kola   'sparrow'   14a. kol   'sparrows'

15. pita   'grain'   15a. pat   'grains'

16. risa   'stone'   16a. ras   'stones'

C. Problems Supplementary to Chapter 3

Problem 188

Instructions:

a. List the types of reduplicatives.

b. Determine whether they are allomorphs of one morpheme or different morphemes.

1. kat   'man'   1a. kakat   'manly'

2. musa   'wind'   2a. mumusa   'stormy'

(Continued on next page.)

3. kori   'stone'   3a. koriri   'hard'

4. mug   'corpse'   4a. mugmug   'smelly'

5. pino   'snow'   5a. pinino   'white'

6. basu   'hill'   6a. basubasu   'hilly'

7. ponus   'wolf'   7a. ponponus   'tricky'

8. kora   'food'   8a. kikora   'happy'

9. oma   'thunder'   9a. oʔoma   'noisy'

10. biga   'fever'   10a. bigiga   'sick'

11. saru   'money'   11a. sosaruru 'wealthy'

Problem 189

Instructions: Describe the reduplicative morphemes.

1. kola 'earth'	1a. kokola 'dirty'	1b. kolala 'floor'
2. paku 'wood'	2a. papaku 'wooden'	2b. pakuku 'firewood'
3. safo 'stone'	3a. sasafo 'hard'	3b. safofo 'pebble'
4. mup 'water'	4a. mumup 'wet'	4b. mupupu 'lake'
5. kopa 'tree'	5a. kopakopa 'forest'	5b. kopapa 'trees'
6. lap 'paper'	6a. laplap 'book'	6b. lappa 'papers'
7. mup 'water'	7a. mupmup 'rain'	7b. muppa 'rivers'
8. kami 'leaf'	8a. kamikami 'hay'	8b. kamipa 'leaves'
9. mali 'goes'	9a. malilif 'went'	9b. maʔali 'goes rapidly'
10. kamo 'runs'	10a. kamomof 'ran'	10b. kaʔamo 'races'
11. zepu 'eats'	11a. zepupuf 'ate'	11b. zeʔepu 'eats rapidly'

Problem 190

Instructions: Describe the type of suffixal morpheme in series 1a–9a.

1. kata   'a dollar'   1a. kat   'money'

2. marro   'deer'   2a. mar   'animal'

3. tisti   'a man'   3a. tis   'mankind'

4. osu   'a person'   4a. os   'someone'

5. pakre   'a tree'   5a. pak   'wood'

(Continued on next page.)

6. minna 'a river'		6a. min 'water'	
7. baru 'dirt'		7a. bar 'earth'	
8. pirka 'a murder'		8a. pir 'war'	
9. kotko 'a shout'		9a. kot 'noise'	

Problem 191

Instructions: Determine the type of morpheme which forms the masculine series.

1. tanu 'man'		1a. tanus 'woman'
2. ama 'boy'		2a. amat 'girl'
3. usi 'horse'		3a. usik 'mare'
4. aku 'ram'		4a. akun 'ewe'
5. tore 'tiger'		5a. torem 'tigress'
6. fomu 'king'		6a. fomus 'queen'
7. more 'bull'		7a. moreb 'cow'
8. kako 'drake'		8a. kakof 'duck'

Problem 192

Instructions: Describe the allomorphs of the infixal morphemes.

1. lep- 'is running'	1a. lop- 'ran'	1b. lip- 'will run'	1c. -lp 'has run'
2. tek- 'is walking'	2a. tok- 'walked'	2b. tik- 'will walk'	2c. -tk 'has walked'
3. trep- 'is seeing'	3a. trop- 'saw'	3b. trap- 'will see'	3c. -trp 'has seen'
4. plet- 'is falling'	4a. plot- 'fell'	4b. plat- 'will fall'	4c. -plt 'has fallen'
5. leit- 'is returning'	5a. loit- 'returned'	5b. lit- 'will return'	5c. -lit 'has returned'
6. senk- 'is growing'	6a. sonk- 'grew'	6b. sink- 'will grow'	6c. -snk 'has grown'
7. temp- 'is sleeping'	7a. tomp- 'slept'	7b. timp- 'will sleep'	7c. -tmp 'has slept'
8. keut- 'is swimming'	8a. kout- 'swam'	8b. kut- 'will swim'	8c. -kut 'has swum'

Problem 193

Instructions: Identify the additive nonroot morphemes.

1. ketil 'working'	1a. kotul 'worked'	1b. aktul 'the worker'	1c. kital 'work'
2. ʔepit 'dying'	2a. ʔoput 'died'	2b. aʔput 'the dying one'	2c. ʔipat 'death'
3. lemis 'running'	3a. lomus 'ran'	3b. almus 'the runner'	3c. limas 'race'
4. gesit 'killing'	4a. gosut 'killed'	4b. agsut 'the killer'	4c. gisat 'murder'

Problem 194

Instructions: Determine the allomorphs of the infixal morphemes.

1. kitüp	'fell'	1a. kitup	'is falling'	1b. kitïp	'may fall'
2. petör	'went'	2a. pator	'is going'	2b. petar	'may go'
3. kemöt	'swept'	3a. kamot	'is sweeping'	3b. kemat	'may sweep'
4. niküt	'sweat'	4a. nikut	'is sweating'	4b. nikït	'may sweat'
5. pisüt	'loved'	5a. pisut	'is loving'	5b. pisït	'may love'

Supplementary information:

1. Plot the morphophonemic vowel relationships as

    i ü ï u

    e ö a o

2. It will be noticed that some stems require high vowels and others require low vowels. The stems may be symbolized as CVCVC and CvCvC, in which V stands for a high vowel and v for a low vowel.

Problem 195

Instructions: Determine the allomorphs of the infixal morphemes.

1. bak	'fish'	1a. bok	'to fish'	1b. -bk-	'fished'
2. pat	'race'	2a. pot	'to race'	2b. -pt-	'raced'
3. pan	'farm'	3a. pon	'to farm'	3b. pən	'farmed'
4. kal	'wood'	4a. kol	'to cut wood'	4b. kəl	'cut wood'
5. tar	'snow'	5a. tor	'to snow'	5b. ter	'snowed'
6. gain	'water'	6a. goin	'to rain'	6b. gin	'rained'
7. dauk	'ice'	7a. douk	'to freeze'	7b. duk	'froze'
8. samt	'house'	8a. somt	'to build a house'	8b. sm̩t	'built a house'
9. fars	'fox'	9a. fors	'to escape'	9b. frs̩	'escaped'
10. bans	'chair'	10a. bons	'to seat'	10b. bn̩s	'seated'

Problem 196

Instructions: Determine the form of the replacive morpheme in series 1a-8a.

1. got	'snow'	1a. goθ	'to snow'
2. tos	'hail'	2a. tos	'to hail'
3. pap	'gun'	3a. paf	'to hunt'

(Continued on next page.)

4. gab   'dog'   4a. gav   'to follow'

5. bek   'money'   5a. bex   'to trade'

6. od   'fish'   6a. od   'to fish'

7. mun   'sheep'   7a. mun   'to herd'

8. feg   'water'   8a. feg   'to rain'

Problem 197

Instructions: Describe the types of stem allomorphs.

1. situ·to 'has worked'	1a. matuto 'is working'	1b. utto 'may work'
2. sida·no 'has followed'	2a. madano 'is following'	2b. udno 'may follow'
3. sibe·lo 'has slept'	3a. mabelo 'is sleeping'	3b. ublo 'may sleep'
4. sisi·no 'has risen'	4a. masino 'is rising'	4b. usno 'may rise'
5. sigo·ro 'has come'	5a. magoro 'is coming'	5b. ugro 'may come'
6. sikə·to 'has gone'	6a. makəto 'is going'	6b. ukto 'may go'

Problem 198

Instructions:

  a. Determine the replacive morpheme occurring in series 1a-6a.

  b. Describe its distribution in terms of the phonological form of the basic stem
     allomorphs.

1. bote·n 'has run'	1a. boto·n 'must run'	1b. bote·nal 'race'
2. pikis 'has arrived'	2a. piku·s 'must arrive'	2b. pikisal 'arrival'
3. ba·nak 'has finished'	3a. ba·na·k 'must finish'	3b. ba·nakal 'end'
4. čo·nos 'has eaten'	4a. čo·ne·s 'must eat'	4b. čo·nosal 'food'
5. tusu·p 'has fallen'	5a. tusi·p 'must fall'	5b. tusu·pal 'injury'
6. rima·g 'has fought'	6a. rima·g 'must fight'	6b. rima·gal 'war'

Problem 199

Instructions: Determine the form of the infixal morpheme.

1. ipi 'was coming'	1a. ippi 'has come'
2. atago 'was rising'	2a. ataggo 'has risen'
3. tixa 'was falling'	3a. tixxa 'has fallen'

(Continued on next page.)

4. bani	'was standing'	4a. banni	'has stood'
5. sora	'was seeing'	5a. sorra	'has seen'
6. ačǔ	'was trying'	6a. aččǔ	'has tried'

Problem 200

Instructions: Determine the replacive tonal morphemes in series 1-9 and 1b-9b.

1. tínó	'was going'	1a. tínó	'has gone'	1b. tíno	'is about to go'
2. sákí	'was riding'	2a. sáki	'has ridden'	2b. sákì	'is about to ride'
3. óma	'was sailing'	3a. ómà	'has sailed'	3b. ómà	'is about to sail'
4. a'á	'was leaving'	4a. a'á	'has left'	4b. a'a	'is about to leave'
5. soó	'was hopping'	5a. soo	'has hopped'	5b. soò	'is about to hop'
6. sanu	'was dancing'	6a. sanù	'has danced'	6b. sanù	'is about to dance'
7. mòrá	'was spinning'	7a. mòrá	'has spun'	7b. mòra	'is about to spin'
8. àlí	'was braiding'	8a. àli	'has braided'	8b. àlì	'is about to braid'
9. tòno	'was cutting'	9a. tònò	'has cut'	9b. tònò	'is about to cut'

Problem 201

Instructions: Describe the replacive tonal morphemes.

1. pátìki	'I go'	1a. pátíki	'he goes'	1b. pátíkì	'you go'
2. omará	'I follow'	2a. omárá	'he follows'	2b. omárà	'you follow'
3. fùsítu	'I see'	3a. fùsítu	'he sees'	3b. fùsítù	'you see'
4. nárìká	'I eat'	4a. náríká	'he eats'	4b. náríkà	'you eat'
5. ìmìkù	'I drink'	5a. ìmíkù	'he drinks'	5b. ìmíkù	'you drink'
6. oríti	'I run'	6a. oríti	'he runs'	6b. orítì	'you run'

D. Problems Supplementary to Chapter 5

Problem 202

Instructions: Describe the future structural series.

1. toni	'will go'	1a. ton-	'to go'
2. potni	'will stay'	2a. pot-	'to stay'
3. kani	'will see'	3a. kan-	'to see'

(Continued on next page.)

4. mirni   'will swim'   4a. mir-   'to swim'

5. gesni   'will loaf'   5a. ges-   'to loaf'

6. motni   'will chew'   6a. mot-   'to chew'

7. rapmi   'will smoke'   7a. rap-   'to smoke'

8. mikŋi   'will talk'   8a. mik-   'to talk'

9. etumni   'will gossip'   9a. tum-   'to gossip'

10. efisni   'will defend'   10a. fis-   'to defend'

11. emar   'will denounce'   11a. mar-   'to denounce'

12. ekop   'will hate'   12a. kop-   'to hate'

Problem 203

Instructions: Describe the structural series 1a-18a.

1. 'rika-   'man'   1a. rika'ma   'of a man'

2. 'atak-   'woman'   2a. atak'ma   'of a woman'

3. 'oret-   'boy'   3a. oret'ma   'of a boy'

4. 'pamat-   'dog'   4a. pamat'ma   'of a dog'

5. 'foršlik-   'cow'   5a. forš'lik   'of a cow'

6. 'antla-   'fish'   6a. ant'la   'of a fish'

7. 'ortil-   'house'   7a. or'til   'of a house'

8. 'ata-   'tree'   8a. a'ta   'of a tree'

9. 'orsik-   'village'   9a. or'sikti   'of a village'

10. 'madar-   'market'   10a. ma'darti   'of a market'

11. 'ofič-   'store'   11a. o'fičti   'of a store'

12. 'imak-   'temple'   12a. i'makti   'of a temple'

13. 'basan-   'field'   13a. ba'sana   'of a field'

14. 'urkit-   'forest'   14a. ur'kita   'of a forest'

15. 'ralić-   'lake'   15a. ra'lića   'of a lake'

16. 'osont-   'cloud'   16a. o'sontum   'of a cloud'

17. 'sana-   'star'   17a. sa'naki   'of a star'

18. 'akar-   'plant'   18a. a'karum   'of a plant'

Problem 204

Instructions: Describe the structural series 1-9.

1. sokosri	'coughing'		1a. -kos-	'to cough'
2. sopitri	'spitting'		2a. -pit-	'to spit'
3. larakri	'crying'		3a. -rak-	'to cry'
4. lametmo	'talking'		4a. -met-	'to talk'
5. larimmo	'whispering'		5a. -rim-	'to whisper'
6. larokmo	'tasting'		6a. -rok-	'to taste'
7. sogogmo	'licking'		7a. -gog-	'to lick'
8. labusri	'swallowing'		8a. -bus-	'to swallow'
9. somugmo	'chewing'		9a. -mug-	'to chew'

Problem 205

Instructions: Describe the following series by setting up stem classes.

1. titoma	'is coming'	1a. tetosi	'came'
2. pipuma	'is returning'	2a. pepusi	'returned'
3. sisama	'is sitting'	3a. sesasi	'sat'
4. rirema	'is pushing'	4a. reresi	'pushed'
5. luma	'is selling'	5a. olusi	'sold'
6. bima	'is buying'	6a. obisi	'bought'
7. muma	'is fighting'	7a. omusi	'fought'
8. koma	'is rushing'	8a. okosi	'rushed'
9. kima	'is falling'	9a. kisi	'fell'
10. puma	'is finishing'	10a. pusi	'finished'

Problem 206

Instructions: Describe the following series by a composite statement.

1. mimito	'working'	1a. mitina	'worked'
2. tutomo	'trying'	2a. tomuna	'tried'
3. kakako	'seeing'	3a. kakana	'saw'
4. bubuso	'falling'	4a. busuna	'fell'

(Continued on next page.)

5. mimeto	'talking'	5a. metina	'talked'
6. kukoro	'rising'	6a. koruna	'rose'
7. gagapo	'calling'	7a. gapana	'called'
8. ramemo	'killing'	8a. memina	'killed'
9. rabuso	'fighting'	9a. busuna	'fought'
10. ragoto	'slaying'	10a. gotuna	'slew'
11. ramaro	'walking'	11a. marana	'walked'
12. ratar	'chewing'	12a. taran	'chewed'
13. ramus	'eating'	13a. musan	'ate'
14. rasam	'drinking'	14a. saman	'drank'
15. ratik	'smoking'	15a. tikan	'smoked'

Problem 207

Instructions: Describe the following series by setting up stem classes.

1. kikel	'to kill'	1a. kukol	'killing'	1b. kikul	'killed'
2. titel	'to shove'	2a. tutol	'shoving'	2b. titul	'shoved'
3. pirel	'to cut'	3a. purol	'cutting'	3b. pirul	'cut'
4. kider	'to rise'	4a. kudor	'rising'	4b. kidur	'rose'
5. simes	'to fall'	5a. sumos	'falling'	5b. simus	'fell'
6. nivet	'to jump'	6a. nuvot	'jumping'	6b. nivut	'jumped'
7. ketem	'to dance'	7a. kotam	'dancing'	7b. ketom	'danced'
8. geret	'to grab'	8a. gorat	'grabbing'	8b. gerot	'grabbed'
9. medes	'to steal'	9a. modas	'stealing'	9b. medos	'stole'
10. metɛt	'to buy'	10a. motat	'buying'	10b. metot	'bought'
11. relɛm	'to sell'	11a. roļam	'selling'	11b. relom	'sold'
12. ferɛr	'to lie'	12a. forar	'lying'	12b. feror	'lied'
13. saras	'to die'	13a. saras	'dying'	13b. seros	'died'
14. lanar	'to speak'	14a. lanar	'speaking'	14b. lenor	'spoke'
15. sagat	'to appear'	-----		15b. segot	'appeared'
16. katal	'to seem'	-----		16b. regot	'seemed'

E. Problems Supplementary to Chapter 6

Problem 208

Instructions: Determine the meanings of the suffixal morphemes.

1. mista	'bamboo'	16. bolri	'boulder'
2. miklo	'plate'	17. tiski	'book'
3. lasri	'ball'	18. palta	'tree trunk'
4. meski	'table'	19. kullo	'tortilla'
5. vitlo	'coin'	20. gosri	'head'
6. pinta	'leg'	21. hutki	'house'
7. masri	'fist'	22. kaski	'box'
8. ladlo	'dollar'	23. milta	'cornstalk'
9. sikki	'rug'	24. sanri	'apple'
10. ranri	'orange'	25. suklo	'flat turtle shell'
11. manta	'arm'	26. monri	'lemon'
12. teslo	'cart wheel'	27. kinta	'banana'
13. kimlo	'watch'	28. siski	'mat
14. sufri	'melon'	29. kovri	'avocado'
15. rupta	'cane'		

Problem 209

Instructions: Determine the meanings of the prefixal morphemes.

1. kisogc	'house'	11. kimiki	'foot'
2. kisoki	'ax'	12. narano	'beauty'
3. nataga	'stars'	13. kilawa	'son'
4. nakoga	'clouds'	14. kitanu	'father'
5. namita	'sun'	15. natimu	'idea'
6. kinatu	'boat'	16. kikano	'wife'
7. narigu	'moon'	17. kileku	'tree'
8. nanama	'life'	18. kimugo	'food'
9. naloka	'death'	19. kikale	'clothes'
10. nadiso	'God'		

(Continued on next page.)

20. kiwaxo   'head'
21. nakila   'sky'
22. napoli   'person dead a long time'
23. kiwata   'daughter'
24. kipota   'bush'

25. nanika   'truth'
26. kilipa   'flowers'
27. kilaxa   'water'
28. naturu   'lie'

Problem 210

Instructions: Determine the meanings of the suffixal morphemes.

1. sonira   'tree'
2. migasu   'horse'
3. mokisu   'bubbling spring'
4. nagisu   'bear'
5. yatosu   'deer'
6. bopira   'chair'
7. nigusu   'skunk'
8. panara   'lake'
9. gawasu   'boiling water'
10. silora   'sky'
11. lukasu   'fire'
12. ligira   'mountain'
13. kolosu   'star'

14. lopira   'well'
15. sogosu   'river'
16. pokira   'bush'
17. lelosu   'elk'
18. tigara   'grass'
19. palora   'table'
20. hulera   'house'
21. tunesu   'fish'
22. terara   'land'
23. pidara   'rocks'
24. nubisu   'cloud'
25. nulisu   'moon'
26. putisu   'wind'

Problem 211

Instructions: Determine the meanings of the first-order suffixes.

1. sominoka   'my wagon'
2. polenoka   'my whip'
3. fusonoka   'my wife'
4. manegika   'my arm'
5. pikanoka   'my clothes'
6. lamagika   'my soul'
7. susinoka   'my traps'
8. tatagika   'my father'

9. waxogika   'my head'
10. nanugika   'my mother'
11. datinoka   'my boat'
12. nunugika   'my son'
13. taragika   'my ear'
14. musanoka   'my cow'
15. paligika   'my leg'

(Continued on next page.)

16. watagika   'my daughter'   21. lahunoka   'my house'

17. yamagika   'my name'   22. walagika   'my horse'

18. kulonoka   'my knife'   23. tigonoka   'my land'

19. vitonoka   'my food'   24. hakanoka   'my axe'

20. pimogika   'my hand'   25. korogika   'my heart'

Problem 212

Instructions: Determine the meanings of the suffixal morphemes.

1. melato   'clams'   11. misito   'sand plums'

2. togoku   'scorpion'   12. fomito   'persimmons'

3. likato   'horse'   13. polito   'deer'

4. nipoto   'grasshoppers'   14. fizuto   'corn'

5. simiku   'wood'   15. simoku   'starfish'

6. natito   'cow'   16. sanato   'blackberries'

7. fameku   'nightshade berries'   17. nisoku   'oak leaves'

8. kagaku   'kelp'   18. naviku   'garter snake'

9. nikoto   'worms'   19. legaku   'salamander'

10. poriku   'grass'   20. maluto   'frog'

Problem 213

Instructions: Determine the meanings of the prefixal morphemes.

1. tisoga   'chief'   10. mitori   'nightshade berries

2. misuku   'spider'   11. tilefi   'son'

3. mipilu   'commoner'   12. tiforo   'sassafras bark'

4. mitine   'scorpion'   13. timino   'hominy'

5. mitudo   'liar'   14. tikobo   'whip snake'

6. tivomi   'honest man'   15. mikake   'old hen'

7. migano   'nag'   16. tivaka   'cow'

8. tiwala   'worker'   17. mimafi   'rattlesnake'

9. mipiba   'thief'   18. tinuse   'horse'

Problem 214

Instructions: Describe the nonlinguistic features which determine the distribution of the suffixal morphemes.[4]

1. komiti   'pigs'   8. bagala   'calves'

2. porula   'colts'   9. tereti   'chickens'

3. nunula   'human babies'   10. koneti   'rabbits'

4. fumuti   'skunks'   11. koleti   'garter snakes'

5. dumula   'fawns'   12. mitola   'elks'

6. borela   'lambs'   13. sibola   'goats'

7. kokoti   'ducks'   14. pipoti   'quails'

Problem 215

Instructions: Determine the meaning of the suffix -ku.

1. taku   'to talk'   11. domiku   'to die'

2. soma   'to be sick'   12. tora   'to fall'

3. nusuku   'to get drunk'   13. nemoku   'to be unconscious'

4. takuku   'to talk a long time'   14. pikuku   'to sniff around'

5. simo   'to smile'   15. domi   'to sleep'

6. makoku   'to stink'   16. piku   'to smell'

7. toraku   'to fall (down a hill)' 17. somaku   'to be an invalid'

8. nemo   'to faint'   18. nusu   'to drink liquor'

9. mako   'to be dead'   19. kisi   'to step'

10. kisiku   'to walk'   20. simoku   'to be happy'

Problem 216

Instructions: Determine the meaning of the suffix -mo.

1. moga   'to step'   6. nuso   'to strike with fist'

2. ropumo   'to shake'   7. lita   'to hit'

3. mogamo   'to walk'   8. zomomo   'to chop wood'

4. haso   'to wink'   9. litamo   'to fight'

5. nasimo   'to be affectionate to'

(Continued on next page.)

---

[4]This distinction exists in Cherokee.

10. torimo   'to dance'   16. zomo   'to hit with an ax'

11. hasomo   'to blink one's eyes'   17. ropu   'to jerk'

12. sumumo   'to jab full of holes'   18. nasi   'to kiss'

13. tori   'to jump'   19. sumu   'to pierce'

14. soka   'to cut with a knife'   20. nusomo   'to pummel'

15. sokamo   'to whittle'

Part II: Table of Phonetic Symbols

The most commonly used symbols for foreign languages are included in the following tables:

Consonants

	Bilabial	Labio-dental	Dental-alveolar	Alveo-palatal	Palatal	Velar	Glottal
Stops							
Unaspirated vl.[1]	p		t		k	ķ (q)	ʔ (ʼ)
vd.[1]	b		d		g	ģ	
Aspirated vl.	p^h		t^h		k^h		
vd.	b^h		d^h		g^h		
Affricated vl.			c (ts)	č (tš)			
vd.			ʒ (dz)	ǰ (dž)			
Laterally released vl.			ƛ (tł)				
vd.			λ (dl)				
Fricatives							
Flat vl.	ꝑ	f	θ		x	x̣	h
vd.	ƀ	v	đ		ǥ	ģ̧	
Grooved vl.			s	š			
vd.			z	ž			
Nasal vl.	m̲ (M)		n̲ (N)	ñ̲ (Ñ)		ŋ̲ (Ŋ)	
vd.	m		n	ñ		ŋ	
Liquids							
Lateral vl.			ł				
vd.			l				

(Continued on next page.)

---

[1] vl. stands for "voiceless" and vd. for "voiced."

<u>Consonants</u>

		Bilabial	Labio-dental	Dental-alveolar	Alveo-palatal	Palatal	Velar	Glottal
Liquids (continued)								
Central	vl.			r̲ (R)				
	vd.			r				
Vibrants								
Flapped	vl.			ř̲				
	vd.			ř				
Trilled	vl.			r̲̃				
	vd.			r̃				

<u>Vowels</u>

	Front Unrounded	Front Rounded	Central	Back
High	i	ü	ɨ	u
Mid	e	ö (ø)		o
	ε	œ	ɘ	
Low	æ		a	ɔ

<u>Diacritical Marks</u>

Tones:

     ′ high tone

     – (′) mid tone

     ` low tone

Stress:

     ′ onset of primary stress

     , onset of secondary stress

     ′ primary stressed syllabic

     ` secondary stressed syllabic

Nazalization:

     Ṽ nasalized vowel

Glottalization:

     V̓ (ʔV) glottalized vowel

     C' (Cʔ) glottalized consonant

Voiceless vowels:

     A, I, U, indicated by caps, or

     a̲, i̲, u̲, indicated by underlining

Vowel length:

     V· long vowel

Relative position:

     C̹ fronted

     C̜ backed

These symbols are only approximations to the actual sounds used in the language problems. Almost all the data are phonemicized, and because of this fact it cannot be expected that the symbol k̲ in one language will stand for the same phonetic sound as the k̲ in another language. In one it may represent a palatal and in another a velar. Distinctions between such sounds are made only when the language itself has these phonemic contrasts.

For some sounds there are alternant symbols, for, wherever possible, we have attempted to preserve the phonemic interpretation employed by the linguist who was the source of the data.

Symbol	Transcription	Key Word	Symbol	Transcription	Key Word
/p/	/píl/	pill	/n/	/nə́t/	nut
/t/	/tíl/	till	/ŋ/	/síŋ/	sing
/k/	/kíyl/	keel	/i/[2]	/fíl/	fill
/b/	/béd/	bed		/fíyl/	feel
/d/	/déyt/	date	/e/[2]	/pén/	pen
/g/	/gét/	get		/péyn/	pain
/č/	/čáyld/	child	/æ/	/pǽn/	pan
/ǰ/	/ǰə́ǰ/	judge	/a/[2]	/pát/	pot
/f/	/fówn/	phone		/báyt/	bite
/θ/	/θín/	thin		/əbáwt/	about
/s/	/sót/	sought	/o/[2]	/bót/	bought
/š/	/šə́t/	shut		/bówt/	boat
/v/	/váyn/	vine		/kóy/	coy
/ð/	/ðén/	then	/u/[2]	/pút/	put
/z/	/ǽz/	as		/búwt/	boot
/y/	/yét/	yet	/ə/[2]	/bə́t/	but
/w/	/wéyt/	wait		/bə́rd/	bird
/h/	/hélp/	help		/bə́tən/	button
/l/	/lówd/	load		/bátəm/	bottom
/r/	/rúwt/	root		/bátəl/	bottle
/m/	/mǽn/	man			

---

[1] The writer's own speech, upon which the transcriptions in this book are based, is a comparatively simple variety of Western American. It lacks certain syllabic contrasts occurring in other dialects.

[2] Additional forms are given in order to indicate the allophonic contrasts preceding /y, w, r, n, m, l/.

/ˊ/   primary stressed syllabic

/ˆ/   secondary stressed syllabic

/-/   phonemic juncture[3]

---

[3]No attempt is made to list all the phonemic features of English, since many of them do not occur in the morphological description.

BIBLIOGRAPHY

Bazell, C. E. "Le Principe de compensation dans les systèmes morphologiques," Garp Filolojileri Dergisi (1947), pp. 59-65.

Bloch, Bernard. "English Verb Inflection," Language, 23 (1947), 4: 399-418.

-------and Trager, George L. Outline of Linguistic Analysis. Baltimore: Special Publications of the Linguistic Society of America, 1942.

-------and Trager, George L. "The Syllabic Phonemes of English," Language, 17 (1941), 3: 223-46.

Bloomfield, Leonard. Language. New York: Henry Holt and Co., 1933.

Boas, F. Handbook of American Indian Languages. Bureau of American Ethnology, Bulletin 40. Washington, 1911.

Denoeu, François, and Hall, Robert A., Jr. Spoken and Written French. Boston: D. C. Heath and Co., 1946.

Frei, Henry. "Note sur l'analyse des syntagmes," Word, 4 (1948), 2: 65-70.

Fries, Charles C. American English Grammar. New York: D. Appleton-Century Co., 1940.

Garvin, Paul L. "Kutenai III: Morpheme Distributions (Prefix, Theme, Suffix)," International Journal of American Linguistics, 14 (1948), 3: 171-87.

Haas, Mary R. "Classificatory Verbs in Muskogee," International Journal of American Linguistics, 14 (1948), 4: 244-46.

-------"Men's and Women's Speech in Koasati," Language, 20 (1944), 3: 142-49.

Hall, Robert A., Jr. Descriptive Italian Grammar. Ithaca, New York: Cornell University Press and Linguistic Society of America, 1948.

-------French, No. 24, Structural Sketches 1 (1948).

-------Leave Your Language Alone. Ithaca, New York: Division of Modern Languages, Cornell University, 1948.

Halpern, A. M. "Yuma" in Linguistic Structures of Native America (Viking Fund Publications in Anthropology, Vol. 6), pp. 249-88. New York, 1946.

Harris, Zellig S. "From Morpheme to Utterance," Language, 22 (1946), 3: 161-83.

-------"Linguistic Structure of Hebrew," Journal of the American Oriental Society, 61 (1941): 143-67.

-------"Morpheme Alternants in Linguistic Analysis," Language, 18 (1942), 3: 169-80.

-------"Structural Restatements II," International Journal of American Linguistics, 13 (1947), 3: 175-86.

Hockett, Charles F. "Potawatomi [Parts I-IV]," International Journal of American Linguistics, 14 (1948), 1-4: 1-10, 63-73, 139-49, 213-25.

------"Problems of Morphemic Analysis," Language, 23 (1947), 4: 321-43.

Hodge, Carleton T. An Outline of Hausa Grammar. Language Dissertation No. 41. Baltimore: Linguistic Society of America, 1947.

Hoijer, Harry. "The Apachean Verb, Part I: Verb Structure and Pronominal Prefixes," International Journal of American Linguistics, 11 (1945), 4: 193-203.

------"Chiricahua Apache" in Linguistic Structures of Native America (Viking Fund Publications in Anthropology, Vol. 6), pp. 55-84. New York, 1946.

------Navaho Phonology. Albuquerque, New Mexico: University of New Mexico Press, 1945.

------"Tonkawa" in Linguistic Structures of Native America (Viking Fund Publications in Anthropology, Vol. 6), pp. 289-311. New York, 1946.

Nida, Eugene A. Bible Translating. New York: American Bible Society, 1947.

------"Field Techniques in Descriptive Linguistics," International Journal of American Linguistics, 13 (1947), 3: 138-46.

------Linguistic Interludes. Glendale, California: Summer Institute of Linguistics, 1947.

------"A System for the Identification of Morphemes," Language, 24 (1948), 4: 414-41.

Pedersen, Holger. Linguistic Science in the Nineteenth Century. Cambridge: Harvard University Press, 1931.

Pike, Kenneth L. The Intonation of American English. Ann Arbor, Michigan: University of Michigan Press, 1945.

------Tone Languages. Ann Arbor, Michigan: University of Michigan Press, 1948.

Pittman, Richard S. "Nahuatl Honorifics," International Journal of American Linguistics, 14 (1948), 4: 236-39.

------"Nuclear Structures in Linguistics," Language, 24 (1948), 3: 287-92.

Sapir, Edward. Language. New York: Harcourt, Brace, and Co., 1921.

------"The Southern Paiute Language," Proceedings of the American Academy of Arts and Sciences, 65 (1930), 1: 1-296.

Slocum, Marianna C. "Tzeltal (Mayan) Noun and Verb Morphology," International Journal of American Linguistics, 14 (1948), 2: 77-86.

Spier, Leslie; Hallowell, A. Irving; and Newman, Stanley S. Language, Culture, and Personality. Menasha, Wisconsin: Sapir Memorial Publication Fund, 1941.

Sturtevant, Edgar H. An Introduction to Linguistic Science. New Haven, Connecticut: Yale University Press. 1947.

------The Pronunciation of Greek and Latin. Baltimore: Special Publications of the Linguistic Society of America, 1940.

Swadesh, Morris. "The Phonetics of Chitimacha," Language, 10 (1934), 4: 345-61.

Trager, George L. "An Outline of Taos Grammar" in <u>Linguistic</u> <u>Structures</u> of <u>Native</u> <u>America</u> (Viking Fund Publications in Anthropology, Vol. 6), pp. 184-221. New York, 1946.

Trimingham, J. <u>Sudan</u> <u>Colloquial</u> <u>Arabic</u>. London: Oxford University Press, 1946.

Voegelin, C. F. "Delaware, An Eastern Algoquian Language" in <u>Linguistic</u> <u>Structures</u> of <u>Native</u> <u>America</u> (Viking Fund Publications in Anthropology, Vol. 6), pp. 130-57. New York, 1946.

------"A Problem in Morpheme Alternants and Their Distribution," <u>Language</u>, 23 (1947), 3: 245-54.

------and Ellinghausen, M. E. "Turkish Structure," <u>Journal</u> of <u>the</u> <u>American</u> <u>Oriental</u> <u>Society</u>, 63 (1943), 1: 35-65.

Watkins, Mark Hanna. <u>A</u> <u>Grammar</u> of <u>Chichewa</u>. Language Dissertation No. 24. Baltimore: Linguistic Society of America, 1937.

Wells, Rulon S. "Immediate Constituents," <u>Language</u>, 23 (1947), 2: 81-117.

Young, Robert, and Morgan, William. <u>The</u> <u>Navaho</u> <u>Language</u>. Phoenix, Arizona: United States Indian Service, 1943.

Allomorph: 14
Allomorphs
 basic and nonbasic: 45
 morphologically defined: 44
Arabic
 Egyptian: 68
 Sudan Colloquial: 16, 41
Aspect: 167
Assimilation: 14-15, 21
 factors in: 283
 of tonemes: 24, 291
Aztec
 Guerrero dialect: 117
 Tetelcingo dialect: 167, 216
 Veracruz dialect: 8, 11, 38, 58, 109, 157
 Zacapoaxtla dialect: 11, 154, 169

Bantu languages: 60, 66, 85, 105, 106, 165,
 167, 183
Bilingual approach: 178
Bloomfield, Leonard: 60, 61, 68, 76, 154,
 174
Bound forms: 81
Burmese: 201

Case, grammatical: 167
Categories, grammatical: 166
Changes
 assimilative: 283
 dissimilative: 285
Chatino: 64
Cherokee: 159
Chichewa: 126, 141, 223
Chiluba: 39
Chinese: 154, 201
Chipewyan: 181
Chiricahua Apache: 225
Chitimacha: 86
Chontal, of Oaxaca: 211
Chukchee: 189
Clitics, 97, 106, 261
Comanche: 167, 197
Comparative linguistics: 3
Compensatory lengthening: 306
Compounds: 127
Congo Swahili: 12, 84, 92, 193, 196
 207
Connotation: 152
Consonant clusters, reduction of: 27, 293
Consonants, weakening of: 301

Constructions
 coordinate: 95
 endocentric: 94
 exocentric: 94
 subordinate: 95
Covert distinctions: 54
Cuicatec: 24

Data, recording of: 188
Delaware: 226
Denotation: 152
Derivational formations: 99
Descriptive linguistics, principles of: 1-3
Descriptive statements, to be avoided: 241
Determined constituents: 111
Determiner, definition of: 111
Dissimilation: 283; of tonemes: 291
Distribution
 observations concerning: 194
 pertinent environment: 87
Distribution classes, definition of: 110
Distributional arrangements, types of: 111

Egyptian Arabic: 68
Ellinghausen, M. E.: 79, 147
Endocentricity: 94
English: 2, 4, 6, 7, 14-17, 30, 44, 54-56, 59,
 65, 72, 74, 82, 83, 85, 86, 89, 91, 93-
 95, 100, 104, 115, 118-20, 122, 123,
 127-29, 151, 155, 162, 174
Environment
 contextual: 154
 linguistic: 153
 nonlinguistic: 152
 objective: 152
 structural: 153
 subjective: 152
Episememe, definition of: 174
Eskimo, Barrow dialect: 78, 82, 88, 98, 167,
 182, 193
Exocentricity: 94
External distribution class, definition of: 110

Files, number of: 199
Filing
 arrangement of sections: 202
 of data: 195
 extent of: 198
 relationship to analysis: 196
Flap phonemes, interchange of: 312

Fluctuations of forms: 3
Form classes, definition of: 107
Frames: 183
Free forms: 81
Frei, Henry: 84
French: 68, 75, 77, 84, 92, 103, 104, 108, 227
Futa-Fula: 53, 110, 114

Garvin, Paul L.: 207, 209
Gender: 167
German: 4, 153, 154
Grammatical sequences, meaning of: 174
Grassman's law: 15
Greek: 2, 15, 27, 69, 77, 84, 98, 104, 167

Haas, Mary R.: 159, 189
Hall, Robert A.: 103, 147, 166, 227
Halpern, A. M.: 235
Haplology: 312
Harris, Zellig S.: 66, 207, 229
Hausa: 22, 36, 70
Hebrew: 66, 229
Historical linguistics: 3
Hockett, Charles: 156, 230
Hodge, Carleton T.: 22, 36, 70
Hoijer, Harry: 28, 34, 80, 96, 225
Homophones: 55
Honorifics: 167
Huave: 17, 66, 112
Huichol: 164, 167
Hupa: 166

Ilamba: 51, 110, 209
Immediate constituents: 86, 89
    combinations of more than two: 90
    determination of: 90
    discontinuous: 90
Indo-European: 147
Infixes: 68, 317
Inflectional formations: 99
Informants
    dialect differences among: 189
    handling of: 190
    qualifications of: 190
Internal distribution class, definition: 110

Junctures
    covert: 86
    overt: 86
    phonemic: 85
    structural: 86

Kekchi: 6, 39, 49, 90, 95, 98, 108, 147, 169, 174, 180, 193
Kissi: 68, 107
Koasati: 189

Labiovelars, development of: 312

Latin: 84
Lengthening, compensatory: 306
Lingombe: 90, 92
Loma: 144, 145, 146, 166
Loss
    of consonants: 26
    of vowel phonemes: 30
    of vowels, in unstressed syllables: 303

Mam: 258
Marshallese: 147
Maya: 3, 107, 147, 148
Mayan languages: 66
Mazahua: 36
Mazatec: 24, 30, 164
Meaning
    definability of: 161
    of grammatical sequences: 174
    procedures in determining: 162
Metathesis: 17, 312
Mode, category of: 168
Mongbandi: 63, 69, 98, 149
Monolingual approach: 175
Morgan, William: 80, 160
Morphemes
    additive: 69
    closing: 85
    complementary: 110
    consisting of segmental and suprasegmental phonemes: 65
    consisting of suprasegmental phonemes: 62
    covert: 54
    definition of: 6
    distribution of: 78
    formal combining of: 85
    internal composition of: 62
    labeling of: 165
    meaning of: 151
    mutually exclusive: 84
    mutually obligatory: 84
    nonclosing: 85
    numbering of: 208
    obligatory: 85
    orders of: 84
    overt: 54
    relative order of: 205
    replacive: 71
    same order: 110
    simultaneous occurrence of: 77
    subtractive: 75
    supplementary: 54, 110
    zero: 46
Morphological structures
    limits of: 102
    types of: 97
Morphology
    descriptive statement of: 222
    practical definition of: 1
    section in file: 200

Morphology (continued)
    technical definition of: 105
Morphophonemics, section in file: 200
Movement, category of: 169
Muskogee: 159

Nasalization: 310
Navaho: 3, 28, 80, 160, 167
Ngbaka: 63, 66, 69, 98
Nida, Eugene A.: 197
Nilotic languages: 60
Nonnuclei, definition of: 83
Nonroots, definition of: 82
Nootka: 82
Nuclear structures, definition of: 84
Nuclei, definition of: 83

Object words: 178
Orthography: 1
Otomi, Mesquital dialect: 219
Outlines
    discussion of: 237
    of grammars: 222
Outlining, systems of: 239
Overt distinctions: 54

Palatalization: 35, 308
Pame-Chichimeca: 216, 217
Paradigms
    complex: 111
    simple: 111
    as supplementary to texts: 197
Peripheral structures, definition of: 84
Person
    category of: 169
    fourth: 169
Phonemes, developed: 307
Phonetic data: 193
Phonological processes: 21
Pike, Eunice V.: 24, 30
Pike, Kenneth L.: 24, 62, 86
Pittman, Richard S.: 167
Popoluca: 37, 98, 166
Portuguese: 178
Potawatomi: 156, 167, 230
Procedures
    analytical: 192
    field: 175
Process words: 182

Quechua: 79, 82, 88, 106, 193; Chanca dia-
    lect: 97

Read, Allen Walker: 57
Reduplicatives: 316
Replacives: 54, 318, 320
Rhotocism: 312
Robertson, A. T.: 2
Roots, definition of: 82

Samoan: 76
San Blas: 69, 84
Sapir, Edward: 103, 231
Semantics: 137
    principles of: 151
    words of related meanings: 56
Sememe, definition of: 155
Semitic: 60
Sequence classes
    compounds: 127
    definition of: 108
    multiple: 130
    single: 111
Shilluk: 72
Slocum, Marianna C.: 16, 23, 46, 68, 95, 100,
    234
Solutions to problems, methods of description:
    48
Southern Paiute: 103, 231
Spanish: 117, 124, 125, 130, 136, 153, 154,
    165, 167, 178
Stems, definition of: 83
Structural classes
    characteristics of: 149
    definition of: 107
    systems of: 147
Structural layers: 98
Subtractives: 317
Sudan Colloquial Arabic: 16, 41
Sudanic languages: 60, 63
Summer Institute of Linguistics: 175
Swadesh, Morris: 82, 86
Swahili, Congo: 12, 84, 92, 193, 196, 207
Symbolics: 137
Symbolization of morphemes, value of: 209
Symbols
    semantic use of: 161
    use of: 207
Synonyms: 151
Syntactophonemics: 200

Taos: 88
Tarahumara: 22, 157, 181
Tarascan: 167, 220
Tense: 167
Terminology: 4, 240; illustrative uses: 242
Texts: 186
Tlapanec: 31
Tojolabal: 18, 26, 67, 69, 70, 147, 214
Tonemes, assimilation and dissimilation of:
    291
Tonkawa: 34, 96, 103
Totonac: 15, 18, 46, 63, 101, 110, 158
Trager, George L.: 88
Trimingham, J.: 16, 41
Tsotsil: 23
Turkish: 79, 82, 88, 103, 147
Turu: 40
Tzeltal: 16, 19, 23, 46, 68, 95, 100, 116,
    129, 174, 234

Unvoicing, final: 290

Verner's phenomenon: 311, 313
Vocalic harmony: 289
Voegelin, C. F.: 79, 147, 207, 226
Voice, category of: 168
Voicing, medial: 290
Vowel length, changes in: 306
Vowel sequences, reduction of: 297
Vowels
    loss in unstressed syllables: 303
    structural relationships: 288
    weakening of: 302

Watkins, Mark Hanna: 126, 141, 223

Weakening
    of consonants: 301
    of vowels: 302
Wonderly, William L.: 75

Yana: 189
Yipounou: 13, 105
Young, Robert: 80, 160
Yuma: 235

Zapotec
    Isthmus dialect: 38, 210, 211, 262
    Sierra dialect: 123, 163
Zero, types of: 46
Zoque: 12, 17, 21, 29, 30, 67, 76, 99, 108,
    171, 205, 207, 209

45

PB-36227
22
G-5